The Book of South Wales, the Bristol Channel, Monmouthshire and the Wye

TO THE

REV. GEORGE ROBERTS, B.A.,

𝕿𝖍𝖎𝖘 𝖁𝖔𝖑𝖚𝖒𝖊

IS DEDICATED WITH FEELINGS OF AFFECTIONATE REGARD

BY ONE WHO HAS PASSED

MANY HAPPY AND PROFITABLE DAYS IN HIS SOCIETY

AMIDST THE

SCENERY AND ANTIQUITIES OF WALES.

NOTE TO THE SECOND EDITION.

THE reception which has been given to this work has been so encouraging as to confirm a belief which I entertained when I undertook it, that I should supply a want. I endeavoured to combine with the machinery of a guide-book what I may call a popular memoir of the country—to bring its Past and Present aspects before the mind of the reader. In this edition the idea is more fully and carefully carried out. A considerable portion has been re-written; very many new facts have been infused into the text; the number of pages has been increased one-fifth; and the actual *matter* at least a fourth. The maps have been materially improved, and several new illustrations introduced. I have spent nearly a month in the spring of 1848 in traversing some of the most interesting districts of the country, and have thus accumulated a good deal of fresh information which is intrinsically valuable, and which will also be found useful to the traveller and the angler. The account of Cardiganshire may be referred to as an illustration of this. Lastly, I have to thank the reviewers for their too favourable estimate of my labours; and also to cordially acknowledge aid that I have received from a number of correspondents, which is the more prized, because it was in several instances unsought.

I am nevertheless conscious that this volume has many imperfections, and I shall therefore be always glad to receive assistance to enable me to correct errors, and accumulate materials which may possibly be again serviceable. A few errors in the spelling of Welsh words have escaped correction; but I think it right to remark, that I have in several places designedly followed the modern mode of spelling names—alterations in fact, which are in most instances of local origin. Carmarthen, for example, is now rarely spelt Caermarthen, and although the vowel omitted has significance, I have not deviated from what has become a usage.

Experience has proved that the price which I fixed for the volume has proved insufficient to reimburse me for the heavy outlay actually incurred in bringing it out, although the sale has been large. I am still as anxious as I was to *open* South Wales; and as a low price is calculated to ensure a large circulation, I have resolved to again try the experiment, which I do hopefully.

GLOUCESTER, June 21st, 1848.

LIST OF ILLUSTRATIONS.

   • An engraving showing the elevation of the proposed Railway Bridge at Aust (p 24), has been withdrawn, in order to admit of the introduction of one of much greater interest.

INTRODUCTION TO THE FIRST EDITION.

Tнıs volume is the result of observations made at intervals in various parts of South Wales during the last twenty years. Sometimes I have resided for several weeks on the sea-coast; at others I have made systematic excursions; occasionally I have roamed through the mountains with a fishing-rod, penetrating unfrequented districts in pursuit of sport. I have thus progressively picked up more information relative to the country than falls to the lot of most men.

The extension of the Railway system to South Wales, together with improvements in Steam Navigation, will open this highly-interesting portion of our island to many thousands who have hitherto never thought of visiting it, or who have been deterred by the time at present required for a tour, and the expense. Perhaps no portion of the kingdom is likely to benefit more, if so much, by the opening of railways, as South Wales, especially its three western counties: its resources are great; it possesses all the elements of prosperity; and, where capital has developed the natural wealth of the land, the return has generally exceeded the expectations of the sanguine.

I have elsewhere observed that sinews of the national strength exist here; and one purpose which I have had in view has been to record the progress already made in unlocking the treasures of the mineral districts. The advance which has taken place within the last fifteen years has been prodigious; the counties of Glamorgan and Monmouth have kept pace with, or even exceeded—as regards rate of progress—the manufacturing districts of the north. There are, however, dark shadows in the picture on which it would be foreign to my present purpose to dwell, but which I must, as a faithful spectator, faintly indicate.

But this is only one phase of South Wales. If the country presents a wide field for the man of Enterprise, it offers equal attractions to those who leave home every year in search of Health or Recreation—to the admirer of fine scenery—of a highly-romantic coast, the explorer of antiquities and national peculiarities,* and the sportsman.

I have, in order to compress superabundant materials within limits which will render this volume generally accessible, been reluctantly obliged to omit much bearing upon the condition of the people that I

* Those who wish to preserve the silent, yet expressive and instructive, records of our forefathers, presented by the Antiquities of a country, will rejoice to learn that a Society has lately been formed under most influential auspices, entitled the " CAMBRIAN ARCHÆOLOGICAL ASSOCIATION." The first congress was held at Aberystwith in September, 1847, when it was determined to hold the next annual meeting at Carnarvon, at a similar period in the following year. A record of its proceedings is given in a quarterly periodical, devoted to the illustration of the antiquities and topography of Wales, which is conducted with great talent and judgment, entitled the *Archæologia Cambrensis.*

should otherwise have introduced. I have been compelled to take the part of a pioneer; and I may observe that I am a labourer in a field that has been long untrodden, and rarely trodden satisfactorily. There is only a single small local *guide-book* in existence, so far as I am aware, relating to South Wales, and this only refers to a particular neighbourhood. Nearly all the " Tours in Wales "—with one exception—are quite out of date, and I have often found it difficult to get any written information about the country.

I have combined with my description of the interior, a novel feature— an account of the Sea which borders it—of the peculiarities of the Bristol Channel—which I have done both in the introductory portion of the volume, and in a description of the Steam-packet Voyages.

The plan I have pursued in describing the country is that which has seemed to me the most natural and clear. Instead of writing a miniature topographical dictionary, I have gone through the counties separately, in regular succession, so arranging the matter as to form an Itinerary for each. I have bestowed the fullest attention on unfrequented districts, and on those counties which are either intrinsically the most important, or which will be traversed by the South Wales and other Railways, and will therefore become the most easily accessible, the most likely to be visited. At the present period, however, by means of the Silent—often boisterous—Highway of the Bristol Channel, great facilities are afforded for gaining access economically and speedily to many of the most interesting districts; and should the projected Pier, near Portishead, at the entrance of the Avon—to which there will be access for the largest vessels at all states of the tide—be completed, the duration of steam voyages will be materially abridged.

I am conscious that this attempt to pourtray, in a popular form, South Wales as it is, is very defective; but where deficiencies or errors are visible, I trust that the reader will considerately take the will for the deed.

I have to express my acknowledgments to many individuals who have kindly afforded me statistical and other information, and I shall be much obliged to any one who will point out errors, or give me new information which may be available at a future opportunity.

At this period of transition, I have not thought it worth while, as a general rule, to give minute lists of public conveyances on land. Cars can generally be procured throughout North Wales at the rate of one shilling per mile and threepence per mile to the driver, which will accommodate a party of four, with a moderate quantity of luggage; the inn-keepers in South Wales have sometimes no vehicle between the ancient post-chaise and gig; and ought to introduce the car as a substitute for the latter. The great mail routes are—1. from Gloucester to Carmarthen by Chepstow, Cardiff, &c.; 2. from Gloucester to Pater (Pembroke Dock) through Monmouth, Brecon, Llandovery, and Carmarthen; 3.

from Gloucester to Aberystwith, by Hereford, Kington, Penybont, and Rhayader. Mails depart from Gloucester to each of these points every morning at a quarter to 2 A.M., soon after the arrival of the London mail-train; and there is a second mail from Gloucester to Brecon and Carmarthen, at 5 A.M., after the arrival of the mail-train from the north. There is also a mail from *Bristol* through Chepstow and Cardiff to Pembroke every morning at 2 A.M.; and a second mail, from Bristol to Swansea only, at 8 A.M. In the summer a coach runs from Gloucester to Builth. Information relative to the conveyances to Aberystwith is given at p. 314.

THE IRON TRADE OF SOUTH WALES.

It was stated by the late Mr. David Mushet, in his valuable work entitled "*Papers on Iron and Steel,*" that in the year 1730 there were only 59 furnaces in all England, the aggregate make of which was 17,350 tons annually, or "little more than five tons a week of pig iron from each furnace." In October, 1847, the "make" of three furnaces at the Witton Park works, near Middlesbro', was 464 tons of good forge iron; and the Cwmbrain furnace in South Wales lately produced, in the same time, 150 tons of cold blast iron. These are illustrations of the present power of production, which is so great that in 1847 the annual value of the iron produced throughout Great Britain was estimated to exceed nine millions sterling. In 1806, the quantity of British iron *made* amounted to 258,000 tons; in 1844, 1,400,000 tons; in 1845, 1,750,000 tons; in 1847, it is said to have reached 2,094,000 tons, viz., in Wales, 884,000; in Staffordshire, &c., 710,000 tons; and in Scotland, 500,000 tons. This estimate, however, is obviously conjectural, and in our opinion exceeds the truth. "To make the above quantity of iron, 14,429,000 tons of material have been consumed, and employment given to 100,000 men."

Perhaps the greatest progress has been made in South Wales, the mineral basin of which offers very great facilities for the manufacture of iron or copper, from the abundance and thickness of coal and iron ore. Until a comparatively recent period, the iron trade has been chiefly confined to the districts connected with the ports of Cardiff and Newport, but two new fields have been opened to the westward, 1. in the group of mountains to the south-west of Merthyr, the outlets of which are Porthcawl, Port Talbot and Neath; and 2. the Swansea, Anman and Gwendraeth vallies, the outlets of which are Swansea and Burry Port. In the first of these groups *Black-band Ironstone* exists to a great extent, by which iron can be produced at a much diminished cost. The area of this immense coal basin has been thus estimated by Mr. Forster, of Newcastle: Monmouthshire, 85 square miles; Glamorganshire, 569; Brecknockshire, 68; Carmarthenshire, 133; Pembrokeshire, 80=935 square miles. The district is intersected by deep valleys chiefly running north

and south, " which together with the elevation of the strata afford unusual
facilities for draining and working *by level* immense tracts of coal and ironstone." The writer quoted estimates " as an approximation" to the
truth " that the quantity of workable coal does not exceed *sixteen thousand
millions* of tons."

The discovery of Black-band ironstone, in South Wales, and that made
in 1836 by the late Mr. Crane, relative to smelting with anthracite coal
(see p. 192) have exercised a most important influence on the progress of
the iron manufacture. Mr. Mushet, formerly of the Calder Iron-works,
near Glasgow, was the first discoverer of Black-band, the ironstone of
which is much more easily reducible than the ordinary ironstone, and
requires less fuel. We learn that in Scotland the income of a single estate
—Airdrie, belonging to Sir W. Alexander—has been increased £12,000
or £14,000 for Black-band ironstone (formerly called *wild coal*) " where
not one single shilling of mineral rent was formerly received." This is
one instance. The existence of Black-band in Monmouthshire and South
Wales was unsuspected until a recent period, when Mr. Mushet had again,
(in 1842 we believe), the honour to be its discoverer in the former. Soon
afterwards, Mr. Charles Hampton, of the Maesteg iron works, sent Mr.
Mushet specimens of Black-band which he had found about the beginning of 1843, in the hills near those works : so that Mr. Hampton may
claim the credit of being the discoverer of this valuable mineral—which does
not exist at all in some of the great districts of the South Wales basin—
in Glamorganshire. We were favoured in March, 1847, by our lamented
friend, Mr. Mushet, with a communication on the subject, of which the
following is the substance :—

" The Black-band that has been found in South Wales, particularly that
in Cwm Avon, Maesteg, the Garth, Tondu, &c., appears much higher in the
coal seams than the Scotch, which correctly considered may form a portion
of the principal part of the coal measures ; whereas the Glamorgan is found
in or near the *Cockshut* rocks and strong *Silurian grit rocks*, at a considerable
distance above the principal seams of coal and even above the upper *rakes* of
ironstone. Near Pontypool the *Cockshut* rocks occupy a range considerably
higher than the *Blackpins* [beds of ore], and these again are found at a
considerable distance above the first, or upper iron-making or white-ash coal.
In Cwm Avon and Maesteg, I think that one bed is above and one below
the two Cockshut rocks ; one, black, compact and clean, the other mixed with
shale, which to a certain extent is detected by burning ; the thickness, viz., 14
and 16 inches, being nearly alike to the Scotch, though when roasted, the yield
in iron is less. There is a bed of clay ironstone which overlays one of the
beds ; it is, I think, 12 or 18 feet thick, and averages from 10 to 12 per cent.,
which, though poor, is yet a curious and valuable deposit. The neighbourhood
now referred to is soon likely to become a flourishing department in the iron-
trade, as the extent of Black-band is great, and the supply of coal fully in
proportion." Mr. Hampton, in a letter which we have since received, informs

us that the Maesteg Black-band veins "lie amongst the upper coals between the *Cockshut* and *Pennant* rocks, whilst the ' Beaufort' (Monmouthshire) vein lies on the ' *Old Coal,*' one of the lowest beds in the series."

The produce of iron in South Wales amounted in 1828 to 297,512 tons ; and in 1836 to 354,912 tons. The *exports* in 1846 exceeded 500,000 tons. In 1847 the exports were probably smaller, owing to the circumstances of the time ; and the *make* will be further reduced in 1848. The chief portion of the exports consists of *bar iron.* This is so at Newport : and at Cardiff the exports are exclusively bars. At Porthcawl and Swansea, nothing but pig-iron is made. We may here observe that the exports do not exhibit the real extent of the make, and that on an average 28 cwt. of pig-iron is required to produce one ton of bars.

In April, 1843, there were 117 blast furnaces in operation in South Wales and Monmouthshire, viz., 57 in the former and 60 in the latter. In 1847, the number of furnaces in South Wales stood thus :—Merthyr Tydvil, 46 ; Hirwain, 4 ; Aberdare, 8 ; Pentyrch, 2 ; Llynvi Valley, 10 ; Cwm Avon, 7 ; Vale of Neath, 4 ; Swansea Valley, 21 ; Anman and Gwendraeth Vales, 16. Total, 118. The number in Monmouthshire was about 70, making a total of about 188 furnaces. The fluctuations of trade are so great that we are unable to state, with any thing like accuracy, the number of furnaces now in blast.

THE SOUTH WALES RAILWAY.

In the year 1824 a prospectus was issued—by whom we know not—for the construction of a Railway from Swansea through Gloucester to the Metropolis, chiefly for the purpose of conveying coal and other minerals to the London market, as well as passengers at coach speed. The idea was then deemed ridiculously chimerical. Twelve years afterwards an embryo company was formed at Gloucester for the construction of a South Wales Railway through Swansea, which was followed by the appearance of a paper scheme—which, however, made some noise—entitled " The England and Ireland Union Railway," a northern line, with a terminus at Fishguard. Mr. Brunel was appointed to make surveys for the first, but the panic of 1837 blighted the project. It was not until the year 1844 that the idea of making a Railway through South Wales became a reality. The Great Western Company proffered warm aid, and the scheme, which was placed in the hands of Mr. Brunel, soon assumed a high rank in public estimation. The line was laid out to run near the coast for the chief part of its length, 162 miles ; and as originally proposed, was intended to form a junction with the Cheltenham and Great Western Railway below Gloucester, where it was to cross the Severn by means of a bridge. This part of the project was strenuously objected to by the corporation and citizens of Gloucester, and by other parties, who memorialised the Board of Admiralty, and opposed the bill in Parliament.

" The Admiralty sent down a commission to inquire into the subject of the proposed bridge for crossing the Severn, and that commission reported against the company. Several attempts were made in the House of Commons to overrule the objection of the Admiralty; but they were unavailing, and the bill, after very great opposition, passed the Legislature, the part for the construction of the bridge having been omitted. The engineer, Mr. Brunel, subsequently proposed to pass the Severn by means of a tunnel, and an application was made to Parliament for that purpose in the following year, but the project was not sanctioned. The company, however, obtained powers to carry their line to Chepstow, with a view to a further extension, so as to form a junction with the Great Western line at Gloucester.—The petition for the bill was introduced into the House of Commons on February 26th, and the bill received the Royal assent on the 4th of August, 1845. The capital of the company was fixed in the bill at £2,800,000, divided into 56,000 shares of £50 each. The bill gave to the Great Western Company power to subscribe the sum of £560,000 towards the capital, which amount was provided by that company.

" Since the above act was passed, another bill has been obtained for extending the line to a point of junction with the Gloucester and Dean Forest Railway, at Hagloe, in Gloucestershire, thus affording (in connexion with that line and the Great Western, to which it belongs) an unbroken broad gauge railway from London to the Irish Channel. The same bill authorised the construction of a short branch from the main line into the heart of Swansea, and another to the town of Haverfordwest." *

In the autumn of 1847, Capt. Claxton, R.N., was employed by the company to survey the Irish channel minutely, in a steamer, for the purpose of ascertaining the best route across. This elaborate survey appears to have led to the abandonment of Fishguard as a terminus; and notice was given of the company's intention to apply to Parliament in the session of 1848, for power to alter the line. The proposed deviation will commence in the parish of Letterston, about six miles to the south of Fishguard, and as at present resolved the terminus will be fixed at Abermawr (*see* p. 283), as indicated in our map. We believe, however, that nothing has been finally settled relative to this most important question.

The length of the South Wales line and branches under the provisions of the acts of 1845, 1846, and 1847, was as follows:—

	m.	fur.	ch.
From Hagloe to Fishguard	155	3	3
Pembroke Branch	19	4	0
Haverfordwest Branch	5	1	0
Monmouth Branch	22	5	0
Swansea Branch	1	4	0
Briton Ferry Branch	1	5	0
Total	205	6	3

* *Railway Monthly Magazine*, Feb. 1847.

The distance from Hagloe to Gloucester being 15 miles, will make the length from the latter to Fishguard 170 miles 3 fur. 3 chains, to which, if the distance from London to Gloucester (114 miles) be added, it will give the entire length of the broad gauge line from the Metropolis to Fishguard 284 miles 3 fur. 3 chains. The distance to Abermawr does not differ materially from that to Fishguard. The length of the railway will be lessened when the Cheltenham and Oxford line is made, which, as a connecting link between the Great Western and South Wales lines, will, of course, be on the broad gauge.

The statistical information which we have accumulated in our subsequent pages in illustration of the vast mineral and other resources of South Wales, and of the progress that has been already made in developing them, shows incontestably that this line must command a very large traffic ; and that the traffic may be expected to steadily increase when the advantages conferred on a country by a cheap and speedy mode of transit begin to be felt. The existing traffic was estimated in 1845 at £127,930 per annum ; and the gross receipts of the line, when it comes into full operation, have been calculated at £422,170.

The principal feeders of the Railway, chiefly mineral lines, will be the Gloucester and Dean Forest, the Llynvi Valley, the Vale of Neath, the Swansea Valley, and the Tenby and Saundersfoot railways. The capital of the company is now £3,000,000, and it has power to borrow one million more if necessary. The average cost of works has been estimated by Mr. Brunel, on experience obtained from contracts, at £8,800 per mile.

The South Wales Railway has passed into the hands of the gigantic " Great Western Company." An agreement to the following effect was ratified between the two companies early in 1847 :—The Great Western are to pay the South Wales shareholders " in perpetuity a minimum interest at the rate of five per cent. per annum upon the share capital expended, besides defraying all the current interest on loans taken up, not exceeding the sums mentioned above. The lease to commence when the line from Gloucester to Fishguard, and the Newport and Monmouth line, shall be finished, provided (as respects the latter) the Great Western Company shall also complete their line from Gloucester to Monmouth by the same time, but not otherwise. One moiety of the surplus profits at the end of five years after the lease commences, is to be divided among the South Wales shareholders in addition to the guaranteed interest."

We shall close this article with a short general description of the railway, which is incidentally noticed in several parts of the text of our work, and faithfully laid down in our *map*.

It will be seen that the line chiefly runs near the western bank of the Severn—passing Newnham and Lydney—from Gloucester to Chepstow. For about three miles below Hagloe, near Blakeney, the rails run under the cliffs, and are protected from the tide by a strong wall. There are heavy cuttings on approaching Chepstow, at which place a bridge will be carried across the Wye a little below the present bridge, and the line then follows the western side of the river until the high ground at its back recedes. From thence the gradients are easy over Caldicot level to Newport, in which neighbourhood, for a distance of about three miles, the works are "remarkably heavy, difficult, and expensive." An embankment a mile in length and 20 feet high leads to the bank of the Usk, across which a wooden bridge, 700 feet in length, was nearly completed in May, 1848, when it was destroyed by fire—a circumstance that will delay the opening of the line. The station is to be nearly in the centre of Newport. The railway is carried across the Monmouthshire canal by a wooden bridge, near which a tunnel of three-quarters of a mile in length commences. Wentloog Level, which intervenes between Newport and Cardiff, is a region of easy gradients. The river Rumney is crossed by a wooden bridge, two hundred and thirty feet in length. The line runs a little to the south of Cardiff, between the head of the Bute Docks and the old town; the station is to be on The Moors, and the river Taff is to be diverted from its present course, and will flow in a straight line to Penarth roads. From Cardiff the line crosses the present mail-coach road, about two miles to the westward, and then bends towards the north, between the villages of Ely and St. George's, passing through St. Fagan's, (not far from Llantrissent) and along the borders of the hill country, by a route distinguished by good gradients. The river Ely is crossed seven times on stone bridges; and much fine scenery is opened, including near prospects of the hills called *Mynydd Garth Mailwg*, *Mynydd Maenddû*, and *Mynydd y Gaer*. After sweeping a little to the south-west, the line passes close to Bridgend on the north-east, afterwards crosses the Llynvi Valley Railway, and runs within half a mile of Pyle. The route originally projected for this part of the country ran by Ogmore and Newton Nottage, close to the coast, but it being apprehended that the sea sand [see KENFIG, p. 155] would be troublesome, a deviation has been sanctioned, [which runs near Margam. For several miles before approaching Neath—where it is necessary to cross the Neath river—the line follows the edge of marshes. The gradients are steep beyond Neath. Some heavy works, including a tunnel, succeed, and cuttings and vast embankments usher the "South Wales" into the Swansea valley, which it will cross at Landore, by a stupendous viaduct, including a bridge over the Tawe. The length of the Swansea branch has already been given (also see p. 184). There will be rather heavy tunnels in this valley and at Loughor. The Burry river is to be crossed by a long bridge a little below the present Loughor bridge. From hence the line will run by Llanelly, and cross the Gwendraeth Vawr, a little below Kidwelly.

The railway, as at first sanctioned, was to run from hence inland to ¯˙rmarthen, but a deviation has been adopted, so that it will nearly follow the course of the Towy, passing Ferryside, up to Carmarthen. There will be an important bridge—below the present—through which vessels will be allowed to pass. There is now a straight run westward to Whitland, to the north of the present mail road; and soon after a fork in the line will commence: a branch is to run in a south-westerly direction not far from Carew Castle to Pembroke Dock, on Milford Haven; and another branch will run from this at Reynalton, a little to the west of Saundersfoot, to Tenby. The main trunk will incline upwards, passing Narbeth in a north-westerly direction; a branch is to be constructed for the Haverfordwest traffic: and finally it will run almost due north to the terminus at Abermawr, curving to the westward towards the last. Powerful steamers will be established between ports in Ireland and those on this side of the Channel, including Pembroke.

It is calculated that the distance from Gloucester to the Western terminus will be performed (by Express Train we conclude) in about four hours, thereby reducing the time for performing the journey from London to the south of Ireland to thirteen hours, an immense saving over the time which it at present occupies.

MONMOUTH AND HEREFORD RAILWAY.

This line, which belongs to the Great Western Company, will command much beautiful scenery, especially during the latter portion of its course to Monmouth. It will commence at a point of junction with the South Wales Railway, eight miles out of Gloucester. From thence it will run westward through the valley at the back of Penyard Hill, behind Ross. The "main trunk" will be carried across the Wye, about a quarter of a mile above the Kerne Bridge; and there will be another crossing at the foot of *Cymon's Yat*, where a tunnel will be carried through the narrow peninsula, described in our account of the Wye. From this point the line will run along exquisite scenery, near the south bank of the river to Monmouth, from whence there is to be a continuation to the South Wales main trunk line, through Usk to Newport, mentioned in the calculation of distances already given, as the "Monmouth branch." There will, on the completion of these lines, thus be a double communication between the ports of Gloucester and Newport. The distance from Gloucester to Monmouth will be twenty-five miles and a half—less than one hour.

THE HEREFORD BRANCH will curve rapidly to the north beyond Penyard Hill, passing Ross—distant from Gloucester twenty miles and a half— to Hereford, eleven miles and a half further on. Length of the line from Gloucester to Hereford, 32 miles.

TAFF VALE RAILWAY.

The main line extends from the Bute Docks to Merthyr Tydvil, 24½ miles. There is a branch to *Aberdare*, which has branches, in all 8½ miles;

and there are also several branches for mineral traffic, including one up the Rontha Valley. The line was partially opened in 1840, and completed on April 12, 1841; it was originally single, but the traffic, which is enormous, has obliged the company to lay down double rails for the greater part of the distance. A glimpse of Llandaff Cathedral may be obtained on the left, soon after leaving Cardiff. The tin and iron works at Melyn Gryffith and Pentyrch, which are next passed, belong to Messrs. Booker and Co. The red round tower on the rock on the right is Castle Coch, an ancient British stronghold. Near Taff's Well Station is a tepid mineral spring, held in much reputation in the district for its medicinal properties. The general characteristics of the river and of Pont-y-Pridd are described elsewhere. The river crossed by the fine railway bridge at Pont-y-Pridd is the Rontha. The river Clydach is afterwards crossed by the line, shortly after which the trains arrive at an inclined plane at Navigation House, nine miles from Merthyr, which is worked by a stationary engine. There is a viaduct over the Taff at Quaker's Yard, nearer Merthyr, 100 feet high and 600 feet long. The works of the line also embrace two short tunnels. Mr. Bush was joint engineer with Mr. Brunel. The cost of the railway, which is on the narrow gauge, has been nearly double the original estimate.

LLANELLY RAILWAY. A mineral and passenger locomotive line (narrow gauge) which runs from Llanelly new docks into the interior; length, including branches, 22 miles.

OTHER RAILWAYS SANCTIONED OR IN PROGRESS IN MONMOUTHSHIRE AND SOUTH WALES.

NEWPORT and PONTYPOOL (narrow gauge) 10 miles.

NEWPORT, ABERGAVENNY, and HEREFORD, (narrow gauge). Length to Pontypool, 32 miles. Extension line sanctioned to Taff Vale Railway. Branches to Usk 4¾ miles, and to Raglan 6¼ miles.

LLYNVI VALLEY (broad gauge). Conversion of Porthcawl tramway into a locomotive line. Length, 16 miles.

VALE of NEATH (broad gauge). Length of main line, 22¾ miles. Four branches, one of which is to join the Aberdare Railway, in all 5½ miles; total 28¼ miles.

SWANSEA VALLEY (gauge not settled).

SWANSEA and LOUGHOR (narrow gauge); will run into Oystermouth tramway; length 5 miles.

SAUNDERSFOOT and TENBY (broad gauge); a branch from the South Wales at Reynalton; length nearly 6¼ miles; branch of a mile from St. Issell's to Saundersfoot.

THE WELSH ALPHABET.—GLOSSARY.

" To read Welsh," observes Mr. Jones, in his *Musical and Poetical Relics,*
" a right knowledge of the Alphabet is all that is necessary; for (not going
to a nicety,) all the letters retain one invariable sound, as there are *no mutes.*
Letters that are circumflexed must be pronounced long, as bôn, like bone in
English; bwn, boon; bîn, been." We subjoin the Alphabet, with the pro-
nunciation of the letters that differ from the English :—

A	B	C	Ch	D	Dd	E	F	Ff	G	Ng	H	I	L	Ll	M	N
		ek	uch		uth		uv	f	eg	ung				lh		

O	P	Ph	R	S	T	Th	U	W	Y.
	uph					uth	ee	oo	ur.

GLOSSARY.—The following explanation of words which often occur in the
names of places, &c., in Wales, will aid the reader :—

Aber, a confluence, the fall of a lesser
  water into a greater.

Avon or *Afon,* a river.

Allt, a woody cliff, the side of a hill.

Bach, Vach, little small.

Banau, eminences.

Bedd, a grave, or sepulchre.

Bettws, a station between hill and
  vale; a chapel of ease.

Blaen, the end or point.

Bôd, a dwelling.

Bryn, a hill or mount.

Bwlch, a pass, a gap. a defile.

Bychan, Fechan, little.

Cader, a hill-fort, a chair.

Caen, an enclosure, a hedge.

Caer, a city, a fort, a wall or mound
  for defence, (Roman).

Capel, a chapel, an old oratory.

Carn, a heap.

Carnedd, a heap of stones.

Carreg, a stone.

Castell, a castle, or fortress.

Cefn or *Cevyn,* a ridge, a back, the
  upper side.

Clawdd, a dike, trench, or ditch.

Clogwen, a precipice.

Coch, red.

Coed, a wood.

Cors, a bog or fen.

Crug, a crag or rock.

Croes, a cross.

Cong, a hillock or mount.

Cwm, a valley, a glen, or dingle.

Cymmer, a confluence.

Dinas, a fortified hill; a British
  camp.

Dôl, a meadow, generally by the side
  of a river.

Drws, a pass, a doorway.

Dû, black.

Dwr, water.

Duffryn, a valley.

Eglws, a church.

Fynnon, a spring, a well.

Gaer. See Caer.

Garth, a hill bending round.

Glan, a shore or brink.

Glas, blue, green, verdant, grey.

Glyn, a glen or vale through which
  a river flows.

Gwern, a watery meadow.

Gwestdg, an inn.

Gwyn, white, fair.

Gwyrdd, green.
Gwyniedyn, *pysgodyn*, a fish.
Havod or *Hafod*, a summer residence.
Hên, old.
Hir, long.
Llan, a church, an enclosure.
Llech, a flat stone.
Llwyn, a grove, a wood.
Llwyd, grey.
Llyn, a lake, a pool.
Llyr, the sea-water.
Maen, a stone.
Maes, a field, a plain.
Mawr, *Vawr*, great, large.
Melin, a mill.
Melyn, yellow.
Moel, a smooth conical hill; naked.
Morva or *Morfa*, a sea-marsh.
Mynach, a monk.
Mynydd, a mountain.
Nant, a ravine, a brook, or river.
Newydd, new, fresh.
Pen, a head, top, or end.
Penmaen, the stone end.
Pentref, a village, a hamlet, or suburb.

Pysgodwr, a fisherman.
Pistyll, a spout, a cataract.
Plâs, a hall or palace.
Pont, a bridge.
Porth, a gate, a port, a ferry.
Pwll, a pit or ditch.
Rhaiadyr, a cataract.
Rhiw, an ascent.
Rhôs, a moist plain, or meadow.
Rhûdd, purple, red.
Rhŷd, a ford.
Sarn, a causeway.
Tal, the head or front.
Tavarn, a tavern.
Tir, the land, earth.
Traeth, a sand.
Trev, *Tref*, or *Tre*, a house, a small town.
Twr, a tower.
Tŷ, a house.
Tyddyn, a farm.
Y, the, on the, of.
Ym, in, or by.
Yn, in, at, into.
Ynys, an island.
Ystrad, a vale or flat formed by a river.

PHRASES.

Bu, an ox.
Ci, a dog.
Ceffyl, a horse.
Merlyn, a pony.
Boreufwyd, breakfast.
Cinio, dinner.
Tê, tea.
Ymenyn, butter.
Caws, cheese.
Bara a'caws, bread and cheese.
Cig mochyn, bacon, ham.
Wy, an egg.
Halen, salt.
Plât, a plate.

Gwydr, a glass.
Cwpan, a cup.
Brandi, brandy.
Gin, gin.
Cwrw (pronounced *kooroo*) ale.
Porter, porter.
Meddyg, a doctor.
Dimai, a halfpenny.
Ceiniog, a penny.
Dwy geiniog, two-pence.
Chwech ceiniog, six-pence.
Un swllt, one shilling.
Hanner coron, half a crown.
Punt, a pound sterling.

DAVIDS HEAD
P E M B R O.
St LAWRENCE
Haycastle
Ambleston
Whitchurch
ST DAVIDS
Brandy
Trefgarn
Spittal
Walte
Clar
R. Alun
Roch Castle
Camrose
Weston Castle
Lapha
 St BRIDES
Nolton
Lambston
Prenderzast
HAVERFORDWEST
Roberton
BAY
Druidston Haven
Haroldston
Cameston
S
Goch
Stack Rock
Broadhaven
Walton West
Boulston
Min
Talbenny
St Brides
Hill
Walwins Castle
Robeston
Pelham Castles
Johnston
Langwm
Marto
Broad Sound
Island
Marloes
St Ishmaels
Haverfordwest
Steynton
Rosemarket
MILFORD
Yerbeston
gwm
Dale
Mullock
MILFORD HAVEN
Llanstadwell
Skokholm Island
St Anns Hd
Light House
Pennar
Rhoscrowther
Pennar Mouth er Ferry
PEMBROKE
Sheep Id
Castle Martin
Langhorn Pill
Hundleton
Ja
Freshwater Bay West
Orielton
St Petrox
Chariton
The Pole
Warren
St Twynnels
Bosherston
Linney Head
Flimston Chapel
Stackpole Park
Danish Camps
Stackpole Elecara
Crow Rock
St Gowans Head
B R I S
The Wash
The Castles
Bullslaughter Bay
The Stack Rocks

CONTINUATION OF THE SOUTH WALES RAILWAY (PEMBROKESHIRE) same Sca
Strumble Hd
British Antiquities
Fishguard Bay
Llanwnda
Goron
St Nicholas
FISHGUARD
Abermaur
Granston
Castellvech Pa
Trefin
Letterston
Punch
Llanrian
St Lawrence
Castell Morris
Davids Hd
Llanhowel

THE BOOK

OF

SOUTH WALES,

&c.

THE SEVERN.

" To princelie Severne first."
DRAYTON'S POLY-OLBION.

THE parent of the Bristol Channel—the fairest stream that gladdens the Vales of merry England—is of mountain origin, cradled amongst the clouds on a wild steep of Plinlimmon, close to the birth-place of its sister the Wye, and three other gushing rivers. It leaps with the joyousness of youth from rock to rock as far as Llanidloes, where it assumes a soberer air. At Welshpool, in Montgomeryshire, it becomes navigable. From thence it sweeps through the counties of Salop, Worcester, and Gloucester, washing " mitred abbeys" and stately towns ; between Gloucester and Newnham its course is exceedingly irregular and serpentine ; near Hock Crib—a place which has become celebrated in consequence of its association with the name of BRUNEL, who here wished to carry out a far greater work than that accomplished by his father in the construction of the Thames Tunnel—the stream expands into an estuary, but we shall still

c

treat it as a river until it meets the Avon in King Road, where the Bristol Channel or " Severn Sea " may properly be said to begin.   Below Newnham considerable tracts of land have been reclaimed from the sea from time to time, partly in consequence of the accumulation of deposits, partly by artificial means.   Old drawings are in existence which show " vessels within a short distance of Berkeley Castle," and the new grounds there " as one expanse of water ;" and between Gloucester and Worcester, the bed of the river is probably four or five feet higher than it once was, and the channel somewhat narrower.

The Severn was called by the Britons, *Hafren*, the queen or chief river, which name it still retains for the first twelve miles of its course.   Its Roman name *Sabrina*, has led to much antiquarian discussion, and is supposed to have been derived from the melancholy fate of Sabra or Sabrina, a daughter of Lochrine, King of Britain, who was forcibly drowned in its waters, and has been made by Milton in " Comus," goddess of the stream—

> " There is a gentle nymph not far from hence,
> That with moist curb sways the smooth Severn stream,
> Sabrina is her name, a virgin pure ;
> Whilome she was the daughter of Lochrine,
> That had the sceptre from his father Brute."

The Saxon name of the river was *Sœferne*, " sea-flowing." It appears to have been a great outlet for trade from a very early period.   The quaint old writer Nennius, who styles it " one of the arms of Britain," complains of the decline that had taken place in its commerce in the seventh century.   William of Malmsbury and other authors describe it as a boundary line between England and Wales.   Its name is associated with many historical events.   Thus Shakspeare, in Henry IV.—

> " Three times hath Harry Bolingbroke made head
> Against my power ; thrice from the banks of Wye,
> And sandy bottom'd Severn have I sent him
> Bootless home and weather-beaten back."

The Wars of the Roses were quenched on the battle field of

Tewkesbury—" now Malvern mountains veil the wearied sun," says Speed, " and yet the combat rages ;" at Gloucester, Charles the First was ominously repulsed ; and at Worcester, the " faithful city," the Royalist cause was finally broken. Berkeley—

> " Mark the year, and mark the night,
> When Severn shall re-echo with affright,
> The shrieks of death through Berkeley's roofs that ring :
> Shrieks of an agonizing king."

The Geological character of the Valley of the Severn has led Sir R. I. Murchison to suppose that it once formed a great channel of the sea—that the Bristol Channel then commenced at the Breiddin hills, near the borders of Wales, and was bounded on either side as it advanced towards the south, by the Malvern and Cotswold ranges. The bluffs of the Cotswold, which often resemble marine headlands, serve to give a popular character to this view. The strait must, therefore, have been reduced to the limits of the present Bristol Channel by some considerable elevation of land. Even now, however, the fall of the river between Worcester and Gloucester, a distance of nearly thirty miles, is only ten feet.

In consequence of the nature of the country through which the Severn and its tributaries flow—soft sandstone and marl—its waters are said to be charged " with a larger amount of turbid deposits than any other river in Europe."* The tidal deposits in the lower course of the stream are also very great. In the deepest reach between Gloucester and Stourport, about six miles above the former place, the mud brought up by the tides often accumulates to the extent of six or eight feet in a year, and remains until a flood occurs of sufficient power to wash it away, although this " scour" is seldom effectual. The Severn is subjected, from its mountain origin and the number of its tribu-

---

* " Hæc erat celebrata illa regio Silurum, tribus validissimis habitata populis, quos inter præ reliquis celebres Silures, proprié sic dicti, qnam ab ora relicta *turbidum Sabrinæ fretum* distinguit." Richard of Cirencester; " De Situ Brit."

taries, to sudden and sometimes very destructive floods, which are
not much to be wondered at when it is borne in mind that the
superficial extent of country which the river drains, down to
Gloucester, exceeds 4,500 square miles. The flood of 1770 inun-
dated the adjacent country to the depth of six feet nine inches.
The fall is very gradual—

> " The wide
> Majestic wave of Severn slowly rolls
> Along the deep divided glebe."

The descent from Buildwas to Gloucester, 72 miles, is only 104
feet three inches, and Mr. T. Fulljames, C. E., states that from
Stourport to Gloucester (42 miles) the character of the stream is
" so continuously similar as to be without a parallel" the course
being almost due north and south, and the width (150 feet) the
same at either end. It may be imagined that the Severn is a
very difficult river to improve, a circumstance which probably
accounts for its having been left in a state of nature until very
recently. The detentions which vessels have sustained have been
serious. Large fleets of river craft have often been detained for
two or three months together, owing to want of water ; and the
average extent of detention has been about three months in the
year, from drought or floods. In 1836 a movement was commenced at Worcester, which does much honour to that city, for
the purpose of rendering this fine river navigable at all periods of
the year ; and after a long struggle, an Act was obtained in 1842,
which placed the river under the control of Commissioners, and
gave that body power to adopt means to obtain a constant average
depth of not less than six feet between Stourport and Gloucester,
and to levy tolls when the improvement should have been rendered effectual. The execution of this national work was entrusted
to Mr. Cubitt, who has deepened the river by means of weirs and
dredging, but the difficulties that have been encountered have
far exceeded expectation ; and it was not until the 1st of January,
1847, that the Commissioners, after expending upwards of
£203,000, were in a condition to levy tolls, which they did in

opposition to remonstrances from the traders, who contended that a depth of six feet had *not* been obtained. The Severn has, therefore, ceased to be a " free river," but its navigation is still imperfect. About 120,000 tons of soil have been removed by dredging between Worcester and Gloucester ; but the experience of 1847 having " practically proved that during a long and dry summer there is not sufficient water descending the river to maintain a depth of six feet in a channel sixty feet wide, without the aid of artificial dams," an act was applied for in 1848 for the purpose of empowering the commissioners to erect locks and weirs between Diglis (Worcester) and Gloucester. The class of vessels which navigate the Severn is peculiar ; they bear the name of " Trows," and are probably the most old fashioned craft in form and rig now remaining in Britain. Some of the largest, of nearly 200 tons burden—few exceed 120 tons—make voyages to Bridgwater, Cardiff, and other channel ports, and many, with gunwales even with the water, may be seen in the Bristol river on their passage to and from the north.

One of the peculiarities of this river is the tidal-wave, commonly called the " *Bore,*" but more properly the " *hygre,*" said to be derived from the French *eau-guerre, i.e.,* " water-war." This wave is the natural result of the contraction of the estuary, which increases the rapidity of the tide at early flood by presenting an obstacle to its advance. The *Bore* excited the attention of some of our earliest writers. In a curious M S. of the Seventh Century in the Harleian collection, written by Nennius, entitled " Wonders of the Island of Britain," we find the following :—

" Another wonder is the *Duong Habren,* or the two Kings of the Severn. When the sea overflows with the tide at the mouth of the Severn, two separate heaps of froth are formed, which strike against each other as if there was a battle between them. Each proceeds against the other, and they attack each other by turns. They then recede the one from the other, and again proceed, and this on the surface of the sea, during every tide. This they have done from the beginning of the world to the present day."

Drayton, in his *Poly-olbion*, gives a vivid idea of the phenomenon :—

> " —— untill they be imbrac't
> In *Sabrins* Soveraigne armes : with whose tumultuous waves
> Shut up in narrower bounds, the *Higre* wildly raves ;
> And frights the stragling flocks, the neighbouring shores to flie,
> A farre as from the Maine it comes with hideous cry,
> And on the angry front the curled foam doth fling ;
> Hurles up the slimie ooze, and makes the scalie brood
> Leape madding to the Land affrighted from the flood ;
> Oreturns the toyling barge, whose steresman doth not lanch,
> And thrusts the furrowing beake into her irefull panch."

The *Bore* rushes onward at spring tides with a head varying from nine to about four feet, and the roar may be heard on a calm day at a considerable distance ; it is very impressive at night. The rapidity with which it covers the vast expanse of sand between Sharpness and Awre Points is often exceedingly striking. The brown waste seems instinct with life in a few minutes—a sea of hissing waters. Many narrow escapes have taken place on these sands, particularly at Purton Passage, about a mile and a half above Sharpness. There are quicksands, which add to the danger of crossing to the Ferry at low water.—The tide before the dredging operations sometimes reached Upton-upon-Severn bridge, 19 miles from Gloucester, but it usually did not flow more than a few miles above that city ; " high spring tides now flow to a height of three feet at Tewkesbury, three feet at Upton, and 18 inches at Diglis, which latter place is forty miles further inland than the high water of neap tides ever flows."—There are other instances of the occurrence of this tidal wave in England, especially on the Ouse, where the country people call it " *The Eager.*"

The Severn is famous for its breed of Salmon ; and owing to the laudable efforts of an Association established in the year 1843, for the purpose of protecting the fisheries from unlawful practices, " fence months" have been fixed, prices reduced, and there is reason to hope that ultimately fish may be as plentiful in this river as they were in the old time, when masters were restrained from feeding their apprentices with salmon more than two days in the week.*   The marine lampreys of the Severn have been famous for centuries ; they have been one of the most highly-prized dishes at King's tables, and until the Reform Bill passed, the city of Gloucester annually sent a lamprey pie with a large raised crust to Windsor Castle.   Even Catherine of Russia sent for Severn lampreys.

·GLOUCESTER,

Within a very few years, has become a large port.   Previously to 1827—in which year the Ship Canal, 16 miles long to Sharpness Point, was opened—sea-borne vessels rarely reached it, owing to the circuitous and shallow nature of the Severn ; now it is computed that sea-going vessels of the aggregate tonnage of three hundred thousand tons annually pass the Old Passage on their way to Gloucester, and some small coal ports (Lydney, &c.), besides an equally large amount of tonnage of trows and small craft, or 600,000 tons in all.   This trade is rapidly increasing, and as the sea-borne traffic is likely in a few years to be doubled, new docks have been constructed.   The Gloucester and Berkeley ship canal has partly created a new trade, partly diverted trade from Bristol.   Vessels drawing 19 feet of water enter the basin at Sharpness, but it is necessary to lighten them a little before they can be drawn to Gloucester.   The canal was originally cut to a depth of 18 feet.   Steam-boats now run regularly from Gloucester to Swansea, Cardiff, and Newport.   The scenery on either side of the Canal is generally very picturesque, and includes the dreamy wooded heights of Dean Forest.   The Barrow Hill, an eminence about nine miles below Gloucester, near the west end of a peninsula four miles long, round which the Severn sweeps to Hock Crib, commands one of the most remarkable river scenes in Britain.   The distance from Sharpness to King Road is nearly

---

* The " Fence time" for the Severn and its tributaries extends from the 14th September to the 31st December. At the latter period the salmon are however unfit for human food.   On the Wye the river is closed between the 14th September and the 10th February.

18 miles. The objects of interest at Gloucester are indicated in our Wye Tour.

THE OLD PASSAGE—RAILWAY BRIDGE.

The Passages across the Severn, of which this is the upper, have long been celebrated, and their history presents many striking incidents. We must, however, chiefly confine ourselves to the present period. In 1845 the "Bristol and Liverpool Junction Railway Company" proposed to construct a Bridge for locomotives over this ferry. At first the scheme was treated as chimerical, but it gradually made its way in the public mind, and its feasibility was proved conclusively. The idea was a magnificent one—truly national; it has been abandoned owing to want of capital; but we entertain no doubt that the government will ultimately construct this great public work. Mr. T. Fulljames, of Gloucester, furnished two designs for a bridge, the second of which was approved by Mr. Walker, the Admiralty engineer, who was appointed to survey the Severn minutely. We annex an engraving of the design selected, and a section of the Severn, showing the rocks, between Aust and Beachley. The rocky nature of the bed of the river presents the best possible foundation for piers; nature has done much to facilitate the erection of a bridge here, in several respects. We abridge from Mr. Fulljames's report, the following description of the design :—
" This plan proposes main piers or towers on the rocks that are chiefly bare at low water; each of the channels, and the shore from Ulverstone, to be spanned by openings of *one thousand one hundred feet each*, the piers being placed as shown on the plan, and of the dimensions and form figured, the height to the platform of the bridge to be 120 feet." The platform to be 35 feet wide, divided into two lines of railway, and with foot-paths between, " to be composed of pierced iron plates stiffened by transverse and diagonal bearers and braces, a system of longitudinal trussing to be connected with the suspension rods as an auxiliary support above and below the platform, and to form the parapets; the platforms to be five feet higher in their centres than at the respective piers. The suspension chains and rods to be of round iron, and so disposed as to present the least surface to the action

of the wind ; there are to be four sets of main chains, each set composed of as many links of wrought iron, three inches diameter, as will give the required strength for passing railway trains ; the deflection to be forty-seven feet ; the chains to be stayed across and tied together ; the longitudinal trussing to be made of hollow cast-iron pipes, through the uprights of which the suspending rods, one inch and a quarter diameter, are to pass and be secured to the platform ; the back stays to be carried a proper distance from the abutments and fastened into masonry along their course, and at the ends to be secured by suitable holding bolts, fixed in chambers of masonry built in the rock." The piers were to occupy 692 feet, and the waterway 4,742 feet. Several works were proposed in connection with this plan, for the improvement of the navigation of the river—which, as a whole, shows Mr. Fulljames to be an engineer of no mean genius.

At present a small iron steamer is used on the Old Passage Ferry, the traffic on which, including the conveyance of the mails, is very great. Many casualties have occurred here with sailing boats ; one of the Messrs. Crawshay, the eminent iron masters, and several other persons were lost in crossing in the year 1840. The distance is about 2,200 yards.

" There is," observes Mr. Walker, in his report to the Lords of the Admiralty, " so far as I know, no *great* communication in this country so bad, or therefore where an improvement is so much wanted, as at this ferry ; and the importance is increased by the fact of there being no bridge below Gloucester, which is 30 miles above the Old Passage, and no crossing below (except the New Passage, which is inferior to the Old) without going down the Avon, from Bristol.........Above and below the Old Passage the river widens rapidly, and is impeded by sand-banks of which the Aust Passage is clear, owing to its contracted width ; but this contraction is again the cause of a very strong run of tide near the place, that of a spring flood being not less than six and a half to seven miles per hour, and the corresponding ebb four miles and a half, with great irregularity in its course, and a heavy tumbling sea when the wind and tide are in opposite directions. There is scarcely any ' still' or ' slack' at low water. Within ten minutes after the strong run of ebb, the flood runs up with nearly equal velocity. The uniformity in the rise of tide during the whole time of flood is remarkable, there being no ' still' at either high or low water.''

NEW PASSAGE. This is a ferry nearly two miles and a half lower than the Old, at a point at which the Severn is nearly three miles wide at high water. Fosbroke, in his " Collections," records the following interesting anecdote :—

" What is called the New Ferry or Passage over the Severn, may dispute antiquity with the Old Passage. The former belonged, time immemorial, to the respectable family of St. Pierre, and was suppressed by Oliver Cromwell from the following occurrence. The unfortunate Charles I. [after staying with the gallant old Marquis of Worcester at Raglan, subsequently to the defeat at Naseby, in 1645] being pursued by a strong party of the enemy, rode through Shire Newton, and crossed the Severn to Chiswell Pill, on the Gloucestershire side. The boat had scarcely returned, before a corps of sixty republicans followed him to the Black Rock, and instantly compelled the boatmen, with drawn swords, to ferry them across. The boatmen, who were loyalists, left them on a reef called the English Stones, which is separated from the Gloucestershire side by a lake fordable at low water ; but the tide, which had just turned, flowed in with great rapidity, and they were all drowned in attempting to cross. Cromwell, informed of this unfortunate event, abolished the ferry, and it was not renewed until the year 1748. The renewal occasioned a lawsuit between the family of Saint Pierre and the Duke of Beaufort's guardians. In the course of the suit depositions taken by a Commission of Chancery, held at Bristol, proved Mr. Lewis's right to the ferry, and confirmed this interesting anecdote."

On the resumption of the traffic, thus interrupted for more than a century, the ferry acquired its present appellation. The mails, &c., to South Wales and Ireland were conveyed across here for many years ; but the loss of time and risk encountered at low water, led to the removal of the chief portion of the business to the Old Passage, which underwent great improvement about the year 1833.—The Bristol and South Wales Junction Railway Company purchased the New Passage from the late Colonel Lewis, and the Old Passage from Duke of Beaufort.

THE TIDES.

The rise of tide in the Bristol Channel is greater than on any other portion of the coasts of the British Isles, and is, we believe, only exceeded in the Bay of Fundy, in North America. The geographical position of the estuary explains this. It tries the strength of the Atlantic. The greatest velocity is attained at " the Shoots" near the New Passage, where the tidal current runs fourteen miles an hour ; but its speed is materially influenced by the wind. Six or seven miles off Hartland Point, spring tides run only three miles and neaps two miles an hour. The average run of tide in the Channel varies in strength from three to five knots, between neaps and springs. There is (we quote Mr. Norie) commonly a northerly indraught into the Channel which sets obliquely towards the shores of Wales ; and " it has been found, that throughout the whole channel, southerly winds augment the tides at high water, and keep them up at low. water, while northerly winds constantly depress them : south and south-westerly winds are commonly prevalent during two-thirds of the year, and these occasion a great influx of water from the Atlantic ocean. " At Milford Haven and St. Gowan's Head, the spring tides rise 36 feet, neaps 24 ; in Barnstaple Bay springs rise 24 feet, neaps 16 ; at the Flatholm, springs 36 feet, and neaps 24 ; at Newport, on the Usk, the rise in springs is about 40 feet ; at Chepstow, on the Wye, 56 to 60 feet (the highest altitude in Great Britain ;) at Rownham Ferry, near Cumberland Basin, Bristol, the *average* depth at springs and neaps is about 25 feet ; at the Old Passage, the rise is 45 and 30 feet ; and at Sharpness Point, the *average* rise exceeds 20 feet. The Wye, which unites with the Severn a quarter of a mile below the Old Passage, tends greatly to relieve the run of tide in that part of the channel. At Chepstow, the tide rose in January, 1768, to an altitude of 70 feet, to the great injury of the old wooden bridge then existing there. Mr. Ham, of Bristol, states that the "water of the channel is of a higher temperature on the Welsh coast than on the Somersetshire side, being 67° Fahrenheit on the former, when 65° near the mouth of the Avon ;" a circumstance which is probably caused by the greater

shallowness of the sea towards the north. The purity of the
water is great at Ilfracombe and Tenby, but it becomes disco-
loured in the upper parts of the channel, although at Weston,
sea-water in a tumbler appears quite clear. From the mouth
of the Usk to King Road, the average quantity of mud held in
suspension, per imperial gallon, is said to be about 40 grs. ; and
the total quantity of mud in an area of 225 miles, on this estimate,
will amount to 700,000 tons.

TIDE GAUGE. About the year 1832, a small instrument, called
a self-registering tide gauge, was placed by Mr. Shirreff, of the
Bristol Institution, in Hungroad, river Avon, in consequence of
a suggestion made by Professor Whewell to that society. Some
years afterwards it was discontinued on account of the erection
of an improved tide gauge, constructed by Mr. T. G. Bunt, (then
of Bristol, now of Fleet-street, London, and calculator of the
Bristol Tide Tables since 1836,) which was placed against the
east side of the Avon, in front of the Hotwell House, Bristol.
An explanation of the action of this instrument for which we are
indebted to Mr. Bunt, will interest many readers. The following
are its principal parts and appendages :—

An upright iron trunk containing a float, and having a small hole in the
bottom to admit the tide. A wheel connected with the float by a cord
and weight, which causes a pencil to rise and fall with the tide. An
upright cylinder, covered with a sheet of paper, upon which the pencil
presses and marks a line. An eight-day clock, which turns the cylinder
round once in twenty-four hours. The combined motions of the cylinder
and pencil draw a curve on the paper which shows the time and height
of each High Water. A minute of time and an inch of height, are the
ordinary limits of error. A fuller description of the instrument, illustrated by plates, will be found in the Phil. Trans. for 1838, and in the
Encycl. Metrop., Article ' Tides,' by the present Astronomer Royal.

Since this instrument has been used, much valuable information has been obtained as to the effect produced by gales in the
Atlantic on the time and height of the tides. During a violent
westerly gale on the 28th of January, 1840, the time of high water,
according to the tide table, was accelerated no less than one hour
and twenty-six minutes ! Mr. Bunt mentions a remarkable fact,

that on this day the *time* of high water only was affected, the mean height of the two tides of the 28th being exactly 20 feet 8 inches, as predicted in the table. The effect of the hurricane which occurred on the morning of the 29th October, 1838, was just the reverse : the " *time* of high water having been retarded about ten or twelve minutes only, whilst the height was augmented by the enormous addition of eight feet" ! Mr. Bunt has found that the variations of atmospheric pressure, as indicated by the barometer, exert a regular and very considerable influence on the height of high water in the river Avon. For example, an increase of atmospheric pressure, by which the mercury was raised one inch, produced a depression of about fourteen inches in the height of high water. We subjoin the material portion of a communication with which we have been favoured by Mr. Bunt :—

" The actual range of the tide is much greater at King Road than it is at the Bristol self-registering Tide Gauge, in consequence of the elevation of the bed of the Avon above the level of the low water line at King Road. Were the Avon to be sufficiently deepened, the range of tide at the Hotwells would be greater than at King Road ; for I found by levelling from the one station to the other, and making simultaneous observations at each, that the tide rises usually about a foot, in absolute difference of level, higher at the Hotwells than at King Road. The time of high water has been supposed by the pilots to be about a quarter of an hour earlier at King Road than at the Hotwells. But by careful observations, during an entire month, made simultaneously at King Road (or rather Portishead) and the Hotwells, I found that the time of high water is sometimes earlier, and sometimes later, by about ten or fifteen minutes, at either station ; and that on the average of the whole, the time was two minutes *earlier* at the Hotwells than at Portishead. The highest tide by far that I have ever registered was that of the morning of 29th of January, 1846, which rose to 38 feet 8 inches above the sills of the gates of Cumberland Basin. At a very low neap tide, the water sometimes reaches only to about 16 feet, making a difference of 22 feet 8 inches in the tidal heights at Bristol."

We may here mention with reference to the English Channel, that during the prevalence of strong westerly winds at its mouth, the difference in the level of the water between the Lizard and

Dover is ten feet; and that during the memorable gale of the 23rd of November, 1824, the tide rose forty feet at Lyme Regis, on which occasion it flowed *one hour* before the time marked in the tide table for low water.—The phenomenon called the *Ground Swell* is occasionally observed in the lower parts of the Bristol channel—a certain precursor of a violent gale then raging in the distant Atlantic, perhaps a couple of days off. The sea on these occasions comes swiftly in, perhaps four or five times in an hour, and as suddenly recedes; small vessels are often carried out by these waves, or violently thrown upon the beach, and vessels at sea-are also materially affected.

CHARACTERISTICS OF THE CHANNEL.

Few estuaries are comparable to the Bristol Channel, in importance, size, and beauty. At its commencement at King Road it is about five miles wide, and it gradually expands, first in a south-westerly direction, then due west,—contracting slightly between the Nass Point, in Glamorgan, and Bossington Point, near Porlock, Somerset, to ten miles and a half; its span between the Worm's Head and Morte Point—two of its chief portals—is 24 miles; and it increases in width to about 40 miles between St. Gowan's Head, in Pembrokeshire, and Hartland Point, the great western landmark of North Devon. Milford Haven and its coast to the westward ought however to be included in the Bristol Channel, and the distance between St. David's Head, the western extremity of Pembrokeshire, and the opposite point of Cornwall— the imaginary line of division between this and the St. George's Channel—is 105 miles. The distance from Lundy Island to King Road is nearly 80 miles. The shores are very irregular —indented by deep bays and small estuaries. The channel feels the effects of some prevailing winds much less than the English Channel, which is exposed to their full force. The high land on the south keeps the sea smooth on that side in southerly, and to a certain extent in south-westerly gales. Lieut. C. Claxton, R.N., in his evidence before a Select Committee on the West India mail question in 1841, laid great stress on the protection which the coasts of Cornwall, Devon, and Somerset, and the opposite coast of Wales, afford to this channel. "From Portishead," he states, "to the West Indies is within half a point only for the first six miles, one course, either one way or the other." The dangerous shoals in the channel, except in its upper parts, and "one fathom bank" a little shoal to the west of the Holmes, are in bays, or out of the straight course westward. The mouth of the estuary is perfectly open, with the exception of Lundy Island. The Great Western steam-ship, when on the Bristol and New York station, never stopped on any occasion in making this channel from America, and, out of eighteen voyages, ran up nine times to King Road in the night, and in thick rainy weather. Lieut. Claxton mentions in his evidence in 1841, that the steamers from Bristol to Ireland had made 8,840 passages, and the coasting steamers 24,248 passages, without accident, except to one vessel, the Frolic. Two or three Irish steamers have since been lost— two in calm weather—owing to carelessness or ignorance, on the south-western coast of Wales ; but no accident of any kind has occurred since the year 1843.—Occasionally ships mistake this for the English channel, especially in thick wintry weather, on returning home from long voyages, and often pay a terrible penalty for their deficient reckoning. The channel is now well lighted ; it was time, for until about the year 1831, the lights were few and far between. A great diminution of casualties has consequently taken place. There are on the north or Welsh side several fine roadsteads, but nature has afforded hardly any shelter on the south. The want of a HARBOUR OF REFUGE is therefore urgently felt ; and a careful examination of the subject has convinced us that such a harbour could be constructed with very great advantage, at Clovelly, on the southern side of Barnstaple Bay. The Commissioners appointed by order of Parliament to enquire into the subject of Harbours of Refuge were strangely ordered not to include the Bristol Channel in their investigation ; but in consequence of the presentation of memorials from Bristol, Newport, Cardiff, Gloucester, and other ports, it is hoped that something will be done. It is believed that, at all events, a Harbour will be formed at St. Ives, in Cornwall. Lundy island, which stretches three miles athwart the prevailing wind and sea, and rises to a height of 500 feet, affords not merely a natural *breakwater*, but on its easterly side valuable shelter for shipping, although comparatively few masters of vessels avail themselves of it. [*See* ISLANDS.]

The depth of the channel, in its centre, between Carmarthen and Bideford bays, varies from 30 to 40 fathoms; opposite the Nass Point it is from 13 to 15 fathoms. The customary route for ships bound upwards is between the islands called the Flat and Steep Holmes, two miles apart, opposite Cardiff, in which passage there are from 5 to 8 fathoms of water; and the depth of the regular channel towards King Road, a little to the north of the Floating Light Ship, between the extensive shoals known as the "English and Welsh Grounds," varies from 16 to 5 fathoms. The English Grounds—we quote Messrs. Norie's excellent Piloting directions—"lie between Saint Thomas's Head or Sand Point, and Blackmore Point, extending from the shore full three miles; part of these, called Clevedon Flats, are dry at low water." The water towards these banks generally shoals gradually. The "Welsh Grounds" are much more extensive and dangerous shoals, "steep to," in nautical language, and partly dry at low water. They commence off the mouth of the river Usk, and extend to Sudbrook Point, a distance of nearly 13 miles E. N. E.

The scenery of the channel is full of variety—fresh as the ocean. Even the tameness of the coasts of Monmouthshire and the upper portion of Somersetshire is relieved by the noble forms of distant mountains or graceful elevations; and when the horizon becomes unbroken, and the eye longs to pierce the dim Atlantic heaving in the far west, a stern and iron-bound shore rises on either side, broken by dark headlands and smiling bays. Gainsborough, in a letter to Uvedale Price, pronounced the coast of North Devon "the most delightful school for a landscape painter that this country can boast;" and Fuseli was so much excited by the sublimity of the rocks of Pembrokeshire, that he was with difficulty restrained from casting himself headlong from their summit, in a moment of wild enthusiasm.

The alternations of storm and calm are greater in this estuary than in most seas. We have seen the treacherous element almost mirror-like for two or three weeks together, but

" —— the smoothness of his brow
Conceals an unquiet bosom."

Often is the hush of evening or sun-rise broken by howling winds and mountain surges.

Vast fleets are occasionally detained for long periods in Milford Haven, and the roadsteads of Caldy, the Mumbles, and Penarth, by adverse winds. This circumstance suggested an enterprise of great interest to the mind of an earnest clergyman, the Rev. Dr. Ashley, who was moved by witnessing the spiritual destitution—almost heathenism—of the sailors belonging to some 300 or 400 vessels thus embargoed in Penarth Roads. He resolved to devote himself to the work of a missionary, refused a living, and for some years pursued his hazardous calling, in a boat, amidst "perils of waters," from which he was often miraculously preserved. His labours attracted the attention of devout persons on shore ; and in 1839 a small vessel appropriately called the *Eirene*, capable of accommodating about 130 persons at a religious service, was constructed. This bark was a floating church and mission-ship, freighted with bibles and prayer books. Dr. Ashley was thus installed the pastor of a vast floating parish, and a remarkable flock ; and his experiences present much that is wild and touching. Differences have unhappily broken out between the Doctor and the Committee of the Society that was formed to support the mission ; the *Eirene* no longer spreads her wings on her errand of Peace ; but we believe that the Missionary still pursues his labour of love undauntedly.

The Corporation of Bristol possess, under a charter granted by Edward III., jurisdiction down the channel as far as the Flat Holm ; and are compelled to "perambulate" their water boundaries every seven years, which the invention of steam navigation has now rendered an easy task. Edward's charter is, we believe, invariably read by the Town Clerk off Portishead, and several hours are usually spent on the island "terminus," where the exact points of boundary, five feet above high water, are care-

D

fully renewed by the Mayor and other dignitaries, who are accompanied on these occasions by the Master and Wardens of the ancient Society of Merchants of Bristol.

The climate along the estuary is exceedingly healthy.   There is nothing to obstruct or to contaminate the Atlantic purity of the westerly breezes ; and the formation of the coast, which is either sloping or of a geological formation that relieves the earth from surface moisture, is favourable to longevity, a striking proof of which is afforded by the vale of Glamorgan.   The winters are less severe on this side of the island than on the eastern, and the temperature of " the western group of climates is rather lower than that of the south coast, but in March and April rises a little higher."

The Bristol Channel was known to the Phœnicians, who carried on a trade in metals with the natives of Devon and Somerset, as well as with Cornwall, which commerce was continued by the Carthaginians and Greeks, and by the Romans, who, " without doubt," observes Mr. Phelps in his recent History of Somersetshire, (vol. 1, p. 136,) "occupied the most prominent British posts on the coasts of the Severn, and established a coast guard, lest their vessels should be intercepted by pirates.   The mouths of the rivers were also defended by earthworks ; vestiges of which are to be seen at the outlet of the rivers Parret, Axe, Yeo, and Avon, near Portishead. "   The *Via Julia* " formed upon a British trackway, derived its name from Julius Frontinus, who succeeded Vespasian, and converted the trackway into a Roman road, to form a more ready communication with Wales, in his campaign against the Silures.   It joined the road to Redland, a short distance beyond Stoke's Croft turnpike gate, Bristol, and then followed the turnpike-road to Sea Mills (the *Trajectus* of the Itinerary) on the river Avon, where was a Roman station, and from whence was the passage over the Severn, forming the communication between *Britannia primâ* and *Britannia secunda*" (Wales).

The Danes frequently made descents here, and many remains of their rovers are discoverable on the coasts of the channel to the westward ; but for centuries the estuary has been free from those incursions to which the inhabitants of the English channel were so long liable. Privateers were afraid of venturing within its jaws. At the beginning of the last century, a Frenchman by means of a stratagem got hold of and sacked Lundy Island ; towards the end of the American war, a corvette ventured up and burnt some Bristol ships, but she was taken by British tars before she could make her escape; and during the last war, Bristol was the favourite port of passengers connected with the West Indies, either outward or homeward bound, owing to its superior safety.

BRISTOL.

Distant from	Miles.	Distant from	Miles.
London, by Railway	118¼	Thornbury	11
Exeter by ditto	75½	Blaise Castle	4½
Gloucester by ditto	37½	King's Weston	5
Cheltenham by ditto	45	Henbury Cottages	4½
Old Passage Inn	11½	Stanton Drew	7
Burnham by Railway	29	Portishead, by water	9
Chepstow by Old Passage	16½	Pill	5
Clevedon by Railway	16	Weston-super-Mare, by Railway	20
Dundry	4½	Wells	20

The expectant shore-haunter, sick of brick and mortar, and panting for the fresh breezes of the Atlantic, is apt to form a strong first impression of " Bristowe, the pride and glory of the western land," as the train which has, perchance, wafted him in two hours and forty-three minutes from the metropolis, slackens its pace—" shuts off steam"—as it glides in sight of the Great Western terminus. The Railroad, disregarding all obstacles, has pushed its way straight ahead, overtopping innumerable squalid tenements and jostling dingy works. The skeleton of some house, not worth pulling down entirely, stares you in the face—you speculate on the physiognomies of chimneys, from the slim giant on your left, which might almost put " tall" Manchester to the blush, or the pursy Aldermanic group of sugar bakers or potters that are hobbing-and-nobbing on your right, to the crazy occupant of a cottage roof with a brace of consumptive chimney pots. Nor will the drive through smoky streets that succeeds, tend to dissipate but to confirm popular prejudices. At last the real city is reached; and although this is not likely to satisfy the admirer of starched rows of stuccoed houses or broad thoroughfares, yet it possesses a character of its own, infinitely more pleasing to the lover of the picturesque in street scenery, than a hundred mushroom towns.   Look up Mary-le-port street—a relic of the old time —where opposite neighbours can almost shake hands from chamber windows—or at the Castle Bank.   Here there is an old Hospital—one of Bristol's innumerable charities—with niches and quaint statues decked in the ruffs and points of the days of good Queen Bess.   That may be some ancient Merchants' Hall, calling up thoughts of Sebastian Cabot or "princelie Canynge."   Now you stumble on a gem of a gable house, with leaden lattices and carved door posts.   The Pit-hay, a human hive, cabinned in an alley like a stair-case.   Churches of fine mezzotinto colour— solemn presence.   The Quays, with forests of masts which relieve the heaviness of huge or odd-looking warehouses.   And then a distant view of the old city : the massive Cathedral tower —the Guardian of the scene—Saint Mary Redcliffe—a host of spires—the long range of steep heights, thickly peopled, stretching for more than two miles until the Old Fashioned softens into the Modern,—Clifton, the ancient *Caer Odor*, or "city of the chasm," again a city in extent and splendour.

We propose to deal thus with Bristol and its district : to give finger-post hints to strangers, to whom time is precious, but who are anxious to see all they can ; to suggest Excursions to those who can afford to spend a day or two in exploring a neighbourhood rife with interest, ere they pass onward ; and to briefly notice those Antiquities which are, perhaps, the most likely to excite curiosity.   There are no ruins at Bristol.   The City was once strongly fortified, but its defences were obliterated by order of Cromwell, after a gallant resistance in favour of the King.

I. POPULATION : 1821, 86,043 ; 1831, 105,528 ; 1841, 126,988 ; at the present time, upwards of 150,000.

II. CHURCHES : *Cathedral*.   Nave destroyed, it is believed at the Reformation, although a groundless tradition exists at Bristol that the destruction was effected in Cromwell's day.   Interesting Monuments.   Bust in memory of Southey, by Baily ; inscription " Robert Southey, born in Bristol Oct. 4, 1774 ; died at Keswick,

REDCLIFFE CHURCH.
View of the Nave, &c., looking towards the East, restored.

March 21, 1843." Chapter House, an exquisite, probably unrivalled, example of late Norman. Daily Service, at eleven and three ; the same on Sundays, except in the Summer months, when Evening Service begins at five.—*Abbey Gate House of Saint Augustine's.* Saint Augustine preached hard by, in the College Green, when he held his celebrated conference with the British Bishops on this spot in the year 603.—*Mayor's Chapel or Collegiate Church of St. Mark, College Green :* Stained glass.— *Temple Church :* leaning tower.—*St. James's Priory Church,* restored : interior, curious example of Norman.—*St. Stephen's :* tower.—*St. Werburgh's :* the Liturgy was first celebrated in English in this structure in 1543.

Church of St. Mary, Redcliffe.

" One of the most famous, absolute, fairest, and goodliest parish churches, within the realm of England. " So spoke Queen Elizabeth in the sixteenth century. The quaintly-worded description was rather under than over the mark. Redcliffe is *the* " most famous" *parish* church in this kingdom. We need hardly tell that this stately example of the piety and munificence of our fore-fathers has fallen into a grievous state of decay ; or that an attempt has at last been made to rescue it from impending destruction. The parochial authorities went the right way to work. They first consulted the veteran John Britton and Mr. Hosking, an eminent architect, who advised a perfect restoration, including the completion of the spire, and gave an estimate amounting to £40,000 ;—the Vicar and parishioners then (July, 1842,) laid the case before the public, heading a subscription list nobly ; and after a lapse of more than three years, it was resolved to commence the work of repair and restoration with the funds then in hand, amounting to nearly £6,000. The architects finally selected were Mr. Britton and Mr. George Godwin, who judiciously advised that the east end should be exactly restored, as a beginning. This has been done with Caen stone, which has been cut to the size of the mouldering stones displaced. The first contract for the restoration was completed in 1847. " The east end, with its curious ' imbricated' window, and one severy

of the chancel on each side of it, have been restored stone by
stone, including parapets, flying buttresses, and enriched pinnacles, which had long ago been destroyed. Withinside the
brickwork which blocked up the archway between the chancel
and the lady chapel has been removed, and a beautiful stone
screen, in that position, in seven divisions, much mutilated, is
exposed to view. The oak roofs of the chancel and aisles have
been renewed and new leaded," and the ground has been lowered
for several feet, to its proper height, all round the church. It was
resolved in 1842 to admit the public to view the edifice without
fee ; to provide attendants, and simply request visitors to write
their names in a book on entering. Within seven months 10,000
persons availed themselves of this privilege, since which vast
numbers have visited the church, many of whom have not
inscribed their names, and we are glad to say that the sacred
structure has suffered no injury.

There are four styles in Redcliffe church. The vestibule is of
a date between 1200 and 1230 (early English) ; the tower and
imperfect spire, of that of Ed. I., (early decorated), and the work,
probably, of Simon de Burton, six times mayor of Bristol, *circa,*
1294. The northern porch was probably built late in the reign
of Ed. III. "An older church was removed to give place to the
present nave and chancel with their aisles and the transept."
This—the main—work, may undoubtedly be ascribed to William
Canynge, Jun., " a religious, charitable, and wealthy merchant
of Bristol," who is believed to have devoted himself to this
" maystrie of a human hande" shortly after the year 1466. The
church is therefore, chiefly perpendicular. The length is 247
feet 6 inches, and that of the transepts 117 feet ; the height of
the middle aisle 54 feet, and of the north and south aisles 25 feet.
It has been conjectured that the south transept is of older date
than the north ; the transition windows in the former are very
remarkable, and the effect of the transepts when seen from
either end is hardly equalled, in its way, in gothic architecture.—
Hogarth executed three large pictures for this Church in 1755—
the only historical pictures that he painted—for which he received
£500. They were placed over the altar, to block up the east end.

The subjects are—*The Ascension, The Three Marys,* and *The High Priest and Servants sealing the Tomb.* Had they not better be sold ?—Some of the monuments are curious and interesting. The altar tomb, with effigies of a man and a woman, under a canopy beneath the centre window, is the first monument to Canynge, and bears a remarkable inscription on its back. Close at hand, is a second altar tomb to Canynge, who appears in priest's robes, as Dean of Westbury. The interesting altar tomb at the end of the south transept, called by some a *third* monument to Canynge, was no doubt erected to commemorate the memory of one of the Canynge family. A monument was erected in 1840 on the outside of the north porch in honour of Chatterton, but it has been removed to one of the vaults.—A marble tablet has been raised to the memory of Sir Francis Freeling, who was the son of a confectioner in a humble way, near this Church.

The Restoration Stone was laid, with great ceremony, by J. K. Haberfield, Esq., thrice Mayor of Bristol, on April 21, 1846. The Committee, in an address issued in the following November, say, " The urgent necessity of *immediate attention* to the whole fabric is strongly evidenced by extreme decay found in those parts now under repair." It is only necessary to examine the *crumbling walls* and *rotten timbers* to be convinced of the truth of this. The restoration already effected is admirable. Mr. George Godwin has forcibly remarked that " St. Mary Redcliffe belongs not to Bristol but to Europe."

An ancient custom is kept up here on Whit-Sunday, on which day the Mayor and Town Council go in procession to the church : the pavement is strewed with rushes, and the pulpit, reading-desk, and pews, very profusely decorated with spring flowers.

In order to aid the restoration fund, we give two engravings. The first shows the design of the proposed spire ; and the second, the interior of the nave, &c. as it would appear if restored. The " existing portion" of the spire is not more than one-fifth of the whole height, or up to the first enriched band. The view of the interior is truly exquisite—" a vista full of the most charming architectural effects." Mr. Britton thinks that it will " bear comparison with the gorgeous chapels of Henry VII., London,

S. E. View of REDCLIFFE CHURCH, with the Spire as proposed to be restored.

and King's College, Cambridge," although not equal in sculptured decoration to those structures. Imagine all the windows of this sublime church filled—as they once were—" with pictured glass, and the ribs, bosses, and capitals of the vaulted ceilings, and of the shafted pillars, with gold and colours ' richly dight ! ' "

III. MODERN STRUCTURES : Exchange. [This is considered, by competent judges, an exceedingly interesting building, especially the quadrangle ; the architect was Wood, of Bath—date 1743.] Council House. New Guildhall.—Victoria Rooms, top of Park Street ; architect, Mr. C. Dyer, of London ; large room 117 feet by 55—48 feet high.—Bishop's College ; Blind Asylum ; near Victoria Rooms.—Bristol Institution, Park Street : an excellent Museum ; Baily's Statue of Eve.—Red Maid's School.— Queen Elizabeth's Hospital, or City School, opened in 1847, on Brandon Hill, (which eminence should be ascended for the sake of the view which it commands, and which was the site of a Roman camp.)

IV. PRINCIPAL INNS : White Lion, Broad Street ;—Royal Western, College Green ; Royal Gloucester, York, Cumberland, and Ivatts', all at the Hotwells ; Bath, and Clifton, at Clifton.

CLIFTON,

During the last ten years, has advanced from a " village" to a goodly town. Builders have hardly been able to keep pace with the demand for houses ; and if the terraces and squares that have sprung up so magically had been laid out with taste and judgment, the place would have been one of the finest in Europe. With all its faults of design, however, Clifton has many good points. Nature has done much to hide defects ; and the tiers of crescents and rocky " Windsor Terrace" of the " early settlers" compose a striking scene. The population of Clifton parish, which in 1821 was 8811, has increased to upwards of 20,000.

The Downs are one of the great attractions : enchanting walks on turf scented with aromatic plants, or on wild furzy commons— graceful prospects of the distant channel, and glimpses of the Avon winding below—are the characteristics. It is a glorious region for Autumn landscapes. Botanists may rejoice here. The *West of England Journal* contains a list of 375 specimens—

only a part of the local flora.   The Rev. J. Evans mentions—we
do not hold ourselves responsible for the statement—that "the
geraneum sanguineum is found native only here and in North
Wales."—Tourists should visit the old tower called "Cooke's
Folly," the road to which is through woods overhanging the
river, at the extremity of Durdham Down, and about which there
is an old legend.—The *Observatory* contains an excellent Camera
Obscura, a self-registering airenometer or wind-gauge, large tele-
scopes, and curiosities.   It stands on the site of *an early British
Camp*, which occupies the whole eminence over St. Vincent's
rocks, and measures 100 yards from E. to W. and 170 from N.
to S.   There was a double foss and tripple agger.   The Society
of Merchants dug a vast hole in it in 1845 for a reservoir, which
has been abandoned, and forms a sad eyesore.   This camp is
part of a chain of ancient fortresses, twenty-five in number, " so
situated as to be capable of communicating with each other by
signal," and extending along the southern vale of the Severn,
from this place, for forty miles in a S. W. direction.   On the
opposite side of the Avon to Clifton camp, are Burwall's and
Stokesleigh camps, of equally early character, and much greater
interest.*   The late Mr. Lloyd Baker, of Hardwick Court, near
Gloucester, traced a series of Roman camps between the Somer-

---

* " Burwall's camp occupies the summit of the rocks, and is separated from
Stokesleigh camp by a deep ravine, whose rocky sides are a defence to each.
Burwall's camp is on the south of the glen, of a triangular form ; two of its sides
are protected by the natural escarpment of the hill, the other being on the level
of the surrounding land and is defended by a vallum, consisting of a double fosse,
and triple agger, which appears to have been raised by stones piled up on it, and
cemented with pure lime, the work of a later period.   The area within the
vallum contains about seven acres, now overgrown with trees and bushes, which
partly conceal its real form.   It is intersected by several ridges of stone, which
seem to convey an idea that buildings stood within its circumvallation.   The
principal entrance to this camp is from the south-west through an opening in the
rampart 50 feet wide.   On passing this entrance, the ground rises, and the remains of a bank appear, thrown up no doubt for greater security to the entrance.
Stokesleigh camp stands on the opposite side of the ravine, and appears a coun-
terpart to Burwall's, in form and character.   The area within the vallum contains
about eight acres.   The fosse is deeper than the one at Burwall's, and further
protected by an outwork in front.   At the entrance appear some ruins and

setshire and the Warwickshire Avon.—It is a " fearful and dizzy thing to cast one's eyes below," from the edge of St. Vincent's rocks : many fatal accidents have occurred, one of the most distressing of which took place in October, 1847, when a young lady named Welsh, who was on a visit at Clifton, most incautiously seated herself on the very brink of the precipice over the Giant's Cave ; in a short time she either grew dizzy or lost her footing, and in a few seconds lay on the ground beneath, shapeless and inanimate.

Sir James Clark, in his work on the sanative influence of climate, speaks very highly of Clifton.   There is less rain, owing to peculiarity of situation, than in other parts of the west of England, and in that respect Sir James considers it " much the same as the south coast."   The spring season is remarkably mild, and the place affords a very favourable winter and summer climate.   The late Dr. Chisholm' remarks that Clifton " seems singularly well adapted for the maintenance of health ; the soil resting on immense beds of limestone rock, exposed to the southerly and westerly winds, for nearly three-fourths of the year ; with an atmosphere elastic, vivifying—not humid."

There are Zoological Gardens near Durdham Down.

THE HOTWELLS once enjoyed very great celebrity, and for more than two centuries formed the chief attraction to invalids in this locality. Sir James Clark says,—" the virtues of this spring were then as much over-rated as they appear now to be under-rated. Yet, I believe that many of the valetudinarians who

foundations, which indicate that it was, subsequently to the Belgic-Britons, occupied either by the Romans or the Saxons. . . . . There are outworks on the river side of these camps ; one of which stands near the spot where the projected chain-bridge is to be thrown over the river. Through the middle of the glen below may be traced the remains of an ancient road, carried on an elevated ridge about three feet high and eighteen feet broad, and leading down to the river, where was a ford, in ancient times, passable at low water. This ford was on a ledge of rock stretching across the channel of the river ; it was partially removed in 1840, but even at the present time, when there is little water in the river, a ripple is discernible over the site of this ford on the rocks."— *Phelps's Somerset*, vol. I. pp. 97-8.

frequent Clifton on account of its climate, might derive benefit from the use of this water. It appears to be a very pure water, having at its natural temperature of 76 a specific gravity of only 1,0007. It contains a very small proportion of lime, soda, and magnesia, in combination with the carbonic, sulphuric, and muriatic acids ; but a considerable portion of free carbonic acid, and a little atmospheric air. The presence of the fixed air, together with its temperature, render this water.grateful to the stomachs of most persons." It is of use in a variety of complaints, particularly dyspepsia. The spring discharges sixty gallons in a minute, from an aperture in the solid rock, near the bottom of the cliffs. On the day on which Lisbon was destroyed by an earthquake in 1755, this spring suddenly became red and turbid, and did not recover its purity for a long period.

CLIFTON SUSPENSION BRIDGE

Is an undertaking which has been suspended since the year 1839, after being talked of for nearly a century. In 1754 Mr. William Vick, a wine-merchant at Bristol, left £1,000 as a contribution towards the erection of a bridge here ; which sum having been swelled by accumulation of interest to £8,000, was at last judged to be sufficiently large to authorise the commencement of the work. A number of local subscriptions were collected in aid of the fund, an act was obtained in 1830, and the first stone laid on the 27th of August, 1836, by the Marquis of Northampton, at a meeting of the British Association. The two hideous piers now standing attest the subsequent labours of the trustees. It is said that the sum of £30,000 is still required, but that the bridge will actually be completed. Numbers have traversed the space between the rocky chasm by means of a basket which runs on an iron bar stretched across. Two London gentlemen stuck fast in the centre on their journey over, on a rather stormy evening in 1842, and were in an agonising state for some time.—Dimensions of the bridge :—Distance between the two points of suspension, 700 feet ; length of suspended roadway, 630 feet ; height of roadway above high water-mark, 230 feet ; total width of floor, 34 feet. Engineer, Mr. Brunel.

Ghyston's or the Giant's Cave

In St. Vincent's Rocks, in an apparently inaccessible situation,
excites a strong feeling of curiosity in the mind of the stranger.
It was, according to a fabulous legend, the abode of a giant,
named " *Saint* Vincent," who clave a passage through the rocks
for the passage of the Avon, during a struggle with another giant
named Goram.   William of Wyrcestre, a native of Bristol, who
wrote in the fifteenth century, states that it was the abode of an
anchorite :—" The hermitage, an oratory or chapel, in the most
dangerous part of the rock, called Ghyston Cliffe, situated in a
cave of the rock 20 yards in depth in the said rock above the river
Avon, in honour of St. Vincent." (Itin. p. 150.)   This Saint
suffered martyrdom at Valencia in the year 305.   William subjoins
a minute description of the interior, in which he speaks of " the
halle of the chapell of Seynt Vincent."   Previously to 1830 the
only apparent means of gaining access to this cave, was by a
narrow ledge of rock a few feet below the entrance, of fearfully
dangerous character, which was removed to prevent accidents.
A few hardy spirits, however, still succeeded in the hazardous
enterprise ; when in 1835, Mr. West, the proprietor of the Observatory above, conceived the idea of blasting a passage from that
structure to it.   A shaft, with steps, was sunk for 35 feet, then
a passage was driven down an incline for 150 feet, and finally
another flight of steps, 30 feet deep, carried to the eastern end of
the cave, which was protected- by an iron railing.   The floor of
the cave was covered with earth and decomposed vegetable matter
in some places to a depth of three feet.   Below this was a layer
of stalagmite, but no bones were found.   In the cavern were
numerous fragments of pottery, supposed by some to be Roman ;
a square glazed tile, like those used in churches ; and a portion
of a mullion of a small gothic window, or probably of a tabernacle
or shrine.   These relics were imbedded under a large flat stone
covered with rubbish.   The cave is 88 feet from the summit of
the rock, and 220 feet from high water mark, which show that St.
Vincent's Rocks rise 308 feet.   Its entrance is a rudely arched
portal 10 feet high and 13 broad ; the roof expands to a height of

18 feet, and there are several cavities, the end of one of which is 49 feet from the entrance.

A large cavern 50 feet deep was found on St. Vincent's Rocks, by the workmen employed in excavating a roadway for the suspension bridge; and a most interesting *Bone Cavern* has also been accidentally discovered on Durdham Down, by men employed in a quarry. Bones of the elephant, rhinoceros, hippopotamus, hyena, bear, &c., were amongst the osseous remains, and may be seen in the Bristol Institution. *Pen Park Hole*, three miles from Bristol, in Westbury parish, derives a melancholy interest from the fate of the Rev. T. Newnam, a minor canon of Bristol Cathedral, who, in 1775, fell into the dreary cavern, fifty yards deep, with eight fathoms of water at the bottom. His body was ultimately recovered by a miner. Rich lead ore has lately been found in the hole.

EXCURSIONS.

To *King's Weston Park* (formerly the seat of Lord de Clifford, now of Mr. Philip Miles, M.P.,) and the adjoining hill of *Pen Pole*, from whence there is a view of extraordinary beauty.—*Blaise Castle*, (so called from a chapel dedicated to St. Blazius) : British and Roman camp on a hill beyond the house; Mr. Harford's famous group of Cottages, at Henbury—a very pretty village—just beyond. These (ten) cottages were erected by the late Mr. J. S. Harford, from designs by Nash, for the purpose of providing "a comfortable asylum for persons advanced in years, and who had a sufficient income to maintain them comfortably, when relieved from the expense of house rent."—*Abbotsleigh*, (3 miles.) In the former manor house Charles II. took refuge after the battle of Worcester. View over channel from church-yard. *Leigh Court*, the seat of Mr. William Miles, M.P., with its superb gallery of pictures, may be seen in this excursion. Application, in the form of a note, must be made on a Monday, requesting orders for the applicant and three friends, addressed to Mr. Miles, the general purport of which had better be indicated outside. This must be sent to Messrs. Miles's counting-house, 61, Queen-square; and orders for four will be issued on the following Wednesday. The collection of pictures was commenced by Mr. R. H. Davis, formerly member for Bristol, from whom it was purchased by the late Mr. Miles. There are two Claudes—the *Landing of Æneas*, and the *Sacrifice of Apollo*—from the Alfieri Palace, which Mr. Davis purchased from Mr. Beckford, for nearly £12,000. The house is closed from April to July.—*Brockley Combe* : residence of Mr. Pigott ; very romantic glen, a mile in length ; road from Bristol 8½ miles ; Nailsea station of Bristol and Exeter railway, near.—*Wick and Abson* : 7½ miles, rock scenery.—*Thornbury* : a beautiful decorated Castle in ruins, built by Edward Duke of Buckingham in 1511. Church. The Yate station, 10½ miles, is the nearest to this town, but the old road is infinitely preferable. —*Badminton*, seat of the Duke of Beaufort, 16 miles.—*Berkeley Castle*. To "Berkeley road" railway station, 22½ miles : thence to the Castle, about 2½ miles. Church : monuments, fine example of very early English windows at west end. Dr. Jenner's house.

Stanton Drew is a Druidical temple, about seven miles south of Bristol. There are three circles of stones, the largest of which, " like Stonehenge, is in reality a sort of ellipsis. Within is a great altar stone as at Stonehenge, placed towards the east." The greatest diameter of the larger circle is 126 yards ; the stones are of various sizes, the largest measuring 9 feet high, and 22 in circumference ; 13 remain, with foundations of others ; the original number supposed to be thirty. The *circle* of eight, on the eastward, is 96 feet diameter ; and the *Lunar Temple*, of Stukeley, on the south-west, 120 feet across. It is supposed that the circles here were designed both for astronomical observations and superstitious rites. " These remains," observes Mr. Phelps, ' may be classed with Abury, in Wiltshire, from the rudeness of their execution, and bear a close resemblance to those at Carnac, in Brittany."—*Dundry* Church, one of the finest of the Somersetshire towers, and one of the most conspicuous landmarks in England, should be visited and ascended in going to Stanton Drew : it is close to the (old Wells) road. There is a very perfect Cistvaen on Dundry Hill.

The neighbourhood of Bristol is very picturesque, and abounds with admirable examples of *English* scenery. Glimpses are frequently obtained of the Severn and the Channel, backed by the Welsh mountains, which give a delicious interest to the landscape. The prospects from Almondsbury Hill, and Milbury Heath, on the road to Gloucester, are glorious ; on a clear day the eye stretches as far as the Brecknock Beacons, the Snowdon of South Wales.

BRISTOL DOCKS—FLOATING HARBOUR.

The Docks were commenced in 1804 and completed in 1809, at a cost of £600,000. Previously to this period, the harbour consisted of the channel of the river Avon, above the present Cumberland Basin, and a short branch of the river within the existing quays of St. Augustine and St. Stephen ; it was therefore dry at low water. A new course for the Avon was excavated in order to effect the improvements, an entrance from which to the docks is obtained at Bathurst Basin. The whole length of •this magnificent floating harbour is nearly three miles. In consequence of the injury inflicted on the trade of the port by dock and other charges, strenuous efforts have been made by the citizens to obtain a reduction of the dues. In 1846, an association was formed for the purpose of making Bristol a nearly *Free Port ;* and the efforts of this body induced the Town Council, after nearly twelve months' deliberation, to make a proposition to the Dock Company (others had been made in former years) for the purchase of the whole of the docks on behalf of the city, in order to secure the great objects sought —low charges, and improved management.—The *Great Britain* was imprisoned here, in consequence of the narrowness of the entrance locks of Cumberland Basin, the chief outlet to the river ; but the Dock Company have since constructed a new lock from a plan by Mr. Brunel, at a cost of upwards of £20,000, 64 feet wide, and therefore capable of admitting the largest steamers afloat.

CUMBERLAND BASIN generally presents an animated scene when the tide is in, as it is the rendezvous of nearly all the steam-packets belonging to the port. The great days of departure are Tuesdays and Fridays. Passengers who wish to go direct from the railway to the steam-packet should avoid the city and order the fly-driver to take the road by the New Cut : distance about two miles ; fly-fare 1s. 8d., in addition to a turnpike charge.

VOYAGE DOWN THE AVON.

An ocean fragrance freshens in the gale,
  And Avon, with full waters winds before,
Like cragged Peneus through his foliaged vale,
  With rampant rocks uprising from his shore.

I mark the turret overtop the wood,
  Whose boughs the sun-rise tips with burnished glow
And the bare upland heath, where oft I stood,
  Watching the sails that glided far below.

Is it the tinted rock, the incumbent shade,
  Trembling upon the tide in ambered gleams ?
Is it the mountain mists that azured fade,
  Where the two rivers blend their sea-tinged streams ?

SIR CHARLES A. ELTON.

We are now afloat. The rope is cast off—we move on at " all
speed"—the crowded pier-heads disappear. The scenery, characteristics, and recollections of the Bristol river, afford materials
for a long chapter ; but, intent on "fresh fields and pastures
new," we must satisfy ourselves with deck gossip. In two or
three hours this fine tidal river, now brim-full, will sink almost to
a rivulet, with immense muddy banks. Despite this drawback—
to which the Wye is also liable below Tintern—the scenery does
not suffer very seriously. The " grand scene" is at St. Vincent's
Rocks, which are impressive even under the flattest light. Dr.
Holland, in his *Travels in Turkey*, says that these rocks convey
a correct idea of the Vale of Tempé, on a reduced scale. The
Peneus, as it flows through the defile, " is not much wider than
the Avon, and the channel between the rocks is of equally contracted dimensions."—The contrast between these " airy cliffs"
and the many-tinted foliage of the opposite heights is striking,
and the combe on the south or Somersetshire side, almost opposite
the " Round Point,"—no longer round—realises its poetical name
of the " Nightingale's Valley." The next reach is terminated
by Cooke's Folly—a tower placed in a position which even Gilpin
would have been compelled to warmly admire. The decorated
engine-house below was erected in 1846, by the Society of Mer-

E

chants, to raise water, and is now the property of a new Water
Company at Bristol, which partly obtains its supply of water for
the city from the Mendip Hills.   At Sea Mills, a muddy inlet—
the ancient Roman haven already described—the small river
Trym, once more important than it is now, joins the Avon.   The
scenery becomes softer from this point.   Before we depart we
must, in common with every admirer of the beautiful rocky valley
we have been passing through, lift our voices against the cupidity
which has remorselessly disfigured it with enormous quarries,
chiefly for the supply of turnpike roads.   Even Saint Vincent's
Rocks have been threatened within the last few years : and the
massive bluff, which was to carry the Suspension Bridge, was
labelled " good road stone at 9d. per ton !''   Where the evil will
stop it is difficult to say.—A large floating dock was commenced
at Sea Mills in 1712, but subsequently abandoned.

Some distance beyond, on the same side, the wooded heights
of Kingsweston Park are seen above the river bank ; the odd little
building below is the Powder House, " where vessels coming to
Bristol leave their powder, and again receive it on their outward
voyage."   This was once the practice ; but it is a rule to which
there are many exceptions.   The next reach, Hungroad, is one
of the most remarkable in the river.   " Hunge-rode," says old
Leland, in the sixteenth century, " is about three miles lower in
the haven than Bristow ; in this rode be some howsys in *dextra
Avon ripa*.   Some think a great piece of the depenes of the
Haven from St. Vincent to Hunge-rode hath been made by
hande."   Until the Floating Harbour was constructed, many
large ships used to lie here and discharge their cargoes into
lighters—hence the origin of the series of massive iron rings
which appear in the rocky wall-like bank of the river.   The
" ancient and fish-like" village lower down is Pill, the abode of
most of the Pilots and Fishermen of the Port of Bristol, whose
vessels (there are thirty-two licensed Bristol Pilot boats) nestle
in an adjoining creek or " Pill."   In consequence of the mal-
practices of its inhabitants, Pill was totally demolished in 1656,
by order of Cromwell ; but rose again a few years later.   Many
sailors have their houses here ; and the population is of a tho-

roughly out-of-door kind—wild and hardy. Great opposition was manifested in 1836 by many of the Pill men to the introduction of steam tugs, previously to which the chief portion of the shipping entering or leaving Bristol were clumsily hauled by horses, or pulled along with the aid of Pill boats. The *Lioness*, the first steam tug introduced, was boarded in piratical style whilst lying at anchor in King Road, cut adrift, and left to her fate. She went down the channel and escaped wreck by mere accident. No steps were taken against the perpetrators of the outrage; but steam steadily went ahead, crushing all opposition.—" Lamplighter's Hall," opposite Pill, adjoining the pleasant village of Shirehampton, is resorted to by many citizens during the summer and autumn. The founder was a contractor for lighting Bristol many years ago—one Mr. Toy—who designed the house for a country abode, but grew tired, and converted it into an Inn.

We now enter Broad Pill, the last reach of the Avon, which here widens greatly, and has always a picturesque character when the tide is up, although the river banks have become low and tame—the " sea-walls" of marsh land. There are two entrances to KING ROAD—the noble roadstead outside,—the southernmost of which, " *the Swash*," can only be traversed by shipping at certain states of the tide, when there is deep water over it ; and as a saving of about a mile is effected by taking this course, the steamers always pursue it when they can. Criminals were formerly hung in chains at the edge of the Swash, and a gibbet-post, which had braved the storms of nearly a hundred years, remained until 1838. One of the most extraordinary murders recorded in the annals of crime was committed in King Road in the last century.

The story is too long to tell at length ; we can give little more than the title of an old narrative : " The right tragical history of Sir John Dinely Goodyere, Bart., who was murdered by his brother, Captain Samuel Goodyere, and assistants, on the 19th of January, 1741, on board his Majesty's ship *Ruby*, 64 guns, then lying in King Road, Bristol." Sir John was a wealthy Worcestershire baronet, who had been at variance with his brother, the next in succession to the estate. The latter feigned a wish for a reconciliation. The brothers dined at the White Hart public-house, College-Green, Bristol. Captain Goodyere's boat was in the river hard by, and the crew had orders to approach the inn at dusk, seize the baronet and put him on board. When the brothers emerged, the crew obeyed their orders ; and although Sir John made a desperate resistance and uttered piercing cries for help, no one interfered. The tide was on the ebb, and the boat shot rapidly down the Avon. The Captain conveyed his brother to his cabin in the *Ruby*, and there succeeded in murdering him—chiefly by strangulation—with the aid of a petty officer, named Mahony : the gibbet which fell in 1838 was his. The first Lieutenant sent for aid to the Mayor of Bristol, and the murderers were, after a most interesting trial, full details of which are preserved, found guilty, and executed.

At last we enter the broad bosom of the Channel.

> " Look round—behold
> How proudly the majestic Severn rides
> On the sea,—how gloriously in light
> It rides ! "

There are few finer roadsteads in this country than King's Road, commonly abbreviated to King Road. It is well sheltered, except from the north-east ; the tide with common springs rises eight fathoms ; there is good holding ground, and the adjoining shore consists of a soft mud bank. The length of the road—which is distinguished by a light-house with a fixed white light—is between two and three miles. The scenery is very beautiful. On the north-west

> " —mingled with the clouds, old Cambria draws
> Its stealing line of mountains, lost in haze."

The dark headland of Portishead encloses the home scene ; and curtains of eminences rise gently in the back ground, finely broken and diversified by soft woods, or picturesque structures, especially on the Gloucestershire side, where the heights of Kingsweston and Blaize Castle compose a Claude-like scene. As a sunset view, it is perfect.

MONMOUTHSHIRE

Is a sort of "debateable land"—England grafted on a Welsh stock. Go to Abergavenny on a market day, and you will see Cambro-Britons to your hearts' content; penetrate the hills and you may still be perplexed by "*dim Sassanech.*" Ever since Gray pictured "delightsome Monmouth," this has been one of the regions of romance amongst home tourists. The "tour of the Wye" is associated with all that is enchanting in hill, wood, rock, and stream.

The county formed a portion of the territory of the Silures—a warlike people, who made "an unparalleled resistance to the Roman armies," and were not finally subdued until the reign of Vespasian, when Julius Frontinus completed the conquest of this region, which was included in the division called Britannia Secunda. Subsequently Monmouthshire comprehended part of *Gwent,* the people of which inherited the courage of their Silurian ancestors, and kept the Anglo-Saxons at bay. In Norman times this border county was included in the "Marches," but its feudal possessors were compelled to build or strengthen at least twenty-five castles for their safety, the ruins of nearly all of which remain; and when the government of the Lords Marchers* was abolished in the reign of Henry VIII., (A. D. 1535), Monmouthshire was dissevered from Wales.

The chief Roman stations were five in number: *Venta Silurum* (Caerwent); *Isca Silurum* (Caerleon); *Gobannium* (Abergavenny); *Blestium* (Monmouth); and *Burrium* (Usk). Many British and Roman encampments exist. "A regular chain of fortresses," observes Archdeacon Coxe, "seems to have been first formed or occupied by the Normans on the banks of the Monnow, the Wye, and the Severn; these are Scenfreth, Grosmont, Mon-

---

* *The Marches.* "These lands being holden, per baroniam, with full power to administer justice unto their tenants, were invested with divers privileges, franchises, and immunities, so that the writs of ordinary justice out of the King's courts were not current among them. But in case of strife between two barons' Marchers, concerning their territories or confines, for want of a superior, they had recourse to the King, their supreme lord, and justice was administered to them in the superior courts of the realm."—*Enderlie.*

mouth, *Trelech,* perhaps *Tintern,* Chepstow, and Caldecot. A second line stretches diagonally from Grosmont to the banks of the Rumney ; these are White Castle, *Tregaer,* Usk, Langibby, Caerleon, and Newport." Abergavenny formed an important out-work of this series. The other castles, some of which may be styled castellated mansions, were erected to keep the natives in awe, at Raglan, Striguil, Dinham, Lanvair, *Lanvaches,* Pen-how, Pencoed, *Bishton, Wilcric,* Greenfield, Rogeston, and Castleton. The fortresses have been wholly destroyed in those instances in which the names are printed in italics. Coxe consi-ders Scenfreth Castle "wholly Saxon." At the Reformation seventeen religious houses, including two hospitals, were in exist-ence ; but the only remains of much interest are at Tintern and Llanthony. Holy Wells are so numerous that there are few parishes which do not possess one " celebrated for its real or supposed medicinal virtues. "

The shores of this highly-interesting county are, with partial exceptions, dull and tame. Extensive levels, named Caldecot and Wentloog, intervene between the uplands and the sea—a " low country" fenced by vast sea walls or earth-works to repel the assaults of tides and storms. These levels are under the control of a Court of Sewers, and " subject to the same laws and regulations as Romney Marsh, in Kent." The county is almost encircled by a chain of heights, often of mountainous elevation, which terminate on the south-east, near Wentwood Forest, and on the south-west, near *Twyn Barlwym,* a conspicuous hill at the back of Newport. The long flat-topped range, called the *Mynydd Maen,* which, on a distant view, forms the apparent boundary of Monmouthshire on the west, is a continuation of the hills which rise near this town. The space within the upland chain, which composes the largest portion of the county, is undulating, but of more fascinating outline than any district of similar character in England. There is something peculiar yet indefinable about it. Graceful home views—solemn landscapes—wooded knolls and shadowy hollows—" blind" lanes, once the public highways—primitive Churches, often half hidden by aged yews or clustering ivy—ruined strongholds—ancient " Courts " converted into farm-

houses with vast homesteads—and misty mountain backgrounds
of ever-varying forms and hues—are the characteristics of Monmouthshire scenery.

The largest group of hills, that lying to the west of the Vale of
Crickhowel, in Brecknockshire, and extending to the borders of
Glamorgan, is full of minerals—coal and iron—two inexhaustible
sources of wealth.   Nature has done much to aid in the development of her riches.   There is a succession of valleys, falling with
a gradual inclination from the hill country towards Newport—the
key of the vale of Usk and the uplands—which are admirably suited
for tram and railroads ; the loaded trams or carriages descend on
gentle inclines towards the shipping place, and are easily drawn
back empty.   Canals—the pack-horses of modern times—exist
in the county ; one company possesses two, 22 miles long, besides
tramways more than 50 miles in length, which have been invaded
by the giant, Railway.

Few counties have undergone more rapid changes than Monmouth.   When Archdeacon Coxe published his tour in 1801, the
iron trade was in its infancy ; and his description of " *the Wilds
of Monmouthshire*," a " region seldom traversed by the gentry,
except for the purpose of grouse shooting," presents a curious
contrast to that region as it now appears.   Capital and enterprise
have done as much as it is almost possible to do in such a district,
to change the face of these wilds—much to the regret of the lover
of scenery, and the sportsman.   The swarthy attendants of the
iron work, the mine, and the railroad, are now occupants of the
deepest solitudes of the last century.   Sinews of our national
strength and prosperity exist here.

The South Wales Coal Field commences in this county, a
circumstance which gives great importance to its *Geology.*   The
country east of a line drawn from Abergavenny to Newport,
consists chiefly of the old red sandstone formation.   Near Usk the
strata of this stone are pierced by the underlying rocks of Murchison's " Silurian System"; and at Chepstow " a tongue of
carboniferous limestone, from the coal basin of Dean Forest, runs
into Monmouthshire, and is bordered on the south by a strip of new

red sandstone, which forms the shore of the Severn." The coal measures of the South Wales Field commence to the west of the line we have indicated, and are skirted by a band of carboniferous limestone, which is used in great quantities—not merely as a building material and for manure—but, when broken small as a flux with the "mine" (iron ore) and coke in the iron works. We learn that in "the selection of limestone for this purpose those beds are preferred which contain the smallest proportion of magnesia," and that about a ton of limestone is required for the manufacture of every ton of iron. The proportion of iron in the iron stone varies from 18 to 55 per cent. Notices of the South Wales Coal Field will be found in other parts of this volume; the area of that portion of it which is connected with the port of Newport is estimated at about 89,000 acres, the *net* yield of which per acre is nearly 40,000 tons.

Monmouthshire does not rank high in an agricultural point of view, although great strides have been made of late years; agricultural societies and farmers' clubs have stimulated improvements, and the late munificent Sir Charles Morgan, by the establishment of the Tredegar Cattle Show, was the means of improving the various breeds of live stock in this and the adjoining county of Glamorgan, to an extent which has produced great public benefits.

The Population of Monmouthshire has increased in an infinitely more rapid ratio during the present century than any other English county. The following are the census returns :—1801, 45,582 ; 1811, 62,127 ; 1821, 71,833 ; 1831, 98,130 ; 1841, 134,355. At the next census the number is expected to reach 200,000 ; in which case the population will have more than quadrupled itself in half a century. Monmouthshire contains 317,440 acres, 123 parishes, is in the diocese of Llandaff, and returns three members, two for the county, and one for the united boroughs of Monmouth, Newport, and Usk. It is in the Oxford circuit ; the Assizes are held at Monmouth, the Sessions at Usk.

The chief rivers are the Wye, the Usk, the Monnow, the Rumney, and the Ebbw. The Honddu and the Trothy are tribu-

taries of the Monnow and the Wye; the Sirhowy falls into the
Ebbw, which joins the Usk below Newport; and the Afon Llwd
meets the Usk near Caerleon.

We begin our itinerary with Chepstow; and under that head
indicate both short and long Excursions; a tour extending in
fact to the Black Mountains, on the north of the county. This
tour—*i. e.* from Chepstow to Llanthony Abbey—cannot be well
accomplished *under* three days; but a week ought to be devoted
to it.—An Excursion from Bristol to Newport and back may
often be made in a day, the steamers remaining a sufficient time
to enable the tourist to visit Caerleon or other places mentioned
after our account of Newport. When the railway system is
perfected, the mountains and antiquities of Monmouthshire will,
no doubt, be often overrun by the motley broods of "excursion"
trains !

CHEPSTOW.

Distant from	Miles.	Distant from	Miles.
Abergavenny by Raglan	21	Monmouth	16
Bristol by Old Passage	16½	Newport	16
Bristol by Steam	18	Raglan	12½
Beachley	3	Raglan by Monmouth	24
Caerwent	5½	Tintern Abbey	5
Caldecot Castle	6½	Wyndcliff	3

There are at present two modes of travelling to Chepstow from
Bristol—by coach, across the Old Passage, and by steam packet.
The latter is infinitely the most agreeable.

THE VOYAGE BY STEAM occupies, at the utmost, two hours.
The *Wye* iron steamer starts from Bristol every morning, except
Sundays, and returns in the afternoon. In the summer the
passages are always arranged, when the tide will permit, so as
to enable the tourist for the day to visit the most striking scenes
on the Wye between Chepstow and Monmouth. Cars, &c., for
excursions are in attendance at the wharf at Chepstow.—When
the steamer nears the entrance of the Wye, the islet of St. Tecla
appears. This rock originally formed part of the adjoining
promontory of Beachley; and the aged and sea-beaten ruin on
its summit—a shrine dedicated to the first female Christian
martyr—has excited a feeling of wistful interest in many a way-

farer. The scenery of the river gradually becomes picturesque ;
and the ivied walls of Chepstow, which are seen to the greatest
advantage on this side, give a favourable first impression of that
steep and romantic little town—the *Strigulia* of the Romans.—
The South Wales Railway, which runs along the side of the
river, across which it is carried by a bridge, affords a suggestive contrast to the ruinous medieval works in the background.
A little beyond, a very pretty iron bridge spans the stream.
This structure, which replaced a crazy wooden erection in 1816,
is 532 feet in length, stands three miles and a half above
Beachley, and is the joint property of the counties of Monmouth
and Gloucester.

The objects of interest in Chepstow are the Church, the Castle,
the Walls, and the ancient Port, some traces of which are disco_
verable at the termination of the " port wall" on the river side.
Slight remains of religious houses and other old buildings can also
be traced. One of the gates is still perfect.

The Church, which is partly Anglo-Romanesque, was once
attached to a Benedictine Priory. Additions have lately been
made to it, of which we cannot speak warmly ; the doorway at
the west front is a very fine example of Florid Norman ; the
ancient structure, as a whole, has been greatly injured by the
" improvements" that have been effected from time to time.
The original tower, which stood at the east end, was suffered to
fall early in the last century. Henry Marten, the regicide, was
interred in the chancel ; he wrote his epitaph, which having
become greatly defaced, was restored in 1812.

𝕮𝖍𝖊𝖕𝖘𝖙𝖔𝖜 𝕮𝖆𝖘𝖙𝖑𝖊 is a noble and massive relic of feudalism.
The boldness of its site, on a rock, overhanging the river—the
vastness of its proportions—render it a peculiarly impressive
ruin. Perhaps the entrance, which is in the best style of Norman
military architecture, is the finest feature. From hence you pass
into the first court, and behold the Stately Hall, and the Keep,
in which Marten the regicide was imprisoned for twenty years,
until his life was terminated by apoplexy in 1680, at the age of
78. Southey, with poetic license, has represented that Marten
was treated very rigorously ; but the reverse is the fact, for he

not merely enjoyed the society of his family, but had permission
to make excursions and visits in the neighbourhood. You next
pass through what may now be called the " garden court;" and
enter that which contains the Chapel, one of the most elegant
ever constructed within a house of defence. This structure, which
is 90 feet long by 30 broad, appears to have undergone alterations
after the Norman period ; some Roman bricks are discoverable in
the eastern wall—not an uncommon circumstance. There are
fifteen rounded arches, about ten feet high and nearly eight broad,
the object of which has led to some rather absurd conjectures ;
but they were designed for the purposes of both decoration and
strength. Within the western gateway, which was strengthened
with three portcullises, and separated by a drawbridge from the
main structure, is another small court. A guide accompanies
visitors ; so we need hardly mention a chamber cut in the rock
overlooking the river, from an aperture in which a very striking
view may be obtained.—The Castle was originally founded by
Fitz Osborne, Earl of Hereford, almost immediately after the
Conquest, as that nobleman was killed in 1070. It passed, temp.
Henry I. into the hands of the famous Strongbow ; and in the
fifteenth century, became the property of Sir Charles Somerset,
created Lord Herbert of Raglan, Chepstow, and Gower, and
afterwards Earl of Worcester. The history of the castle, during
the civil war, is stirring. Cromwell was repulsed here, by a
gallant Royalist officer, Sir Nicholas Kemeys, who had a garrison
of only 160 men. " He then left Colonel Ewer, with a large
force, to prosecute the siege. But the garrison defended themselves valiantly, until their provisions were exhausted, and even
then refused to surrender under promise of quarter, hoping to
escape by means of a boat which they had provided for that
purpose. A soldier of the Parliamentary army, however, swam
across the river, with a knife between his teeth, cut the cable of
the boat, and brought it away ; the castle was at length forced,
and Sir Nicholas Kemeys, with forty men, slain in the assault."

HOTELS at Chepstow,—the Beaufort Arms ; the George.

An enjoyable *Excursion* may be made to the south of Chepstow,
to Caerwent, Caldecot Castle, and other old places.

Caerwent,

Once a British city, and subsequently the *Venta Silurum* of the
Romans—a military station of great importance—is now a poor
village. Its antiquities, however, are exceedingly interesting ;
few Roman posts in this country remain in so perfect a state.
The fortifications, which are about the size of *Segontium* in North
Wales, are defended on all sides except the southern, by a deep
moat. The facings of the walls, which are composed of oblong
limestone grouted with lime, are in many places visible ; the
height of the walls appears to have varied from twelve to twenty-
four feet, and the thickness from twelve to nine ; the existing
remains of the south wall, which is in much the most perfect
preservation, are in several places twenty feet high, and to some
extent almost entire. There are three pentagonal bastions
towards the western end of this wall, which, according to some
authorities, were added at a later period than the Roman invasion. The antiquities that have been found at Caerwent have
been, as is generally the case, scattered far and wide. The
remains of two tesselated pavements still exist, and many others
have been discovered ; in 1689 three pavements of great beauty
were found in a garden. Large quantities of coins, some of
the reign of Severus, fragments of columns, statues, sepulchral
stones, tesseræ, and other relics of the Roman conqueror, have
come to light at various periods ; and much must now be hidden.
Mr. Seyer, the historian of Bristol, justly thinks that the site of
the Prætorium may be traced near the western gate. The high
road to Newport intersects Caerwent at right angles on the line
of the Roman trackway, passing through openings which were
once the eastern and western gates. The south wall is locally
called the *Portwall ;* and the people on the spot entertain the
belief that the place was once a port. There is reason to believe
that the river, which now runs nearly half a mile from Caerwent,
was formerly a tidal " pill," which has undergone great changes
since the days of the Romans ; and that galleys floated near the
walls. The people aver, indeed, that rings have been discovered
in them.—Caerwent Church is partly Norman, with a lofty
embattled tower.

The *Via Julia* runs from Caerwent to *Caerleon*, another Roman city of still greater consequence, distant nine miles. This road is an example of public works which were constructed to endure for ages. It may be here mentioned that the Britons usually prefixed *Caer* to the names of Roman stations, the word being derived like the Saxon Chester, from *castrum*.

Between four and miles to the north of Caerwent on a hill forming part of a small farm, called *Gaer Llwyd*, about a mile from Newchurch—in which parish it is situated—is the *Cromlech*, depicted in the accompanying sketch.

The upper stone is twelve feet long and about three feet and a half broad, and the uprights vary from four to five feet. Vestiges of a trench and bank are discoverable round this Cromlech, which is the only one in the county, and has been strangely overlooked by Coxe and other topographers.

The new road from Chepstow to Usk intersects the parish of Newchurch. The most interesting road to the Cromlech *from Chepstow* is by *Devaudon Green* (to which there are two routes), an eminence centrally situated amidst the hilly range that runs in a north-easterly direction through the south of Monmouthshire, between Caerleon and Monmouth. Devaudon commands one of the finest prospects in the county. The Cromlech stands near the junction of two roads beyond Newchurch.

A very large *Camp*, called *Gaervawr*, may be traced in the parish of Llangwm, about a mile from the Cromlech ; a mile and a half to the east is a British camp, called *Bryn Eurawg*, at a place called Golden Hill ; a third camp, called *Curtygaer*, said to be of Danish origin, and of circular form, stands about a mile to the north-east of Gaervawr.

Caldecot Castle

Is a magnificent stronghold, chiefly Norman, but with some Saxon work, situated a short distance to the southward of Caerwent. Its history is obscure ; but it was long in the hands of the Bohuns, Earls of Hereford. Camden terms it " a shell belonging to the Constables of England," by whom it was held by the service of that office. It now belongs to the Duchy of Lancaster. The general design is oblong ; round towers strengthen the angles ; the entrance is grand ; the baronial hall, keep, and other ruined structures distinguish the interior.

THE FOREST OR CHASE OF WENTWOOD

Is an elevated wooded tract, of nearly 2,200 acres, belonging to the Duke of Beaufort—a portion of the range just indicated. It was once of much greater extent, and abounds with pleasing scenery. Nearly midway on the road between Caerwent and Usk, about the point of intersection with the Newchurch, &c. road, is PEN Y CAE MAWR—on which a British trackway has been found—a hill which commands an exquisite view of the vale of Usk, the mountains, and the channel.—Wentwood Forest was defended by six agrarian fortresses, most of which were built by the Clares. The ruins of five remain :—

DINHAM CASTLE stands on rising ground, about a mile to the north of Caerwent ; the ruins, which are small, are nearly hidden by wood.

LLANVAIR ISCOED CASTLE occupies an eminence two miles from Caerwent, near the Usk road. The walls are seven feet thick ; there are two round towers and a ruined keep.

STRIGUIL CASTLE (locally called Troggy, from a brook that runs here) stands in a field in the neighbourhood of *Pen y Cae Mawr*, about three miles beyond Llanvair. It has been greatly injured ; its chief feature is an octagonal tower.

The other two castles stand near the southern side of the road to Newport, west of Caerwent, about two miles apart. The first,

PENHOW CASTLE, is romantically situated, between three and four miles from Caerwent. Its chief portion, a square tower, is blended with a farm-house. The church is nigh at hand. On the road side opposite is the Rock and Fountain Inn.

PENCOED CASTLE is the most ancient as well as the most interesting of its compeers—a very early Norman edifice. An old mansion, now a farm-house, occupies the site of the keep.

The tourist who is fond of antiquities may also explore the ruins of *Sudbrook Chapel*, a little way below the New Passage, overlooking the coast ; near which is *Sudbrook Camp*, a British fortification, defended by triple ramparts, in the form of a stretched bow, on the edge of a cliff. *Portascuyth*, a Roman station, stood near.

MATHERN PALACE (until 1706 the residence of the Bishops of Llandaff, for about three centuries) stands near the sea, a mile and a half from Chepstow, below St. Pierre. It is quadrangular, and the tower and some other portions were built early in the fifteenth century. The present Bishop of Llandaff lives at Hardwick House, Chepstow.—*Moinscourt*, another old house built by a former Bishop of Llandaff, in this vicinity, is a good example of domestic architecture.—*Mathern Church* is worth visiting. Some portions are Saxon, and there is a tablet in the chancel, with an inscription by Bishop Godwin, to the memory of the British Prince and Christian Martyr, Theodoric, whose stone coffin was found here some years ago. The skull was fractured, probably by an axe at the battle of Tintern, A. D. 600, but the rest of the skeleton was perfect.

EXCURSION UP THE WYE.

The road out of Chepstow to Monmouth commands a succession of lovely views. About a mile and a half out of the town on the right is the entrance lodge of *Piercefield*, admission to which may be obtained by making a written application to the occupier, Mr. Wintle.

THE WYNDCLIFF rises in the back ground. The best mode of ascending is to proceed up a lane just beyond a sudden turn of the road—which commands a prospect of extreme beauty—a short way above St. Arvan's turnpike. A carriage may be driven up this lane for some distance, and can rejoin the party at the "Moss Cottage," about half a mile onward, where the Duke of Beaufort has placed a servant, who admits visitors into the steep zigzag walks that lead to the summit of the rock, 970 feet high, but which must be descended by those who, on their way *from* Chepstow, adopt our suggestion. We have described Piercefield and the Wyndcliff in our sketch of the Lower Wye Tour.— A gradually descending road, chiefly amongst woods, two miles and a quarter long, leads up the valley of the Wye to

Tintern Abbey.

A friend who has recently written a sketch of this ruin judiciously observes, that Tintern owes the celebrity it deservedly enjoys, perhaps as much to the scenery by which it is surrounded, as to its own intrinsic merit. "How different from the severe Llanthony, in its mountain cradle, is the sister institution in the same county! While every thing there is rugged, bold, secluded, wild, and tempestuous, here we have softness, sunshine, repose, and richness. The graceful Wye, filled up to its banks, and brimming over with the tide from the Severn sea, glides tranquilly past the orchards and fat glebe of ' Holye Tynterne.' On every side stands an amphitheatre of rocks, nodding with hazle, and ash, and birch, and yew, and thrusting out from the tangled underwood high pointed crags as it were for ages the silent witnesses of that ancient Abbaye and its fortunes ; but removed at just such a distance as to leave a fair plain in the bend of the river, for one of the most rare and magnificent structures in the whole range of Ecclesiastical architecture. As you descend the road from Chepstow, the building suddenly bursts upon you, like a gigantic stone skeleton ; its huge gables standing out against the sky with a mournful air of dilapidation—as though they were only waiting for some friendly hand to take pity on their lonesomeness, and to consummate their ruin by dashing them down headlong into the gloom beneath. There is a stain upon the walls, which bespeaks a weather-beaten antiquity ; and the ivy comes creeping out of the bare, sightless, windows ; the wild flowers and mosses cluster upon the mullions and dripstones, as it were seeking to fill up the unglazed void with nature's own colours....The door is opened—how beautiful the long and pillared nave—what a sweep of graceful arches—how noble the proportions, the breadth, the length, and the height. How massive are the centre arches, clustered, bound, and tied together with knots of stone work, as though to support something most exquisite...the once glorious and elaborate Lanthorn Tower ; and, then, with what stately elegance does the eastern window close the perspective—one slender, and that the principal, shaft alone left, where formerly there were eight...but now that tall slender shaft, 70 feet in height, runs up like a dilapidated rose, and seems to fall like a thread upon the woods and lichen-stained rocks....As you walk up the nave on the smooth velvet turf which nature laid down in the place of the encaustic tile, when she took charge of the hallowed spot, after man's greedy sacrilege had desecrated it, your eye meets with relics and broken fragments, dug out of the ruins at several times, and reverently placed at the foot of the columns." Amongst these is the effigy of a crusader in chain armour—popularly conjectured, but erroneously, to be

F

that of the famous Strongbow, conqueror of Ireland in the reign
of Richard II.—and which in Grose's day had five fingers and a
thumb on the right hand, now mutilated from exposure to the
weather. "Here is a truncated Virgin and Child. Here is a
beautiful fragment of the screen—another of the rood-loft—a
key-stone, tumbled from the roof, elaborately worked—a crozier
handsomely chiselled upon a broken slab—an exquisite morsel of
fretwork—a delicate specimen of tracery. Few tombs remain—
no complete tombs, only memorials of the dead—some nearly
perfect, others mutilated, principally of Ecclesiastics. We have
the names but of three Abbots. As you return from the East,
you must admire the great Western Window, which is almost
perfect. It has been objected that the breadth is too great for
the height—this may be true, if spoken of the window as a
detached portion, but it is not true when considered in respect to
the doors below, the smaller windows above, and the general
harmony of the whole building. Thoroughly to appreciate
Tintern you must see it at all seasons, and in all weathers, and
at all hours of the day ; but be not absent in the September and
October full moons, for then the moon's disk, crossing the east
window just below the rose, floods the church with a light which
no painter can transfuse upon canvass, but which a devotional
frame of mind appropriates to itself, as the true medium for asso-
ciating the works of the past, with the shadowy and fancied forms
of those who raised them. The Cloisters, the Sacristy, the Crypt,
the Chapter House, the Dormitory, and especially the Refectory,
with its Lectern in the wall, for the convenience of the 'reader'
during the meals, are well worth inspection." Tintern was built
on the spot where Theodoric, King of Glamorgan, was killed
whilst fighting under the banner of the Cross, against the Pagan
Saxons, in the year 600. An abbey, dedicated to the Blessed
Virgin Mary, was founded here in 1131, by Walter de Clare, for
a Cistercian community ; but the existing structure was not
finished until *Circa* 1287. Roger de Bigod, Earl Marshal, the
founder, bestowed great wealth on the abbey, in which a superior
and twelve brethren ministered, and at the Dissolution the land
revenues were £256 11s. 6d. The history of Tintern, strange to

say, is involved in obscurity.—Some interesting discoveries have been made in the Chapter House, until lately choked with ruins. It is to be hoped that the area of the Cloisters will also be cleared.

The remains of a large oblong building supported by a row of pillars, the lower parts of which appear in a perfect state, were discovered early in 1847, in making an excavation in an orchard which adjoins the Abbey. "The situation of this adjunct (nearly adjoining the Refectory) marks it as the Hospitium, or smaller convent, in which the monks were wont to entertain strangers and travellers of their order, who passing thence, through the cloisters, entered on the more solemn duties of the Abbey ; and its extent suggests the scale of liberality on which every thing was done at this once splendid monastic place."

There are two humble inns at Tintern ; we can speak well of that below the Abbey, called the "Beaufort Arms." It is just the place for a pedestrian tourist. Many interesting excursions may be made in this neighbourhood : we indicate *Saint Briavel's Castle*, at the edge of Dean Forest, and *Trelech*, on the summit of the hill of that name, where there are Druidical remains near the parish church—three stone pillars, hence *Tre-lech*. A cross and very early tombstone in the church-yard deserve notice.

MONMOUTH.

Distant from	Miles.	Distant from	Miles.
Abergavenny by Raglan	16	Hereford by Wormelow Tump	18
Abergavenny (old road by Llanvapley)	14	Newport	24
		Pontypool	20
Chepstow	16	Raglan	8
Cymon's Yat	5½	Ross	10
Goodrich Court	6	Scenfrith Castle	7
Gloucester	26	Tintern Abbey	10½
Ditto by Kerne Bridge	24	Usk	14
Grosmont	10	White Castle	10

Monmouth is situated in the midst of a region which has been poetically described by Gray, as "the delight of the eyes and seat of pleasure." It was successively a British and a Roman station (*Blestium*)—although the latter is doubtful—a Saxon fortress to restrain the inroads of the Welsh, and a Norman walled town. In

the reign of Henry VIII. four gates, most of the walls, and the
moat, existed ; now, the "Welsh gate" on the Monnow Bridge—
one of the most perfect and interesting relics of its kind—is nearly
the sole remain ; a portion of the "English gate," on the old Ross
road, still exists.   The Castle, which stands on the site of the
British fort, has also fared badly.   More of it remains than the
tourist who takes a superficial view is apt to suppose, but still
only fragments.   It passed into the hands of the Crown, temp.
Henry I., and afterwards into those of John of Gaunt, father of
Henry IV.   We need hardly mention that the fifth Harry was
born here, in 1387.   Tradition points to the spot—part of an
upper story in ruins.

The ecclesiastical antiquities consist of the *expressive* spire of
St. Mary's Church—a relic of a Benedictine priory founded in the
reign of Henry I., part of which—known by the name of Geoffry
of Monmouth's House or Study—overlooks the Monnow at the
edge of the church-yard, and is chiefly used for the purposes of a
National School.   Geoffry, the author of a celebrated History of
Britain, was created Archdeacon of Monmouth, A.D. 1251, and
afterwards became Bishop of Saint Asaph.   The body of the
present church, a very tasteless edifice, was built in 1740.—
St. Thomas's Church, Over Monnow, is one of the most beautiful
Saxon structures now in existence, and has been restored.

The Free School and Alms Houses, the latter of which were
rebuilt in 1842 at an expense of £7,000, were founded by William
Jones, a native of the neighbouring parish of Newland, who made
a large fortune in London, temp. James I.   This "worthy" then
returned to his native place, in disguise, pretended poverty, and
was refused relief ; he experienced a friendly reception at Monmouth, where he soon assumed his real character, and testified
his gratitude by founding this charity, which now belongs to the
Haberdashers' Company.   Two yearly exhibitions of £30 each,
at either of the Universities, have been established for the boys.
The alms houses contain twenty aged men and women, who each
receive eight shillings per week.

Monmouth is a well-built and altogether a pretty town, and
has been much improved within a few years, especially by the

construction of a new entrance on the Ross side, and by the erection of an excellent market-house. The river Monnow joins the Wye a little below the town, washing one side of Chippenham Mead, on which well-attended Races are held in the autumn.

Population in 1841, 5,446 ; market, Saturday.—HOTELS : the Beaufort Arms, the Swan, the King's Head.—One of the county papers, the *Monmouthshire Beacon*, is published here.

EXCURSIONS. Monmouth is an excellent central point for Excursions, and few places command so many beautiful walks. *Troy House* is described in our Wye Tour. The *Kymin Hill* (on which there is a trumpery monument in commemoration of naval victories) commands a view of extraordinary beauty, embracing portions of the counties of Monmouth, Gloucester, Hereford, Worcester, Salop, Somerset, Brecon, Radnor, and Montgomery.

The Buckstone.

The *walk to* the Buckstone, which is seen on a lofty hill at a considerable distance, is through Beaulieu Wood, from whence you emerge on the high road to Coleford. A little before reaching Stanton turnpike (three miles) an avenue has been recently cut through the Forest hill above, at the top of which the DRUIDS'

STONE stands, poised almost between earth and sky—we know nothing of the kind so strange and striking. Walk up this avenue and return by Stanton village, keeping the road all the way to Monmouth.

Our sketch speaks for itself; we need do little more than give dimensions : extreme length of the stone 22 feet ; top 19 feet by 13 ; circumference 53 ; height 13. The apex is about three feet in diameter where it touches the foundation. This is probably the most celebrated *Rocking Stone* in the kingdom, except the Logan Rock in Cornwall. Dr. Paris, in his work on the Land's End, observes that those "who are in the habit of viewing mountain masses with geological eyes will readily discover that the only chisel ever employed" in forming monuments of this nature, "has been the tooth of time—the only artist engaged, the elements."* The Druids, no doubt, perceived that this stone might, with some trouble, be made to answer an important purpose ; but the extent of their work must be left to conjecture. The pedestal on which the Buckstone stands *slopes ;* it is probably "retained in its place merely by the roughness of its surfaces," and the density of the lower part has been supposed to be much greater than the upper. The weight of a man at the top, when at the edge, does not perceptibly affect the stone. Deer used to shelter here from storm or heat—hence the name.—There is a *Maen Hir* in the parish of Stanton, on the left of the road to Coleford.

The view from the Buckstone is one of the finest in the world.

Stanton Church is an interesting old structure, with a stone pulpit.

THE VALE OF THE MONNOW

Is characterised by some of the most lovely scenery in the county —a combination of softness and grandeur. The river, from a point above Treget's Bridge, forms a boundary between Monmouth-

---

* Dr. Paris thinks, and we agree with him, that when the Druids perceived a stone possess so uncommon a property as to oscillate when pushed, "they dextrously contrived to make it answer the purposes of an ordeal, and by regarding it as the *touchstone* of truth, acquitted or condemned the accused by its motions."

shire and Herefordshire, and lovers of ecclesiastical antiquities should proceed up the right bank, ascend the *Garway Hill*, and find their way to *Kilpeck Church*, which is about 11 miles from Monmouth. There are other churches of high interest in the *Golden Valley*.—We must keep the left bank. SCENFRITH CASTLE is a very picturesque little Saxon structure, with a keep in good preservation.

GROSMONT, once a town of importance, which stands on high ground, beyond the *Graig Hill*—a prominent feature in Monmouthshire scenery—overlooking one of the finest scenes on the Monnow, is a place of historical interest. Llewellyn and Henry III. had a famous encounter here ; and Owen Glendower was defeated under the walls of the *Castle* in 1405. This structure was a favourite residence of the Earls of Lancaster. The *Church* is a miniature Cathedral. There is a good road to Llanthony Abbey from Grosmont ; and within a few miles is a well-known fisherman's inn, called the " *Monmouth Cap*," (the last of the " *Caps*" for which Monmouth was once famed, as all who have read Shakspeare's Henry V. know). This inn is the headquarters of the Kentchurch Fishing Club, which preserves the Monnow, we believe, about two miles above and about four below the Monmouth Cap. An angler must obtain a member's ticket : day tickets are not issued—an injudicious regulation, not in accordance with the system generally pursued in Wales. There is excellent fishing in the Monnow, which takes its rise at the head of a romantic Cwm in the Black Mountains, or Hatterel Hills, near the Hay end.

The road from Grosmont to Llanvihangel Crugcorney runs for some miles along a lofty ridge, which commands prospects of exceeding beauty of the shadowy bluffs of the Black Mountains. The descent to Llanvihangel is two miles long, and now a superb scene breaks upon you. The Holy Mountain in the front is foreshortened to a sharp bare peak, which rises over vast masses of wood in the park of

LLANVIHANGEL COURT,

a remarkable old mansion, belonging to the Hon. W. P. Rodney, and which, with the exception of a short interval, has been the

property of the noble family of Harley, since the reign of Anne.
The very picturesque gable and terrace front seen at the head of
the avenue of firs was built by Rhys Morgan, A. D. 1559, but a
part of the building is of much older date.   This avenue is the
finest of its kind in the kingdom ; the firs are not of the common
Scotch species, and about forty years ago the government offered
£10,000 for them.   Venerable oak and chesnut trees also abound
in the park.   At the hamlet of *Llanvihangel Crugcorney*, (the
church of the angel with the twisted horn, *i. e.* St. Michael), close
at hand, there is a good old-fashioned inn, on the road from Abergavenny to Hereford.   *Oldcastle*, four miles from Llanvihangel,
near the slope of the Hatterel, was the abode of Sir John Oldcastle, Lord Cobham, a truly illustrious martyr of the early
Reformation.   The castle was taken down some years ago ; there
are vestiges of circular entrenchments connected with it near the
church.   At *Longtown*, a rather picturesque little place, further
on, are the remains of a Castle.

Before we proceed, it is desirable to state, that besides the
roundabout road by Grosmont, there are two other routes from
Monmouth to Llanthony:—1. By the western side of the Graig
Hill to a point of junction at a turnpike into the Grosmont road,
already described.   Distance to the Abbey (properly Priory)
nearly 23 miles. 2. By Abergavenny, which is the best for a
carriage, and also embraces Raglan, 26 miles.

Llanthony is a long six miles from Llanvihangel.   In 1800,
Archdeacon Coxe had considerable difficulty in making his way
up the Vale of Ewias ; a carriage road is now constructed as far
as the Abbey, indeed a carriage may be driven—although in many
parts the way is narrow and rugged, at least as far as *Capel y
Fin*, a small church upwards of four miles above the ruin,
near the base of a vast bluff which we shall indicate presently.

Near the entrance of the Vale, on the left, is a conspicuous
Roman Camp, of large extent, called the *Gaer*, crowning a hill
that is worth ascending if only for the view that it commands.
You now enter the deep Vale of Ewias.   The "chrystal Honddy,"
a true mountain stream, is often seen—sometimes flowing in a
darksome channel furrowed by winter storms and shaded by lofty

trees—far below. As you proceed a singular curve or recess in the hills, called *The Yoke*, strikes you forcibly on approaching *Cwmyoy*, a romantically situated church on the slope of the mountain opposite. The views of the Vale of Ewias, which is apparently terminated by the grand mountain bluff already mentioned, that succeed, are truly fascinating. The eye ranges along a narrow valley for a distance of at least eight miles, with towering hills and precipices on either side, and constant variety is given to the prospects by changes in wooded foregrounds. Solitude is on the surface—it is a valley of shadows—dreamy repose.

Llanthony Priory.

"There stands in a deep valley a conventual church, situated to promote true religion, beyond almost all the churches in England; quiet for contemplation, and retired for conversation with the Almighty; here the sorrowful complaints of the oppressed do not disquiet, or the mad contentions of the froward do not disturb, but a calm peace and perfect charity invite to holy religion and banish discord." These words were written by a Monk of Llanthony at the beginning of the thirteenth century, and form the opening of an elaborate Latin M S. account of the Abbey, which exists in the Cottonian Library. The good ecclesiastic's description of Nature is true; the history of the Church is a history of Man.

It is said, on authority which has been rather doubted, that St. David built a cell here A. D. 600, which fell to ruins and was deserted for several centuries. In the reign of William Rufus, a kinsman of Hugh de Laci one day chased a stag into the Vale of Ewias—then a deer forest—and killed it near the ancient hermitage. He rested awhile, and became so deeply impressed with the grandeur of the solitude which he had penetrated, that he resolved to take up his abode there, and devote himself to religious exercises. He wore a shirt of hair cloth beneath his armour, girded himself with a rope, and led so austere a life that another man of enthusiastic mind, Ernesi, chaplain to Queen Maud, joined him. They succeeded in finishing a chapel A. D. 1108, on the site of David's cell, for a time resisted rich endowments that were proffered, but ultimately Hugh de Laci prevailed. The foundations of a grand monastery of Black Canons of the order of Saint Augustine were laid, with the sanction of the Archbishop of Canterbury, and the stately structure was completed about A. D. 1120. Ernesi was the first Prior, and presided over forty monks collected from the most celebrated religious houses. The church was styled Llandewi Nant Hondeni, the Church of David on the river Honddu, or "Black-water,"—hence Llanthony. The successor of Ernesi was Robert de Betun, afterwards created, sorely against his will, Bishop of Hereford, of whose life a most interesting M S. account is preserved. This very delightful example of medieval biography was translated for the first time by the Rev. George Roberts, for his admirable work on Llanthony, which appeared in a popular form in the year 1847. Betun's departure was followed by a train of misfortunes. The wild Welsh were troublesome neighbours, had frequent feuds amongst themselves, and the defeated at last sought and obtained sanctuary in a body within the abbey walls. The sufferings of the community were grievous, and the cold, the tempests, and the mists of winter—here protracted to a great length—rendered Llanthony truly a dwelling in the wilderness. The good Bishop of Hereford gave the poor monks shelter for two years, and induced Milo de Laci to grant them lands near Gloucester, in the fertile vale of the Severn, where partly with the aid of De Betun they erected a "cell" to the parent monastery, as a place of temporary refuge; the Daughter Church, however, possessed greater charms than the Mother; and the latter fell from its high estate, and became little else than a place of banishment for refractory brethren from Gloucester. These occurrences took place between 1108 and 1136; a case without a parallel in ecclesiastical history—a magnificent monastic establishment, "founded, built, endowed, flourishing, and deserted," within less than thirty years. Notwithstanding this, its records probably surpass in fullness and interest those of any other conventual church—that is, more has been preserved.

The form of the church was that of a Roman cross; length 212 feet; breadth of nave 50 feet; length of transept 100 feet. In

the year 1188, Giraldus described the building as an elegant one, roofed with stone, and covered with lead. Value at the Dissolution £71 3s. 2d. ; at which period the Gloucester Llanthony had an annual income of £648 9s. 11d. The church and manor were granted to Richard Arnold, in whose family they remained until Queen Anne's reign, when the property passed into the hands of the Oxford family, who retained it until Mr. Walter Savage Landor became the possessor.

The engraving, for which we are indebted to Mr. Roberts's work, gives a most accurate general idea of the ruin as it now stands. In 1774 when Wyndham made his Tour, the east window was in existence ; about thirty years later Archdeacon Coxe found it destroyed, and the views given in his *Historical Tour in Monmouthshire* show that during the present century neglect and spoliation have wrought many ravages, the most deplorable of which was the fall of the arches on the southern side of the nave, which took place in 1836. Since that period Mr. Webb, the agent of Mr. Landor (the owner of the ruin and a large adjoining tract), has laudably taken pains to stay the progress of destruction ; and several gentlemen commenced a subscription in 1846 to clear the choir and transepts of rubbish, and to strengthen the fabric generally ; Mr. Webb, at the Abbey, will take charge of any sums that may be contributed towards this meritorious design.

Some of the earliest—perhaps the earliest—examples of the Pointed Arch, *i. e.* of that form of construction as applied to ecclesiastical architecture, exist here. Part of Saint David's Cathedral, and Buildwas Abbey, in Shropshire, are nearly contemporaneous structures. " The great Bell Tower has lost much of its massive strength and majestic height"—the western window has fallen in, like the eastern—" but the west entrance still presents a rich and fresh appearance, and altogether its singular simplicity, combined with boldness of design and massive effect, harmonises with the everlasting hills, which look down upon and enfold, as it were, with a fond, but melancholy embrace, the holy spot. "

Part of the old Priory is converted into a romantic inn, where comfortable accommodation may be obtained.

The rapid river Honddû was once a capital fishing stream, although too much hidden with foliage ; the water is now so much "flogged" by local fishers, that the sport has been much injured.   May is the best month.

EXCURSIONS from Llanthony : To *Capel y Fin*, afterwards ascend mountains on the right, to source of the Monnow.—To summit of *Pen Cader* (six miles, nearest route) ; commence the walk from Llanthony up Cwm Bychan, opposite the abbey, cross the next valley and the river Gruny, at a rude bridge, enquiring carefully at farm-houses.   Or, after gaining the height of Cwm Bychan, go round the tops of the hills, on the right, keeping the "Cader" in view.   By taking this course, which, however, is several miles round, you avoid the severe ascent involved by the near route across the valley.   [See BLACK MOUNTAINS of Breconshire.]

ABERGAVENNY.

Distant from	*Miles.*	*Distant from*	*Miles.*
Brecon	20	Llandrindod	50
Blaenavon	6	Llanthony Abbey	11
Caerleon	19½	Merthyr	20
Chepstow, by Raglan .. .. ..,	22	Monmouth	16
Crickhowel	6	Nant y-glo	9
Grosmont	11	Scenfrith	12
Hereford	24	Usk	11

The situation of Abergavenny is enchanting.   Standing at the entrance of one of the fairest Vales in Wales, almost surrounded by a group of mountains of singular beauty and variety of outline, and washed by the merry Usk, it realises the idea of a pleasant land.

The small river Gavenny here joins the Usk—whence the name, *Aber* meaning confluence.   Roman coins, and bricks, inscribed " *Leg. II. Aug.*," which have been found, attest that this was *Gobannium*.   Subsequently Abergavenny, a sort of Warder on the edge of the hill country, played a conspicuous part in border warfare.   The Norman de Brosses and the house of the Welsh chieftain, Sytsyllt ap Dyfnwal, had many struggles.   Owen Glendower burnt Abergavenny almost to ashes in 1403.   Charles

1. exercised false clemency here to traitors. William III. deprived the place of its ancient charter in 1688, in consequence of the disaffection of the inhabitants. Most of the perriwigs of the beaus of a past day were made here ; and a rural woollen manufacture is still successfully carried on in the neighbourhood—simple hand-looms in which old Welsh patterns and durable plaids are woven.

Leland (temp. Henry VIII.) describes this as a " fair waulled town." The last or Tudor's gate was recklessly destroyed a few years ago, but fortunately Sir B. Hall has perpetuated its memory at *Porth Mawr*, the chief entrance to Llanover. Churchyard the poet (1587), sings of the " most goodly towers" of the *Castle*, but as a ruin it is now uninteresting—hidden by ivy, and blended with a modern mansion, erected by the Earl of Abergavenny, about fifty years since, on the site of the Keep, which was pulled down for the purpose. The view from the Castle Hill is a " grand scene" with tourists.

The Priory Church—once the property of a Benedictine com-munity—is one of the finest in the county, but has been half ruined or injured by modern " restoration." There are many curious monuments—Norman effigies, especially of the Herbert family.—St. John's, the original parish church, was converted into a free grammar school by Henry VIII. The remains of the Priory, which is on the south-eastern side of the town, form part of the residence of Mr. C. Kemys Tynte, which contains some curious tapestry.—There are five meeting-houses in the town, and a Roman Catholic chapel.

The establishment of the " Abergavenny Cymreigyddion So-ciety," in 1832, for the purpose of continuing, on an important scale, the ancient *Bardic Festivals*, has been very beneficial to the town and neighbourhood in several respects. The objects of the society are expansive ; and embrace not merely the cultivation of national historical studies, traditions, and music, but the encou-ragement of native manufactures, rural economy, &c., for which end prizes and rewards are given, varying in value from one to ninety guineas, and including several harps. There are many Cymreigyddion societies in Wales, but this is the only one of practical utility, with the exception of a society of more recent origin in North Wales. Essays on subjects of Celtic research have been sent from France and Germany ; a revival has been established through a distinguished Breton, M. Rio, of intercourse between Wales and Brittany ; the chief prize at this national congress has more than once been awarded to Foreigners. Harpers from all parts of the Principality attend the annual meetings, and there is reason to expect that the use of the national or three-stringed harp, by far the finest instrument of its kind, will again become universal in Wales. Welsh families will once more possess Harpers like Highland chieftains their pipers. A great impetus has been given to the manufacture of Welsh woollens and hats by the Cymreigyddion—a name which means a society of Welshmen, although it numbers many English members.—A *Hall*, capable of holding 2,000 persons, has been built, chiefly for the use of the society ; the annual congress is held in October, and is of course a great event. The procession on these occasions is rendered national by attention to costume, and extends for a mile ; the meeting lasts two days, but the festivities at Llanover and other neighbouring seats, are of greater duration.

The Population of Abergavenny in 1841 was 4,253. The market on Tuesday is thronged, the population of the neighbouring iron-works being great consumers. HOTELS—The Greyhound, the Angel.

There is good society here, and many fine seats in the neighbourhood, amongst which are *Llanover* (Sir B. Hall), four miles on Pontypool road. In the grounds of Mrs. Waddington (mother of Lady Hall), at Llanover, is a Rhododendron, 150 feet in circumference.—*Coldbrook*, the ancient seat of Mr. Ferdinand Hanbury Williams, under the *Scyrryd Vach*, near the town, once the abode of the famous Sir Charles Hanbury Williams ; gallery of portraits by Vandyke, &c.—*Clytha*, seat of Mr. W. Jones, five miles on Raglan road ; *Llanarth*, seat of Mr. Philip Jones, the head of a very old Roman Catholic family, the original seat of which, *Tre Owen*, now a farm-house, visible from the Monmouth and Raglan road, is a fine specimen of Inigo Jones's style.

PWLL-Y-CWN WATERFALL. Follow the Merthyr road, passing the Clydach iron-works, which are four miles from Abergavenny.

When about half-way between Clydach and the village of Pwll-y-Cwn (which is a mile beyond the works) diverge along a tram-road on the left, and on reaching a public-house called the "Morning Star," make enquiries for the Waterfall of *Pwll-y-Cyn*, the approach to which is across a brook up a very romantic glen. When the rivulet is low, its course can be followed with advantage. Pwll-y-Cyn means "Pool of the dogs." This wild spot is the haunt of superstition—a favourite resort of the Spirit called the *Pwcca*, commemorated in Miss Williams's contributions to Croker's *Fairy Legends*.

THE MOUNTAINS.

The SUGAR LOAF, or *Pen y Val*, 1856 feet high, a miniature Vesuvius, stands enthroned on four lofty spurs, called the Llanwenarth Hills, viz., the *Deir*, the *Rholben*, the *Graig*, and to the north-east of the first, the *Bryn Arw*, or rugged hill. An excursion to the summit of the Sugar Loaf and back occupies upwards of three hours. Tourists usually commence the ascent by climbing the Deri, about a mile on the Hereford road, and descend the side of the Rholben; some follow the course of a brook, which takes its rise within about 100 feet of the summit of the mountain in three springs, which are intensely cold in the hottest weather. You can ride on horseback almost to the extremity of the peak, which commands views of great extent and magnificence, bounded on the east by the Malvern Hills, and including the Vales of Crickhowel and Usk, but which are not so interesting as those from

The HOLY MOUNTAIN, or *Scyrryd Vawr*, 1498 feet high, nearly three miles from Abergavenny. At Llandewi Court, a great farm-house near the base of the hill beyond Llandewi Scyrryd church, horses can be put up. There is an air of sublimity about this wild rugged mountain, on the north-east point of which was an ancient chapel, dedicated to St. Michael, some of the foundations of which are discoverable. To this elevated spot Roman Catholics in the vicinity are said to repair annually to perform their devotions. The fissure near this end has evidently been produced by a Landslip, but is the subject of superstitious legends; some aver that it took place at the Crucifixion, when the "rocks were rent." The scenic effects along the lofty ridge, especially of the Black Mountains, dwell in the memory. An ancient mansion, called *Wern-ddû*, now a farm-house, about two miles from Abergavenny, on the road to the Holy Mountain, was "the cradle" of the noble family of the Herberts.

The LITTLE SCYRRYD *(Vach)*, a pretty eminence, 765 feet high, near the town on entering from Raglan, commands lovely prospects.

The BLORENGE *(Blawrenge,* grey ridge) is a very conspicuous feature in Monmouthshire scenery, and under fine lights assumes an air of grandeur that much exaggerates its height, which is 1720 feet. It stands between the entrance of the vale of Crickbowel and the Pontypool or Avon Llwyd valley. Inclined planes and other utilitarian signs on its sides show that the traveller has reached the Mineral Basin of South Wales. A round may be made from Abergavenny by the Blaenavon Iron Works, six miles —the road to which slants up the side of the Blorenge on the left, above the town—to Pontypool, altogether about eleven miles.

LLANTHONY ABBEY. There are two roads from Abergavenny ; the old road, which runs along high ground, is nearly two miles nearer than that by Llanvihangel.

Raglan Castle.

" A famous castle fine,
That Raglan hight, stands moted almost round ;
Made of freestone, upright as straight as line,
Whose workmanship, in beautie doth abound,
The curious knots, wrought all with edged toole,
The stately tower, that looks o'er pond and poole ;
The fountain trim that runs both day and night,
Doth yield in shewe a rare and noble sight."

Churchyard's " Worthines of Wales," 1587.

This peerless ruin stands on a gentle elevation, partly hidden with foliage, a short way from the village and church of Raglan, on the right of the Abergavenny or great road into Wales.

It is the most perfect decorated stronghold of which this country can boast—a romance in stone and lime. No portion of the structure can be assigned to an earlier period than that of Henry V., from which transition styles can be traced down to the first quarter of the seventeenth century.

A castle was founded here by one of the Clares in the thirteenth century, from which period its history for more than two hundred years is obscure. ' It successively belonged to the Berkeleys and the Herberts, and in 1491, on the death of the Earl of Huntingdon, better known as the Earl of Pembroke, the castle and manor passed into the hands of his son-in-law, Sir Charles Somerset, a very distinguished soldier and statesman of royal lineage, in the reign of Henry VII., who, in right of his wife, the heiress of the House of Herbert, bore the title of Baron Herbert of Raglan, Chepstow, and Gower. This eminent person died in 1526, " full of honours"; and the castle progressively rose in dignity, especially during the time of Henry, fifth Earl and first Marquis of Worcester, who was born in 1562. The records of the Civil War present few events so touching of their kind as the struggle made here by this gallant and good old man in favor of the King. When created a Marquis in 1642, he raised an army of 1,500 foot and 500 horse, which he placed under the command of his son, the celebrated author of the '' Century of Inventions'' and the discoverer of the steam engine. He maintained the cause of the the King bravely, and advanced large sums for that object. Charles visited his faithful subject several times. The King sought a refuge here in July, 1645, after the disastrous battle of Naseby, and remained until the 15th of September, when he took an affecting leave of the venerable Marquis. The style which was kept up at Raglan was princely, and interesting accounts of the method of living, as well as of the visit of Charles, are preserved.

Raglan was the last castle throughout this broad realm which defied the power of Cromwell. Fairfax's lieutenant, when he summoned the garrison to surrender in June, 1646, wrote thus :— " His excellency, Sir Thomas Fairfax, having now finished his work over the kingdom, *except this castle*, has been pleased to spare his forces for this work." The Marquis—then eighty-five —in reply stoutly said, that he " made choice (if it soe pleased

God) rather to dye nobly than to live with infamy." The siege lasted from the 3rd of June until the 19th of August, during which period a number of characteristic notes passed between Fairfax and the Marquis, who evidently feared, and justly, that the Parliament would not keep faith. The main works of the besiegers were pushed forward to within sixty yards of the fortress, and the place where their chief battery was planted may still be seen in the "Leaguer Field" on the east side. The garrison harrassed the besiegers greatly with sallies, although only 800 strong. A capitulation was effected on honourable terms; the Marquis and his followers, including several persons of note, marched sorrowfully out, the former proceeding to London, where, contrary to the articles of surrender, he was seized and imprisoned. He lingered for a few months, and soon before his death, at the age of eighty-six, when informed that parliament would permit him to be buried in the family vault, in Windsor chapel, he cried out with great sprightliness of manner, "Why, God bless us all, why then I shall have a better castle when I am dead than they took from me whilst I was alive."

The castle was literally "spoiled" after the siege; the farmers in the vicinity emulated the parliamentary destroyers, and no effort seems to have been made by the Somerset family to preserve their ancestral house until rather late in the last century, since which, like all the Duke of Beaufort's other castles, it has been carefully preserved. Twenty-three stone stair-cases were taken away during the interval; and the great Hall, the Chapel, and other grand features of the sumptuous building, grievously injured. Enough, however, is left to convey a vivid idea of its olden grandeur; and much of the masonry is as fresh as when first exposed to the elements. The motto on the time-worn arms as you enter, speaks eloquently of the Past—" *Mutare vel timere sperno,* "—I scorn to change or to fear. The machicolated Gateway Tower on the right contains a few fragments of armour and a vaulted -room, which possesses very fine properties of sound. After lingering in the great *Stone Court*—now paved with turf—120 feet by 58, the buildings on the right of which were greatly damaged at the siege, visitors usually proceed to the *Kitchen,* which occupies a tower at the upper extremity, below which is the *Wet Larder*, approachable by an underground passage. The *Stately Hall*, 66 feet by 28, is the grand feature of the Stone Court. In a line with this Hall, was a dining-room of smaller dimensions on the north. Beyond the great hall are the remains of the *Chapel*, the west side of which has been destroyed, so it is now open to the *Fountain Court*, which, though smaller than the first court, is almost the most fascinating portion of the ruin. Pass through the elegant doorway opposite, and ascend the stairs to the summit of the tower, which is said to have been a favourite resort of Charles I. From hence there are passages and other means of access to the state apartments, the chief of which, the long room with bold windows in a tower looking north, was the state room of Charles I. After making a circuit as far as the kitchen tower, the visitor can either return by the way he came, or descend to the Stone Court, and pass through the Fountain Court to the *Pleasaunce*, or *Grand Terrace*, 260 feet long, and 77 broad, which was once exquisitely laid out. The *Cellars*, which are of vast extent, excite interest in returning, for the purpose of exploring the *Citadel* or *Yellow Tower of Gwent*, access to which is gained by a foot bridge across the moat that still surrounds it. The walls of this structure are ten feet thick, and its five stories rise to a height of 128 feet, which are easily accessible by a wide and massive geometrical staircase. An admirable idea is obtained of the castle from the summit. Before you depart do not omit to walk round the Terrace which surrounds the Tower of Gwent, and which is suggestive of the days of gallant cavaliers and high-born dames of another age—fail not, either, to traverse the dry moat round the Castle, to visit the Leaguer Field, and if the day be favourable, to linger until evening. Sunset, from the battlements of Raglan! Under fine lights we know of few scenes in Britain, especially at such an hour, that can compare with this —a region below which, long as it has been disafforested, is still chase-like—a back ground of mountains, sentinels of the hill-country—perfect in form, in colour, and in grouping.

Inn at Raglan—The Beaufort Arms.

We recommend the pedestrian tourist to cross the country

from Abergavenny to Raglan, ascending the Holy Mountain and visiting White Castle, on his route. The same advice will apply to those who walk *to* Abergavenny by Raglan.

𝖂𝖍𝖎𝖙𝖊 𝕮𝖆𝖘𝖙𝖑𝖊 is a rude and gigantic ruin, partly of a date anterior to the Normans, moated, and situated on a ridge of land about six miles to the east of Abergavenny, one and a half from the village of Llantillio Crossenny, and five from Raglan. It is of immense strength, and, with one exception, the only apertures in its walls, which are flanked by huge round towers, are arrow holes. There is an extensive barbican. A Sir Gwyn [White] ap Gwaithvold is said to have been its possessor when the Norman invasion took place ; temp. Henry II. William de Braose was its owner ; Henry III. granted it to his favourite, Hubert de Burgh ; it was '' a place of great renown and magnificence" early in Elizabeth's reign ; and " ruinous and in decay," temp. James I. White Castle is seldom visited, except by those who diverge from beaten tracks.

NEWPORT.

Distant from	*Miles.*	*Distant from*	*Miles.*
Bristol by Steam	28	Chepstow	16
Bassaleg	3	Llantarnam Abbey	3
Caerleon	3½	Monmouth	24
Caerphilly	12	Pontypool	9
Caerwent	11	Tredegar	3
Cardiff	12	Usk	10

The average PASSAGE BY STEAM from Bristol occupies nearly two hours and a half, but the trip has been accomplished in one hour and fifty minutes ; the Old Company's boats leave Cumberland Basin ; those of the New Company, Bathurst Basin. Both run daily except Sundays. Fares, 3s. saloon ; 1s. 6d. fore cabin. There are steamers to Gloucester and Liverpool. The rock called " the Denny," which at a distance looks something like a seamonster floating on the waters, rises in mid channel, near the track pursued by the Bristol and Newport steamers. A lighthouse marks the entrance of the Usk, about five miles up which river stands Newport, discernible at some distance by its "forest" of masts.

Few places have risen more rapidly during the present century than Newport, called by Giraldus *Novus Burgus,* or New Town, after the decline of Caerleon. Leland (temp. Henry VIII.) styled it " a town in ruin"; and Archdeacon Coxe, nearly fifty years since, described it as "dirty and ill paved." The commencement of the Monmouthshire Canal in 1792, gave the first impetus to the trade of the port, for mules formed the only means of conveying mineral produce for shipment previously. The Tredegar, Rhymney, and other tramroads were afterwards constructed. In 1791, Newport was a village containing only 750 persons, and only exported 6,939 tons of coal ; in 1841, half a century later, the population of Newport and Pillgwenlly amounted to 13,737 ; and now it cannot be far short of 20,000. At the opening of the new docks in 1842, the chairman spoke of Newport as " an infant Liverpool," and little doubt can be entertained that it will become a large and very important place before the end of the present century. The traffic of five great mineral valleys—Crickhowel, Pontypool, Ebbw, Sirhowy, and Rhymney—converges at this, their natural outlet to the sea ; and when we state that the mineral wealth thrown off by Monmouthshire now amounts to nearly three millions annually, our prospective view cannot be deemed extravagant. Newport, now a fifth-class port, commands another advantage in a magnificent river, with spring tides varying from 36 to upwards of 40 feet, and it will very soon possess railways to the east, west, and north. Bristol, now rising from her lethargy, begins to be jealous.

The docks, which were opened on the 10th of October, 1842, after a sum of £180,000 had been expended in their construction, are the key-stone to the prosperity of the port, which previously was a dry harbour. A fine ship of 1,200 tons, with sails set and yards manned, floated through the lock, with perfect facility, on the occasion. The area of the dock is four acres and a half, but there is another dock of similar size close at hand, which is temporarily used as a reservoir. The width of the main lock is 62 feet ; length 202 feet ; and vessels of 1,080 tons *register* have with ease entered and been loaded in the dock.

The exports of minerals approximate to those of Cardiff. In

1829 they were—iron, 108,726 tons; coal, 471,625 tons. The annual average exports of iron in the four years 1842-5, amounted to 188,381 tons; in 1846 the quantity exported was 215,014 tons. The annual average export of coal between 1842-5, was 631,901 tons; in 1846 it was 647,816 tons.—In addition, a large quantity of tin plates and merchandize, including oak timber and bark, is annually exported. The value of the iron during the years 1846-7 probably averaged £8 10s. per ton; and the coal, 8s. 6d. per ton. There has been a slight declension in the exports of coal of late, in consequence of several coal owners, whose trade was previously confined to Newport, having partially removed their shipping trade to Cardiff. During the first four years after the Taff Vale Railway was opened, the coal trade of Newport increased only two per cent., whilst at Cardiff the increase was 65 per cent. The chief increase in the coal trade at Newport has taken place in the white-ash coal, which is largely used for steam purposes. Until the coal duty was repealed, Newport and Cardiff, under the powers of an act passed early in the present century, possessed a peculiar advantage, viz., a right to ship coals free of duty, which was extended to all ports " east of the Holmes," thus shutting out all the ports to the westward. The annual shipments from Newport to Bridgewater alone, under this monopoly, exceeded 100,000 tons; but under " free trade" in coal, the price at Cardiff has been reduced 1s. 6d. per ton—a little below the level of Newport—hence the increase we have indicated. The imports of Newport chiefly consist of iron ore from Lancashire, Cumberland, and Cornwall, and foreign timber for ship-building, which is extensively carried on. In 1846, 84 vessels of 9,831 tons belonged to the port.

The antiquities of Newport are the Castle, and St. Woollos Church. The town was once walled, and three gates existed in Leland's day, the last of which was destroyed about half a century ago. The Castle was built by the celebrated Robert Fitzhamon, in the reign of William Rufus, chiefly for the purpose of defending the passage across the river, but also to aid him to maintain the newly-conquered lordship of Glamorgan. It formed part of the dowry of Mary, heiress of Sir William Herbert, on her marriage with Lord Herbert of Cherbury. The square tower, which now forms the principal feature, was probably the keep ; the remains of the baronial hall are worth looking at ; but the commercial character which has been given to the structure—now an ale store—discourages the archæologist.—*St. Woollos Church* stands on an eminence, and is an interesting structure with a Saxon nave. The western doorway, which leads from a chapel dedicated to St. Mary (in which there are ancient monumental effigies), is also Romanesque, highly enriched. The tower, from whence there is a fine prospect, was built by Henry III. " in gratitude for the attachment of the townsmen to his cause."—Some remains of a House of *White Friars*, chiefly consisting of the northern transept of the chapel, and the fratry, may be seen in a low neighbourhood near the bridge, called " Friars Fields." On Stow Hill are several curious old houses. St. Paul's church, a poor modern structure, finished in 1836, stands near the south entrance into the town, and there is a chapel of ease subservient to it at Pillgwenlly, supported by the Church Pastoral Aid Society. A Roman Catholic chapel, in the Early English style, was opened in 1840 ; and there are about twelve other chapels belonging to Protestant dissenters.

The descent of the Chartists on Newport on the 4th of November, 1839, belongs to the romance of history. The ringleader, Frost, was blinded by deadly hatred to the then Mayor, Mr. Phillips, now Sir Thomas Phillips, on whom he hoped to wreak his revenge ; no mere political agitator would have engaged in so mad an enterprise. The men whom he and his confederates led astray had no pretence for disaffection, for the majority were earning wages nearly three times higher, on an average—some much more—than agricultural labourers ; but Frost had brute ignorance and intemperance—mighty aids to the demagogue—to deal with. Still it seems hardly credible that the bulk of the working men of a district should deliberately rush on a career of murder, robbery, and incendiarism ; for their avowed object at the outstart was to take Newport by surprise, sack and burn it. Arrangements had been made to start for Newport, and it is believed Monmouth, on Sunday evening, so as to reach those places at the dead of night ; but the plan was most providentially frustrated by a fearful storm, which tore up trees by the roots, deluged the country with rain, and compelled the mass of the Chartists to remain at home until the following morning, when the idea of attacking Monmouth was abandoned.   The utter discomfiture of the modern Jack Cade's band of five or six thousand followers, armed with almost every conceivable species of weapon, by twenty-eight soldiers and a few special constables, is a striking proof of the value of discipline and steady courage in the hour of difficulty.   The attack on the King's Head Hotel, at Newport, was over in a quarter of an hour—Mr. Frost's host* scattered to the winds.   It is believed that many men died of their wounds on their return home, who were buried by their comrades, and never again heard of, for there was a very great disparity between the number of killed and disabled, and the number missing.   As it was, the scene in Newport was fearful. Both Newport and Monmouth—where the state prisoners were confined—presented for many months after the rising almost the appearance of besieged towns.   The Westgate Hotel, at Newport, still bears marks of the conflict, and will long be an object of curiosity.   Sir Thomas Phillips behaved nobly, and although seriously wounded, saved his life miraculously.

Newport returns one member to Parliament in conjunction with Monmouth and Usk, and is a borough by prescription.—It possesses a Mechanics' Institution, with a good library ; an Exchange and Reading Room in the Town-hall, erected in 1842 ; a Dispensary ; and a National Training School.   The *Monmouthshire Merlin* is published here.—Races are annually held on the Marshes. —Saturday is the market day.   The area of the cattle market—

---

* The following list of the weapons of the rebel host is taken from an excellent local history of the outbreak, " The Rise and Fall of Chartism in Monmouthshire : "—" Guns, pistols, blunderbusses, swords, bayonets, daggers, pikes (spears about a foot long, with two sharp hooks attached to poles about two yards in length), bill-hooks, reaping-hooks, hatchets, cleavers, axes, pitchforks, blades of knives, scythes and saws fixed in staves, pieces of iron, two and three yards in length, sharpened at one end, bludgeons of various length and size, hand and sledge hammers, mandrils (a kind of light pick-axe,) &c." Many of the multitude, who marched twelve abreast, carried ammunition in bags.

in which the annual Tredegar cattle show is held—is four and a half acres.

Principal INNS—The King's Head, and the Westgate Hotels.

Amongst the objects of interest in the neighbourhood of Newport is *Tredegar Park*, the seat of Sir C. M. R. Morgan, a house erected in the reign of Charles II. The late Sir Charles Morgan was perhaps the most perfect remaining example of " the fine old English gentleman." A very large revenue is derived by the Tredegar family from the tramroad that partly passes through the park, which is skirted by the Ebbw river, is extensive and well stocked with deer. One of the principal rooms, 42 feet long and 27 feet broad, was floored and wainscotted from a single oak. There is a fine collection of pictures.

Llantarnum Abbey, seat of Mr. R. J. Blewitt, M. P., adjoining the Pontypool road. The only remains of a Cistercian structure that existed here are the gateway, some of the cells, and the old garden walls; but the mansion is of Elizabethan date.—Some relics of a Priory of Black Friars can be traced at *Basselleg*, on the old road to Cardiff, where there is an aged church. About a mile from Basselleg, on Wentloog Level (which contains St. Mellon's, St. Bride's, Marshfield, and Peterstone churches), is an ancient *Encampment*, said to be Saxon. At *Goldcliff*, a small headland near the channel, nearly three miles from Newport, are vestiges of a Priory, founded in 1113; and there is an important encampment, said to be Roman, about a mile and a half from the town, towards Caerphilly, called " *The Gaer*."

Caerleon.

The walk from Newport to Caerleon runs up the pleasant vale of the Usk, here a stately river. On an opposite eminence, nearly half-way, St. Julian's, the abode of the famous Lord Herbert of Cherbury, carries the mind to another age. It has undergone many alterations, and is now a farm-house; part of the chapel has been converted into a barn. The ecclesiologist has hitherto halted on his way to visit the rude early Norman church of *Malpas*, once the chapel of a cell of Cluniac monks, but we believe

that the structure either has been pulled down or is about to be
so ! The mansion near, *Malpas Court*, is the seat of Mr. Prothero.
On nearing the bridge, we ascend the brow of the hill before passing through *ultra pontem*, to *Christchurch*,* a structure of various
periods, commanding an exquisite prospect.   Caerleon is impressive when approached near sun-down on a summer evening.   A
lofty mound—a *Pretorium* to an imaginative mind—looms above
old-world buildings in the foreground ; it seems a place for day
dreams.

This, then, was Antonine's *Isca Legionis Secundæ Augustæ*—
the ancient metropolis of Wales ! Here, when the iron-hearted
Roman became elegant and luxurious, he was wont to resort,
and disport himself in the fair region of *Britannia Secunda*.   It
was a place of great note—the " city of the legions.''   Listen
to the glowing account which Giraldus Cambrensis gives more
than seven centuries after the Romans had left this island :—
" Many remains of its former magnificence are still visible ;
splendid palaces, which once emulated with their gilded roofs the
grandeur of Rome, for it was originally built by the Roman
princes, and adorned with stately edifices ; a gigantic tower,
numerous baths, ruins of temples, and a theatre, the walls of
which are partly standing.   Here we still see, within and without
the walls, subterraneous buildings, aqueducts, and vaulted
caverns ; and what appeared to me most remarkable, stoves so
excellently contrived, as to diffuse their heat through secret and
imperceptible pores. "   Nearly seven more centuries have elapsed
since this was written : how are the mighty fallen !   Can this
mean town, scarcely rising above the rank of a village, be the
place of which Giraldus speaks ?   But still there is much to repay
curiosity.   The mound, 300 yards round at the base and 90 at
the summit, on which the " gigantic tower " stood, exists and

---

* " The Church contains a curious sepulchral stone of the fourteenth century,
on which are carved two rude whole length figures of a man and woman, with
their arms folded, standing on each side of a cross.   A superstitious belief
prevails amongst the lower class of people in these parts, that sick children who
touch this stone on the eve of the Ascension are miraculously cured.   They remain all night in contact with it."—COXE. This superstition has nearly died away.

ought to be surmounted,—ruins lie about it, the garden in which it stands is full of Roman antiquities. The Amphitheatre may still be traced in the *Round Table* field, associated by many with the famous Arthur. Its form is oval, 222 feet by 192. In the last century stone seats were discovered on opening the sides of the concavity, but they are now covered with turf. The walls of Caerleon are not nearly so perfect as those of the sister city, Caerwent. Those near the amphitheatre are the most remarkable ; none now exceed 14 feet high, but their thickness, 12 feet, is great. " The shape of the fortress appears to be oblong, inclining to a square ; three of the sides are straight, and the fourth, like the northern wall of Caerwent, curvilinear ;" they inclose a circumference of 1,800 yards, "with corners gently rounded, like most of the Roman stations in Britain, and the four angles nearly correspond with the cardinal points of the compass." The mound, already described, is supposed to have been greatly enlarged by the Normans, who built a fortress here, the ruins of which were about 40 feet high in the middle of the last century. Amongst the other features of Caerleon may be mentioned remains of the works of the castle overhanging the Usk—ruins near the bridge—and a round tower near the old-fashioned inn— famed for its ale—the " Hanbury Arms." Many of the houses are partly constructed with Roman bricks. The Market-place is supported by four *Tuscan columns*—grim memorials of the ancient conqueror. In 1847 Sir Digby Mackworth granted the Old Town-hall as a Museum for the preservation of local antiquities, to forward the objects of which an association was formed. The railway excavators have lately discovered a number of stone coffins.

After the departure of the Romans, Caerleon became a British city—the capital of Gwent-land—in the sixth century, one of the abodes of King Arthur. Its ecclesiastical history is highly interesting :—it was stained with the blood of martyrs in early times—it was the seat of an archbishopric, once held by the famous Dubricius, and which was removed by Saint David, his successor, to Menevia, in the wilds of Pembrokeshire.

A few years ago, Mr. John Edward Lee published a thin

quarto, with twenty-seven excellent engravings, illustrative of the history and antiquities of Caerleon.

About half-way between Caerleon and Usk, near the west bank of the Usk, is *Tredonnoc Church*, in which there is a Roman inscription to the memory of a soldier of the second Augustan legion.—*Llangibby Castle*, seat of Mr. W. A. Williams, a descendant of Sir Trevor Williams, stands on the left of the main road, about two miles and a half further on. The ruins of the fortress stand at the back of the present mansion, hidden by wood.

USK.

Distant from	Miles.	Distant from	Miles.
Abergavenuy	11	Monmouth	14
Caerleon	7	Pontypool	6
Chepstow	11	Raglan	6

Usk is a small place of great antiquity, very prettily situated on the left bank of the river of that name, at a point where it is joined by the Olwy. The salmon fishing is superb, and there is also good trout fishing. The Castle stands on an eminence commanding the town, and commands a lovely view of the Vale of Usk. Its remains are considerable.

Owen Glendower unsuccessfully attempted to take this fortress, and sustained under its walls a signal reverse, which compelled him to retire to the mountain fastnesses of North Wales. In the fifteenth century, the castle was the favourite abode of Richard Duke of York, father of Edward IV. and Richard III., both of whom were, it is said, born here. In the church, a large structure, is an inscription on brass, which has long puzzled antiquaries. We gather from a paper in the *Archæologia Cambrensis* for January, 1847, that the style of the poetry ,is that of the fourteenth or fifteenth century, and that it is all Welsh, with the exception of two words. Some remains of a Priory to which the church was attached, and which was founded in the thirteenth century, may be seen near.

INN—The Three Salmons.

ENCAMPMENTS. *Craig-y-Gaeruyd* (Roman), on the brow of a precipice on the right bank of the Usk, one mile and a half north-west from the town, near Pontypool road. *Campwood*, two miles and a half from Usk, on left of road to Raglan, on a wooded emi- nence ; form oval. *Coed-y-Bunedd*, 1,440 feet round, on the top of a lofty elevation, not far from Clytha Castle, near the junction of the Usk and Abergavenny and Monmouth roads.

PONTYPOOL.

Distant from	Miles.	Distant from	Miles.
Abergavenny	10	Newport	9
Monmouth	20	Usk	6

This large, dirty, straggling town stands near the entrance of the Vale of Avon Llwyd—once highly picturesque, but which is deformed by iron-works and collieries, seamed by tramroads, a canal, and other appliances of a mineral district. The name was originally *Pont ap Hywel*, the bridge of Hywel, a small hamlet in the vast parish of Trevethin, the old church of which stands in the mountains. Population in 1841, 14,942.—*Pontypool Park,* the fine seat of Mr. Capel Hanbury Leigh, occupies an eminence near the town.

A charcoal furnace and forges were commenced at Pontypool in the sixteenth century (about A. D. 1565), by Capel Hanbury, Esq., so this is one of the earliest seats of the iron trade ; but there is reason to believe that the Romans worked iron ore in these hills, then covered with wood, as they undoubtedly did in Dean Forest, ancient heaps of slag being occasionally struck upon. In consequence of the destruction of timber for fuel being carried to a serious extent in the reign of Elizabeth, acts were passed prohi- biting the erection of iron works, except in districts specified. Many years elapsed before coal could be successfully applied to the smelting of iron, but in 1740, after nearly a century and a half had been wasted, this great result was attained by Mr. Abraham Darby, at the Coalbrookdale iron works, in Shropshire. In that year Monmouthshire only contained two furnaces, the make of which was 900 tons annually, and so slowly did the trade pro- gress, that in 1788, only one more furnace had been put up, but the aggregate make of the county had increased to 2,100 tons, owing to the use of the steam engine. Charcoal furnaces were, however, still in operation at Pontypool and Tintern. Three furnaces were erected at Blaenavon by T. Hill and Co. in 1790, in which year furnaces were also erected at Ebbw Vale, and Blaendare. The Nantyglo works, now almost the greatest in the world, were commenced in 1795, but did not succeed, and were suspended in about a year. Mr. Joseph Bailey was then a youth, under his uncle, Mr. Crawshay, at Merthyr. The latter, at his death, left him a share in the Cyfarthfa works; but soon after, his sons bought Mr. Bailey out, paying him a very large sum. Mr. Bailey, with intuitive sagacity, perceived the capabilities of Nantyglo, which has thriven uninterruptedly under the management of himself and his brother, Mr. Crawshay Bailey, another " iron king," who retired from the management in 1846, and commenced new works at Aberdare.

The success of Blaenavon gave a vast impetus to the iron trade in the Monmouthshire Hills; and a range of works sprung up to the westward, almost in a line near the heads of valleys that stretch towards Merthyr. The Beaufort, Ebbw Vale, Clydach, and Varteg works, were in operation in 1803; Tredegar in 1805; Nantyglo in 1811: Coalbrooke Vale in 1821; Blaina in 1824; Pentwyn in 1825; Abersychan (British) in 1827; Bute in 1828; Golynos (now united with Pentwyn) in 1837; and Victoria in 1838. Besides these leviathans there are several smaller works. The first iron work of the South Wales series is at *Clydach*, a small concern about four miles from Abergavenny; and the works can be visited in succession, to Merthyr, the distance of which from Abergavenny is about 20 miles.

Mineral property on the hills, which, when the Monmouthshire Canal and its tramroads were constructed, was only worth five shillings an acre surface rent, soon increased in value to £1,500 an acre, or more, underground. The area of the Monmouthshire coal field exceeds 89,000 acres, and the various seams of coal that can be profitably worked are said to average about 50 feet, which produce a gross yield per acre of nearly 73,000 tons. The total quantity now worked annually is estimated at about 2,200,000 tons; at which rate there is a sufficient supply left for the next

1,500 years.   The net quantity available for export has been estimated at about 3,000,000,000 tons ! Great Britain now annually consumes from all her collieries about 21 million tons.

Tourists who visit Pontypool will find the Pentwyn, and British works at Abersychan the nearest at hand ; the Blaenavon works stand on the hills at the head of the valley. A visit *at night* makes an impression not easily effaced.

INNS at Pontypool—The Red Lion, the Clarence.

The mountain parish of *Aberystwith*, in which Nantyglo and some other works stand, contained in 1841, 11,272 persons. *Bedwelty* is another vast parish, which stretches for many miles on the western boundary of the county.   It contained in 1841, 22,413 persons ; and a market town has sprung up at *Tredegar*, near the northern extremity, 21 miles from Newport.   Another considerable place, called *Newbridge*, has also sprung up in the Ebbw Vale.

This region formed the head-quarters of the Chartist legion ; and the population which have been forced in a rank hot-bed, have been too long left in a lamentable state of ignorance.   Several of the iron-masters, however, have of late years laudably exerted themselves to provide churches and schools, but much remains to be done.   In 1847, a new ecclesiastical district, in the diocese of Llandaff, called " Beaufort," was formed out of the parishes of Aberystwith, Bedwelty, in Monmouthshire, and Llangattock, and Llangynider, in the county of Brecon.

We have crossed the country from Pontypool to Caerphilly ; first following a long valley in which there are two immense reservoirs or artificial lakes, then intersecting the Ebbw and Sirhowy vales, and finally descending a mountain by Bedwas, a church and village near the Rhymney river, on the other side of which we entered Glamorganshire.

This is a fatiguing walk, alternately dreary and exciting ; but it is a judicious route for those who wish to economise time, and also to diverge from beaten tracks.   Such tourists ought to proceed from Caerphilly to the Bridgewater Arms, Pont-y-Pridd, pass the night there, and then go on to the Vale of Neath, through Ystrad-y-Vodog.

GLAMORGANSHIRE.

IF a history marked by events which influenced the fate of a nation—if an extraordinary abundance of antiquities—if great variety of scenery, and objects of natural history—if a profusion of mineral wealth—can render a county interesting to the archæologist, the lover of nature, the scientific observer, and the capitalist, Glamorgan is entitled to distinction in an eminent degree.

Gwlad Morgan was once an independent sovereign principality, comprising the country between the present county of Carmarthen and the river Wye, including the southern and eastern portions of Brecknock. "The principality of South Wales" proper, consisted of the three western counties, the remaining part of Brecknock and Radnor. The two provinces were often rent by the feuds of their rulers, and soon after the Norman conquest of England the dissensions between the Welsh princes had arrived at so great a height, as to give the Normans an opportunity, which they had long been anxious to obtain, of placing their mailed hand on this rich and romantic region. The circumstances of the conquest are remarkable.

A revolt broke out towards the close of the eleventh century in the territory of Rhys ap Tudor, Prince of South Wales, which was mainly fomented by a knight called Einion ap Collwyn, who had seen much service on the continent, especially under William the Conqueror in Normandy, where he had contracted a friendship with several barons, who followed their sovereign to England. The rebels were signally defeated by Rhys, who although of the great age of ninety, manifested extraordinary energy, and all the leaders fell except Einion, who fled to Jestyn in Glamorganshire. The latter was then at war with Rhys, and inflamed by jealousy and ambition, promised Einion his daughter in marriage, with a rich dowry, if he would bring him aid from England to conquer western Wales. Robert Fitzhamon, a Norman knight of princely birth, eagerly listened to Einion's proposals ; and soon induced twelve other knights to march under his banner, with whom, and according to some accounts, 3,000 followers, he joined Jestyn in the spring of the year 1091. They then carried fire and sword into the dominions of Rhys, but the gallant old prince met them on the lofty common of Hirwain Wrgan, two miles north of Aberdare, on the borders of Glamorgan, where he was defeated, and according to some accounts killed. Jestyn rewarded his Norman auxiliaries so liberally, that the place where they were paid—all in gold pieces—a common three miles to the east of Bridgend, is called the *Golden Mile* to this day. Fitzhamon and his followers proceeded to the coast to embark at Penarth, near Cardiff. Einion demanded *his* reward ; but Jestyn, flushed with success, told him that his daughter should never wed a traitor. Acting on the impulse of sudden revenge, Einion galloped after the Normans ; they had embarked, but were baffled by a light wind. Perceiving the Welsh knight frantically waving his mantle on the shore, Fitzhamon put back, and Einion related his story, exposed dissensions which existed in Jestyn's camp, and told the Norman that he might win South Wales. It was a fortunate opportunity ; questions of right and wrong were not closely canvassed in that age ; there was, moreover, a pretence—a " grievance" to redress. Jestyn was taken by surprise ; made a feeble resistance, was routed, and fled to England. He ended his days at the religious house of Llangennys in Gwent.

So the Normans won the lordship of Glamorgan.

Fitzhamon fixed his chief abode at Cardiff, which he fortified, gave his twelve knights—the ancestors of many of the present Glamorganshire families — princely estates, including several castles, and with sound judgment confirmed or made grants to members of Jestyn's family, and the native chiefs who had assisted him.   The following is a list of the grants :—Robert Fitzhamon took Cardiff, Kenfig, and Lantwit ; Ogmore was awarded to William de Londres ; Neath to Richard Grenville ; Llanblethian to Robert de St. Quintin ; Penmark to Gilbert Humphreyville ; St. Athan's to Roger Berclos ; Sully to Reginald Sully ; Peterston super Elwy to Peter Le Soor ; St. George's to John Fleming ; Fonmon to Oliver St. John ; St. Donatts to William de Esterling ; and Coity to Payne Turberville. Caerphilly, with a barren district, was awarded to Einion the traitor, with Jestyn's daughter, the prize at which he aimed, in marriage ;

H

Caradoc ap Jestyn obtained Aberavon ; and Rhys ap Jestyn the country between Neath and Tawy. The Welsh could not stomach the feudal system ; and in 1094, whilst a Norman army was engaged in Gower, they rose suddenly, and headed by Payne Turberville, who had married a Welsh heiress and entertained ambitious views, took several of the Norman strongholds, and laid siege to Fitzhamon, who, unprepared for violence, was at his castle of Cardiff. The latter was in consequence obliged to remove several of the rivets he had clenched, and restore ancient laws and privileges which had been abrogated. The history of South Wales, for a long period subsequently, abounds with incidents of border warfare, and many years passed before the indomitable spirit of the mountaineers was subdued.

We cannot wonder, then, that there should still remain the ruins of at least *thirty Castles* in Glamorgan. The conquerors had to maintain their ground with their swords ; and the stern memorials of the massive middle age, which are now one of the great charms of the country, each telling a wild warlike story, attest the bravery of their foes. The district, too, was richer than other Welsh counties, in religious communities, the civilizers of a rude era. The Cathedral of Llandaff, the Abbeys of Neath and Margam, and the Priory of Ewenny, are beautiful and interesting remains ; there are other monastic relics, and curious parish churches ; and the ruins of Lantwit Major are records of a vast seminary of learning frequented by a large body of students in the sixth century.—" The antiquity of the cottages," observes Mr. Malkin, with his usual discrimination, "is a strongly-marked feature in this county. There is little doubt that many of them are as ancient as the castles, to which they were attached. The pointed door-ways and pointed windows sufficiently evince their date......they carry with them the recommendation of a venerable exterior, and a portion of internal room, comfort, and security from the elements, rarely enjoyed by their fellows in any part of the world." Malkin's description stills holds to a considerable extent.—Druidical remains of considerable importance exist in Glamorganshire ; and the Romans had several stations in it, for the *Via Julia* ran from Cardiff to Loughor, and was joined at

Neath by the *Sarn Helen*. The first station is supposed to have existed at Caerau, near Cardiff ; the site of the next *(Bovium)*, has been fixed both at Boverton and Ewenny ; *Nidum* (Neath), succeeds ; Loughor is *Leucarum*.

The scenery of Glamorganshire possesses very great variety— is " full of pictures " from end to end. It has a coast of extreme interest, ninety miles in length ; its hill country often strikingly resembles Merionethshire, one of the most picturesque counties of North Wales, the mountains appearing larger than they really are, owing to their noble forms, their abruptness. It is a county of wild valleys and flashing streams ; there are very few parts of the Principality that exceed Ystradyvodog (the Green Vale) in all the concomitants of scenery of the highest class; and be it remembered that magnitude is not essential to beauty, and that even sublimity is not always to be measured by yards and feet. The Vale of Glamorgan is popularly known as the " Garden of South Wales." The landlords are anxious to promote improvements, and there is consequently some good farming. The Glamorgan or native breed of cattle are hardy, and possess good points.

A striking change has taken place in the character of the people since the commencement of the present century, especially during the last fifteen years, a circumstance which has partly arisen from the intermixture with the English in the large towns and works. In the Vale, English is almost universally spoken ; but in many of the sequestered valleys and nooks of the hills, Welsh still prevails. The language of the southern portion of the Principality differs materially from that of North Wales, so that the people of those districts often cannot understand each other without difficulty. The South Wallian dialect contains many words used by the people of Brittany, and Breton sailors can readily keep up a conversation with the Welsh at sea-ports. The introduction of Railroads will break down national peculiarities, and South Wales, which presents vast capabilities, will, no doubt, be gradually " revolutionised" in a peaceful sense.

Full information relative to the state of Education in Wales may be found in three Blue Books which were issued in December 1847—the fruit of the labours of three Government Commissioners. The report relative to the counties of Glamorgan, Carmarthen, and Pembroke, was drawn up by Mr. Lingen, who commenced his enquiries at Llandovery, in October, 1846, and concluded at Merthyr Tydvil, in April, 1847. The district contains 345 parishes; a population (in 1841) of 365,558 persons; 712 day schools, attended by 30,918 scholars; 913 Sunday schools, attended by 79,392 scholars; and of the aggregate number of scholars, 23,417 are returned as "common both to the day and Sunday schools." The scholars are thus classified:— 12,338 in the Church of England (National) Schools, 2,096 in British schools, 1,356 Independent, 746 Baptist, 640 Methodist, 276 Wesleyan, 449 other denominations, 9,622 "private adventure," 338 workhouse, and 3,007 in workmen's schools. Mr. Lingen considers the use of the Welsh language very injurious to the interests of the people.

"It would be impossible," he says, "to exhibit a greater contrast in the aspect of two regions, and the circumstances of their inhabitants, than by comparing the country between the rivers Towy (Carmarthen) and Teifi (Cardigan) with Merthyr, Dowlais, Aberdare, Maesteg, Cwm Avon, and the Vale of Neath and Swansea. Yet the families which are daily passing from the one scene to the other do not thereby change their relative position in society. A new field is opened to them, but not a wider. They are never masters; and, if the rural portion of them does not grow in numbers, nor manifest any fresh activity, while the other portion is daily augmented, and put upon fresh or more extended enterprises, the difference is to be sought in the classes to which they are severally subjected, and not in themselves. It is still the same people. In the country the farmers are very small holders, in intelligence and capital nowise distinguished from labourers. In the works, the Welsh workman never finds his way into the office. He never becomes either clerk or agent. He may become an overseer or sub-contractor; but this does not take him out of the labouring and put him into the administering class. Equally in his new, as in his old, home, *his language keeps him under the hatches*, being one in which he can neither acquire nor communicate the necessary information. It is a language of old-fashioned agriculture, of theology, and of rustic life, while all the world about him is English." This picture does not apply to Welshmen who speak English.

The number of schools in Glamorganshire is 327; 228 of which are let on tenure at will, ten for terms of years, and twenty-two are in trust for ever. Number of scholars, 21,194.

Glamorgan embraces the greatest portion of the mineral basin
of South Wales, which will last at least 2,000 years. The "coal
measures and the associated beds, the mountain limestone, and
the old red sandstone, occupy all the northern part of the county ;
they are bounded on the south by a line drawn across Gower
peninsula from Whitford Burrows to Oystermouth, by the shore
of Swansea bay, and by a waving line drawn eastward from
Margam on that bay by Llantrissent and Caerphilly to the river
Rhymney." The deepest portion of the South Wales coalfield
extends from Neath, its centre, to Llanelly in Carmarthenshire.
Owing to the nature of the country, which is mainly composed of
valleys running north and south, the miners are to a considerable
extent enabled to obtain coal and iron by driving levels into the
hill sides, but this does not prevail on the western side of the coal
basin. Most of the coal is bituminous, but the upper parts of the
Vales of Neath and Tawe yield excellent stone coal or anthracite.
A "fault" or "dyke" of great thickness, filled with fragments
of the disjointed strata, exists near Swansea, traversing the coal-
field, and raising the strata on one side no less than 240 feet.
There are many other faults. Ironstone is found in great abundance in the Merthyr and Aberdare districts, and in the group of
hills to the south-west, which abound with black-band ; this
mineral also exists in the Vale of Neath. Lead is to be found in
the carboniferous limestone region near Llantrissent, Cowbridge,
and in some other places. Calamine abounds at Maenllwyd ; and
manganese on the northern side of Gower, and at Newton. The
country adjoining the mineral formation is chiefly composed of
white limestone, which also occupies nearly the entire peninsula
of Gower. In this peninsula, and also in the Rhymney Valley at
the other end of the county, the old red sandstone crops out from
below the carboniferous limestone. The stratification of the limestone is remarkably horizontal, especially along part of the coast
between Cardiff and Swansea bay. The conglomerate or newer
magnesian limestone, " the lowest rock before coming to the coal
measures," appears frequently in the cliffs, varying in thickness
from thirty to three feet. Sir John Stradling, in a ballad in praise

of this county, written in the sixteenth century, sums up, with slight poetical licence, its mineral treasures :—

> " And in Glamorgan's hillie parts
> Cole greatly doth abound,
> For goodness and for plenty too
> Its equal never was founde.
>
> With wood and iren, ledde and salt,
> And lime aboundantlie,
> And everything than mankind want,
> This land doth well supplie."

The Llangeinor Mountain (1859 feet) is usually considered the highest in the county, but Craig-y-Llyn appears loftier.

The largest rivers rise in the mountains of Brecknock and Carmarthen. On the eastern boundary is the Rhymney, the length of which is more than 30 miles. The Taff, the most important stream in the county, is about 40 miles long, and has three chief tributaries, the Taff Vechan, at Merthyr, the Cynon, which joins about seven miles lower down, and the Rontha Vawr, at Newbridge. The river Ely, 21 miles long, also joins the Taff at the sea-side. The Thaw, 12 miles long, flows past Cowbridge to the sea at Aberthaw. The Ogmore, 18 miles long, washes Bridgend, and is joined by the Ewenny, a stream about a third shorter. There is a rapid stream at Pyle. The Avon, which rises on Llangeinor Mountain, and runs into the sea, 16 miles off, is next in succession. The Neath comes next ; then the Tawe, like the last, a Breconshire river ; lastly, the Loughor, which properly belongs to Carmarthenshire.

Few portions of the kingdom offer so wide and attractive a field for the naturalist as this. Those who visit the coast will observe that Samphire, called in Welsh *corn carw 'r mor*, or " sea buckhorn," grows in extraordinary profusion on cliffs of lias formation.

The area of Glamorgan, which is the largest of the Welsh counties, except Carmarthen and Montgomery, is 792 miles ; and it contains at least one-sixth of the population of the Principality. In 1801, it contained only 71,525 persons ; in 1831, 126,612 ;

the census of 1841, gave 171,188 ; and at present the number must considerably exceed 200,000 ! This rapid advance, like that of Monmouthshire, has arisen from the development of vast mineral resources. There has been of late years a decrease of population in almost all the parishes which are purely agricultural. The number of persons per cent.·engaged in trade, commerce, and manufactures, was in 1841, 14.0, and in agriculture 5.9. The waste lands amount to nearly 100,000 acres.

Glamorgan returns two county, and three borough members, viz., for Cardiff, Merthyr, and Swansea. It contains 128 parishes, all of which, except twenty-two in the deanery of Gower, are in the diocese of Llandaff. The Assizes are held alternately at Cardiff and Swansea.

The Canals are the Glamorganshire, between Cardiff and Merthyr ; the Aberdare, the Neath, the Swansea, and the Penclawdd. We have described the Railroads under a distinct head.

CARDIFF.

Distant from	Miles.	Distant from	Miles.
Bristol, by Steam	32	Llantrissent, by Llandaff	11
Bridgend	20	Merthyr Tydvil, by Railway	24½
Caerphilly	7	Merthyr, by Road	24
Caerau	3	Newbridge, (Pont-y-Pridd)	12
Cowbridge	12	Newport	12
Llandaff	2½	St. Nicholas (Cromlechs)	6¼

THE VOYAGE BY STEAM—usually a very charming trip—occupies from two hours and a half to three hours, and has been done in two hours and three minutes. The fares are 4s. and 2s. The Holmes form one of the main features of the channel, in running down ; the Flatholm, the island nearest the shore, is four miles N. ¼ E. from Penarth Roads, off Cardiff—so called from the headland, surmounted by a church, at one extremity. At early flood, the steamer, passing a numerous fleet lying outside, runs up the new channel, three-quarters of a mile in length, cut to the Bute Docks, which, with their long vista or forest of masts, rise in the background, and give a most favourable impression of the port.

Until the BUTE DOCKS were constructed, the only outlet for the mineral district of which Merthyr is the capital, was the Glamorganshire Canal, the access to which was very imperfect, and the dimensions wholly inadequate for the rapidly-increasing trade of this great iron and coal country. The Marquis of Bute was the owner of a large tract of land that intervened between the town and the sea, called " Cardiff Moors," and conceived the idea of converting it into a harbour on a scale commensurate with the prospective wants of the neighbourhood. In 1830, he obtained an Act for constructing a new port, the " Bute Ship Canal," and steadily proceeded amidst many difficulties, to carry out the design at his individual cost. The works—then considered a " wild speculation"—were commenced in 1834 with the construction of a feeder from the river Taff, the first stone of the docks laid on the 16th of March, 1837, and the docks opened on the 9th of October, 1839.

At the entrance of the sea-gates, 45 feet wide, there is a depth of 17 feet at neap and 32 feet at spring tides. The area, of the outer basin is about an acre and a half, and a lock, 36 feet wide, connects it with the inner basin,. which stretches almost up to Cardiff, possessing an area of nearly 200 acres of water, in which between 300 and 400 vessels of all classes can be accommodated. This splendid dock—which is now hardly sufficient for the trade of the port—is 1,450 yards long and 200 wide, is in direct communication with the Taff Vale Railway, of which it forms the water-side terminus ; and great improvements have lately been made on the east side. The foundation of the outer or sea-wall gave way more than once, which greatly increased the expense ; but the undertaking, which at first languished under an injudicious tariff of rates, has prospered beyond all expectation ; and a plan which was adopted for keeping the roadstead clear, has perfectly succeeded. The outlay in money on the whole of the works has, it is understood, exceeded £300,000 ; to which should be added, the value of the ground, and of the lime, stone, and piles, all of which belonged to the Marquis. The noble lord is a true patriot. In October, 1847, we counted 160 vessels in these docks at one

time, of an aggregate burden of 31,000 tons.   Th following
figures show the advance of the traffic at the Bute Docks :—

	Vessels entered Inwards.	Vessels entered Outwards.	Registered Tonnage.
1844	2,115	2,132	184,405
1845	3,227	3,439	298,576
1846	3,805	3,816	327,637

The exports of coal and iron at these docks were as under in
the following years :—In 1844, 256,332 tons of coal ; 8,497
tons of iron.—In 1845, 353,890 tons of coal ; 70,085 tons of
iron.—In 1846, 415,115 tons of coal ; 66,171 tons of iron.

Until the Taff Vale Railway was opened in 1840, the produce
of the mineral districts found its way down the Glamorganshire
Canal, which also follows the line of the river.   It was opened in
1794 : length 25 miles ; rise 611 feet.   The traffic of this valley
has so euormously increased of late years that the canal company,
notwithstanding railway competition, can hardly carry all that is
offered, and in 1847 carried 1,000 tons a week more than it ever
did before.   The following figures show the number and registered tonnage of vessels that have entered the canal for three years,
exclusive of others that have loaded outside :—In 1844, 2,795
vessels, 180,341 tons ; in 1845, 2,888 vessels, 148,455 tons ; in
1846, 3,087 vessels, 162,840 tons.   Shipped on the canal in 1845,
272,553 tons of coal, and 152,406 tons of iron.

The following statistics illustrate the advance of Cardiff :—

Exports of coal : in 1826, 40,718 tons ; in 1843, 350,000 tons ;
in 1845, 626,443 tons.   Exports of iron : in 1826, 64,303 tons ;
in 1843, 140,615 tons ; in 1845, 222,491 tons.

The value of the exports in 1843 was, coal, at 8s. per ton,
£140,000 ; iron, at £6 per ton, £843,690 ; tin plates, at 40s.
per box, £160,000.   Total, £1,143,690.   In that year it was
estimated by Mr. Booker, at a meeting of the Cardiff Chamber of
Commerce, that the annual consumption in the works, collieries,
and districts connected with Cardiff, amounted to a million
sterling, half of which was earned by the miners and workers in
iron.—In consequence of the increase that has taken place in
the trade, and the increased value of iron, the exports of minerals

here must now amount on an average to between two and three millions.

Captain Smyth, R. N., in his "Nautical Observations on the Port and Maritime Vicinity of Cardiff" in 1840, gives a picture of the state of things near the close of the last century, which affords a curious contrast to the foregoing statistics :—

"This port was held to be in extreme activity half a century ago, when the comparatively scanty supply (of iron) was brought down from the hills in waggons, each bringing two tons, drawn by four horses, and attended by a man and a boy. Even Mr. Bacon's contract guns in the American war were thus conveyed for embarkation to the side of *Gwlad Quay*, which from that circumstance was known for some time afterwards as the 'Canon Wharf,' though that name has long been lost; and it is a proof of the growth of the town since that time, that the guns used to be proved from the street before this Quay (St. Mary's), against the earth bank of the South Wall, across the end of the street; there being no houses beyond the then gate, called *Port Llongy*. Coals, at the same time, were brought chiefly from Caerphilly Mountain, in bags weighing from 100 to 130 lbs., on horses, mules, and asses, with a woman or a lad driving two or three of them. This was principally done in fine weather, for it was customary to avoid the incidental delays of frost, snow, or bad weather, by bringing in the winter stock at a particular time; and this provident collecting was called a *Cymmorth*, from a Welsh word, signifying help or assistance."

It may be gathered from the facts which we have grouped, that Cardiff has been running a friendly race with Newport. Not many years ago it was a small, ill-built, dirty, Welsh town; now it is a respectable town of its class, with less of a sea-port look than any other trading place we have seen on this coast, a circumstance which arises from the distance of the docks from the bulk of the population. The force of a good example is strikingly manifested here. The spirit of the Marquis of Bute has been caught by the people; everything wears a cheerful air; and the corporation have made many improvements, including an *Abattoir*, or public slaughter-house. Cardiff is the "county town," and contains the county gaol. The census returns give, perhaps, the best idea of the progress made : in 1801, the population was about 2,000; in 1831, 6,187; in 1841, 10,079. The number must be now about seven times as large as it was about half a century ago.

The Welsh name of Cardiff, *Caer Dydd*, is said to be derived from *Caer Didi*, the camp of (Aulus) Didius, a Roman General, who succeeded Ostorius in the command of the legions in Britain. Roman relics have been found within the walls of the present castle, which stands on the line of the Roman coast road through South Wales. Jestyn ap Gwrgan had commenced to build walls round Cardiff, at which he must have had some stronghold, when he was driven out of Glamorgan by Fitzhamon *(ante* p. 97), who, according to Sir Edward Mansel, then built " his new castle by the west gate. " Cardiff was subsequently strongly fortified, and its history presents many vicissitudes. The wretched Robert Curthose, Duke of Normandy, ended his days in the castle, after a confinement of twenty-eight years, at the instance of his inhuman brother, Henry I. His place of imprisonment was the existing tower, at the left of the gateway on entering, the restoration of which was commenced in 1847.

Owen Glendower took the castle and destroyed the town. In the civil war of the seventeenth century, Cardiff was alternately held by both parties, and it is said that Cromwell was so much baffled by the resistance which he encountered, that he would have been compelled to retire, had not a deserter, whom he afterwards hung as an example to traitors, disclosed a subterraneous passage. Doubt, however, has recently been thrown on this " stock " story by Mr. Dorney Harding *(Cymmrodorion Trans.* Vol. IV. 1843), who thinks that Cromwell was never here. Be this as it may, picturesque incidents and severe struggles have occurred at Cardiff. The octagonal keep, 75 feet wide, stands on an eminence within the old ramparts, which have been planted, and form a very agreeable walk, commanding extensive views. On the western side of the castle is a " modern " castellated mansion—in which there are some good pictures—the residence of Lord James Stuart, a brother of the Marquis of Bute. Access to the ruins cannot be obtained when this nobleman is at home. The Marquis of Bute is the possessor of a great portion of Fitzhamon's estates in this district, his grandfather, John Stuart, Marquis of Bute, Baron Cardiff, having married Charlotte Jane Herbert, daughter and heiress of the last of the ancient lords of Glamorgan. The noble marquis means to carry out princely improvements in Cardiff castle and grounds.

The tower of St. John's Church is the finest in Wales, except Wrexham, in Denbighshire, and reminds one of the Somersetshire towers, in the loftiness of its proportions, and the elegance of its pierced battlements and airy pinnacles, but is of somewhat earlier date.   The church has been altered at various periods ; the decorated west window, a statue of Edward III. on the same front, and a monument in honour of Sir William and Sir John Herbert, are the chief features worth noticing.—The objects of antiquity are slight, and chiefly consist of the fragments of two religious houses, occupied by Black and White Friars.   A very fine church, near the edge of the river, was undermined and washed away about two centuries ago, and the parish annexed to St. John's.   St. Mary's, the modern church, on the road to the Bute Docks, is in strange taste, although not finished until 1842. Lord Bute subscribed largely towards it, and in 1847 built in addition a Burial Chapel for the town of Cardiff, at a cost of £1,500.—There is a well-conducted Infirmary at Cardiff, open to the counties of Glamorgan and Monmouth ; the Marquis of Bute and Daniel Jones, Esq., of Beaupré, have been the chief bene-factors.—The educational statistics of Cardiff are encouraging. The Marquis of Bute, when he came into his property, founded a school with some aid from other individuals ; four others have since been erected, and upwards of 1,000 children receive educa-tion.   The number of beer-houses produces injurious effects on the population.—There are nine Dissenting chapels in the town.

New Law Courts in St. Mary-Street, were projected in 1848.

The river Taff, the course of which has been diverted by the South Wales Railway Company, washes the town on the westward, and meets the Ely in Penarth roads.

Amongst the " worthies " of Cardiff are King Arthur and Wilson the painter.—The town returns one member in conjunc-tion with the boroughs of Cowbridge and Llantrissent.—News-paper, the *Cardiff and Merthyr Guardian.*—Principal INNS—The Angel, and the Cardiff Arms.

EXCURSIONS FROM CARDIFF.   1. To Llandaff.   2. To Caer-

)
-
r
t
,

ᴐ
ʙ
-
ɔ
t
ʙ
l
ʙ
,
r
ө
ө
.
g
ө
!-
ff
d
d
ө
.ө
ıt
k
ıa
l-
f,
n
n
ıd
ʙ,

philly Castle. 3. To Pont y Pridd, up Taff Vale Railway.—
thence up Rontha Valley to Ystradyvodog, &c. 4. To Merthyr
Tydvil. 5. To Caerau, and Druidical Antiquities near Saint
Nicholas. 6. To Western Coast. 7. To Margam, Vale of Neath,
and Swansea.

Llandaff.

The Vale of the Taff, which for the greater part of its course
is fretful and turbulent, alters its character when it fairly enters
the lowlands, when the stream expands, and moves onward tranquilly, laving wooded banks and grassy meads, as if reluctant to
depart after a very brief experience, from scenes so fair. At
Llandaff Bridge there is a long reach, which Mr. Malkin has
well described as "a scene of sylvan beauty perfect in kind and
exquisite in degree." It is just the spot for the site of a House
dedicated to GOD—for religious contemplation, reverential feeling,
contentment, tranquillity. Even the natural history of the river
is suggestive to the moraliser. Here, in the first half of the
fifth century, Myric, King of Glamorgan and Siluria, founded the
episcopal see of Llandaff, said to be the oldest in the kingdom.
The celebrated Dubricius was consecrated the first Bishop, owing
to his zeal in opposing the Pelagian heresy, and elevated to the
Archbishopric of Caerleon or Primacy of Wales. St. David succeeded him at Caerleon, and according to some writers Llandaff
was not created a separate bishopric until after St. David removed
the metropolitan see to Menevia, and the first bishop was Eliud
or Teleiaù, a man of eminent piety, who was canonised. The
late Dean of Llandaff, in an address to the clergy of the diocese
relative to the restoration, quotes Bishop Godwin's statement that
a church was founded here about A. D. 180—which we think
very apocryphal—but he adds that "it is certain that Dubricius
presided here in 436." At the end of the seventh century, Godwin says "that so much riches had been bestowed on Llandaff,
that if it enjoyed the tenth part of that which it had been
endowed with, it *would* be one of the wealthiest churches in
Christendom." In 1108, Urban, thirtieth bishop of the see, found
a very different state of things in existence,—the church in ruins,

the revenues confiscated. He set to work in earnest, obtained large funds, and commenced the present cathedral in 1120. The styles prove that the progress of the work must have been slow. Dean Conybeare is of opinion (1847) that from the commencement by Urban, " at least sixty years must have elapsed before the completion of the nave' '—probably eighty—" and another eighty in addition before the eastern chapel was appended. " We think that John de Monmouth, appointed bishop in 1296, made considerable alterations in the church ; and Bishop Marshall also " beautified it greatly," particularly with a new altar piece, and frescoes, *circa* 1480. Browne Willis, in 1715, says, " the glorious structure has fallen into a most deplorable state of decay within these few years," yet a print which he gives shows that the exterior, except the south tower which was ruinous, and the pinnacles which were almost destroyed by the great storm of 1703, was nearly perfect in all essential particulars. Nothing was done to repair it ; the decayed tower fell, and the Chapter, in the middle of the century, at last obtained funds to the amount of £7,000—sufficient to have effected a perfect restoration—which they expended, partly in pulling down, partly in casing the ancient structure. An elevation resembling a *Town Hall*—" classic" run to seed, with *urn* " pinnacles, " rose in the centre of this exquisite gothic edifice ! The nave was left roofless, and St. Mary's or the " Welsh " chapel deserted. Even during the debased taste of the last, and early part of the present century, when " gothic " was a term of reproach, this act of barbarism provoked indignant comment. Few persons are aware that it was proposed to remove the see of Llandaff to Cardiff in 1717-18. The ancient fane remained in its state of desolation until 1839, when the late Dean (the Very Rev. William Bruce Knight) made an eloquent appeal to the clergy of the diocese, and the church at large. A sufficient sum was soon obtained to enable the Chapter to commence the work of restoration.

The Cathedral stands retired from the village in a hollow, partly shaded by foliage, not far from the bank of the river—a site chosen with the usual exquisite taste of our forefathers. The structure, which is dedicated to St. Peter, St. Dubricius, St. Teilo, and St. Odoceus, is 270 feet in length from east to west ; there are no transepts, and the breadth of the nave and its aisles corresponds with that of the choir and its aisles, 65 feet ; the choir is upwards of 35 feet broad ; the dimensions of the eastern chapel are 58 feet by 25. The building of 1751 chiefly occupies the choir, and it has been ascertained that the old walls were then *encased*, so that by removing the plaster and new stone work, the edifice resumes its former character. A " sublime antiquity" breathes through the nave ; " every arch infuses a solemn energy, as it were, into inanimate Nature ;" the western front is, in part, one of the most beautiful examples of the Early Pointed style, which, when fully developed, was distinguished by its " extreme depth and multiplicity of moulding, high-pitched roofs, acute arches, long and narrow windows, slender and isolated shafts." In the first story is a round-headed door, the work of Urban ; three Early English windows, divided by arcades, rise above the centre higher than the others ; another lancet window, on either side of which are four trefoil-headed arcades, form the third story ; and the design is completed by a trefoil window under the gable cross. The northern or remaining tower of this front, which was finished by Jasper, Duke of Bedford, *circa* 1480, has been injured by some additions, and should be ascended in order to obtain the view which it commands. Nearly all the upper portion of the nave has been destroyed ; the arches have very rich mouldings ; and the south door (the porch has been demolished) is one of the most exquisite existing examples of deeply-recessed Romanesque work.—The Chapter House, on the south side of the choir, has a groined roof, springing from a central column, and produces the effect of a transept, on a superficial view. It is not now used for its original purpose.

There are several monuments of great antiquity in the church, chiefly of bishops, which have been partly defaced. The most remarkable are the following :—A recumbent effigy of William de Braose (an ancestor of the late Dean), who died *circa* 1287, which was found in clearing out the rubbish that blocked up the Lady Chapel. The words " William de Brusah" are carved in rude letters round a mitre, in blue lias stone, of which the monument, is composed. It is placed on the north side near the altar.

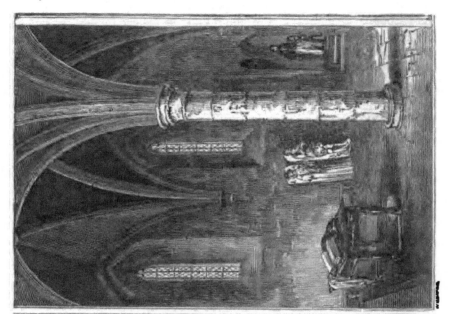

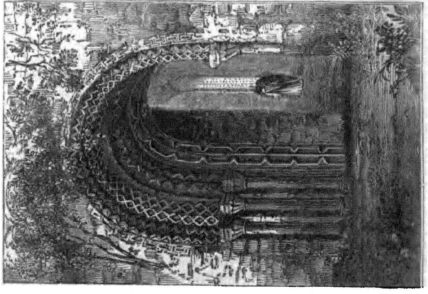

An effigy of Dubricius, which lies on a raised pedestal next to a figure of Bishop Brumfield. A representation of an emaciated female in her winding sheet "designed to perpetuate the memory of an unfortunate person who fell a victim to disappointed love." An alabaster figure of an armed knight, named Christopher Matthews, 6 feet 2 inches high, who distinguished himself and fell in the civil wars. There are also effigies of the following bishops: John of Monmouth, who succeeded de Braose ; Paschal, 1361.

The Lady Chapel has been restored with great taste at an expense of £1,165 12s. ; and the eastern extremity of the south aisle, with its fine windows and open-work parapets, and part of the choir, are undergoing restoration. "A noble arch of Bishop Urban's work has been opened out, commanding a striking perspective into the Eastern Chapel ; the mouldings of this arch are very interesting, and in the most perfect preservation. Beneath this, a very beautiful screen of Bishop Marshall's work, A. D. 1480, has been exposed. A sepulchral recess, in which the capitals of the side shafts are most beautifully executed, in the style of 1200, is likewise now again disclosed to view in the south-east wall of the choir. Tradition assigns this as the tomb of St. Teilo, or rather, of one of his three corpses ; for the legends of the *Book of Llandaff* relate, that on his decease, three churches with which he was connected, contested for the possession of so precious a relic. It was on this miraculously multiplied for the satisfaction of all their pious desires ; the parties having agreed to refer the controversy to the decision of a sign from Heaven. They spent the night watching on their knees round the single corpse ; but the first rays of the morning disclosed three corpses before them absolutely identical in every lineament ! " Bishop Teilo's bones were discovered in a very dilapidated leather coffin ; a statue was found in the grave, a well-executed figure of a bishop with a crozier, &c. It was estimated in January, 1847, that the cost of restoring the *cased* choir would not exceed £600 ; and it is expected that in 1850, "a very complete restoration of everything under the roof will have been effected." The Chapter propose at present to leave the roof as it stands, but we trust it will ultimately be replaced by one suited to the style of the structure,

I

and *that the Nave will be restored.* But these objects cannot, of course, be effected without considerable funds.

The Library of the Cathedral, which contained inestimable manuscripts, was removed for security to Cardiff Castle, during the civil wars ; where it was burnt by Cromwell's supporters, "with a great heap of prayer books." "The cavaliers of the country and the wives of several sequestrated clergymen were invited, on a cold winter's day, to warm themselves by the fire, which was then made of the books there burnt."

The cathedral has long sunk to the condition of a parish church ; but a revival of the daily service must follow the restoration of the material fabric. The architect, under whose directions the Lady Chapel was restored, and who has the charge of the works in progress, in conjunction with Mr. Wyatt, is John Prichard, Esq., son of the Rev. Richard Prichard, vicar of Llandaff.

The " city " of Llandaff stands on a gentle eminence, and is now a mere village. It is an old-world spot, and some years ago possessed a larger number of quaint houses than almost any place of its size that we can call to mind. There is an air of comfort about the village green ; it is one of those nooks which people who are sick of life's turmoils might dream of. The old cross was restored some years since ; but the ancient episcopal palace, a castellated mansion of considerable extent, is in ruins, and long ago passed from the possession of the bishops of the diocese into that of laymen, the present owners being the heirs of Sir Samuel Romilly, who have a good estate in the county. An impression has always prevailed that Owen Glendower destroyed the bishop's residence at Llandaff, but doubts have recently been thrown on the circumstance, which rests merely on tradition. In all probability, Glendower "spoiled" this house, and it was not afterwards thought worth while to repair it, for we find that the next bishop in succession fixed his abode at Matherne. The gateway of the ruin possesses great merit in an architectural point of view, and the Editor of the *Archæologia Cambrensis* is disposed to refer it to the thirteenth century, although Bishop Urban, the reputed founder of the edifice, is said to have built it A. D. 1120. "The sloping buttresses, which are characteristic of the castles in South Wales, will not escape notice."

Llandaff is two miles from Cardiff, by a pleasant field-walk which commences close to Cardiff Bridge ; the distance by the turnpike road is nearly half a mile more.

There are some large mansions in the parish ; that near the village, on the path from Cardiff, is Llandaff Court, the residence of the Rev. George Thomas.

ST. FAGAN'S, hitherto a sequestered place, two miles to the N. W. of Llandaff, but now on the line of the South Wales Railway, was the scene of a battle, which had decisive results, between a Welsh royalist army of 8,000 men and a large force under Cromwell—who narrowly escaped defeat—in 1648. The Castle here is rather a castellated mansion than a stronghold.

LLANTRISSENT—the Church of three saints—is a town of great antiquity, most picturesquely situated on a lofty eminence, near the verge of the hill country. There are some remains of a castle, and the church is a fine old Norman structure. It is four miles and a half from Pont-y-Pridd ; and within easy distance of the South Wales Railway.

The Vale of Ystradyvodog may be entered here through the vale of Ely, more easily than by the route already described.

Caerphilly Castle.

No ruin in Great Britain affords so impressive an idea of the Feudal Age as Caerphilly. Carnarvon, Edward the First's master-piece, although externally more perfect, more graceful as a finished example of Gothic military architecture in its palmy days, is not nearly so large. These old Baronial strongholds—grand in their desolation—almost defying Time in their strength—are Histories in stone. Speaking evidences of a massive system, which with all its vices, its tyranny, its defects, can never be regarded by the people of an " old country " like ours, without mingled feelings of earnestness and romance—a system, like the monastic, admirably adapted to a period when the world, after the overthrow of the great nations of antiquity, began to emerge from an era of barbarism and slumber—heave with mighty impulses, the forerunners of civilization.

Caerphilly is seven miles north of Cardiff—within an easy excursion, and its situation amidst an amphitheatre of bleak mournful-looking hills is impressive, especially on a distant view.

But little is known of its early history. A smaller castle stood here originally. Daines Barrington, in an essay published seventy or eighty years ago, which excited more attention than it deserved, attributed the erection of the present structure to Edward I., merely because it had been recorded that that monarch had passed through South Wales ; but there is no reason to doubt, after an examination of authorities, that Gilbert de Clare, the last but one of that name, was the *founder, circa* 1270. The next Lord of Glamorgan in succession fell at Bannockburn, and having no male issue, his immense estates were divided between his three sisters ; Caerphilly falling to the portion of Eleanor, who married Hugh le Despenser the younger, the well-known favourite of Edward II. About the year 1320, it was recorded that the younger Despenser had been for some time governor of this castle, which he greatly enlarged and strengthened. Six years afterwards the king and his two "minions" fled to Bristol, where the elder Spenser was barbarously executed, and the king, accompanied by the other, embarked in a vessel on the Channel, with the intention of taking refuge in the wild and almost inaccessible seclusion of Lundy Island. But the elements were against him, and baffled by storms and opposing gales, he was compelled to land near Neath, in Glamorganshire. His subsequent movements until his capture are narrated so variously that it is impossible to thread the maze. These facts are certain : that he took refuge for a time at Neath Abbey and at Margam, and that he was captured owing to treachery, with his friend Spenser, near Llantrissent. Whether the latter event occurred after or rather in the midst of a siege of Caerphilly Castle seems a matter of uncertainty. We confess that we are inclined to think that it did. The preparations that had been made to withstand a siege were prodigious, and it is hardly likely that the king would have altogether deserted such a shelter.

The siege is the most memorable episode in the history of Caerphilly. Despenser had a son, the second Hugh Despenser the *younger*, a youth of twenty, who, according to the generally-received accounts, seems to have been old in judgment and resolution, although in an elaborate essay on this Castle, which appeared in the *West of England Journal*, a periodical published at Bristol in 1836, this view is controverted. It is there asserted that Hugh Despenser, jun., did not act as military governor of the castle during the siege, but resided there supinely; and it is certain that in 1327 a pardon was issued in favour of John de Felton, " for holding out Kerfilly against the Queen and Prince Edward." It is said that before the siege, " of live cattle, there were lodged within the Castle walls, two thousand fat oxen, twelve thousand cows, twenty-five thousand calves, thirty thousand fat sheep, six hundred draught horses, and a sufficient number of carts for them; two thousand fat hogs, of salt provisions two hundred beeves, six hundred muttons, one thousand hogs, two hundred tons of French wine, forty tons of cyder and wine, the produce of their own estates, with wheat enough to make bread enough for two thousand men for four years." We are surprised to find that so accurate a writer as Mr. Malkin should adopt this most improbable statement; but no doubt can exist that the castle was well victualled.

Roger Mortimer, who claimed Caerphilly Castle and its estates, as heir at law, commanded the besieging army, which is said to have consisted of 10,000 men. The Despensers had rendered themselves exceedingly unpopular in Wales, a circumstance which favoured the besiegers. The accounts of the siege are contradictory and obscure, like every other fact connected with the place, but it is certain that the resistance was obstinate and prolonged. At last a breach was made in a tower which had been filled with salt. There was a furnace near at hand for smelting iron [lead ?] for the purpose of pouring it on 'the besiegers, who, " whether purposely or accidentally is not known, allowed the fused metal to escape and poured water from the moat on it; the result was a tremendous explosion, which forced the tower into its present position." This is Mr. Malkin's version of the origin of the celebrated *Leaning Tower*, and Mr. Harding, the author of the article on the Castles of Glamorgan which appears in the *Cymmrodorion Transactions*, justly remarks that "its accuracy is strongly corroborated by marks which resemble those of metal dashed against the wall with considerable violence, when in a state of fusion, which are still to be seen." Mr. George T. Clarke, the able writer of the Essay on Caerphilly already alluded to, differs from this opinion, and ascribes the inclination of the tower to the explosion of a mine at its foot, during the civil war, when, as it has been supposed, the castle was dismantled. *Leland* does not mention a leaning tower here.

The besieged, availing themselves of the confusion which ensued at the time of the breach, drove back the assailants with great loss; and ultimately the garrison capitulated on honourable terms. Hugh le Despenser, the last of his name, was present at the coronation of the new monarch, Edward III., and "delivered up," says Kington, "the castle of Caerphilly, which he had from his father, to the king, and placed himself at his disposal, who, in return, 'granted him safety of life and limb," and a portion of his paternal estates, though not the castle of Caerphilly, which appears to have withstood another long siege in 1329. Soon afterwards, however, the castle was again granted to the Despensers, who defended it against Owen Glendower. Leland (temp. Henry VIII.) writes thus : " In Isaibac is Cairfilly Castelle sette among marisches, wher be ruinous walles of wonderful thickness and tower kept up for prisoners as to the chief hold of Senghenith." The castle was not repaired during the civil war. It is now the property, by marriage, of the Marquis of Bute.

The etymology of Caerphilly, according to Mr. Clarke, seems to be, Caer, *a castle ;* Pwll, *a morass.* The Essay in the *West of England Journal,* which—with some exceptions as to historical details— is a model for a *Castellarium,* is illustrated with an engraving of the castle as it originally stood, which gives a palpable idea of the strength of its position. Advantage was skilfully taken of the small river Nant-y-Gledyr and an adjoining rivulet, to insulate a peninsula surrounded by low and marshy land, which was slightly elevated above the adjoining ground. First, there was a broad moat, defending the eastern or grand facade, " one of the finest and most complete specimens of a feudal line of defence extant in this or any other country," composed of a curtain wall 360 feet long, strongly buttressed, with a vast gateway in the centre, and clusters of towers at either end. Then there was an inner moat communicating with a lake and encircling an island, on which were the main fortifications. Another island, converted into a hornwork, adjoined this to the westward : and on the main land, to the north-west, was a redoubt of vast size and strength. There were, without the last, three distinct lines of defence. The weakest portion of the castle was the southern. We borrow the following abridged description of the whole from Mr. Lewis's work. " The buildings in the several courts, together with a spacious area, were enclosed within a lofty outer wall of great thickness...defended by square towers at intervals, between which a communication was kept up by an embattled corridor. In the outer court were the barracks for the garrison, and from it was an entrance through a magnificent gateway, flanked by two massive hexagonal towers, leading by a drawbridge over the moat into an inner ward, from which was an eastern entrance into the extensive court that contained the state apartments, by a massive gateway, strongly defended with portcullises of which the grooves are still remaining ; the western entrance to the court was also over a drawbridge, through a splendid arched gateway, defended by two circular bastions of vast dimensions. The court, in which were the superb ranges of state apartments, is seventy yards in length and forty in width, enclosed on the north side by a lofty wall strengthened with buttresses, and in the intervals pierced with loop-holes for discharge of missiles, and on the other sides by the buildings and the towers which guarded the entrances. The great hall on the south side of the quadrangle is in a state of tolerable preservation, and retains several vestiges of its ancient grandeur : this noble apartment was 70 feet in length, 30 feet wide and 17 high, and was lighted by four lofty windows, of beautiful design, in

which the ogee-headed arches, richly ornamented with fruit and
foliage, are finely wrought in the Decorated style : between the
two central windows are the remains of a large fire place, of which
the mantle is highly embellished in beautiful and elegant detail :
on the walls are clusters of triple circular pilasters resting upon
ornamented corbels at the height of 12 feet from the floor, and
rising to the height of four feet, for the support of the roof, which
appears to have been vaulted.   The suite comprises various other
apartments of different dimensions and of corresponding elegance,
in a greater or less degree of preservation.   Near the south-east
angle of the central building is the armoury, a circular tower of
no great elevation ; and almost adjoining is the leaning tower."
This tower, which is still called " the Mint," is 70 feet high, is
at least 11 feet out of the perpendicular, and divided by a fissure.
" Near the armoury is a spacious corridor, about 100 feet in
length, in the wall of the inner enclosure communicating with
the several apartments, and affording a direct intercourse with the
guards who were stationed in the embattled towers, which protected the walls."   The remains of the stabling afford a striking
idea of the strength of the garrison, and far exceed anything of
the kind in existence.   There is not a scrap of iron left throughout
the vast structure, but it is in a more perfect state than could be
expected, when it is borne in mind that nothing has ever been
done to guard it from injury.   Such is an imperfect outline of the
history and present state of this magnificent ruin ; and we are
anxious to respectfully impress upon its noble owner, the Marquis
of Bute, the necessity of efficiently protecting a castle so interesting and so national, from further dilapidation.   This can be easily
effected ; an annual outlay of a few pounds would preserve the
ruins—which have been much injured by mischievous persons
and the elements during the present century—for some hundred
years to come, in nearly their present condition.

The small town of Caerphilly—in which there are two inns, the
best of which is " the Castle"—adjoins the fortress.   The Rhymney, which divides the counties of Glamorgan and Monmouth,
runs a short way to the eastward, down a spacious valley to the
sea.   Newbridge or Pont-y-Pridd, on the Taff, is seven miles

from Caerphilly ; and the Castle is seen to much the greatest advantage from a point on this road, about half a mile from the town.

THE VALE OF THE TAFF

Abounds with picturesque scenery, especially along its upper half, where the wild beauty of the country offers a refreshing contrast to the noisy public works and ugly assemblage of dwelling houses, said to be 3,000 in number, which are scattered about Pont-y-Pridd or NEWBRIDGE.   The Taff falls rapidly, the descent between Merthyr Tydvil and Cardiff, a distance of 24 miles, being 568 feet.

Tourists should halt at the Newbridge Station.   The singular Bridge, from which the place derives its name, is worth inspecting. It was the work of a self-taught mason and architect, named William Edwards, who became before his death one of the most famous bridge builders of the last century.   He failed twice here —first in 1746, when he built a bridge of three arches, which was swept away by a flood ; secondly in 1751, when he constructed a single arch with too thin a crown.   The third attempt succeeded perfectly.   By introducing three circular openings in each of the abutments the weight was reduced, and the key stones relieved. The span or chord of the bridge is 140 feet, forming the section of a circle of 175 feet in diameter, the height from the water 34 feet, and the width of the roadway about 11 feet.   There is an echo under the bridge, which is said to repeat a single sound nine times. The well-known work called " the Pursuit of Knowledge under Difficulties," contains a good sketch of William Edwards.—A short half mile above this bridge is a fall of the river, which especially in a flood, or in the evening, is strikingly beautiful.

In 1816, Newbridge was an insignificant village ; but the advantages of its situation became visible to capitalists, who erected iron and chain-cable works here, and since the opening of the Taff Vale Railway, the progress of the place has been wonderfully rapid.   Objects of interest : the tin-works of Messrs. Crawshay, at Treforest, said to be the largest in the kingdom ; the chain cable works of Brown and Lenox.—INNS : The New Inn, near the Railway Station, and the Bridgewater Arms, once a famous roadside house.

YSTRADYVODOG.

Very few persons who visit the county of Glamorgan—nay, few of its inhabitants—are aware of the existence of a Valley in the heart of the hill-country, which is the gem of South Wales, and hardly surpassed throughout the alpine North.

At the Newbridge Station of the Taff Vale Railway, the Rontha (Rhondda), one of the joyous mountain streams that excite the ardour of the fly-fisher, joins the Taff. The distance from hence to Glyn Neath, which we shall describe anon, cannot be far short of thirty miles; and the difficulties presented by the rudeness of the road, but above all by the pass over the mountains at the head of Ystradyvodog parish, are such that almost every one prefers travelling by the round-about-way through Aberdare, more to the north. Into this wild solitude we shall conduct the reader; premising that those who do not wish to proceed to the Vale of Neath may explore Ystradyvodog, to the source of the Rontha Vawr, and return to Newbridge in the course of a summer's day. An early start is indispensable, and it is advisable to take provisions, for there is only one hostelrie in the Vale, which is not always well prepared for hungry and thirsty guests.

The road up the Rontha Valley lies for some miles along a tramway, the outlet of an extensive colliery at Dinas, about six miles off, and other works of a similar nature. The scenery along this part of the Rontha is wooded and pleasing. About three miles up there is a famous salmon-leap worth looking at. Wild river scenes succeed—fretful "runs"—lanes of deep still water —lofty banks half undermined by floods—fantastic rocks. The mountains begin to open abruptly. You approach the foot of a hill, near which the greater Rontha is joined by the lesser (Rontha Vach) which flows along another beautiful valley, almost parallel to that of its sister stream, in a direction north by east. You leave the tramway—cross a rude bridge of one arch, and ascend the hill on the right, round which the Rontha Vawr curves; it is desirable to enquire the road to Ystradyvodog here. The hill is steep and lofty, and forms the south-east end of the long chain *Cefyn Twym Rontha*, which divides the rivers.

We shall never forget our first impression of Ystradyvodog, when we had walked about a mile and a half over this hill. It was a fine morning after a heavy day's rain. The clouds, which had been down on the hills, began to "lift;" and suddenly the glorious " *Green Valley*," for that is the translation of its unmusical Welsh name, unfolded itself before us with one of those exquisite effects peculiar to mountain scenery—which a Claude could not transfer to canvas. The Vale stretched for a distance of eight or ten miles between two nearly parallel lines of hills, broken by a succession of bluffs of singular beauty, apparently terminated by a vast alpine headland feathered with trees or copse wood to its summit—a mountain chief keeping watch. As we descended, the emerald greenness of the meadows in the valley below was most refreshing. At last we got into a narrow cart road, and soon reached the tavern of the district, an ancient place, the "sitting room" of which has a mud floor, kept by a true specimen of a mountaineer, with an exceedingly limited idea of English, one John Pickernell, where we obtained comfortable refreshment for " man " but wretched fare for " horse." Rest here. A rough cart road runs parallel with the river, which is fringed with much brush-wood, to Blaen Rontha, a large farm near the head of the Vale, the last trace of "civilization." The scenery when explored in detail realizes the first impression ; there are some fine waterfalls, and when you reach the frowning headland that towers at the end, which like most of these hills seems loftier than it really is, owing to its perpendicularity, the composition of the landscape is dignified and bewitching.

The people of this solitudinous and happy valley are famed for hospitality—a pastoral race, almost entirely dependent on their flocks and herds for support. The chief farmer, Mr. Edwards, has no less than three thousand sheep, but most of the farm houses are rude and small—the population thin and scattered. The parish church stands near the middle of the vale, and we believe that the Dissenters have only one meeting-house.

The air is aromatic with wild flowers, and mountain plants—a sabbath stillness reigns.

The country now becomes "untameably wild." You ascend a steep, narrow, broken path on the right, leaving the infant Rontha Vawr far below ; and hard work it is to thread your way on foot,

or to lead a horse, if so encumbered, along the shaggy sides of
the huge mountain—a chaos of rocks.   A glen of the wildest
beauty carries the eye to the source of the river—the sweetest of
the many *pistylls*, the silver threads or chords of the hills, which
have charmed the heart of the wayfarer with their music, on his
day's journey.   You halt, with a feeling of awe, at a modern
cairn by the side of the path.   A winter rarely passes without
the occurrence of two or three deaths on these mountains.   This
cairn commemorates the death of a poor fellow who had lost his
way and perished here in the gloom of a snowy March evening
in 1838, and whose body was not discovered for three weeks.   We
followed the time-honoured custom, and threw a stone on the
heap.   At last we reached the moorland or peat moss, diverged
to the left to *Cairn-y-Moesey* (said to be the grave of a Bard) at
the edge of *Craig-y-Llyn*, the highest mountain of Glamorgan,
which makes a bold horse-shoe sweep here, visible at great
distances.   Our path, however, lay to the right, so we descended
a break in the hills—were refreshed by some country people
milking, a couple of miles from their farm—and after encounter-
ing many difficulties reached the " Lamb and Flag," at Cwm
Neath, in about twelve hours after leaving Newbridge.

Under Craig-y-Llyn there are two small lakes, some distance
apart, the largest of which, *Llyn Mawr*, nearly a mile round, is
passed on descending the way we have described.   There is, we
believe, good fishing, with a breeze.   The Rontha rivers are
limed or poached by the men from the iron works at Hirwain and
Aberdare, so the sport is indifferent.

There is a small hamlet, the centre of a parish of 12,000 acres,
called *Glyn Corwg*, in the depth of the hills about two miles and
a half south-east of Cairn-y-Moesey, and nine from Neath.   We
once descended with horses to the Vale of Neath, about two miles
beyond Craig-y-Llyn, but we advise no one to attempt to thread
the mazes of the ravines of this chain of hills.

During the mania of 1845, a company was formed to carry a
Railway from Blaen Rontha down the Vale to the entrance of the
Ely Valley on the south side, from whence the course of the Ely
was to be pursued to a point of junction with the South Wales

Railway below Llantrissent.—These hills are of the carboniferous group, and will no doubt ultimately be invaded, and perforated with coal levels. We trust that it may not happen in our day.

ABERDARE,

Which is connected with the Taff Vale Railway, by a line and branches, eight miles and a half long, has long been famous for its iron works and its collieries. There is also a canal. The scenery of the Vale of Cynon, through which the line runs, is charming. The increase of Aberdare during the last few years has been so great, that there is a prospect of its ultimately becoming a second Merthyr. Early in 1847 there were eight blast furnaces in operation, six of which belong to Messrs. Thompson and Co.; and in the spring of that year Mr. Crawshay Bailey commenced new iron works at Aberaman, on an extensive scale. The Aberdare Railway, which joins the Taff Vale line at the foot of the incline, was sold to the latter Company, on an estimated dividend of ten per cent.,—a proof of the extent of the traffic.

The Vale of the Taff contracts beyond the inclined plane at Navigation House, and there are many picturesque scenes in the journey—a gradual ascent—to

MERTHYR TYDVIL.

Distant from	Miles.	Distant from	Miles.
Aberdare, by Railway	15	Hirwain	6
Brecon	18	Newbridge	12
Cardiff, by Railway	24½	Neath	25
Glyn Neath, or Lamb and Flag	14	Pont Neath Vaughan	12½

Merthyr is like an American city—the creation of yesterday. Its name thus originated: a Welsh prince named Brychan, who appears to have embraced Christianity, retired hither towards the end of the fifth century, with his son Rhun, and daughter Tydvil. They were soon assailed and murdered by a body of Saxons and Irish Picts; and a church, which was subsequently erected on the spot where they were put to death, was dedicated to Tydvil the Martyr—hence Merthyr Tydvil.—A Castle called *Morlais*, the

rude remains of which are to be traced on a hill about three miles
to the north-east of the town, was subsequently erected by Gilbert
Lord of Glamorgan, on the site of an early British camp, as an
outpost on the frontier of the Lord of Brecknock, a turbulent
neighbour. The modern history of Merthyr dates from the middle
of the last century,* about which period the importance of pre-
paring iron by means of pit coal had been fully demonstrated.
In 1755, Mr. Anthony Bacon, subsequently member for Aylesbury,
obtained, in conjunction with some other individuals, a lease for
ninety-nine years, of a mineral tract here about eight miles long
and four broad, full of valuable coal, and iron ore. Shortly before
the commencement of the American war Mr. Bacon erected a
smelting furnace and forge for making bar iron at Cyfarthfa ; and
afterwards, having obtained a contract for supplying government
with cannon, put up a foundry and works for that purpose (see
Cardiff, *ante* p. 106). The contractor reaped a large fortune by
his bargain ; but the Carron Company in Scotland obtained a
renewal of the contract just before the close of the war. In 1782,
Mr. S. Homfray took a lease of a portion of this concern ; but,
owing to some disagreement with Mr. Bacon, soon disposed of it
to Mr. Tanner, of Monmouth, who in turn sold his interest to Mr.
Richard Crawshay, who was practically acquainted with the iron
trade. Mr. Homfray established in 1784 the Pen-y-darren works,
which were a source of very great profit ; and a few years afterwards he was the projector of a canal to Cardiff, which, however,
was constructed under the direction of Mr. Richard Crawshay,
Mr. Homfray having retired from active life in consequence of
some misunderstanding with the gentlemen with whom he was
associated in carrying out these improvements. The Plymouth
works were now in operation ; and before the end of the century
Mr. Richard Crawshay became, on the demise of Mr. Bacon, the
owner of the whole of the Cyfarthfa works, which he rapidly

---

* In the seventeenth century, and no doubt earlier, rude attempts were
made to smelt iron ore here. In the former a small work was founded at
Pen-y-Darren, at which the bellows was worked by a water wheel. Charcoal
was used instead of coke, hence the destruction of the woods which formerly
covered the head of the Taff Vale.

extended.* The rise of Merthyr has subsequently been fluctuating, its inhabitants like all communities dependant on trade, having had to encounter periods of severe depression. The census return in 1831 was 22,083; in 1841, 34,977; and it is believed that at present the number is at least 45,000. The parish runs for a distance of ten miles from north to south, and is on an average three miles broad. The whole population of the Vale of Taff and its dependencies must now amount to about 100,000 persons.

* Mr. Crawshay, at a dinner which was given to him in 1847 by the people of Merthyr, gave so graphic and interesting an account of the rise of his family of "iron-kings," that it deserves to be perpetuated. "My grandfather was the son of a most respectable farmer in Normonton, Yorkshire. At the age of fifteen father and son differed. My grandfather, an enterprising boy, rode his own pony to London, then an arduous task of some fifteen or twenty days' travelling. On getting there, he found himself perfectly destitute of friends. He sold his pony for 15*l.*; and during the time that the proceeds of the pony kept him, he found employment in an iron warehouse of London, kept by Mr. Bicklewith. He hired himself for three years for 15*l.* the price of his pony. His occupation was to clean the counting-house, to put the desks in order, and to do any thing else that he was told. By industry, integrity, and perseverance, he gained his master's favour, and was termed—"The Yorkshire Boy." He had a very amiable and good master; and before he had been two years in his place, stood high in his master's confidence. The trade in which he was engaged was only a cast iron warehouse; and his master assigned to him, the Yorkshire Boy, the privilege of selling flat irons—the things with which our shirts and clothes are flattened. The washerwomen of London were sharp folks; and when they bought one flat-iron they stole two. Mr. Bicklewith thought that the best person to cope with them would be a man working for his own interest, and a Yorkshireman at the same time. That was the first matter of trading that ever my grandfather embarked in. By honesty and perseverance he continued to grow in favour. His master retired in a few years, and left my grandfather in possession of his cast iron business in London, which was carried on on the very site that I now spend my days—in York-yard. My grandfather left his business in London, and came down here; and my father, who carried it on, supplied him with money almost as fast as he spent it here, but not quite so fast. What occurred subsequently this company knows perfectly well. Who started with humbler prospects in life than my grandfather? No man in this room is so poor but that he cannot command 15*l.* Depend upon it that any man who is industrious, honest, and persevering, will be respected in any class of life he may move in. Do you think, gentlemen, there is a man in England prouder than I am at this moment? What is all the world to me unless they know me?"

In the years 1846–7 the place was in a higher state of prosperity than it had ever been before. There were four iron works in operation, viz. : the Dowlais works of Sir J. Guest and Co., at which there are nineteen blast furnaces ; the Cyfarthfa works of Messrs. Crawshay and Sons, at which there are thirteen furnaces ; the Pen-y-Darren works of Messrs. Thompson and Co., at which there are six furnaces (this firm possess two other large iron works) ; and the Plymouth works of Messrs. Hill, at which there are eight furnaces. There are always some furnaces out of blast. Messrs. Crawshay also possess the Hirwain works, six miles from Merthyr, at which there are four furnaces.

The Plymouth works are seen to the right of the Taff Vale Railway, shortly before reaching the station from Cardiff ; the Pen-y-Darren works stand near the commencement of the long defile which leads up to Dowlais ; Cyfarthfa is situated on the outskirts of the town, near the Neath and Hirwain road.

The Cyfarthfa works form one of the most perfect examples in existence of an immense manufacturing establishment. Although, including colliers, upwards of 4,000 men are employed, such is the admirable disposition of the buildings and machinery—the vastness of which must be seen to be comprehended—that there appears to be no bustle ; the whole of the complicated operations seem to go on with the regularity of the action of a watch. But it is necessary to walk up to Dowlais to obtain a clear idea of the *character* of this great seat of the iron trade. And here let us say a word or two about the position of Merthyr.

The town, which mainly consists of workmen's houses, is of an irregular form, and lies in the midst of a group of bleak mountains : Dowlais occupies the upper part, near the edge of a table-land, and is approached by a long street stretching for considerably more than a mile, up a steep ascent beyond the Pen-y-darren works. This narrow valley is blocked up to a great extent by enormous black banks of cinders, &c., compared with which the largest railway embankments are mere pigmies. Additions are of course constantly being made to these banks, and it appears to a looker-on a hazardous operation to bring a horse and tram close to the edge of the lofty ends or "tips" for the purpose of shooting

the contents over the precipice. As the "tips" in progress are
formed of hot cinders, they are on fire from nearly top to bottom
—glow like lava.   Rivulets of *hot* water wash the bases of these
gloomy banks.   The scene is strange and impressive in broad
day-light, but when viewed at night it is wild beyond conception.
Darkness is palpable.   The mind aids the reality—gives vastness
and sublimity to a picture lighted up by a thousand fires.   The
vivid glow and roaring of the blast furnaces near at hand—the
lurid light of distant works—the clanking of hammers and rolling
mills, the confused din of massive machinery—the burning headlands—the coke hearths, now if the night be stormy, bursting
into sheets of flame, now wrapt in vast and impenetrable clouds
of smoke—the wild figures of the workmen, the actors in this
apparently infernal scene—all combine to impress the mind of the
spectator very powerfully.

A sketch of the processes carried on in the works would involve
much dry technical detail.   Merthyr is one of the great seats of
the *bar iron* trade ; and so extensive are the rolling mills, of late
years almost exclusively occupied in the production of railway
bars, that it has been found necessary to import a quantity of pig
iron, chiefly from Scotland, to supply the demand, as well as large
quantities of iron ore of various qualities.   The exports at Cardiff
afford an idea of the extent of the iron trade ; but the quantity of
iron produced is of course much larger.   The chief firms sometimes accumulate large stocks, which they work up when times
are very prosperous.'   The make of blast furnaces varies greatly
according to circumstances, and according to the quality of iron
produced.   Thus a furnace that will make 120 tons of forge iron,
is not capable of producing more than 65 tons of foundery iron.
The average make of pigs at Dowlais (where no foundery is
made), amounts, we believe, to between 80,000 and 87,000 tons of
pig iron per annum ; the average make of pigs at Cyfarthfa and
Hirwain somewhat exceeds 60,000 tons.   " The strata of coal are
of excellent quality, accompanied by parallel veins of argillaceous
iron ore, which penetrate the mountains to a great depth, and
yield upon an average about thirty-five parts of metal out of 100 ;
the mines are worked by levels."   There is no *black band* here.

K

In the spring of 1847, the rate of wages was nearly 40 per cent. higher than it was two years previously, owing to the advance in the value of iron; yet the workmen were dissatisfied, and there were many mutterings about a strike. The variation of wages in the mineral districts is very great. An average is struck every five or six years, at periods when wages are at the lowest; but it is so difficult to arrive at accurate conclusions, that we shall only give the highest rates. Colliers have earned from £3 to £5 10s. per month, averaging about £1 per week. Miners about 18s. per week. Furnace men at the blast furnaces, 20s. to 30s. Finers and Pudlers, from 25s. to 35s. Ballers from 20s. to 45s., averaging 30s. Rollers, from 25s. to, in a few cases, *five pounds*, averaging about 50s. per week. The average earnings are considerably reduced through the "hill country" of Glamorgan and Monmouth by intemperance, which leads to much loss of time.

Almost the only assemblage of houses in Merthyr deserving of the name of a street—tramroads generally run along the lines of dwellings—is the High-street, in the lower part of the town, which is the creation of the last few years. In 1836, the site of the present commodious Market-house—which was built by two individuals—was a fine hay field. Some attention is now paid to appearances; but there is great room for improvement. There are gas-works, but no public lights! The sanatory regulations are wretched, notwithstanding the advantageous natural situation of the town; bad ventilation, bad drainage, prevail. Merthyr, however, is not externally so dirty as some of the English mining towns, in consequence of there being much less smoke from the coal. Fever frequently exists to a great extent, so much so that Merthyr is said to be the most unhealthy town in Wales. The interiors of the workmen's houses have been improved within the last ten or twelve years; more attention to comfort is displayed. The workmen's wives know very little of housekeeping, and do not take their meals with their husbands, circumstances which drive the latter to the beer-shops. The truck system does not exist here; but many of the sub-contractors at the works keep public-houses, where they pay the workmen's wages, much to the injury of the latter.

The old Church, dedicated to St. Tydvil, is an uninteresting structure, and was the only church until the year 1847, when a new Church on the east side of the High-street (St. David's), the funds for which were chiefly raised by subscription, was opened, and forms the chief ornament of one of the most thoroughly utilitarian places in the world.   The proprietors of the Dowlais iron works have erected a church at Dowlais, with 450 sittings, half of which are free.   On the death of the present incumbent it is intended to subdivide the parish of Merthyr into parochial districts ; the Marquis of Bute is patron ; value £675.   In Merthyr and Dowlais there are about twenty large meeting-houses, the majority of which belong to the Baptists and Independents. A Roman Catholic chapel has lately been erected.   Vavasour Powel, a celebrated non-conformist preacher, established here in the year 1620 the first congregation of Dissenters that assembled in Wales, and "while preaching to this congregation, was apprehended, and committed to Cardiff gaol.   According to a curious journal kept by the incumbent of the parish at that time, the Dissenters were not contented with the liberty of paying only what they pleased for tithes, but were in the habit of entering the church in a body, during the performance of divine service, and forcibly wresting the Book of Common Prayer from the hands of the officiating minister : and when he ascended the pulpit to preach, a teacher of their own sect would climb up into one of the yew trees in the churchyard, and commence an address to his followers."

Some serious riots, which led to loss of life, occurred here in 1831, owing to certain differences between the masters and men. Until the Chartist outbreak occurred in 1839, education was at a low ebb, but the wealthy employers have since "for the most part done much"—we quote the substance of Mr. Tremenheere's report—"to improve the moral and social condition of their workmen."   The "small" employers, a numerous class possessing collieries in various parts of the hill country, have however done nothing for the mining population, and drunkenness and other vices prevail to a lamentable extent.   Dowlais alone is said to contain 200 beer shops !   Clubs abound.   In cases of

accident, the workmen are generally exceedingly kind to one
another ; but the people of different counties keep up a sort of
clanship, living together as much as possible in different districts.
There are four National Schools in Merthyr and Dowlais, and
other day and many Sunday schools are maintained.   New
National Schools and a British School were projected in 1848.
A book canvasser informed us in the year 1847, that there
is little or no taste amongst the people for modern publications, such for instance as those of Messrs. Chambers, but that
the books in demand are the " Pilgrim's Progress," Baxter's
" Saints Everlasting Rest," in Welsh and English, and other
works of a similar character ; and that the "religious " part of
the community are the chief book buyers.—There has been *no
Savings' Bank* at Merthyr for several years, the Actuary having
appropriated about £2,000 of the deposits to his own use ; but
surely' this invaluable institution could be revived on a safe basis.
There are several Benefit Societies, which are well supported, and
sick funds ; forethought, however, is not an element in the character of the mass of the people.

The markets are held on Wednesday and Saturday ; but the
latter is the best day to visit Merthyr, as the people from the
surrounding country to a distance of at least twenty miles visit it
then, and peculiarities of national character can be observed.

Dowlais contained in 1841, 9,867 persons ; and it is said that
on an average between 5,000 and 6,000 men are employed at
the Dowlais iron works.   Messrs. Guest have erected a Market
House ; a Mechanics' Institute was established in 1829, at
at which weekly lectures are given ; and a " Tradesmen's and
Workmen's Library " was commenced in 1845.   There are
schools at Dowlais for boys, girls, and infants, supported by a
monthly stoppage of 4*d.* in the pound upon the people's wages.

Merthyr, with the parish of Aberdare, and the village of Coed-
ycymmer in the adjoining parish of Vaynor, were constituted a
Borough under the Reform Bill, with the privilege of returning
one member.—Cyfarthfa Castle and Park, and Pen-y-Darren
House and gardens, are agreeable objects at opposite extremities
of the town.—The HOTELS are the Castle and the Bush.

We return to Cardiff. The enormous length of the mineral trains on the Taff Vale Railway strikes a stranger forcibly. We have seen an up-train drawn by one engine, consisting of ninety-nine waggons, twenty-one full of iron ore, the others empty, the length of which was 585 yards, and the weight 365 tons. This enormous mass was drawn on a rising gradient at the rate of eighteen miles an hour.

Druidical Antiquities.

Some Druidical antiquities which are well worth visiting exist in the parish of St. Nicholas, a small village on the road to Cowbridge, six miles from Cardiff. Walk down the lane to the left leading to Duffryn House (the seat of Mr. Bruce Pryce), for about half a mile, then enquire at the first cottage. The principal Cromlech stands just within the edge of a wood, two fields from the lane. It was first noticed by Mr. Malkin, and is, so far as we are aware, *the largest Cromlech in Britain.*

The superincumbent stone, which is cracked about six feet from its narrow end, is supported by five others of large size, which enclose it entirely on the east, west, and north sides, thus forming a low room, open to the south, 16 feet long, 15 wide, and 6 high, in the loftiest part; but rubbish has accumulated to the extent of probably 3 feet, in which case the height would have

been 9 feet. Some other rubbish, with a heap of stones, is placed
about it to a greater height on the outside.   The supporting stone
on the north is 16 feet long ; that on the west 9 feet ; the three
stones on the east are set closely together.   The roof or horizontal
stone is 17 feet in the widest part, 10 in the narrowest, 24 in
length, and about 2½ thick.   It overhangs about two feet, and
is partly covered with ivy.   This stone is computed to contain
324 square feet ! The Cromlech appears once to have been covered
with a heap of small stones—a remarkable circumstance.—The
second *Cromlech* at Duffryn, in an adjoining field, is uninteresting,
and consists of only four stones.—These Cromlechs, and some
others in Glamorganshire, are known by the "uncouth term of
greyhound bitch kennels ; " Mr. Malkin conjectures that "in all
probability, the first British Christians, by way of showing their
detestation, wherever they met with Druidical or heathenish places
of worship, converted them into dog or bitch kennels." But there
are also instances in which Cromlechs are called churches,

The district abounds in Druidical antiquities, some of which
are to be found in a field at Cotterell, five miles from Cardiff :
and the whole of the valley from St. Nicholas to a place called
Highlight *(Ychal-ola)* is still called *Duffryn Golych* or the *Valley
of Worship.* A large collection of human bones was found in
February, 1847, at the Doghill Farm, in St. Nicholas Parish, in
graves cut deep in the lias rock.

THE VALE OF GLAMORGAN.

The old mail-coach road from Cardiff to Neath intersects for
twenty miles of its course the Vale of Glamorgan, an irregular
country that intervenes between the hills and the sea, varying in
breadth from eight to ten miles.   Travellers on the road can only
form an imperfect idea of its character ; on the right or north, the
landscape often stretches to the roots of the mountains ; and
there are frequently sweet landscapes, but perhaps the scenery as
a whole does not equal expectation.   The pedestrian, however,
who penetrates the country on either side, will in most cases be
rewarded for his pains.   There is a rare store of Norman antiquities—churches, crosses, castles, farm-buildings ; rural hamlets,

and many gentlemen's seats, with pretty wooded parks. Several
of the old castles are "modernized" and still inhabited. Then
there are refreshing shady dingles, feathered to the rivulet's
edge, and often ending in the sea ; and wide commons, which
command prospects of vast extent.

The distance from Cardiff to Neath is nearly 40 miles, viz. : to
Cowbridge 12 ; Bridgend 7 ; Pyle 6 ; and Neath about 13.

EXCURSION TO BARRY ISLAND, LANTWIT, OR ST. MARY CHURCH, &c.

The pedestrian who wishes to embrace the prettiest scenery
should first follow the Cowbridge road about three miles, until he
sees a church (Caerau) at the top of a hill to his left. This was a
Roman camp and station, many remains of which are still visible.
The high ground of St. Lythian's Down, to the south-west, commands very fine views ; below which is Wenvoe Park and Castle,
the residence of Mr. Jenner. A vale leads to a small sandy estuary,
at the mouth of which is Barry Island, divided from the mainland
when the tide is out, by a fresh-water stream. It will be described
in our chapter on the Channel Islands. About three miles to the
east is Sully Castle, nearly opposite Sully Island. Those who
mean to follow the coast must take the road that runs westward
from Barry Church. Between two villages, called Porthkerry and
Rhoose, is a modern villa—a beautiful object from the sea—
occupied by one of the sons of Sir Samuel Romilly. The Church
is dedicated to St. Curig, and there is a fine cross in the churchyard. Proceed to Aberthaw, a small port, with a fortnightly
vessel to Bristol, from which much limestone, that possesses the
valuable property of immediately hardening under water, is shipped. It is five miles and a half from Aberthaw to Lantwit Major.
The headland which protects the harbour is Breaksea Point.

There is a pleasant alternative road by Cowbridge, for those
who wish to thoroughly explore the country. Ascend the hill
from Barry, near which are some remains of its Castle in a farm
yard, and proceed to Penmark, where there are the ruins of a
Castle built by Gilbert Humphreyville. About half a mile to the
west is Fonmon Castle, a large Norman structure modernised,
and the residence of Oliver Jones, Esq., a descendant of a distinguished Parliamentary officer who was related to Cromwell. It

contains a fine original portrait of the Protector.—Cross the river Thaw to St. Athan's, in which parish are the remains of three Castles or castellated houses—East and West Orchard, and Castleton. The two former took their names from some celebrated orchards managed by Flemish cultivators in the reign of Henry I., fruit and trees from which were long sent to the royal table and gardens. From hence there is a pretty road through St. Mary Church to Cowbridge. The church of Eglws Brewis is only 33 feet long by 21 feet wide.

Beauper (Beaupré) **Castle**, about half a mile from St. Mary Church, affords a singular example of the classic style of architecture engrafted on the gothic, and is a structure worth visiting. An ancient Welsh fortress, which was enlarged by the Normans, existed at this place. Mr. Harding (*Cym. Trans.*) says "there is a vague tradition that Magna Charta was here composed." The "classic" additions were made in the years 1586 and 1600, by a Welsh artist, originally a stone mason, who acquired great skill in Italy. A romantic love story is associated with his name. This individual and his brother, also a stonemason, were both enamoured of the same damsel, quarrelled, and vowed never to speak to each other again, which vow they rigidly kept. On learning the fact, the fair cause of the quarrel would have neither ; a determination which drove the eldest abroad, where he acquired great reputation.

COWBRIDGE

Is an old-fashioned town, chiefly consisting of one long street. It was attached to the neighbouring lordship and castle of St. Quintin, and walled by Robert St. Quintin in 1090 ; the walls and three gates—only one of which now exists—were perfect in Leland's day. The church is rude and massive, and is a chapel of ease to Llanblethian, Cowbridge not being a distinct parish. The plan of this structure is singular ; there is a north aisle to the chancel, and a south one to the nave ; the tower has an immense staircase turret attached to its north-east corner, and a "huge and incomprehensible" buttress at the north-west. The windows and some other parts of the church have been recently restored. A Grammar School, founded by Sir Leoline Jenkins, Secretary to the Admiralty in the reign of Charles II., stands close to the church. It is in the patronage of Jesus College, Oxford, and the state of its endowment, and fallen condition, having lately excited much attention, it has been placed under most efficient management. These are exhibitions to Jesus College. Thirty or forty years ago this school enjoyed great celebrity ; about seventy boys, one of whom was the Vice Chancellor Knight Bruce, have been educated here at the same time. —INN, the Bear.

There are three castles near Cowbridge, all which are inhabited. *St. Quintin's* or *Llanblethian* (which was twice destroyed by the Welsh mountaineers) the property of Colonel Turberville ; the river Thaw, which falls into the sea at Aber-thaw, commences here. *Llandough,* (one mile and a quarter south), a castellated mansion ; and *Penlline,* originally a Welsh stronghold, on the top of a hill on the right of the road to Bridgend : the ancient castle is hidden by a modern house which is inserted in it, and which has lately been purchased by Mr. Homfray.

LANTWIT MAJOR.

There are two roads from Cowbridge to Lantwit ; the shortest (five miles) and prettiest is by Llanblethian ; the best for a carriage is by Nash (six miles). The western extremity of the Vale of Glamorgan, with the exception of its coast, is less interesting than the eastern ; table land, gradually falling towards the sea, but diversified by many picturesque bits.

The original name of Lantwit was *Caer Wrgan,* which was altered to Llan-Illtyd in the fifth century, in consequence of the dedication of the parish church to St. Illtyd or Iltutus, who was placed here, A. D. 448, at the head of a monastery and college chiefly for the education of young men for the priesthood, by Germanus, a prelate sent to Britain to suppress the Pelagian heresy. Iltutus led a life of exemplary piety, and is said to have presided for ninety years over this school, which became the most famous of that age, and maintained its celebrity until the time of the Norman conquest, when its resources were chiefly transferred to the Abbey of Tewkesbury by Robert Fitzhamon ; but it did not become extinct until the Reformation, at which period the remainder of its tithes and endowments were bestowed on the newly-created Chapter of Gloucester Cathedral.   In the year 1080, Jestyn ap Gwrgan, Lord of Glamorgan, who resided at Boverton in this parish, was patron of Lantwit.   Amongst the pupils of Iltutus—once 2,000 in number—were Gildas the historian, St. David, Paulinus, Archbishop Sampson, Talhaiarn, and Taliesin, the celebrated Welsh bard.   The sons of seven Princes, and of many nobles both of Britain and Brittany, were educated here at the same time.   Iltutus gave instruction in the useful arts as well as theology, and invented the common plough still used in Wales, and called St. Illtyd's.   Some remains of the schoolhouse and other buildings occupied by St. Iltutus exist behind the churchyard, including a ruinous structure called the Tithe Barn, in a field called the Hill Head, which has of course been much altered since its original foundation.   The *Liber Landavensis* contains a list of the Abbots of Lantwit, several of whom were bishops of Llandaff.   According to an old MS. of Mr. E. Stradling's, "the saints of Lantwit Monastery had for their habitations 400 houses and seven halls."   .

The church and churchyard are full of curious relics of antiquity.   First, there is a building in ruins, 40 feet and a.half in length, called the Lady Chapel, at the *west* end, once decorated with many statues of saints ; next, the "Old Church," a structure 64 feet and a half long, which, according to tradition, was abandoned on account of the dampness of its site, a story which cannot be true, because if it were so a new church would not have been added ; lastly, the most recent church, which is dedicated to St. Illtyd, and according to an old MS. was erected by Richard Neville, Earl of Warwick and Lord of Glamorgan, temp., Henry VI., but is of much earlier date, although the style of the windows and other features indicate alterations down to the perpendicular period.   This structure is 98 feet long by 53 broad, and consists of a nave, aisles, and chancel.   An embattled tower, containing six bells of exquisite tone, rises between the churches.

The old church is undoubtedly one of the most ancient in this

country, and some of its details deserve an elaborate description.
It is now a place of tombs, and has been much mutilated.
Several of the monuments are of high antiquity; and we copy
from a MS. the following description of two that were brought
here A. D. 1730, by Thomas Morgan, a schoolmaster, from the
" Great House," a place in the parish where a chapel once stood:
—" One of the stones is in the form of an ancient coffin, with a
hole in the upper end. It is not flat, but polygonal, three sides
of a decagon, adorned with curious carvings of foliage in a tolerable Roman style, that indicates its great age, and that it was
wrought in the time that the Romans had possession of Britain. (?)
On one side of it is the following inscription in Monkish rhyme, a
circumstance that affords an objection to its antiquity:—' *Ne
patra calcetur que subjacit istatuctur.*' The characters are purely
those of the lower empire. The other stone has on its recumbent
side the effigy of a man in a sacerdotal habit as large as life.
Round its side are these old French words in rude characters:—
' *Willm Rhchllo gyt ici Deu de sa alme eyt merci*;' William de
Rhchllo lies here, may God have mercy on his soul. "

A beautiful stone screen is placed in the chancel of the new
church, within about three feet of the east end. Twelve compartments or niches, now vacant, were once (according to local
tradition) filled with twelve figures of the apostles, of gold, which
remained until the civil troubles of the seventeenth century (?)
when they were removed for safety and buried in the Lady
Chapel. The late parish clerk spent much time in digging for
them. In the space at the back of the screen is a stone figure,
six feet two inches high, which until recently was in a recumbent
position, bearing a mutilated inscription behind the head, " Prince
Richard Hopkin." There is no record in existence of such a
person. The costume is that of the reign of Henry VIII.—Some
portions of the canopy of the screen exist in this place.

In the north side of the churchyard is the shaft of a *cross*,
which was erected early in the sixth century, by Archbishop
Sampson, to the memory of Iltutus. Its present height above
the ground is six feet three inches; and its breadth diminishes
from two feet six inches to one foot ten inches. The carving is

finely executed ; and the west side is divided into compartments, in which the following words occur :—" *Crux Iltuti;* " " *Samson redis,*" " *Samuel egisar'* [*excisor*].   On the east—" *Samson posuit hanc crucem pro anmia* [anima] *ejus.*"   The head of this cross was destroyed by the Puritans.   Amongst the antiquities are the shafts of two other very interesting *crosses,* one of which was found in 1789, after a search instituted on the strength of an ancient tradition.   It stands on the east side of the porch, is nine feet in height, and bears a Latin .inscription, which refers to Juthakel King of Glamorgan, and Artmael King of Gwent.   The other cross is of similar date and style to that of Iltutus, and we gather from the inscription that it was set up by Howel, Prince of South Wales, on his absolution by the Church for the murder of his brother Rees.   It was discovered in 1730, " in an old curious place, where tradition says that seven churches "—probably chapels of colleges—" stood."   A curiously carved pyramidal stone, seven feet high, which stands near the wall of the old church, is reputed to be a part of a heathen altar. (?)   There is a cross on the south side of the churchyard, and one in the village.

Some of the flat stones in the church attest the longevity of the inhabitants of Lantwit, which is one of the healthiest places in the kingdom.   We copy one : " Here lieth the bodi of Mathew Voss, Bured 1584.   Ætat 129.᾽᾽   At Llanmaes Church, in this neighbourhood, there is a monument to a man who is *said* to have reached the age of 150.   Few districts equal the Vale of Glamorgan in point of salubrity.—Many old buildings exist in the decayed town of Lantwit, which is now a straggling village.   The population of the parish and its hamlets is about 1,200.

The Town Hall, or " Hall of Justice," was built by Gilbert de Clare, Earl of Gloucester, shortly before he was killed at the battle of Bannockburn.   This building and also several other houses in different parts of the Vale of Glamorgan, " which go by the name of *Church Lofts,* was erected for the purpose of keeping a market every Sunday (?) morning for flour, bread, cheese, and flesh, and at other times for holding parish meetings and festivals for dancing."   About forty years ago, a table ran from wall to wall in the upper room of Lantwit Hall, having seats all around, which were in good preservation. This large room, the ascent to which is by two flights of steps outside the east end, is now used as an Odd Fellows' Lodge. An ancient gable bell, on which a clock strikes, bears the inscription " *Ora pro nobis, Sancte Iltute,*" and is said "to have been presented to St. Iltutus by one of the Popes of Rome." A curious story connected with it is recorded in *Holinshead's Chronicles*, vol. 1, p. 161.

BOVERTON, a village a mile distant to the south-east, was probably the *Bovium* of Antoninus, a station on the *Julia Strata*. A large number of Roman and silver coins, and other antiquities, have been found in this and other parts of the parish of Lantwit. The remains of the castle or castellated mansion of Jestyn ap Gwrgan, and Fitzhamon, still exist; when the former resided here, the demesne consisted of 900 acres. It was one of the chief residences of the Lords of Glamorgan until the reign of Richard III., when it fell into the hands of the Crown. Henry VII. gave the Lordship of Glamorgan and its estates to Jasper Duke of Bedford, who afterwards lay in concealment at Boverton, in consequence of having killed " one of the Herberts of the Friars at Cardiff." He gave a life interest in Boverton to his tenant there, one Griffith Voss, through whose exertions he obtained pardon for this and two other murders that he had committed. Sir John Guest, who has purchased several of the demesnes of the old Norman barons, is now the proprietor of the manor and estate.

Two camps supposed to be Roman, about two miles apart, exist on the coast, one of which called the " Castle Ditches" stands on the west side of the little Valley of Colhugh, about half a mile from the lower extremity of Lantwit, and consists of three lofty parallel embankments about 100 yards long. These camps have probably been occupied by the Danes. A field adjoins the Castle Ditches on the west, of extraordinary richness—three times the value of any land in the vicinity. The land, however, in this parish, and generally in this part of Glamorgan, is amongst the richest in the kingdom. It is indifferently cultivated in many parts.

EXCURSION ROUND THE COAST.

The encroachments of the sea on this exposed portion of the coast have been very great within the memory of many persons now living.   Sixty years ago the land sloped to the sea, so that carts could be driven to the water's edge, far beyond the present line of perpendicular cliffs.   The work of destruction is constantly going on.   At the mouth of the Colhugh, a small stream which runs from Lantwit, are vestiges of an *ancient port*, chiefly consisting of some piles of oak on the beach, called the "*Black men,*" an outwork of a pier.   A considerable trade with Somersetshire was carried on ; and vessels came here for protection in the reign of Henry VIII.   The regularity of the stratification of the limestone—generally horizontal, sometimes curved—gives the coast quite an artificial appearance, and the shore often appears like a floor or pavement ; indeed the country people send their carts to the beach for natural paving stones.

The number of *caves* is unusually large.   From Dimhole to Tressilian—a little cove a mile and a half from Lantwit, where there is a gentleman's house, and a curious ebbing and flowing well—there are twenty-nine.   "The Tressilian Cave, called Reynard's Cave (or by the country people, St. Reynard's Church, as a tradition exists that formerly marriages were celebrated there), is a very large cavern, eighty-five yards from the end to the mouth."   Dr. Nicholl Carne, the writer of this passage, some years ago disproved a legend that a passage from this cave led to St. Donatt's Castle.   A portion of the interior, called *Dwynwen's Bow of Destiny*, is distinguished by a singular superstition. The unmarried person who succeeds in throwing a stone three times through this arch in the rock will be married within the year ; every failure involves a delay in marriage for a year. Large numbers of persons have for centuries visited the place to "try their luck."   The father and mother of the celebrated Sir Thomas Picton were married in this cave.—"Very few caves," observes Dr. Carne, "occur in the cliffs between this place and St. Donatt's, whilst from St. Donatt's all the way to Dunraven, a distance of nearly four miles, hardly a cave occurs.   There are two sorts of caves in limestone ; sea caves, in the cliffs adjoining the shore, and dry or inland caves." The former are chiefly caused by the sea; the origin of the latter " may probably be found in the influence of acid vapours (carbonic acid?) rising through fractures adjacent to these corroded portions of the limestone."—Many foxes inhabit the sea caves; hounds are brought down when the tide is in, and reynard is ensconced in some adjoining cover on the main land. Fox-hunting in Glamorgan is conducted in primitive style. The hours for the "meets" are very old-fashioned—often at six in the morning.

St. Donatt's Castle, which overlooks this part of the channel at a short distance from Tressilian, is an extensive and romantic pile—a gem for a landscape painter. It was founded by Sir Wm. le Esterling, or Stradling, in whose family it continued for 684 years. Their arms remain over the outer gate. The present possessor, Mr. Tyrwhitt Drake, lives in Buckinghamshire; and the Castle and adjoining farm are tenanted by the Misses Thomas. The mother of these ladies, an eccentric person, died at the end of 1846, and was in the habit of letting a portion of the castle to sea bathers during the summer, although we believe that she was never visible. Tourists were not admitted for some years before her death. The structure is nearly quadrangular, and the state apartments, which are in a dilapidated condition, contain some fine examples of carving in wood, by Grinling Gibbons and other artists of his age. A celebrated mantel-piece, carved by Gibbons, has been nearly carried away piecemeal by curiosity hunters. Terraces lead to the shore below; to which there was formerly a covered way to an extensive series of barracks for men and horses, surrounding an oblong nook of two acres on all sides except that to the sea, which often dashes over and injures the outer wall. We heard on local authority that these barracks were occupied, during a visit paid by Queen Anne (?) to this castle. The Queen's room is still pointed out.—A *Watch-tower*, nearly fifty feet high, in a shattered condition, occupies a height on the western side of a very pretty wooded dingle, on the edge of which the castle stands. This tower was erected to enable the lord of the manor to obtain early intelligence of wrecks [*see* DUNRAVEN]. The walls of the Norman Deer-park are of vast extent.—*St.*

Donatt's Church nestles in this dingle, under the protection of the castle. It contains paintings of the fifteenth century, and monuments commemorative of the Stradling family. A *Cross* of great beauty stands in the south side of the churchyard.

A short distance beyond the watch-tower is the Nass Beacon, on the edge of the cliff, and the *Lighthouses* on the *Nass Point* [*see* SWANSEA]. The coast now sweeps to the north-west, and gradually rises. We recommend those who are fond of walking along downs overlooking very grand coast scenery, to keep near the edge as far as Dunraven : the occasional intervention of deep dingles renders the walk somewhat fatiguing, but the fine air and the scenery afford ample compensation. The beautiful headland of Dunraven is seen to much the greatest advantage from this side.

DUNRAVEN CASTLE is a house in the bad taste of the last century, the residence of Lord Adare, M.P., eldest son of the Earl of Dunraven, who married Miss Wyndham, the sole heiress of an ancient family of that name, who possessed large property in this district. A castle of great antiquity, said to be the oldest in Wales, and once the abode of Bran ab Llyr and his son (the celebrated Caractacus), formerly stood here. Fitzhamon gave the castle and manor to William de Londres, who bestowed them on Sir Arnold Butler, one of whose female descendants married the father of Walter Vaughan, who then became the possessor. The latter disposed of it to an ancestor of the Wyndhams. Strangers are permitted to enter the walks that have been tastefully made round the partly-wooded headland, or "Witches' Point." The watch-tower which exists here is not the tower mentioned in the following legend, scarcely a vestige of which, we believe, exists.

A Legend of Dunraven.

A wild and a cheerless coast is that of Eastern Glamorgan ; terrible to the mariner, not merely for banks and rocks and perpendicular cliffs, but for wrecking. This practice, happily now on the wane, was once made a system, *a trade* ; and we select, out of many old legends and "modern instances" that we have heard, a story of strange catastrophes which has been alluded to by several of the old topographers, and which invests the headland of Dunraven with a tragical interest.

Walter Vaughan, lord of Dunraven, commenced life under the fairest auspices. Soon after he came to the estate he signalised himself by swimming off with a rope to the crew of a stranded ship, whom he saved—a rare act of humanity in those days. The success of this attempt turned his thoughts into a new channel ; he busied himself in devising plans for preserving life in cases of shipwreck—he constructed boats, and finally gave his mind to navigation and astronomy. In the lofty watch-tower which adjoined his castle, he loved to spend the night in reading the stars. At last he laid his plans before the Government, by whom they were slighted and rejected. Treatment like this produced a re-action in a character which, although ardent and enthusiastic, was strongly disfigured by vanity. Walter Vaughan returned home an altered man. The deserted halls of Dunraven once more resounded with revelry ; the watch-tower was deserted ; the bowl and then the dice engrossed its owner. He was pronounced, on all hands, to have revived the hospitalities of the old Welsh chieftains, and gained what he coveted—distinction. In the meantime he had married. It is uncertain whether he broke the heart of his wife or not, but she died as his fortune began to fail, leaving four boys, the eldest of whom was on the verge of manhood, and the youngest a child of four years old. Man is the same everywhere ; the Welsh gentry turned their backs on their prodigal friend when poverty struck him. The castle was nearly shut up, and its lord, with one attendant, a faithful harper, again betook himself to the watch-tower. His eldest son—no longer heir, for there was hardly any inheritance left—determined to seek his fortune on the broad ocean, and in foreign parts. The parting was painful ; the affections of the father, long deadened by dissipation, returned in the hour of desolation with redoubled force to their natural channels—he had loving children left, although he had lost wealth, friends, and reputation ; anxiety and remorse made him prematurely old. Who could recognise in that stooping form and haggard countenance the manly youth of

L

five and twenty years ago ?   A wreck occurred about this time, which bettered the condition of Vaughan, who as Lord of the Manor, possessed under charters that had descended from Saxon times, a right to property " cast up by the sea " *(seupwerk)*, although the rights of owners remained in force for 366 days, if anything living, except vermin of course, should be found on board—a law which was practically a dead letter.   This event gave birth to a new passion in the mind of the broken landlord. Could not sufficient property be accumulated by wrecking to reclaim the estate for the eldest son ?   There lived in the neighbourhood a man of desperate habits, nicknamed "Mat of the Iron Hand," who had once been the captain of a piratical vessel, which, when in port, was seized by order of Mr. Vaughan, a magistrate, soon after he came to his estate.   There was, however, a desperate struggle with the crew ; and the captain, who lost his hand in the fight, turned wrecker, and carried a stone in his bosom against the man who had ruined him.   Strange to say, Mr. Vaughan, notwithstanding the protestations of his faithful dependant the old harper, formed an alliance with this ruffian, who had gained notoriety by hanging out false lights to mislead vessels.   They were never seen together in the day-time, but those who were abroad in the dark averred that they had observed the confederates in company.   The lord of Dunraven and his harper now spent much of their time in a sea-beaten grotto—a wild place which commanded a boundless view to the south-westward.   One day as the sun was descending gloomily towards the horizon, the watchers saw the ill-omened form of Mat of the Iron Hand near them.   He was looking steadily towards a rock called " the Swinkers," which was dry at dead low water, but covered with the tide at half flood.   A gleam of exultation shot athwart the wrecker's face.   There was a sharp cry.   What boat is that drifting out to seaward ?   The fatal truth flashed on the mind of Mr. Vaughan.   His two boys were on the rock— their boat had drifted away under the influence of a raging spring tide.   The distracted father rushed to the beach—his sons saw his agony, but his voice was lost amidst the roar of the sea and the hoarse sighing of the wind.

" Twas vain : the loud waves lashed the shore,
　Return or aid preventing ;
The waters wild went o'er his child,
　And he was left lamenting."

Both the young Vaughans were drowned. This was not all.
The old man rushed home to seek his youngest—he had one left.
" In the confusion," says an old topographer, " the youngest
child, left alone, fell into a vessel of whey, and perished at the
same time. " The bereaved parent was stunned by a loss so
fearful and so sudden ; and the people of the neighbourhood spoke
of it as a just retribution, many declaring that gain gotten by
those who followed wrecking as a trade—who lured men to
destruction by false lights and other evil practices—never came
to any good. After this event Mr. Vaughan wished to amend
his life, and endeavoured to shake off his associate the pirate,
fixing his hopes on his eldest son, of whom he had heard nothing
since his departure from home. One evening the old man observed
a distant vessel standing slowly up the channel, the movements of
which seemed characterised by uncertainty, as if the master
hardly knew what course to take. She was soon hidden by the
gloom of the night, which became gusty. Mr. Vaughan felt
anxious about this vessel, for it is believed that sorrow had worked
repentance ; and he went down to his cave by the shore, accompanied by the harper. The latter, dreading evil from Mat of the
Iron Hand, whose hatred to his master had broken out unequivo-
cally of late, took arms. They 'had not been long near the sea,
before the ruffian's false lights cast a lurid gleam over the rocks.
The night grew thick and drizzling ; but the old man moodily
refused to stir. Presently crashing sounds were heard above the
howling of the wind ; wild and broken cries followed ; and in half
an hour Mat the pirate entered the cave. A few words hurriedly
passed ; the wrecker declaring that the ship's boat had been
swamped by the waves, and that every living thing in it had been
drowned. The captain, he said, remained alone on the wreck,
which drove on the rocks after the crew had deserted her ; and
stated that he was a Welshman, and that his birth-place was
off this coast. " Did you help him, villain ? " interrupted Mr.

Vaughan.   The wrecker did not answer, but, with a fiendish
laugh, thrust a cold hand into that of his questioner.   Mr.
Vaughan started at its clay-like coldness.   A gleam of light fell
from the wrecker's fire into the cave, and revealed a ring.   The
one-handed man had achieved his *revenge*—the hand was that of
the corpse of the heir of Dunraven, whom he had murdered on the
wreck.   The broken-hearted father soon after left the district
[*see* TENBY].   Some say that the pirate was shot by the harper,
others that he was executed a few months after for another
murder, committed on a shipwrecked seaman.   The gifted author
of the "Mountain Decameron" has woven this legend into a most
interesting tale, which will be found in the *Cambrian Quarterly
Magazine,* a periodical of limited circulation, which was discontinued many years ago.

SOUTHERNDOWN

.Is a rural "watering place," situated on an extensive slope nearly
a mile beyond Dunraven, and five from Bridgend.   There are a
few lodging houses, the rates asked for which are very high;
and an Inn, "the Dunraven Arms Hotel and General Bathing
House," kept by Mr. Evans, at which the charges for boarding
and lodging are also high for the locality; but at present the
demand for accommodation much exceeds the supply.   The construction of the South Wales Railway will, however, exercise a
favourable influence on the interests of this very healthy spot;
several houses have lately been built, and others are projected.
There are no public conveyances, but in the summer an omnibus
runs to Bridgend.   The beach in Dunraven Bay is small, and chiefly
composed of shingles; there is no bathing machine.   In 1841, a
lamentable accident occurred.   Two young ladies, the only
daughters of Mr. Gething, of Newport, went down to bathe at
that portion of the beach which is appropriated exclusively to
ladies.   They ventured out too far, although warned by their
mother, who was also bathing, got into a deep pool formed
by the junction of two strong currents, were carried round the
dangerous point called *Trwyn-y-witch,* and drowned.   A board,
warning strangers of the peculiarities of the place, was soon

after put up ; and there is no danger within the prescribed limits.

Three remarkable *Caves* exist nearly a mile and a half to the westward of Southerndown. " *The* Cave " is a passage worn through a projecting stack of rocks, with two entrances on the east and south, the latter of which produces a very impressive effect. To the eastward of " the Cave " is a cavern called the " *Wind Hole*," fully 77 yards deep from the entrance ; there are some narrow fissures to the down above, through one of which a current blows that will often carry away a hat placed over it. The third and farthest is styled the " *Fairy Cave*," " from the various icicles, petrifactions, and .grotesque shapes which the strata assume." These caves can only be visited with safety at the first ebb of *spring* tides ; the recession of the tide for three days after the highest " spring" is greater than at any other period. The coast for some miles is perpendicular—frequently overhangs—and is sometimes more than 300 feet high, and the limestone measures are still disposed horizontally, and vary from two to eight feet, but are interspersed with calcareous and argillaceous earth.

The distance from Southerndown to Newton, across the mouth of the Ogmore, when the tide is out, is about five miles ; a great saving in distance is effected by taking this route, as compared with that by the road. Enquiries should be made on the spot. Sutton stone quarry, near Sloan House, has been celebrated for centuries ; the stone for most of the arches, &c., of the local castles and abbeys have been taken from it. Near the western end of the long down, close to the Ewenny river, which joins the Ogmore near Ogmore Castle, a very large spring of water, 15 feet wide and 3 deep, forming two streams—one hard, the other soft—boils up under the hill. The people call it Sheweel.

Those who do not wish to follow the coast from Lantwit to Southerndown or Dunraven have the choice of two country roads ; one by Marcross and Monknash, the other by Wick. Near Marcross there is a *cromlech* called the *Old Church ;* and there are fragments of a Castle at Marcross, and other relics of antiquity in the neighbourhood, including a monastic barn.

Ogmore Castle stands at the junction of the rivers Ewenny and Ogmore. It fell at the conquest of Glamorgan to the share of William de Londres, who built the keep, and otherwise strengthened the outworks. The keep is in the earliest style of Norman military architecture, and resembles Gundulf's tower at Rochester, although on a smaller scale. The castle is commanded by the brow of a hill near at hand, but in other respects its situation was exceedingly strong; it was annexed to the Duchy of Lancaster at an early period.—On the opposite side of the Ogmore, higher up, in the distance, is *Merthyr Mawr*, the seat and park of Mr. Nichol. A road up the side of the river leads to

Ewenny Priory, distant about two miles, which was founded by Maurice, son of William de Londres, A. D. 1140, for a community of Benedictines, and afterwards became a cell to Saint Peter's, at Gloucester. The church, conventual buildings, and precincts, were surrounded by lofty walls and other strong defences, which still exist to a considerable extent. The chief gateway was defended by a portcullis, and is in good preservation. The care taken to defend the brethren proves that they were set in the midst of a half-conquered country.—The Priory Church is an exceedingly massive Norman structure, of rude construction. It was originally cruciform, but the north transept has been destroyed, as well as the aisles of the nave, and the roof lowered. The nave, which is now used as the parish church, contains four round-headed arches, with early Norman capitals. The south transept is as long as the nave or choir, so the church formed a perfect Greek cross. Here is an altar tomb bearing the mutilated effigy of a knight in armour, with the following inscription to some friend of the de Londres family, which was first deciphered by Sir R. Colt Hoare, previously to which it was supposed to refer to Paine Turberville :—" *Sire Roger de Remi Gist isci. Deu de son alme eit merci. Am.*" The style and orthography of this monument closely correspond with those of an altar tomb in the choir, to the memory of the founder, which bears this inscription :—" *Ici gist Morice de Lundres, les fundur deu li rende sun*

labur. Am." The choir, which is entered through a nearly perfect screen, is the most remarkable and impressive we ever saw
in a church of this class.   It is very dimly lighted by two narrow
round-headed windows on either side of the altar, and by one at
the east, now partly blocked up.   There is a roof of stone, with
ribbed mouldings.   The small number of windows, and very
massive character of this church, show that its founder contemplated that religious rites would often be celebrated here during a
siege—with fear and trembling.   There are several monuments
of the Carne's—to which family the Priory was sold at the Reformation—in the choir.   A member of the Turberville family
became the possessor by marriage with one of the daughters of
Edward Carne, Esq.—The tower is low and exceedingly massive.
At the dissolution, the value was £87 per annum.

A modern mansion, the residence of Colonel Gervase Turberville, closely adjoins the church, and stands on the site of the
ancient manor house, the hall of which is, we believe, still preserved.   The keys of the church are kept here.   In the grounds
is a very fine Norman arch, an entrance to one of the conventual
buildings.—There is a square *camp* on a hill near Ewenny village.

The Priory stands near the edge of an extensive marsh, which
might be profitably drained, and is bounded by the river *y Wenwy*,
or the White Stream.   The nearest way to Bridgend is across this
marsh ; on the other side of which enquiries should be made.

BRIDGEND.

Distant from	Miles.	Distant from	Miles.
Cardiff	19	Llautrissent	7
Cowbridge	7	Margam	8½
Dunraven Castle	6	Pyle	6
Ewenny Priory	1½	Southerndown	5

A thriving, irregularly-built, market town, called in Welsh,
Pen-y-Bont-ar-Ogwr.   The river Ogmore divides the town into two
parts.   That on the western side (chiefly a steep street) forms the
"Lower" hamlet of the parish of Newcastle ; the eastern, or
larger half, which is called Oldcastle, stands in the parish of
Coyty.   Newcastle Church (St. Illtyd's) forms a picturesque

object, seen in conjunction with the Castle, near the edge of an
eminence ; and the Chapel of Ease for the part of the town which
is in " Coyty Lower," also stands within the verge of Newcastle.
Scarcely any vestiges of the *Old Castle* exist ; it was probably a
Welsh fortress, and a part has been converted into a barn, in a
farm-yard, about half a mile from *New Castle*. The latter is of
much later date, and occupies a considerable area, but is reduced
to a mere shell of quadrangular form. The chief feature, in an
architectural point of view, is the doorway, which consists of a
segmental arch, within a semi-circular one, of considerable beauty,
as well as singularity. This door probably formed part of the
Old Castle, and was brought here when that structure became
ruinous.—It is stated that '' on a hill above New House, to the
north of Bridgend, is one of the largest and most ancient encampments in South Wales.''

The elections for the County are held here, and a new County
Hall, a very creditable building, has been lately erected. The
National School is attended by about 150 children. The South
Wales Railway runs very near the town. A tramway for coal
traffic, 4½ miles long, joins the Llynvi Valley line. Market,
Saturday.—INN, the Wyndham Arms.

The only objects worth mentioning on the road from Cowbridge
to Bridgend are the *Golden Mile* (see p. 97), about three miles
of the latter place, and *Ewenny Priory*, two miles further on.

This is the fishing station for the rivers Ewenny and Ogmore.
The former is partly preserved, but we believe that the proprietor,
Colonel Turberville, of Ewenny Priory, will grant permission to
any gentleman angling with rod and line, who sends in his card.
The fishing in the Ewenny is better than in the Ogmore. Sewin,
trout, and a fine-flavoured fish called the *Gwyniad* abound. The
latter is in season only at the end of April and in May ; it is
broader than the trout, is as red when cut as a salmón, and is
very highly flavoured. The weight of this fish varies from half
a pound to a pound ; it is supposed to be a cross between the
sewin and the trout, and to be peculiar to this river ; perhaps so,
as regards South Wales, but the *Gwyniad* is found in some of the
lakes and rivers of North Wales, and we have taken a fish which

we believe to be it, in one of the former.   Sewin are caught with
the fly at the beginning of March until the end of summer; but
when the month of May arrives, the fishermen use their nets until
the end of the season.

A very remarkable custom, said to be one of remote antiquity,
exists here.   The Ewenny joins the Ogmore a little below Ogmore
castle; the river is shallow, contains a number of pools, and at its
sea-side diffuses itself over the sand.   When the river is low and
the tide is on the ebb, the fishermen station themselves with their
cur dogs at the mouth, and "club" the sewin and salmon as
they endeavour to escape across the shallows to the sea.   The
dogs are trained to seize the fugitives, and the struggles of men
and animals constitute an animated and entertaining scene; the
dogs often leave an ugly mark in the back of the fish.

The Ogmore is a much larger river than the Ewenny, and is
one of the best salmon streams in the Principality.   Trout and
Salmon Pink are caught from April until June; Sewin, which
vary from about 2 to 8 lbs., from May till July; Salmon—the
season for which is very late—from August till November.   We
indicate the best seasons, of course.—The length of the river
from Bridgend to the sea is about 3½ miles; which portion, with
another which extends for a mile above the town, is preserved,
i. e., let by the proprietors to several fishermen, who make a living
by their vocation, and either of whom will grant leave to a fair
angler.   A douceur is required.—Hansard, in his *Angler in Wales*,
gives an interesting account of the mode adopted of spearing the
fish by night, during the spawning season, which begins in October and ends in January, when the fish run up in shoals, twenty
or thirty together, "rooting up the bed of the river like hogs."

Coyty Castle.   The distance to Coyty from Bridgend by the
fields is a long mile and a half; by the road it is more than
double that distance.   In Tours and Guide Books this castle is
described as one of the most "magnificent" in South Wales;
and we are disappointed to find it an uninteresting ruin, of considerable size, of various styles, but in a sad state of dilapidation.
It belongs to the Earl of Dunraven.   The history of Coyty is

distinguished by a romantic incident, which is thus narrated by
Sir Edward Mansel :—

" After eleven of the Knights had been endowed with lands for their
service, Pain Turberville asked Sir Robert where was his share ? to which
Sir Robert answered, ' Here are men, and here are arms, go get it
where you can.' So Pain Turberville with the men went to Coity, and
sent to Morgan, the Welsh Lord, a messenger to ask if he would yield up
the Castle; upon this Morgan brought out his daughter Sara in his hand,
and passing through the army with his sword in his right hand, came to
Pain Turberville, and told him, if he would marry his daughter, and so
come like an honest man into his Castle, that he would yield it to him
quickly; and if not,' said he, ' let not the blood of any of our men be
lost, but let this sword and arm of mine, and those of yours, decide who
shall call this Castle his own.' Upon this, Pain Turberville drew his
sword, and took it by the blade in his left hand, and gave it to Morgan,
and with his right hand embraced the daughter; and after settling every
matter to the liking of both sides, he went with her to church and
married her, and so came to the Lordship by true right of p ssession, and
being so councelled by Morgan, kept in his Castle two thousand of the
best of his Welsh soldiers. . . . . Upon account of getting possession by
marriage, Pain would never pay the noble that was due to the chief Lord
every year to Sir Robert, but chose to pay it to Caradoc ap Jestin, as the
person he owned as chief Lord of Glamorgan. This caused hot disputes
about it, but Pain, with the help of his wife's brothers, got the better, till
in some years after that, it was settled that all the Lords should hold of
the seignory, which was made up of the whole number of Lords in
junction together."

he Castle was surrounded by a deep fosse, and we were told
that copper (?) pipes have been lately found in the vicinity, which
conveyed water from the hills to fill it, and for the use of the garrison, who had also a well, 160 feet deep, which still exists.   A
passage, said to run for a great distance, has been traced under
the Round Tower.—Coyty Church, one of the best structures that
we have seen in Wales, has been judiciously restored.

PYLE INN,

The next stage, is a commodious and comfortable house, which was
erected by J. M. Talbot, Esq., father of the present proprietor,
for the accommodation of tourists and travellers.   The parish is

consolidated with Kenfig; in the churchyard, by the side of the coach road, is a very elegant Cross. We observed a very interesting custom, which prevails in Wales and its borders, *Grave flowering*, carried out here to perfection. On Palm Sunday especially, the demand for flowers for the decoration of church-yards is universal, and the market towns on Saturday are always abundantly supplied. EXCURSIONS may be made from Pyle to Kenfig; Newton; Porthcawl; and Margam.

KENFIG.

A walk to Kenfig may embrace—1. The Church. 2. The fragments of the ancient Castle. 3. A singular Pool by the sea shore; and 4. the Ogham Stone; but those who wish to econo-mise time may walk first to Newton and Porthcawl; then follow the road that leads by *Nottage* near the coast till they come to the Pool, and from thence proceed to the other objects named, walking on to *Margam* after passing the Ogham Stone. Or, there is a middle road across the country to Margam. The walk is a long one and will occupy the greater portion of the day, or if Margam be included, a whole day.

The coast on the eastern side of Swansea Bay was desolated by an overwhelming inundation of the sea in the middle of the sixteenth century, hence the extensive tracts of sand that abound in this district. Fitzhamon enlarged a castle belonging to Jestyn ap Gwrgan at Kenfig, which place became a town of considerable importance, and is still a contributory borough with Swansea in returning a member to Parliament; but it was ruined, with many other places, by the calamity alluded to. An arch of the ancient castle, and part of the ancient church and churchyard—in which human bones are often exposed—may be traced amongst the sand hills. The sand banks and rabbit warrens extend from Sker Rocks to Briton Ferry; and have been preserved from further assaults of the sea by planting the *arundo arenaria*, which binds them together, the tenants of the adjoining land being compelled to enter into covenants to plant a certain quantity of it annually. The road from Cardiff to Swansea originally passed through Kenfig; but was, after the encroachment of the sea, diverted a

mile and a half inland, by Pyle. These facts will be interesting
to travellers on the South Wales Railway. The meaning of
Kenfig is a ridge of land above a bog, which *bog* " has from time
immemorial formed a lake or pool, nearly two miles in circumference ; and though situated close to the sea-shore, and encompassed with sand, never imbibes any muriatic properties. "

The present church of Kenfig stands on an eminence. About
a mile and a half to the north, on the left side of the parish road
to Margam, which at the commencement runs over sand hills, is
an inscribed Stone about five feet high and one broad, which
stands, as is supposed, near the line of the *Via Julia Maritama.*
We were told by a farmer that his father had this stone removed
from an adjacent ditch where it formerly stood, to its present
position, about thirty years ago ; and that another stone of twice
the size, but without an inscription, is to be seen in a field about
a mile nearer Kenfig Church. The inscription on the Kenfig
Monument has long puzzled antiquaries.

The letters " *Pumpeius Carantorius* " have by some been considered " the name of a Roman or Romanised Briton ;" by others,
" a genuine Welsh inscription, honourable to the spirit of the

ancient inhabitants of the Principality." The question, however, has been virtually set at rest by the discovery, in 1839, of a stone with an undoubted Roman inscription, which was dug up near Port Talbot :—IMPCFLAV (MCL) MAXIMINO INVICTO AVGVS. This Maximiamus or Maximus, was a Briton, or to use words of Fabyan, " a Knyght of the British bloode, the sonne of Leonyn, and cosyn German to Constantine the great," who conferred upon him the government of Britain. Mr. J. O. Westwood, in a communication to the *Archæologia Cambrensis*, has drawn attention to a very interesting fact, viz., that the marks between two and three inches long, occurring on the lateral angles of the Kenfig stone, are " no other than Ogham letters, and which are now for the first time proved to exist out of Ireland. That they should be found in Wales will not, however, be deemed very surprising when the long intercourse between the early Welsh and Irish is taken into consideration." [See CRICKHOWEL.] These rude inscriptions are highly interesting, because " *they afford evidence of the employment of certain characters, distinct from the Roman Alphabet, by the early Britons.*" The distance of the Kenfig stone from Pyle Inn is upwards of three miles.

NEWTON

Is a decayed bathing village, spoken of by the Swansea Guide (1823) as a place of "fashionable" resort. The houses have been gradually suffered to go to decay ; but fortunately Sir John Guest has recently purchased the village and much property in the neighbourhood, and has commenced to build. The knoll on which the village partly stands is pretty, and capable of improvement. The Church, which is rude and massive, stands close to the sea shore. Near this is a well which flows when the tide is out, and ceases when it is in, called Sandford's, mentioned by Camden. A new school, sanctioned by the Educational Board, was finished in 1848. The sea has made great encroachments here within the memory of man. There is a good beach. The range of high land in the vicinity, called Newton Down, commands magnificent views, and was traversed by the *Via Julia*.

NEWTON NOTTAGE is a cluster of farm houses and cottages about half a mile inland. There are no lodgings. At *Ty Mawr*, or the Great House, which has been restored by Mr. Knight, Neath, it is said that Ann Boleyn resided for a short time.

PORTHCAWL,

One mile from Newton, is the water side terminus of the Llynvi Valley Railway, sanctioned in 1846 ; length of the main line 16 miles. A breakwater was constructed in 1827 for the purpose of making the port efficient for the coal traffic of the Duffryn Llynvi and Porthcawl tramway, now amalgamated with the Llynvi Valley line, and a large trade has thus been created. The exports in 1846 were—Pig iron, 25,554 tons ; coal, 22,913 tons. In 1847, iron, 36,705 tons ; coal, 18,340 tons. In 1847 thirteen blast furnaces were at work near the railway, belonging to the Maesteg Company, the Llynvi Iron Company, Sir R. Price, (Tondu), and Malins, Rawlinson, and Co., (Cefyn Cwse). Considerable extensions of the Llynvi Valley line are projected, including a junction with the Cwm Avon Railway, which runs to Port Talbot, eight miles from Maesteg. Porthcawl is the natural outlet not merely for the Llynvi but other vallies abounding with coal and iron (both argillaceous and carboniferous or Black-band) ; and it " will afford some idea of the riches of this district when it is known, that the coal alone which it contains is estimated to exceed one thousand million tons, which would not be exhausted in less than five hundred years if 3,000 tons per day were shipped, and a like quantity consumed in the manufacture of iron." It is however the discovery of *Black-band* which has mainly led to the extension of the iron trade in these hills, especially at Cwm Avon.

The Maesteg works are capable of producing 15,000 tons of pig iron per annum, with the means of converting 120 tons per week into refined metal, and 70 tons per week into railway chain. The royalty upon the chief portion of the minerals, including Black-band, is only 6*d*. per ton. There are eight furnaces at these works, which stand in the heart of the hills.

Porthcawl Harbour is artificial, formed by two substantial arms of masonry, which enclose a bed of soft mud, with 20 feet water at spring, and 12 at neap tides. It is capable of accommodating about 20 vessels, and is to be improved. A piece of water from

B to 10 feet deep exists at the back of the present harbour, and if the sand hills were cut through and a channel made, a sheltered dock of vast extent and utility might apparently be formed at moderate cost.—There are two inns at Porthcawl, and good bathing ; and several very convenient lodging-houses were erected in the autumn of 1847.

Margam

Was once called Pen-dar or the Oak Summit ; an expressive appellation, for few oak-woods can compare with that which covers the mountains and sweet shady dingles which form the great charms of the demesne. This is one of the most delicious retreats in the world, full of enjoyable influences, sometimes marred, however—like life by clouds—with the smoke of the distant copper-works of Taibach. Nature has done much ; and art has completed what she has left undone. · What a site for an Abbey ! And here, amidst these solemn woods, there once existed a religious house of high repute. Robert Earl of Gloucester, when sorely pressed by adversity, bethought himself, *circa* 1147, of providing an asylum in this calm retreat for a brotherhood weary of the world ; and before his death, which happened soon after, this wealthy noble munificently bestowed a portion of his worldly goods in forwarding the work. Maud, the daughter and heiress of the famous Robert Fitzhamon, married the Earl of Gloucester, and it is said that both were buried here. Giraldus styles this monastery a noble community of Cistercians, and says " that it exceeded all others in Wales for the reputation of liberality in relieving the distressed." Leland speaks of it " as an Abbey of White Monks, where was a very large and fair church." Its revenues were valued at the Dissolution, when Sir Rice Mansel, Knight, an ancestor of Mr. Talbot the present owner, became the purchaser, at £181 7s. 4d. Sir Rice converted, in 1552, part of the abbey into a dwelling-house, which for two centuries continued to be the family mansion. After the male line became extinct in 1750, considerable alterations were made, and the house was finally pulled down in 1782, and the materials or furniture partly removed to Penrice Castle in Gower, and partly used in the erection of the Pyle Inn. When Mr.

Wyndham visited Wales in 1774, the Chapter House, which was one of the most elegant buildings of its class, as may be seen from a large engraving in his Tour, was perfect. The plan was a duodecagon, fifty feet in diameter ; a central column of great beauty supported a fan-shaped roof. " The just proportion of the windows, " observes Mr. Wyndham, '' and the (24) delicate ribs of the arches, which all rise from the centre column and the walls, gradually diverging to their respective points above, must please the eye of every spectator, and what is uncommon in light gothic edifices, the external elevation is as simple and uniform as the internal perspective. '' In the year 1799 the outer walls were so much decayed that the roof fell, and the exquisite structure became a ruin—which calamity the outlay of a few pounds would have averted,—nothing except the shell of the outer wall, and a part of the central column, being now in existence. The work of decay is still proceeding.

Very little is left of the Abbey Church. The present structure, which is now used as the parish church, was chiefly erected by the late Mr. Talbot in 1809, on the site of the nave, which had become ruinous ; the west front was preserved. There are several interesting altar tombs of the Mansel family ; and the mutilated effigy of a crusader, and monuments of some of the abbots, exist in the ruins. The south door of the Lady Chapel remains, near which a grave stone and tiles have lately been found. The church when entire must have been of large dimensions. The ruins of the Cloisters, the chief entrance to which is perfect, are exquisite. Several mutilated tombs, and a great wheel cross, will engage attention. A stone bearing a flat cross has a rude Latin inscription, which may be thus translated :—" The cross of Christ, which Eilniaum erected for the soul of Guergoret " (Gregory). The wheel cross, which formerly stood in the village street, and is of great beauty, bears some rude and imperfect characters, which have very lately been thus deciphered : *Con. delin avit.*

The largest orangery in the world exists here. A Spanish vessel, bearing a cargo of orange trees and other exotics, as a present from a Dutch merchant to Queen Mary, consort of William III., was wrecked on this coast ; and in 1787, T. Mansel

Talbot, Esq., built a conservatory, 327 feet in length, for their reception and better preservation. There are three rows of trees, 74 of which are of large dimensions (some 20 feet high) and include about 12 of the original stock, the girth of the largest of which is 2 feet 3 inches. The oldest trees are still good bearers, but only a small quantity of fruit is grown. There are also Pomegranates, Lemons, Citrons, and Shaddocks, in the collection. In the summer the trees are removed into a circular spot in the open air.

The vigour of the evergreens and other trees in the surrounding plantations is remarkable, and evinces a very fine soil and climate. An enormous bay tree, 60 feet high and 45 in diameter, with many stems from one root, supposed to be the largest in Britain—hollies like timber trees—Camellias which encounter the severest winters unscathed—are amongst the leafy curiosities.

The modern mansion of Margam, which has been erected within a few years in the Tudor style from designs by Mr. Hopper, of London, at a cost, according to rumour, of £100,000, is a splendid monument of the good taste and spirit of Christopher Rice Mansel Talbot, Esq. Its chief external features are two grand façades, broken by bays, and a tower. The interior is superbly furnished, and contains several curiosities, including some Roman antiquities found in the neighbourhood, and several valuable statues and other antiques from Italy.

A spur of the mountains rises at the back of the house, the summit of which exhibits interesting traces of a Roman encampment. The adjacent hills contain more Roman and other antiquities ; one of which, known as *Y maen Llythrog*, or the lettered stone, bears the following inscription :—" *Bodvacus hic jacet filius Catotis Irni pro nepos Æternali Domo.*" Domus æterna was a common designation for a sepulchre in ancient Rome. Some writers are of opinion, from the style of the Latin, that this monument was erected subsequently to the departure of the Romans from Britain. It stands on a mountain about two miles from the Abbey. Local directions are requisite. One of the stones at Margam is thus inscribed :—" *Senatus populusque veromanus divo Tito, divi Vespasiani, F. Vespasiano, Augusto.*"

M

Four Chapels were attached to Margam Abbey ; one of which belonged to a nunnery on the road from Margam to Kenfig, *Eglwys Nunyd*, part of which has been converted into a farm-house.

One of the gems of Margam, in the estimation of tourists, was its picturesque village street, and ancient cross, leading to the church. We rubbed our eyes on our last visit. The village no longer exists ! It has been wholly swept away, the surface altered, and the ground enclosed within Mr. Talbot's gardens.

The parish of Margam is very extensive, and as it includes the works and collieries at Taibach, &c., the population is large.

A dense cloud of smoke, and a long line of white-washed cottages called " Constantinople," mark the position of Taibach, two miles from Margam on the Neath road, at which Messrs. Vivian have large copper works.

PORT TALBOT.

VOYAGE BY STEAM. A steam communication between Port Talbot and Bristol was commenced in November, 1847, on a most efficient scale. The voyage from Swansea to the Mumbles, where the vessel usually waits for tide, is often done in 4½ hours.

Port Talbot, better known as Aberavon, is a port and trading place about a mile from Taibach. The parish, which includes the town of Aberavon, and most of the inhabited houses at Port Talbot, contains about 2,500 persons ; in 1847 there was church room for only 230. It is the outlet of the mineral produce of Cwm Avon, a valley in the adjoining hills, in which are situated the copper, tin, and iron works of the " Governor and Company of the Copper Miners of England," incorporated in 1691—a large and important concern. In 1845, the company raised 134,556 tons of coal at Cwm Avon, and sold 52,689 tons ; they made in that year 36,412 boxes of tin plates, and smelted and refined 2,389 tons of copper. Besides this they raised and partly sold 42,136 tons of coal at their works on the Swansea river.—There are 7 blast furnaces in Cwm Avon, 6 mills, 68 puddling and 20 balling furnaces. In order to facilitate the transit of minerals between the works and the harbour, a distance of about four miles and a half, locomotives have lately been used. The smoke of the

Cwm Avon Copper-works is carried up the side of a mountain *(Foel)* through an enormous flue or chimney, the head of which is visible at great distances.   The herbage on the hills has thus been blasted for three or four miles.   A water-wheel of 90 horse power, the water for which is conveyed by a fine stone aqueduct across a deep valley, furnishes power for some of the blast furnaces.   The English Company's Works, which include iron, copper, tin, and chemical works, are under the superintendence of Mr. T. R. Guppy, late of Bristol, the builder of the *Great Britain* steam-ship.   The population in this recently secluded valley exceeds 5,000 ; no less than 500 new workmen's cottages were built in 1847.—In the Port Talbot district are also other tin, iron, and mixed metal works.   · : ·

A fine piece of (natural) civil engineering was executed at Port Talbot in 1836.   The course of the river Avon from the village to the sea was circuitous and shallow ; the harbour bad.   Mr. H. K. Palmer, C. E., who was employed to effect an improvement, made a straight channel to the bay, by cutting a trench through marshy land which intervened, ● 20 feet wide by 10 deep, into which the mountain torrents were directed ;—the channel soon became sufficiently large to admit the whole body of the river, which is now turned into that track, and free access obtained to a commodious harbour, calculated for the wants of a rising port—thus using the powers of nature to accomplish a work of art.   The new channel is a mile long, at least 100 feet wide, and free from shoal.   The sea-lock of the docks is 45 feet wide, and vessels of large burden are now able to come here on spring tides.

Before we quit Aberavon we must tell an amusing story which we heard in our boyhood.   Many of the " contributory boroughs " in Wales are " decayed " towns or villages ; but it sometimes happens that the Portreeve (Mayor) and Aldermen assume greater airs than civic functionaries of higher consequence in the world —something like the Po-rochial Beadle of Dickens.   In these small boroughs it of necessity happens that the largest number of " aldermen " belong to the working class.   Very ludicrous incidents have occurred in consequence, especially before the Reform Bill.   The story of the Cornish Portreeve, who was found

plastering a house when summoned to preside at the election of
the candidate for the borough, is well known. A similar incident
occurred at Aberavon. Lord Nelson happened to stop at the
village on a journey to Pembroke Dock Yard, for the purpose of
changing horses, and sent a message that he should be most
happy to pay his respects to the Portreeve. Unluckily his worship was totally unprepared for the honour, being busily engaged
in repairing the roof of a neighbouring house. He contrived,
however, to slip on his best clothes, and after due congratulations
had passed between the parties, the naval hero was attended to
his carriage by our dignitary ; and just as he was going to order
the postillions to proceed, his worship advanced, made a bow,
stammered, and touching his hat said, he "hoped his lordship
would please remember the portreeve!" The admiral could no
longer check the mirth that was uppermost—"I will remember
you, by —— ! I never shall forget you to the last day of my life!"

The scenery from Port Talbot to Neath, although injured by
copper smoke, is eminently beautiful, especially at Baglan and
Briton Ferry, one of the grand scenes of old Welsh Tourists.

By crossing at Briton Ferry—which is the property of the Earl
of Jersey—and pursuing a route to *Swansea* near the coast, over
Crumlyn burrows, the pedestrian may save about five miles.
Briton Ferry has become a place of commercial consequence ;
powerful rolling mills were opened in 1847, at which a good deal
of the iron made in the Vale of Neath is converted into bars.
The engine is three hundred horse power.

NEATH.

Distant from	Miles.	Distant from	Miles.
Bridgend	19	Merthyr	24½
Brecon by Pont Neath Vaughan	33	Pyle Inn	13
Lamb and Flag	11	Pont Neath Vaughan	13
Margam	10½	Swansea	8½

VOYAGE BY STEAM. Passengers for Porthcawl and other places
are embarked or landed in boats according to circumstances, and
the steamer frequently crosses to the Mumbles to wait for tide
within five hours after leaving Bristol.

Neath, the *Nidum* of Antoninus, is a thriving sea-port, on the left bank of the river from which it derives its name, and possesses but very slight attractions for the tourist. Its situation, at the entrance of one of the most lovely valleys in the Principality, is pleasing; "picturesque" ideas are, however, banished by clouds of smoke from large copper and iron works. The town is irregularly built, but has been much improved. There are a well-supported Philosophical Society, Museum, Library, and Mechanics' Institute here. A large Market-house was constructed in 1837. Wednesday is the market-day.

The Castle, which belonged to Jestyn ap Gwrgan, was enlarged by Richard de Grenville, a near relation of Fitzhamon's, and an ancestor of some 'of our great English families, but has been nearly destroyed. The Church, which is supposed to have been, in part, the garrison chapel of the castle, is hardly worth visiting.

As the town is situated about two miles and a half from the shore of Swansea Bay, it has been found necessary to improve the navigation of the river to enable vessels of burden to come up to the quays. This has been partly effected by confining its course between huge banks of copper slag and by improved buoying; and ships of 300 or 400 tons can now come up on spring tides; at neaps they lie at the old harbour of Giant's Grave (Briton Ferry), from whence goods are sent up in barges. Giant's Grave is virtually the port of Neath—the canal terminus. There is a bar outside, over which are 17 feet at high water, spring tides, and 11¼ at neaps; the best channel is on the western side. Steam tugs have been of vast service to the port. The Neath canal was commenced in 1791, and extends from Giant's Grave to Abernant, a distance of 14 miles up the Neath Valley. Tennant's canal, chiefly constructed in 1822, branches off to Aberdulais, two miles up the vale, is carried across the river by an aqueduct of eleven arches, and runs near the Neath Abbey and other works to Port Tennant near Swansea, altogether a distance of eight miles. The exports of coal to France, Ireland, London, and the counties of Cornwall, Devon, and Somerset, have exceeded 200,000 tons annually; and a great quantity is sent to Swansea.

In 1847, 49,858 tons of coal, and 70,676 tons of culm, were exported. The produce of the iron, copper, tin-plate, fire-brick, chemical, and other works in this neighbourhood, also constitute a large amount of traffic.

A local writer thus accurately sketches the district :—" Towards the north, looking from Neath, the broad top of March-Howel towers above all the surrounding hills ; and southward, the view is bounded by two lofty eminences called the Foel and Mynydd-y-Gaer, the former distinguished by the smoky chimney of the copper-works in Cwm Avon, and the latter crowned with an ancient encampment, from whence it derives its name. Neath is nearly the centre of the great coal-basin of South Wales, and veins of this valuable mineral may be seen cropping out on the hill-sides in the neighbourhood. Much of the coal is anthracite. Iron-stone is also found in considerable quantities, and the hard sand stone of the coal formation affords a cheap and durable material for building. The hills are penetrated with coal-levels, and the atmosphere, even of secluded and romantic glens, is darkened with the smoke of various manufactories, which always flourish most where coal is plentiful. "

The population of Neath in 1841 was 4,970 ; it must now be 6,000. INN, the Ship and Castle.—Knoll or Knole Castle, the residence of H. J. Grant, Esq., occupies a wooded eminence to the east of the town, and is a fine addition to the scenery.

CADOXTON is a parish on the north-western side of the river, which extends for a distance of fifteen miles from Briton Ferry to Pont Neath Vaughan. A suburb of Neath, the Neath Abbey Iron-works, the copper-works of the Crown and Mines Royal companies, and many other large mineral or manufacturing establishments, stand in this extensive parish. At the Neath Abbey works of Messrs. Price and Co. steam-engines and iron steamboats are constructed.—Cadoxton Church is dedicated to Saint Catwg ; and is remarkable for a monument containing the pedigree of the family of Williams, engraved on sheets of copper, a copy of which occupies four large pages of Evans's Tour. The proverb "as long as a Welsh pedigree" is here palpably exemplified.

The Neath Abbey Iron Company have two blast furnaces at Abernant, and Messrs. Jevons and Ward, two furnaces at Venalt ; the exports of pig iron in 1846 were 5,700 tons ; in 1847, 4,070 tons. The annual make is about 10,000 tons.

Neath Abbey.

Little did Richard and Constance de Granville, the first bene-factors of the Abbey of Neath, when in the year 1129 they witnessed the solemn dedication of the sacred structure to the Holy Trinity—little did the community of Grey Friars, from Savigny, near Lyons, who had taken up their abode in this fair spot at the earnest wish of the Norman Lord and Lady—imagine that it would be desecrated by the worship of Mammon, become a smoky ruin, scarcely distinguishable by the passing traveller from the forges, the furnaces, the chimneys, or the squalid out-works of manufacturing establishments by which it is surrounded ! The Anthem of Praise and Thanksgiving has been superseded by the clank of the steam-engine and the roar of fires. Strange mutation ! Yet the old Abbey is pleasant to look upon. It is a memento amidst the turmoil of life. It speaks eloquently of a Future. It is full of interest to the lover of antiquity.

The *Fratres Grisei* soon became Cistercians, and never appear to have been subject to the foreign monastery from whence they sprung. The architect of the Abbey was named Lalys, one of the most eminent of his time, who also built Margam Abbey, and other structures, ecclesiastical and military, in South Wales. The building must have undergone extensive alterations and additions subsequent to its foundation. Leland speaks thus of it in Henry the Eighth's days :—" Neth, an Abbey of White Monks, a mile above Neth town, standing also in the ripe [bank] of Neth. It seemed to me the fairest Abbey in all Wales. " In his *Collectanea*, however, this accurate old topographer expresses a preference in favour of Margam. The Abbey possessed the privilege of Sanc-tuary—hence Edward the Second's preference. " The celebrated Welsh bard, Lewis Morganwg, who flourished about the year 1520, composed a very elaborate Ode in praise of Lyson (Lleision) who was abbot of this place in his time." *(Cym. Trans).* The subjoined extracts, from a recent translation,* give a vivid picture of the Abbey :—

" Like the sky of the vale of Ebron is the covering of this monastery : weighty is the lead that roofs this abode—the dark blue canopy of the dwellings of the godly. Every colour is seen in the crystal windows, every fair and high-wrought form beams forth through them like the rays of the sun.—Portals of radiant guardians!

" Pure and empyrial, here is every dignified language, and every well-skilled preceptor. Here are seen the graceful robes of prelates, here may be found gold and jewels, the tribute of the wealthy.

" Here also is the gold-adorned choir, the nave, the gilded tabernacle-work, the pinnacles, worthy of the Three Fountains. Distinctly may be seen on the glass, imperial arms ; a ceiling resplendent with kingly bearings, and on the surrounding border the shields of princes! the arms of Neath, of a hundred ages ; there is the white freestone and the arms of the best men under the crown of Harry ; and the church walls of grey marble. The vast and lofty roof is like the sparkling heavens on high, above are seen archangels' forms ; the floor beneath is for the people of earth, all the tribe of Babel, for them it is wrought of variegated stone. The bells, the benedictions, and the peaceful songs of praise, proclaim the frequent thanksgiving of the white monks."

Just before the Reformation it was intended to found an University at Neath, and a Charter was actually obtained. At the time of the Dissolution there were only eight monks here ; and the revenues were, according to Dugdale, £132 7s. 7d., and to Speed, £150 4s. 9d. The Abbey and its demesnes were granted to Sir Richard Williams, in the 35th Henry VIII. ; and in 1650, the Abbey House " formed an admired seat of the Hobby family." Few ruins of a large class have undergone greater injury ; yet the Church—although a mere broken shell—still looks stately ; and the chapter-house, the refectory, and some of the chief apartments, also present interesting architectural studies. The conventual buildings are very extensive, and although somewhat altered, afford a good idea of the structure as it once stood.

* " Original Charters of Neath and its Abbey," &c. By George Grant Francis, F.S.A., &c. Vol. 1, 8vo. Swansea, 1845. (Not published.)

THE VALE OF NEATH

Extends in a south-westerly direction from the head of the Neath river—which is formed by the confluence of many mountain streams—for a distance of about thirteen miles, and although it varies in breadth very considerably, preserves a much straighter course than most of the valleys of South Wales.

In ascending from Neath, the surface of the vale is flat and marshy, but bounded by mountains which soon assume a bold character. At Aberdulais—where there are a cascade and other favourite studies for the artist—the vale contracts for a distance of about three miles, and the railway is carried through some very romantic scenery. From Aberdulais there is on the west or left side a succession of woods for about five miles, belonging to Mr. J. Dillwyn Llewellyn, of Penllergare, who is the owner of Ynisygerwn, the old Welsh mansion of the Llewellyn's, which is almost hidden by trees in the vicinity of the road. You now enter the property of Mr. N. V. E. Vaughan, whose mansion—*Rheola*—eight miles from Neath, is happily placed in one of the most exquisite scenes in Wales. The *Aberpergwm* estate, the fine property of Mr. Williams, succeeds, shortly before the traveller reaches the hamlet of Glyn Neath, where a new church and parsonage have recently been erected. As you proceed upwards the scenery, which although generally wild and graceful has been injured by the straight line of a canal and the intervention of public works, becomes more secluded. The echo of mountain rivulets is unbroken by the turmoil of commerce ; there is nothing to mar country associations.

We know few things more delightful than *the descent into this Vale*, on a calm summer's evening, after passing through the untameable wilds of the Glen of Llia on the road from Brecon —one of the most solitary tracks in the Principality,—we know few scenes more refreshing than that presented from the rapidly-descending road to Pont Neath Vaughan, as the Vale opens its arms before you near sunset. On the left, *Craig-y-Llyn*, King of the Glamorgan mountains, sweeps boldly, yet with singular elegance, over a continuous line of shaggy woods ;—and dark groves which also partly clothe the opposite heights for many miles, complete the delicious effect of the scenery. In a word : the characteristics of the Vale are pale and russet mountains, with steep sides broken by exquisite ravines and many rills, rising majestically over a succession of *wooded bases.*

The Roman road, called the *Sarn Helen,* runs from the *Gaer* near Brecon, over the mountains on the westerly side of the Vale of Neath. We have only traced it partially ourselves ; but it is stated to be remarkably perfect in many parts. At the head of Glen Llia is a huge upright stone, lozenge-shaped on one side, called *Maen Llia,* visible at a distance of five miles ; and on the top of the hill about a mile and a half above Ystradyvelte, we were informed that there is a stone pillar, still larger, on which are Roman characters ; we conceive, however, that our informant must have referred to a stone with a Roman inscription *(Marci Caritani filii Berici)* which used to stand near this road, and was first mentioned in Mr. Llwyd's contributions to Gibson's Camden, but which has been removed to the Gnoll, at Neath.

The inhabitants of the upper portions of the Vale are of a remarkably primitive and hospitable character, and few can speak English. They manufacture plaids, some of which give a very tasteful effect to female costume. Superstition lingers in this congenial neighbourhood—soon to be dissipated or weakened by a railroad ! Miss Williams, of Aberpergwm, sent a most entertaining account of the superstitions of the vale and hill country to Mr. Crofton Croker, at the period when he published his Fairy Legends. We can only afford room for a few passages. Parents used to caution their children when setting out for the mountains to look after cattle or sheep, " to avoid treading near the Fairies' Ring, or they would be lost." Some "old secluded mountaineers" still see the *Tylwyth Teg* (Fairies), and hear their enchanting music. "They are also familiar with ghosts and strange noises, behold supernatural lights, and always foretell death by certain signs...Mamma remembers a meeting of twenty preachers assembled on a hill not far from this, to combat with the wicked spirit which had enticed so many to sinful practices, by tempting them with bars of gold, which were dug up near a Roman causeway called Sarn Helen. A farmer, a tenant of ours, was commonly supposed to have sold himself to the evil one. Many of. my friends are highly respectable in their line of life ; farmers and farmers' wives, of stout veracity on all topics save supernatural agencies ; and they relate these stories with an earnestness and an air of truth that is perfectly confounding. Some have actually seen the fairies, and among this number is old Shone, of Blaen-llanby, in the Vale of Neath," who not many years ago observed a long cavalcade of very diminutive persons, riding four abreast, and mounted upon small white horses, not bigger than dogs. They disappeared near the Sarn Helen, which they seemed to be traversing. Another case is related of a Welsh Rip Van Winkle, " who had been twenty-five years with the fairies, and who, when he returned, thought that he had been only five minutes away."

AT GLYN NEATH

Is a well-known but humble public-house, called the " Lamb and Flag." The travellers' room is hung with eight views of the Waterfalls, which were early productions of the celebrated artist, Penry Williams, who has in vain attempted to advise the land-lord to part with them. This is the only house in the Vale, so far as our experience has gone, at which the tourist can be accom-modated with any approach to comfort ; although many, who do not mind "roughing" it, have taken up their quarters at the primitive hostelrie called the " Angel" at the hamlet of PONT NEATH VAUGHAN, two long miles higher up, which in point of situation is infinitely preferable, as it is on the edge of

THE WATERFALL DISTRICT.

PONT NEATH VAUGHAN is romantically situated just within the boundary of Brecknockshire, nearly at the confluence of five rivers and several lesser streams. These resolve into the *Neath Vaughan* or *Fychan* (which divides the counties of Glamorgan and Brecon,) and the *Melté*, which form the double head of the Neath river at this spot, mentioned by Drayton. The channels of the streams are deep wooded ravines—the roots of the moun-tains—with so rapid a descent that each river is distinguished by one or two waterfalls of considerable size and great beauty, besides smaller cascades. It is possible to combine all these falls in one day's Excursion, which must, except for a mile or two at the outstart, be performed on foot, and under the direction of a guide, who may be hired at the Angel Inn. The actual distance traversed does not much exceed ten miles—*i. e.* if Porth yr Ogof be left out,—the ruggedness, steepness, and in wet weather, dirtyness of the path, and the attractions of the scenery, consume the time. It is hardly necessary to say that waterfalls cannot be seen with effect in dry weather, and those who are disappointed under such circumstances, must not accuse us of exaggeration when we state that this series of waterfalls is perhaps the most beautiful and interesting in Wales. A guide is indispensable.

You first proceed to *Craig-y-Dinas*, the "fortress precipice," a lofty rock of singular conformation, which commands home and distant views of very great beauty, stretching beyond the extremity of Swansea Bay. The little river Sycrhyd, on which there is a minor fall, runs in an extensive dingle below—an outwork· of Craig-y-Llyn. The *Bwa Maen* or Bow of Stone, consisting of curious strata of marble in concentric lines, is an interesting object here. You now ascend high bare land to

THE FALLS OF THE HEPSTE,

the approach to which down an exceedingly steep wooded bank is difficult. It seems no easy matter when you get below, either to advance or return, but *your path lies under the waterfall*, beneath which Mr. Warner took refuge from a shower of rain. If there is much water in the river, however, few will wish to linger more than a few moments. The country people regularly use the ledge of rock under the fall, as a foot-path ; and sheep and, it is said, cattle are sometimes driven across by this odd route. The accompanying illustration will give some idea of this remarkable cascade, the height of which is fifty feet.

The *Lower Falls* of the Hepsté, which in fact consist of a series about 300 feet in length, will be found just below. You then ascend the hill by a path through the woods, and visit

THE FALLS OF THE MELTE,

or *Clungwyn*. The *Lower Falls* consist of four in succession, and are very pretty but not striking. The *Upper Fall* is a considerable distance up, and as the Melté is a larger river than the

Hepsté, and the descent is longer (70 feet), there is a greater body of water ; but the fall, in beauty and originality, is not equal to the Upper Fall of the Hepsté ; and it cannot be seen *from below,* which greatly injures the effect.   Some cattle and a horse have been carried over this fall, and escaped without injury.

THE HEPSTE FALL.

Those who do not mind fatigue, and cannot spend a second day in the neighbourhood, should now walk up the river to the cavern
PORTH YR OGOF.

A short way above the rude little village of Ystradyvelté, four miles above Pont Neath Vaughan, (where there is an inn kept by Watkin Davies, a guide) the river Melté disappears suddenly.   Its underground course can be traced on the surface, which is always swept by floods ; and it re-appears in a vast cavern called Porth yr Ogof, which cannot be safely explored without a guide, who provides candles for visitors. The entrance to this darksome passage is 43 feet high and 19 wide, and forms a striking rock scene. Here, during the floods which sometimes rise and rush in angry torrents down the vale, after only two or three hours heavy rain on the hills, the recoil of the water is awful,—large trees are dashed against the rocks, and ultimately forced into the winding depths of the cavern. In the month of June, 1842, when the Melté was exceedingly low, we succeeded in penetrating more than 500 yards through Porth yr Ogof, walking occasionally by the side of the stream, as far as the " White Cave," a point which our guide, Watkin Davies, had only succeeded in reaching once before. Here we saw the light gleaming through an aperture at some distance from us ; and as the water becomes deep, it is, we were told, impossible to proceèd further. The fatigue is great, as it is necessary to assume a stooping posture for most of the distance. Amongst the curiosities of the cavern are two " chimneys " in the rock.

You now diverge over high land to the right, crossing the Brecon road, and descend to

THE FALLS OF THE PURTHEN,

which are the most elegant of the Vale of Neath group. The *Upper Fall* or *Ysgwd Einon Gam* (crooked waterfall) forms an enclosed scene of extreme beauty—contrasted rock and foliage. An air of grandeur is cast over the glen by the profoundness of its depth, the richness of its colouring, and breadth of shadow. The descent is fatiguing and difficult towards the last. Above you, the agitated Purthen leaps over the rock, under the shade of a trembling oak, to a depth of nearly ninety feet. It is difficult to tear oneself away from this delicious waterfall.

The Lower or *Lady's Fall* of the Purthen is within less than a mile and a half of Pont Neath Vaughan. Its height does not exceed 40 feet, but it possesses a singularly graceful character, and bounds over the rock so rapidly, that on most occasions you can, as in the case of the Melté, pass below without receiving more than a few drops of water.—The guide will point out a *rocking stone* near the Lady's Fall. This closes the day's excursion.

Mr. Hansard, in his " Trout and Salmon Fishing in Wales," speaks well of the fishing in these rivers, and we shall extract his remarks, having never had a favourable opportunity of angling here ourselves. We observed, however, that the trout of rivers which adjoined each other closely, as the Hepsté and the Melté, were of an entirely different species. " Fish," says Hansard, " directly under the various falls. There is abundance of trout, &c., in this wild but hospitable neighbourhood. The spring of the year affords the most diversion, as in dry summers the rapid streams become very shallow. At such times a bottom of single stallion's hair, a very fine light hook, and a tough brandling, thrown out like the artificial fly, will be very successful. Artificial flies—the blue, the red, the brown—the oil fly, and the sky blue."

There is a waterfall, 70 feet high, on the small river Llech, four or five miles above the upper fall of the Purthen, which is worth visiting after heavy rain.

Five miles above Neath, on the eastern side of the vale, is a famous Waterfall called *Melincourt*—a descent of the Cleddau river over a rock eighty feet high.

SWANSEA.

Distant from	Miles.	Distant from	Miles.
Briton Ferry	5½	Margam	19
Carmarthen	26¼	Neath	8½
Gower Inn	8	Pont-ar-Dulas	9
Mumbles	5	Rhosilly	18

THE VOYAGE BY STEAM. The distance from Bristol to Swansea is about 66 miles. In consequence of both ports being tidal harbours, the voyage occupies nearly double the time that it would do were there water at all times in either port ; but this difficulty will be remedied if a Pier at Portbury be constructed. The steamers, however, make for the Mumbles Roadstead, where they remain until there is water over Swansea Bar ; and passengers are landed on a " hard" under the headland, in the steamers' boats, if they

wish ; a crowd of " poor Jacks " watch for the luggage on the
beach (which is stony and somewhat slippery), and omnibusses
wait about a mile off, which convey passengers to Swansea for
sixpence.   Numbers avail themselves of this advantage, which
abridges the voyage nearly one half.

After leaving the Holmes, the vessels make a pretty straight
run, with an inclination towards the Welsh shore, for 15 miles,
as far as the Nash or Nass Point.   Shoreward, the objects passed
are Sully and Barry Island, and the small port of Aberthaw,
the headland beyond which is graphically called Breaksea Point.
The coast from hence to Nass Point is stern and inhospitable
until the beautiful wooded dingle of *St. Donatt's*, with its castle
and watch-tower, opens with an effect like an oasis in a stony
desert.   On reaching Nass, the steamers, except in very stormy

THE NASS LIGHTHOUSES.

or thick weather, take what is called the "inner passage"—*i. e.* the channel between the *Nass Sand*, a formidable bank fully six miles long, which extends in a north-westerly direction—and the mainland, on which are two most important light-houses. These lights have a melancholy origin. During the night of the 16th of March, 1831, the steamer *Frolic*, on her voyage from Haverford-west to Bristol, with nearly 80 passengers on board, struck on the Nass Sands, and immediately went to pieces. Every soul perished. Amongst the passengers were military officers of rank, and fourteen respectable tradesmen of Haverfordwest; the captain, Lieutenant Jenkins, R. N., had invested his property in the vessel, and left a widow and nine children. Amongst the bodies cast on shore were those of a mother and her infant, who were fast locked in each other's arms. This event put the Trinity House on the alert, and the erection of the light-houses followed.

The contrast between the heavy surge on the Nass Sands, over which, especially if there is any wind, immense and tumultuous masses of breakers constantly roll, and the calmness of the narrow channel which the steamer securely traverses, is very impressive. *The Lords of the Admiralty* got on these sands on a fine summer's night in 1840, whilst on their annual tour of inspection in the *Black Eagle* steam ship. Their escape was miraculous in the extreme; had not the night been perfectly calm, Lord Minto and his colleagues must have inevitably perished. The officers of the vessel seemed ashamed of their stupidity; for although the Swansea steamer *Bristol*, on her passage up, proffered assistance, and cast anchor for some time, making signals within a quarter of a mile of the royal ship, not the slightest notice was taken! Next tide the *Black Eagle* got into Bristol, seriously strained.— A portion of the eastern end of the Nass Sand is uncovered at half tide; it has two ordinary buoys and a beacon buoy.

It is believed that the extent and character of the Nass Sands are materially affected by the sea in stormy seasons. We lately heard an extraordinary fact—that soon after the wreck of the *Frolic*, they were visible for three or four days to a great extent; and that on a remarkably calm day some gentlemen from Dun-

N

raven Castle took a boat, landed on the sand-banks, and walked about them for a distance of 12 or 15 miles, the boat being rowed close to the edge, as they proceeded.

A very considerable distance is saved by taking the inner passage to Swansea, for vessels pursuing the "outer" route are obliged to make a wide sweep round the Nass shoals, and another most dangerous bank, called the *Skerweather Sands*. The inner channel is in its narrowest part about a quarter of a mile wide, and at dead low water there is three fathoms in the shallowest part.

The coast beyond the Nass Point runs in a northerly direction, and is exceedingly bold and interesting. We know nothing in Great Britain more truly "iron-bound." On the high land, Dunraven Castle and Southerndown now become visible, after which a formidable reef of rocks called the *Tuskar* (five miles from Nass Point) show their teeth; many distressing shipwrecks have occurred here. Presently the church and village of Newton and Porthcawl are seen; and the attention is directed to the *Skerweather Sands* which extend for about five miles in a direction west-north-west, and over which there are always breakers. A strip of this shoal dries to six feet above low water; and a Light-ship ought to be placed on the "tail" of the north-west end, the want of which has fatally misled many a mariner.—A small shoal called *Hugo Bank* lies beyond the Skerweather. The steamer is now abreast of *Sker Point*, the bearing and distance from which to *Mumbles Point* are north-west half-north, nine miles. This is a fine run. We cast anchor under the shelter of the Mumbles. At night the eye can guess the line of Swansea Bay from the glimmering lights in the habitations on the high ground along shore. Vessels have been lost in this bay and elsewhere, in consequence of conspicuous lights from dwellings having been mistaken for a light-house; and persons living on the coast should be careful, particularly when the weather is fresh, in not unnecessarily displaying lights at their windows.

SWANSEA (*Aber-tawy*), the most important place in the Principality, is happily situated between two hills on the western side of the river Tawy, and has been much improved and greatly extended during the last twenty years, but there is still room for improvements, which the South Wales Railway will probably be the means of accomplishing. The resort of visitors during the season is not very large, in consequence of the vicinity of the town to the copper-works; otherwise its natural advantages, the beauty of the semi-circular bay, which has been compared to that of Naples, the extent of the sands, which are generally excellent for a distance of three miles, and the cheapness of living, would no doubt render it one of our most popular watering places. It is, however, rather hot in summer. Still, Swansea will always hold a respectable rank amongst a section of sea-bathing people. The lodgings are generally good, and not dear.

There are but few antiquities. The Castle is unfortunately so much concealed with houses that it is only visible at particular points—the best is on the quay, not far from the Liverpool Steam Packet Wharf. It was erected, *circa* 1113, by Henry Beaumont, Earl of Warwick, the conqueror of the lordship of Gower, and is distinguished by a very elegant open parapet of arches, of which there are, so far as we are aware, only two other examples—the Episcopal Palaces at St. David's and Lamphey in Pembrokeshire. This parapet was very possibly the work of the same architect as those structures, the munificent Henry Gower, Bishop of St. David's, a native of the seignory of Gower. On this story were the state apartments, which, with a massive tower still in existence, command an extensive view. The castle passed through various hands. In the reign of Edward IV. the heiress of William Herbert, Earl of Huntingdon, the then possessor, married Sir Charles Somerset, an ancestor of the Beaufort family, in which it is still vested. The structure is appropriated to the purposes of a barrack, a prison, and a warehouse.

Swansea was frequently taken and re-taken during the civil war of the seventeenth century. In 1646 it was ordered " that Swanzey Castle be disgarrisoned and the works slighted ; " but it was strengthened by Major General Laugharne, a Royalist, in 1648, in which year, after Laugharne's defeat at St. Fagan's, Cromwell marched here, and remained some time, during which he frequently prayed with a singular old woman in the neighbour-

hood. He subsequently conferred a long charter, a copy of which
is given in Mr. Dillwyn's " Contributions towards a History of
Swansea, " on the inhabitants.

Swansea is called a Borough by Prescription, in consequence of
the supposed loss of the Charter of Creation granted to it by
King John (which, however, exists amongst the Records of the
Tower), and William De Breos, who assumed a sovereign jurisdiction over Gower very early in the same reign, probably gave
Swansea its next charter. Few towns have received so many
charters. Under the new Corporation Act of 1835, the borough
is divided into three wards, under the government of a mayor, six
aldermen, and eighteen councillors.

Swansea Church, with the exception of the chancel, which
belongs to the " Decorated " era of architecture, is a structure
in the worst taste of the last century. It was built in 1739, when
the old church " fell down." In the chancel is a very fine brass,
now inserted in the north wall, to the memory of Sir Hugh
Johnys and Dame Mawde Cradock. Sir Hugh was Deputy
Knight Marshall of England during the fifteenth century, and
aspired to the hand of Elizabeth Woodville, afterwards Queen of
Edward IV.

" Praye for the sowle of Sir Hugh Johnys knight and dame Mawde his
wife which Sir Hugh was made knight at the holy sepulchree of our lord
ihu' crist in the city of Jerusalem the xiiij day of August the yere of oure
lord gode Mt CCCC XLJ And the said Sir Hugh had co'tynuyd in the
werris, ther long tyme before by the space of fyve yers' that is to sey
Ageynst the Turkis and sarsyns in the p'tis of troy grecie and turky
under John yt tyme Emprowre of Constantynenople and aftir that was
knight marchill of ffrawnce under John duke of som'set by the space of
ffyve yere. And in likewise aftyr that was knight marchall of Ingland
under the good John Duke of Norfelke which John gyave unto hym the
mano' of landymo' to hym & to his heyr' for ev'rmore uppon whose
soullis ihu' have mercy."—[The label issuing from the lady's mouth has
these words]—" Fiat mi'a d'ne super nos."

The Rev. Thomas Bliss and Mr. G. Grant Francis have published an interesting account of Sir Hugh Johnys,—who lived at
Landimore Castle, in Gower, with an engraving of the brass.

There are only six or eight sepulchral brasses in Wales, one of which exists in Landough Church, near Cowbridge.—A very interesting altar tomb stands in the Herbert Chapel (formerly the chapel of St. Ann) in Swansea Church ; on which are to be seen the effigies of Sir Matthew Cradock and the Lady Catherine his wife, the widow of the famous Perkin Warbeck. The Rev. J. M. Traherne, a very eminent Glamorganshire antiquary, has published a curious account of Sir Matthew. There are other sepulchral memorials in the two ancient chapels on the north of the chancel, adjoining which is a large modern mausoleum of the Vivian family. A monument has been erected by subscription to the memory of the late Rev. Dr. Hewson, for thirty-two years Vicar of the parish, who died in 1845.—There are two other churches in Swansea ; St. John's, a poor building, which occupies the site of an ancient chapel of the Knights of Jerusalem ; and a recent structure in a nondescript style of architecture.— New National Schools for 800 children have been erected in the Elizabethan style, in consequence of active efforts which have been made by the present Vicar, the Rev. E. B. Squire, and were opened in May 1848.

The town contains many meeting-houses. In 1846 a very handsome Wesleyan Chapel—the finest in Wales—was built ; and a new gothic Roman Catholic Chapel dedicated to St. David, and an Unitarian Chapel, in the Tudor style, were opened in 1847. —The " Normal College for all Wales," established on the Voluntary principle, which has hitherto been located at Brecon, has been recently removed to Swansea, and strenuous exertions were made in 1848, through the Principality, to raise funds for the erection of a building at Swansea, for the College Students.— We are informed that it is probable that an effort will be made to erect a Normal School on a larger scale than this, by the party which advocates government grants, as there is a large and influential body, comprising both churchmen and dissenters, who think that no voluntary effort will be adequate for the education of the Welsh people without aid from the legislature.

The quadrangular Mansion of the Lords of Gower stood near the castle in Temple-street, but has been recently demolished.

The Market, which is on a scale suited to the wants of the district—a model for other towns—was opened in 1830 by the Corporation, at a cost of £20,000, on ground given by Calvert Richard Jones, Esq. The area is 320 feet long by 220 wide. A walk through this abundantly-supplied market, on Wednesday or Saturday, especially the latter, will be found amusing. The prices of provisions are moderate, and considerably under the average of England, especially for butter, poultry, and fish. The supply of fish is not, however, very large. A new fish market, and an illuminated two-dial clock—the latter presented by T. B. Essery, Esq.—were added in 1847.

On the westerly side of the town, towards the Mumbles and on Mount Pleasant, there are a great many agreeable residences, principally new.—The Lodgings are chiefly near the Burrows, but the construction of docks in that vicinity will render the Mumbles side increasingly popular.—The Baths are on a small scale.—The Assembly Rooms, in Cambrian Place, Burrows, consist of handsome ball, card, and concert rooms, on the first floor; and reading, billiard, and coffee rooms on the basement story. There is also a well-managed and well-supported Theatre open in the summer months.—Amongst the other public buildings is an Infirmary, and a House of Correction, which has lately been enlarged.—It was determined in 1848, to erect a Lunatic Asylum for the counties of Glamorgan, Carmarthen, Cardigan, and Pembroke, on a site near Swansea, at a cost of £15,000.

The Town Hall stands near the river, adjoining the Burrows. It was erected in 1827, but in consequence of the inadequacy of its size, particularly for the business of the Assizes, which are held at Swansea and Cardiff alternately, the Town Council determined in 1847 to make extensive improvements, which, when complete, will render this structure one of the finest in the Prin_cipality. These additions consist of a Nisi Prius Court, Town Council chamber, consultation rooms, &c.; also offices for the Town Clerk, Paving Commissioners, and other public boards. The designs of the south, west, and east fronts are rich elevations in the Corinthian order of the Palladian school; Bath stone is the material used. The architect is Mr. Thomas Taylor, of London.

A Chamber of Commerce has been established with great advantage to the port.

ROYAL INSTITUTION OF SOUTH WALES. A Philosophical and Literary Institution was established at Swansea in the year 1835, which prospered so much beyond the hopes of its founders, that in about three years the members subscribed a sufficient sum for the construction of a building, worthy of the place and of the Principality, and which led to a change in the designation of the society, which was expanded to that of " The Royal Institution of South Wales." A design was furnished by Mr. F. Long, architect, of Liverpool, and the first stone laid on the 24th August, 1838, on a piece of detached ground granted by the corporation, near the Burrows. The principal front, which is of Bath stone, extends 100 feet from east to west, in the centre of which is a prostyle portico of four fluted Ionic columns, " which order is continued in antæ. The entablature has an architrave of three faciæ, and a dentelled cornice, and is surmounted by a very deep blocking course. The portico, which has a low pediment, is elevated five feet and a half above the level of the pavement," which produces a good effect. The depth of the structure varies ; that of the east end is 44 feet. " On the right or east side of the vestibule is the theatre, 38 ⋈ 35, (independently of the large segmental recess for the lecturer) and 20 high ; and behind it is the laboratory. On the opposite side of the vestibule is the library." There are four chief rooms on the upper floor, viz. :— the museum of zoology ; the museum of antiquities ; the council room ; the museum of geology and mineralogy. The library includes, perhaps, the largest collection of books relating to Wales extant, and large additions are constantly being made. The cost of the whole structure was £3,500. A regular series of lectures is given every seasorr; and the museum presents claims to attention not only for the very valuable collection which it contains of objects illustrative of the antiquities, the geology and mineralogy, and the natural history of South Wales, but for its general collection of curiosities. The spirit with which the institution has hitherto been supported is exceedingly creditable to the people of Swansea and the neighbourhood. The illustration and preservation of local antiquities—the development of local resources, of the mineral treasures of the country—useful statistical enquiries—researches in natural history—have profitably occupied the attention of the members ; and the Annual Reports afford abundant proofs of industry.   An useful branch of the Royal Institution was established in the year 1845, under the title of "The Swansea Literary and Scientific Society," the members of which meet weekly in the library, and annually publish a report with a selection of the papers read during the year.   "The Society for the Acquirement of Useful Knowledge," and likewise other societies like the foregoing, hold their meetings in this fine building, a fact which proves that Swansea well deserves the selection made by the British Association for the Advancement of Science, for its meeting of 1848.   Strangers are admitted to the museum on payment of a shilling ; but a member's order will give free admission to the building.   Sometimes the institution is thrown open to the inspection of the inhabitants of the town and district, when scientific experiments are made : nearly 12,000 persons availed themselves of this privilege on Whit-Monday and Tuesday, 1847.   In the museum are many specimens from the Paviland and other bone caverns of Gower ; and several Roman antiquities, including a stone found near Pyle Church in 1832, with the following inscription :—"IMP. MC. PIAVONIO. VICTORINO. AVG."

The Bay is admirably suited for sailing matches, and the Regatta here are more than usually interesting.   Races are held on Crumlyn Burrows, two miles from the town.

The population has increased rapidly.   In 1801 Swansea contained 6,099 persons ; in 1811, 8,166 ; in 1821, 10,255 ; in 1831, 14,931 ; and in 1841, the parish of Swansea, including St: John's, (1,037) contained 20,152.   The population connected with the town, including the copper district, now amounts to between 35,000 and 40,000.

Swansea returns a member to Parliament, in conjunction with the boroughs of Neath, Aberavon, Kenfig, and Lloughor.

The Passenger Station of the South Wales Railway here is in the Pottery Field, near the High Street ; the Goods' Station stands near the Old Brewery, Strand.

The principal INNS are the Mackworth Arms, the Castle Hotel, the Bush, the Commercial Inn, and the Packet Hotel.

Swansea possesses two newspapers, the *Cambrian*, and the *Swansea and Glamorgan Herald*.

Natural History. Mr. Dillwyn's work contains an alphabetical list of nearly 200 of the rarer flowering plants and ferns—some almost unique—which have been found within twenty miles of Swansea; and also a series of zoological memoranda. Amongst the fish that have, at various periods, been taken in Swansea Bay, are the Anchovy, Sucking fish (Echineis Remora), Sun fish, Ballan Wrasse or Old Wife (labrus maculatus), Torpedo, Sting Ray (Raia Pastinaca). A number of rare fish have been caught in Oxwich Bay; and in July, 1824, many thousand shells of Janthina, and skeletons of the Medusa Velella and of Medusa Navicula, were thrown, during very hot weather, on the shores of the same Bay. Many very rare birds have been shot in Gower, and in this part of South Wales.

THE PORT. "Of all the ports in the Bristol Channel," remark the compilers of the Admiralty Surveys, "there are perhaps none more favourably situated than Swansea; for it is an important fact that Swansea Harbour is accessible to any stranger that may arrive in the bay, when blowing too strong for pilots to get off." A town so situated, with an immense coal field at its back, possesses most important elements of prosperity—elements which will be soon fully developed by railway and dock accommodation —for strange to say, Swansea has hitherto been a dry harbour. A large sum of money has been laid out by the Harbour Trustees in forming a new channel or cut for the river Tawe; the old channel being dammed up by a wall between the town and the copper works. For some years there was a great and constantly increasing accumulation of mud in the latter, which baffled all attempts to dredge it away; gates have, however, been inserted in the wall, by which means the river now scours the old channel efficiently. The total expenditure of the Harbour Trustees in improvements is said to amount to about £100,000.

The stone piers that enclose the outer harbour were erected under an act passed in 1791, and stretch on the east side, or

" Fabian's bay," 600 yards—beyond which is Port Tennant, with two small docks for vessels of 200 tons, communicating with the Neath canal—and on the west side 300 yards ; the width between the pier-heads is 75 yards.   This spacious basin is dry for two hours before and after low water.   When there is eight feet water over the bar, a black ball is hoisted on a lighthouse on the western pier-head, which is three miles from the Mumbles light.   The highest spring tide in the harbour rarely exceeds 24 feet ; and the lowest is generally more than ten feet.   Observations are taken by one of Mr. Bunt's tide-guages.   The Tawe is navigable for sea-borne vessels for more than two miles.

The " dock question," which was for many years *the* question here, was at last taken up in earnest.   A Company was formed and an Act obtained in the session of 1847, for the construction of docks on the western side of the Harbour, in front of the Burrows. The works include a basin 100 yards long, and a dock 480 yards by 100 yards.   There is room for another dock of equal size at the back.   The land is fortunately of very little value ; so that the cost of both docks is only estimated at between £100,000 and £130,000.   The engineer is Thomas Page, Esq., and the Secretary, George Grant Francis, Esq.

The increase in the trade has been steady.   In 1819, 1652 ships entered the port ; in 1830, 2,277 ; in 1840, 2,728 ; and in 1845, 4,569.   The foreign trade, which has chiefly arisen since 1827, when the first cargo of foreign copper was brought here, has advanced very rapidly. . The number of ships trading to foreign ports in the year 1814 was four only ; in 1834, 46 ; in 1840, 328 ; in 1844, they amounted to, inwards 168, and outwards 437—with cargoes.   In 1847, 158 foreign vessels of an aggregate burden of 38,967 tons with cargoes, and 148 vessels of 15,296 tons in ballast, entered Swansea.   The following is a statement of the number and registered tonnage of vessels " inwards" frequenting the port during three years, *not* engaged in the foreign trade :—

Years.	Vessels.	Register Tonnage.
1844	4,017	261,698
1845	4,132	268,243
1847	3,651	217,882

Total quantity of coals of every description, shipped in 1847, coastwise :—Coal, 107,371 tons ; culm, 90,886 tons ; stone coal, 7,916 tons ; total coastwise, 206,173 tons; coals exported in foreign vessels, 34,182 tons ; total exports in 1847, 240,355 tons. We believe that no *stone* coal is shipped for foreign parts. The duties paid at the Custom House in 1831 were £4,767 ; in 1846 they exceeded £70,000.

Nearly 140 vessels belong to the port of Swansea. There are ten pilot boats, which are celebrated for their build—the remains of a fleet almost superseded by steam-tugs.

Extensive Potteries have been carried on here for many years. Large works were erected in 1848 by the Patent Fuel Company—an undertaking of national importance,—and which has entered into a large contract with Government for the supply of this valuable steam-packet fuel ; and also by an Iron Ship Building Company, which means to devote much attention to the construction of steamers.

THE COPPER WORKS.

The Swansea Valley is the chief seat of the copper trade in Great Britain. There are eight works here (the Whiterock, the Middle Bank, the Hafod, the Upper Bank, the Morfa, the Landore, the Rose, and the Forest), two at Neath, three near Port Talbot, one opposite Lloughor, two at Llanelly, one in Anglesea, and one at Liverpool, for smelting foreign ore.

Until the year 1827, the ore smelted at Swansea was exclusively British, at which period the consumption for *South Wales* was about 200,000 tons annually ; in 1845, the imports of foreign ore exceeded 45,000 tons ; and, in 1846, this quantity was increased to 58,456 tons, which yielded £668,267 1s. in money ; the quantity of fine copper exceeded 9,174 tons, average produce 15⅜ 1-16, standard £87 3s. The highest produce was from Chili ; but the South Australian ore appears to be on an average, as rich as the American.* The two first cargoes of Australian ore

* " Among the Australian mines, the Kapunda, 831 tons of ore yielded 221 tons 18 cwt. 1 qr. 16 lbs. of copper, produce 26⅜ 1-16, standard £83 15s. Burra Burra, 1,038 tons of ore yielded 231 tons 8 cwt. 2 qrs. 1 lb. of copper, produce 22¼, standard £88 8s."

which reached this country were used in the autumn of 1846, and manifested great docility in smelting. The imports of foreign copper ore in 1847 amounted to 35,939 tons, of which 5,039 tons were from Australia. The eight copper companies at *Swansea* purchased in 1847, 153,120 tons of *Cornish* ore, at a cost of £873,436 10s., producing 12,490 tons of fine copper. In addition to this, 47,611 tons of Welsh, Irish, and foreign ore were purchased here in 1847 at a cost of £641,056 10s. 6d. Besides these quantities, many private transactions take place in Cornish ore, but the foregoing show an annual outlay for raw material to the extent of nearly a million and a half sterling, of which one firm (Williams, Foster, and Co.) furnished £413,557. The gross produce of fine copper is estimated at about 25,000 tons. The total quantity of copper ore sold in Cornwall by public ticketings during the four years 1844–7, was 613,076 tons, which produced £3,390,997 7s., an average of £5 14s. 1d. per ton. During the same period (1844–7) the quantity of foreign ore sold was 170,288 tons, the value of which was £2,583,244 8s. 6d. This trade is therefore "one of the most important branches of British industry''—and employs an immense amount of labour and capital —machinery and shipping. It has been calculated that the Cornish mines alone give employment to 20,000 tons of shipping, and 1,200 seamen in the carrying trade. A considerable decrease took place in the production and consumption of copper ore in the years 1846–7. The value of Cornish cake copper per ton in the latter year varied from £93 to £98. The repeal of the differential duties on the importation of foreign ores will make a considerable difference to the smelters ; it is stated that one firm at Swansea will clear £15,000 a-year by the reduction. The American ore, in consequence of the quantity of sulphur which it contains, appears to the eye much richer than the Cornish, and is so on an average.

The art of manufacturing copper in this country was lost for a very long period. There is no reason to doubt that it was practised in a very rude form by the Romans in Britain, to which people excavations in the Anglesea and other copper mines are attributed. In 1670, a Sir Clement Clarke erected copper smelting

works in Cornwall; but as that county possesses no coal, it was
soon found necessary to remove the trade elsewhere, and a place
on the Avon, below Bristol, was fixed upon.   Other works were
soon after erected at Crew's Hole, near Bristol, and at Redbrook,
below Monmouth.   It is a curious fact, that the Cornish miners
were entirely unacquainted with the nature, and therefore the
value, of copper ore until a comparatively recent period.   Dr.
Paris, in his admirable "Guide to the Land's End" district,
places the date of the discovery considerably later than Sir
Clement Clarke's day, but erroneously.   He states that about
the year 1735, Mr. Coster, a mineralogist of Bristol, observed a
quantity of ore, which was called by the miners *Poder*, lying
amongst the heaps of rubbish around the tin mines, "and formed
the design of converting it to his advantage; he accordingly
entered into a contract to purchase as much of it as could be
supplied.   The scheme succeeded, and Coster long continued to
profit by Cornish ignorance."   A windfall of this kind, on a
smaller scale, was recorded in 1846.   Copper generally occurs at
a much greater depth than tin; and the first miner, in the latter
half of the seventeenth century, who discovered it, abandoned the
mine, because he fancied that it "*spoilt the tin*," an expression
long used.   A Mr. Turner erected a small copper smelting work
near Neath Abbey in 1700; soon after which another work was
built at Melyngryddon by Sir Henry Mackworth and Co.   These
were the first works in South Wales, and it was not until 1719
that a copper work was erected (by a Mr. Phillips) at Swansea,
near the site of the present Cambrian pottery.   The Landore
works were the next.   There are now several extensive copper-
rolling establishments in the Swansea valley, and in 1846 Messrs.
Vivian erected a silver mill.   The American ore, especially, often
contains a considerable quantity of silver.   The assaying of the
ore, by which its value is determined, is a very important process; and is confided to a gentleman of great skill, who resides
at Swansea.

The manufacture of copper is not so attractive as that of iron,
the metal being softer; but some of the processes are interest-

ing.*   The ore is first stamped or pulverised, and then goes through seven processes before it becomes pure copper.   The difference in its appearance, as it becomes progressively purified, is great; in one furnace it remains twenty-four hours : metal for copper wire is dropped into water.   The refuse, scoriæ or " slag," is remelted, to extract any metal that may remain, before it is deposited on the vast " banks " which form so prominent a feature in the scenery of the district.   Immense quantities of this slag are cast into moulds for copings of walls, corners, &c., and in this district houses are occasionally constructed of it.

The trade gives employment to a large population.   Messrs. Vivian, who have one of the largest works near Swansea (the Hafod, which is the most easily accessible), employ about 500 men, and 300 women and boys.   The women are chiefly engaged in wheeling the ore in barrows to be crushed, and receive 9s. or 10s. per week ; children earn from 3s. 6d. to 6s. 6½d. ; furnacemen from 28s. to 32s. ; and the men whose duty it is to ladle the liquid metal from burning fiery furnaces into moulds, are paid £2 and upwards.   The wages are paid at the Messrs. Vivian's works, and we believe at others, every Friday—an excellent plan. A certain number of the men rest on Saturday, and work a given task, to keep the furnaces in, on the Sunday ; tasks are called " watches."   Children are not employed during the " night watches."   The people appear more healthy than could be imagined, but those not bred to the work from childhood cannot stand the sulphureous atmosphere and heat, and generally die early.   A variety of instances of longevity are recorded.   An old woman lately died at the age of 103, in " full possession of her faculties ; " and a number attain the age of 80 years and more.

---

* A discovery was made in 1846 which was expected to produce an extraordinary change in the copper trade. A process was patented for smelting copper ore by means of *electricity*, which, it is averred, is so rapid and simple in operation, that copper can be produced in a state fit for use in thirty-six hours. The enormous saving of fuel and labour which would thus be effected would, of course, produce a corresponding reduction in price; but experience has proved that the process will not answer on a large scale *practically*.

A woman in one of the works told us, in answer to a question, " Sure, we live always, sir." A very large capital is required to conduct a copper work.—Mr. Vivian, M.P., has set a noble example to those who employ many workpeople, by erecting, near the Hafod works, at his sole cost, schools with appropriate offices, capable of accommodating nearly 800 children. The British and Foreign system is carried out ; no religious test is enforced.

The copper smoke is a serious nuisance to the country around, injurious both to cattle and herbage, and has on several occasions afforded employment to the gentlemen of the long robe ; tall chimneys are of little or no avail. Several efforts have been made to counteract its deleterious effects on vegetation, but hitherto without success. Several of the plans proposed have been successful in the laboratory, but have not proved workable on the gigantic scale required here. The grass called *Melica Cœrulea*, " which is not anywhere uncommon " in the neighbourhood, will perfectly withstand the sulphureous fumes of the copper works.

THE SWANSEA VALLEY.

The appearance of copper as well as iron works is of course the most impressive at night ; and the Swansea valley forms no bad representation of the infernal regions, for the smell aids the eye. Large groups of odd chimneys and ricketty flues emit sulphureous arsenical smoke, or pure flame ; a dense canopy overhangs the scene for several miles, rendered more horrible by a peculiar lurid glare. The day-light effect is not much more cheering. All vegetation is blasted in the valley and adjoining hills, and immense swellings on the joints of horses and cattle occasionally attest the pernicious nature of the vapour. On a clear day the smoke of Swansea valley may be seen at a distance of 40 or 50 miles, and sometimes appears like a dense thunder cloud.

This valley, from Swansea upwards for many miles, is a scene of busy industry. The quantity of coal required for the consumption of the copper works alone is enormous ; and when it is borne in mind that the back freight of the vast fleets that arrive at the port is coal, some idea of the extent of the trade may be entertained. The bituminous or binding coal field is near the town :

the collieries of stone coal chiefly commence about 13 miles up the valley, near the Twrch river.

Mr. Logan has made a geological discovery of much interest with regard to the carboniferous strata in this valley. He has ascertained that the upper beds " abound in rolled pebbles of coal itself ; implying the prior existence of land, containing beds of perfectly-formed coal. If the enormous periods of time which all geologists admit to be requisite for the conversion of vegetable matter into coal are granted, these pebbles can scarcely be referred to the earlier beds, even allowing for the unsuspected thickness which Mr. Logan has ascertained that the carboniferous group in this basin exhibits.''

The late Mr. Crane, of the Yniscedwyn Iron Works, near the head of the vale, made a most important discovery in 1836, viz., that by using hot blast (heated air) he could melt iron ores with anthracite coal. The result has been an extension of the pig iron trade on a large scale, to the west of the Taff Vale ; the discovery affecting a district more than 60 miles long, and six to eight in breadth, which abounds with anthracite or carbon coal, lime, and ironstone. Pig iron to the extent of more than 600 tons a week is now produced in this valley. Mineral property has thus, perhaps, been trebled in value. In addition to a number of large iron works that now exist in the Swansea Vale, there are tin, zinc, alkali, and earthenware works.—The mineral produce of this valley has hitherto been chiefly conveyed by a canal, completed in 1798, which runs for 17 miles to an elevation of 373 feet, a rise which involved the construction of thirty-six locks. The Swansea Valley Locomotive Railway, to Abercave in Breconshire, will, in connexion with another new and important line, the " Swansea and Anman Valley Junction, " fully develope the capabilities of this rich mineral district.

CARN LLECHART. Near the top of *Mynydd Maen Coch*, in the parish of Llangyfelach, near Swansea, is a stone circle called Carn Llechart. We have not explored it ourselves, but a correspondent of the *Archæologia Cambrensis* states that it is in a state of almost perfect preservation. " From Swansea the way to it is up the vale to Pontardawe, and then a lane on the left may be safely followed for a mile or so." Enquire of the first cottager you meet.

At the "Lamb and Flag" Inn, near the head of the canal, Hatfield, who seduced the maid of Buttermere, was apprehended. The scenery from this point to the "Carmarthenshire Beacons" and Lakes, a few miles further on, is striking. [*See* LLANDOVERY.]

GOWER

Is one of the "ends of the world"—one of those secluded districts, destitute of high roads, which always invite and generally repay investigation. The circuit of the Peninsula exceeds fifty miles ; and its coast is much indented, so that the sea-shore scenery is characterised by great variety. There are, too, many beautiful inland landscapes, although the prevailing character of all the northern side is wild, and often dreary. This arises from the large extent of common ; for owing to peculiar reasons, there is a wider surface of unenclosed land in this region than in any district similarly situated in Wales. Camden, however, says that in his day, "Gower was more famed for corn than towns."

The early history of Gower (so called, it is said, from *Gwyr*, *recurvus* or crooked) is interesting ; but it is not our province to enter into historical disquisitions, and the details given in accessible works are confused and often conflicting. In British times, the Druids had an important station here ; and subsequently to their era, a prince named Cyndaff, who had embraced Christianity, appears to have conquered the Peninsula, to have become a religious anchorite, and to have been canonised for his piety and his miracles. Some of the churches in Gower are, we believe, dedicated to local Saints. The Normans entered Gower soon after the conquest of eastern Glamorgan by Fitzhamon in 1091 ; but the Welsh disputed the ground so fiercely that it was not until about 1099 that the conquest was completed, in which year the redoubtable Henry de Newburgh, Earl of Warwick, who had obtained a grant of the Peninsula, engaged the sons of Caradoc ap Jestyn near Penrice Castle, when the death of Rhys, the eldest

o

Welsh prince, and the almost total destruction of his army, enabled the Normans to maintain possession. They were, however, much harassed by incursions from the Welsh, and when, in 1103, a numerous body of Flemings, who had been driven from the Low Countries by an inundation of the sea, landed like a swarm of bees in the south of England, it occurred to Henry L. that he might be able to hold South Wales with greater ease if he planted this hardy and industrious people in Gower, and in the opposite peninsula of Pembrokeshire, but they were long compelled to keep their ground with the sword.

This race have in a great measure preserved their national characteristics throughout a period of nearly seven centuries and a half. They have held aloof from and rarely intermixed with their neighbours, the Welsh; their physical form is different, their costume somewhat peculiar, and their language an English dialect, the prevailing radical of which is Saxon, although abounding with obsolete, sometimes Flemish, words. The Gowerians are generally more cleanly than the Welsh, but perhaps not so much so as the English peasantry. Their character is good; they are temperate, and their pursuits are chiefly pastoral, although many, like the inhabitants of the Danish marshes, are sailors, or pass part of their time in deep-sea fishing. The plough and the net may often be seen together. The inhabitants on the eastern side of Gower are as intelligent and well-behaved a race, of primitive habits, as any in Great Britain; as you advance westward the people appear to deteriorate. They have imbibed the superstition, and also, it is said, the love for litigation, of the Welsh; but their popular superstitions are not so poetical as those of the Celtic race. Their garments are chiefly home-spun; some of the plaids are pretty, although not equal to those of the Vale of Neath; and most of the women wear a *whittle*, generally dyed scarlet—a sort of scarf-like shawl, with a fringe at the bottom called Ddrums, which has often a very picturesque appearance, and within which infants are bound and carried on the shoulder, in order to enable their parents to use their hands in household duties, or knitting. In the old time the whittle was fastened with the prickle of the black thorn. The peaked beaver hat so common in Wales, but which the maidens in many parts, especially in Carnarvonshire, are discarding, is used by the women of Gower. It is not generally known that the female peasants of the Tyrol wear the same head dress as the women of Wales. The honesty of the people is strikingly exemplified in the narrative which we give in another page, of the wreck of the "City of Bristol" steamer ; *wrecking* is said to be almost unknown in Gower, although it deforms the character of the inhabitants of the neighbouring coasts. Some of the vehicles and agricultural implements are primitive, especially the sledges and a peculiar species of cart, occasionally still made with solid wooden wheels. Dissent is weaker in this peninsula than in any other part of South Wales. We visited four churches during a recent excursion, and found in three instances large congregations. Most of the churches are of one era, early Norman—apparently the work of one architect ; the chancels are deep and secluded, and there is little or no light admitted into the edifices on the north side. Some are of earlier date.—In local legal proceedings, the distinction between the Flemish and Welsh population is still strictly kept up. At Swansea (which is within this lordship) there is now an old Court in operation, where the Gowerians do suit and service twice a year, called the Court of Gower *Anglicana ;* a similar but distinct court for the Welsh inhabitants of the seignory is styled the Court of Gower *Wallicana.* A short charter granted by King John, in the tenth year of his reign, witnesses—

" That we have released the Welshmen of Gower from the custom which our Sergeants of the Castle of Sweinesey had of taking their food with the aforesaid Welshmen ; and our will is that they be not herein by any one henceforward molested or aggrieved."

A similar charter was granted by John to " the Englishmen of Gower." The lordship or seignory passed into the hands of the Crown late in the reign of Henry II. It was granted by John to William de Breos, " to be held in capite by the service of one Knight's fee." A descendant of this Norman baron in the reign of Edward II. sold a considerable part of the district to various proprietors, but broke his faith, might then being right, and put the younger Spenser in possession in order to please the king—a step which led to important consequences, injurious to the crown.[*] Gower afterwards became vested in Herbert, Earl of Pembroke, and (temp. Henry VII.) in Charles Somerset, an ancestor of the Duke of Beaufort. Gruffyth de Gower, a decendant of a Welsh prince, according to Malkin, was a founder of a family in the peninsula, "distinguished by its great authority and opulence about the end of the twelfth or beginning of the thirteenth century. The celebrated John Gower, the contemporary, friend, and panegyrist of Chaucer, was a descendant of Gruffyth," and a native of the seignory. Henry Gower, an eminent Bishop of St. David's, and distinguished for his skill in architecture, is believed to have been of the family. He died in 1347.

The long mountain region of Cefyn Bryn and other uplands still belong to the Crown ; but the peninsula is now chiefly vested in the Duke of Beaufort, Mr. Talbot, M. P., and two or three other large land-owners. The Duke is Lord Paramount of the seignory ; appoints a coroner and bailiff ; and is entitled to a quit rent from 600 farms formerly included in the lordship. There are about 700 pieces of waste land that have not been granted out, to which the Duke of Beaufort has a title as Lord of the Manor. These commons are valuable aids to the farmers, who all possess a right of turning stock upon them, subject to a payment of about 6d. per acre. In order to protect the common property, and to prevent encroachments from strangers, it has been the custom to appoint haywards, who once every year scour the commons, and take possession of all cattle, sheep, &c., that are not claimed by the tenants, and if the estrays are not demanded within a year and a day, the hayward retains possession of them by paying the sum of 2s. 6d. to the duke's steward.

AN EXCURSION THROUGH GOWER

Cannot be satisfactorily or conveniently accomplished under three or four days. The Mumbles headland and other objects of interest in South-east Gower should be first visited ; and the

[*] The title of Baron de Breos of Gower is now assumed both by the Duke of Norfolk and the Earl of Berkeley."

pedestrian, who has followed the coast from Caswell Bay towards Pwldie Point, the highest headland in Gower, and who does not mind fatigue, may proceed after walking *up* Bishopston Valley, to the Gower Inn (nearly three miles from Bishopston Church), where he may pass the night. This is much better than returning to Swansea, and proceeding the next day by the regular road to the Gower Inn.—In order to give clearness to our arrangement, we shall describe the castellated and other antiquities under distinct·heads. We begin our excursions with

THE MUMBLES ROAD, which follows the line of Swansea Bay closely, and affords a delightful drive. The graceful wooded eminences which rise throughout the distance to the right are studded with gentlemen's seats, and country "boxes." *Singleton Abbey,* the residence of J. H. Vivian, Esq., M. P. for Swansea, is one of the most perfect places in the kingdom on a moderate scale—a triumph of art. The situation of the house, which replaced a residence called Marino, is unfortunately rather too low ; but the grounds afford enchanting prospects. The pleasure gardens are extensive, and laid out with remarkable taste and judgment. A series of imitative *fonts* are placed about the mansion, and serve the purpose of flower pots. This is in bad taste. In an Abbey Church, a font was always treated with the highest reverence ; the use of a font is associated with the holy Sacrament of Baptism. In the house, which is most elegantly fitted up, is a very fine portrait of Sir Hussey *(*afterwards Lord*)* Vivian, who was a brother of the munificent owner of Singleton ; and pictures that illustrate stirring passages in his military career. There are ten or twelve lodges in Singleton Park, one of which is a fac simile of a celebrated Swiss cottage, another of an American log-hut.—Amongst the other seats on the Mumbles road, *Woodlands Castle,* the residence of Mr. Berrington, may be specially mentioned. Beyond this is the pretty village of Norton, succeeded by Oystermouth Castle, a majestic object from almost all points of view.

THE MUMBLES HEADLAND—OYSTERMOUTH.

There are few natural places of shelter for shipping on the British coasts comparable to the Mumbles roadstead. In a

channel destitute of a harbour of refuge it is invaluable ; and
occasionally 400 or 500 sail of vessels are anchored in this small
road, which is well sheltered from all except north-easterly
winds.   The length of the rock is about a mile.   At the eastern
end are two islands, which in effect form part of the promontory,
as the tide usually leaves a dry passage between, at low water.
On the farthest is a well-known Lighthouse ; below which to the
south is a vast cave, locally called " Bob's Cove," accessible
when the tide is out.—The Mumbles headland consists chiefly of
excellent limestone, much of which has been quarried and exported
(price 1s. 3d. to 1s. 6d. per ton) ; and a valuable vein of iron ore
was discovered in 1845, which has been worked to the disfigure-
ment of this romantic spot, which commands home scenes of great
beauty, and a view of the channel from Nass Point to Lundy
Island on one side, and Swansea Bay, backed by graceful hills
and studded with many sails, from the three-master to the pilot
boat, on the other.   On the south of the headland, just in the
track of ships, is a shoal called " the Mixon," distinguished at
its western extremity by a buoy.   In strong weather, at early
flood, the sea runs " mountains " over this sandbank.

The village is primitive—a genuine " fishing village "—and
has retained its original character, although omnibusses are
constantly running to and fro to Swansea at " the small charge
of sixpence."   The INNS are—the Mermaid and the George.
Lodgings may be procured of various kinds ; a few are good.
Comfortable lodgings may also be obtained at moderate rates at
the adjacent and very healthy hamlet of NORTON (we can strongly
recommend Williams's), and at houses, surrounded by gardens,
close to the shore along the Swansea road.   It is said that the sun
does not shine on the village of Oystermouth, which straggles under
and up the side of the headland for three months in the year.

To those who are fond of breezy downs, scented with thyme
and other wild plants, sloping to an iron-bound coast broken by
bluffs, and vast headlands—of delicious little bays where one can
dream away the day in gladsome sunshine and be lulled by the
music of the sea—of heathy upland commons—this neighbourhood is full of charms.   The large number of vessels that daily

leave Swansea, Neath, and other ports, always give animation to
the marine prospect.   There are no bathing machines ; but many
lady visitors bathe, nevertheless.—A rude path runs along the
coast for many miles ; but the downs are often preferable.

The OYSTER FISHERY AT THE MUMBLES gives employment, in
the height of the season, to upwards of 400 men ; and the appearance of the fleet of boats, 60 or 80 in number, is often very picturesque.   Every boat is manned by four men, who each pull a
heavy oar—hard work against tide—but sail is set whenever practicable.   The oyster beds extend from off the Mumbles headland—
under shelter of which the " fleet is moored"—almost to the
Worm's Head, at the other extremity of the Gower coast ; and
the boats in dredging are usually kept in two divisions.   The take
varies from 500 to 3,000 for each boat, in a day ; and the boat's
crew get 2s. each per 1,000 for their labour.   Prices vary considerably ; and the fishermen must be in some degree at the mercy
of the factors' or " middle men" at Swansea, who supply Bristol,
Liverpool, London, and other great markets.   The large oysters
fetch from 12s. to 15s. or 16s. per 1,000 ; small, from 9s. to 12s.
The quality is excellent : the Tenby and other large oysters in
this channel are coarse ; in the higher part of Milford Haven,
towards Haverfordwest, however, the oysters are nearly equal to
the best " natives," and are very frequently passed off as such
by fishmongers, who must make enormous profits, " natives"
being three or four times as dear in the London market.   The
dredging season at the Mumbles begins on the 1st of September,
and closes at the beginning of May.   Immense quantities of these
oysters are sent to London in March and April, but Liverpool is
the best market.   The shore within the Mumbles head is divided
into regular partitions by large " shingles," within each of which
the week's produce of a boat is piled.   Sometimes a boat dredges
18,000 to 20,000 in a week ; so that the aggregate number in the
heaps, even reckoning only 10,000 in each, must be enormous.
A watch is kept at night.   The oyster dredger is heavy and
strongly constructed.   The best oysters lie in beds near low
water mark in spring tides within the headland, and sometimes
300 or 400 persons—men, women, and children, some of whom go

into the water almost up to their necks—are engaged in gathering
the fish.   Altogether, the oyster fisheries of. this channel afford
employment to a large body of hardy seamen.* We may here
mention that the Welsh sailors are generally a very fine body of
men.   Their reputation is so good, that a few years ago the Emperor of Russia desired that a crew of thirty Welsh sailors should
be engaged to man a yacht, which was built for him at Cowes.

CHIEF EXCURSIONS FROM THE MUMBLES.—1. *To Langland Bay*
(where there is a lodging-house), about a mile.   Some beautiful
shells may be found here, but not by a casual explorer.—2. *To
Caswell Bay*, one of the gems of the coast, resembling Lulworth
Cove, about two miles by the village of Newton.   These bays are
best seen at low water.   On the western side of Caswell Bay there
is a remarkable instance of surface-earth being changed into rock
by the action of sea water.   The violence of the sea has undermined a portion of the acclivity, and large masses of earth may
be seen lying on the beach in various stages of change.—3. *To
Pwldie Point and Bay, and Bishopston Valley.* Rock scenery
at Pwldie.   Proceed up wooded dingle on right.   Enter Bishopston Valley at a striking enclosed scene.   Beautifully contrasted
scenery.   Appearance of river below rocks, after *running underground* for about two miles.   Two vast *pits* at upper end—some
of the curiosities of Gower—depressions in the limestone ; there

---

* *Pickled Oysters* are the greatest delicacy of the place.   The fish are washed
three times in water, and then put into jars with spices.   If Cayenne pepper be
added, and the air excluded, oysters thus prepared will, it is said, keep some
time perfectly fresh.   The price for the best is 2s. per 120.

Sea-weed Bread, or *Laver Cake*, if not one of the delicacies, is one of the
edible curiosities of the Gower coast.   A great sensation was made some years
ago, by a statement that thousands of the peasantry in the " wild west" of Ireland were obliged, for some months in the year, to live mainly on *sea weed*.
In Gower and at Swansea sea weed is rather a popular article of food.   Women
attend Swansea market with baskets of laver cakes, which are sold at 1d. and
2d. each.   This weed *(ulva porphyra laciniata)* makes an excellent ingredient
in sauce for mutton.   It is got close to low water mark; washed well in sea
water to free it from sand, then boiled twelve hours, and seasoned with salt.
In winter it is only necessary to boil it two hours.   The weed grows rapidly
except in winter, and is renewed every other spring tide.   It is also used in
several parts of the Scottish coasts and islands, where it is called *sloke* or *slokum*.

are other pits of this nature in the peninsula.　Bishopston formerly belonged to the Bishops of Llandaff.　A peculiar custom relative to copyhold prevails ; " and there is an ancient tenement called Culver House, which is held by service of grand sergeantry at the King's coronation, the tenure having been recognised by the Court of Claims, William IV." Great quantities of lead ore have been raised here.　The Rev. E. Davies, the learned author of the " Celtic Researches, and Mythology of the Druids," was long rector of Bishopston, and died here in 1831.—4. *To the Moors*—a wild upland common of great extent, covered with heath and gorse, a mile above Norton ; views magnificent.

THE GOWER INN

Stands at the head of a dingle, eight miles from Swansea, and six from Oystermouth, at the back of Oxwich Bay, and within two miles of the base of the east end of Cefyn Bryn.　It was built by the late Mr. Penrice, of the adjoining demesne of Kilvrough, —along the edge of the woods of which the road descends for a mile—expressly for tourists.　Here, unless the rooms be occupied by lodgers, excellent accommodation may be obtained.　There are no carriages or horses to let ; so those who cannot walk, must arrange to keep the vehicle that they hired at Swansea, during their exploration.　The *Green Combe*, a woodland scene two miles long, of singular beauty, affords a pleasant walk from the Gower Inn.—At Langrove Farm, and the Court House, one mile from this inn, are examples of Flemish architecture ; the latter supposed to have been a Flemish court of justice.

OXWICH BAY

Is within a mile of the Gower Inn.　There are two roads to it, one over the sandhills to *Pennard Castle*, and the Eastern Cliffs ; the other on the right side of the river towards the Tors.　Obtain a guide ; and take the first road, when after visiting Pennard Castle, proceed to two CAVERNS of great interest, and difficult of access, a mile and a half on the coast to the left.　Both front the sea, almost to the level of which it is necessary to descend down very steep and lofty declivities.　They are *Bone Caverns*, and that which lies most to the east, *the Bacon Hole*, is still rich in osseous remains, remarkably disposed ; a large number have been removed, and the floor of the cave, which is about twenty feet above the sea, has been much altered in consequence. Some very large stalactites have been almost destroyed. Several rare plants may be discovered here. The conformation of the entrance is depicted in the accompanying sketch. The second Cave, the *Mitchen Hole*, is much the largest and most impressive—of perfectly dissimilar character to its neighbour. It is of dome-like shape—the perforation, in fact, of a vast headland; the remains of stalactites are prodigious. The guide may be dismissed on returning towards Oxwich Bay, or rather Three Cliffs Cove, a picturesque scene, with an arch-like perforation. If the tide be out, cross to " the Tors ; " but as the sea only recedes for a short period below the Great Tor, it is generally necessary to climb the hill and descend towards the sands of Oxwich Bay proper. Keep straight along the line of rocks till you come to a causeway at the head of a salt

THE BACON HOLE, GOWER.

water inlet ; then cross towards Penrice Village, which stands on
a wooded knoll in the distance.

A field near the eastern extremity of Penrice comprehends
one of the finest coast scenes in Britain. On the left the long
moorland ridge of Cefyn Bryn rises over masses of foliage in the
park of Penrice Castle ; the shoreward prospect embraces a line
of bluffs and jagged tors—progressively changing their character
from graceful to stern,—the colours gradually softening from
sombre grey and dark green to the warm tints of heath, gorse
and wild rose, relieved by the delicate green of young fern and
bent, and terminating in the bleached limestone of the vast eastern
heights, capped by Pwldie Point.—Penrice Church is a cruciform
Norman structure. This and most of the other churches in Gower
have lately undergone restoration. The other objects of interest
are the Castle and luxuriantly wooded Park of Penrice, one
of the seats of Mr. Talbot, M. P. for Glamorgan. The modern
house is a tasteless structure of the last century, placed close
below the ruins of the ancient Castle ; the grounds are in many
parts most judiciously laid out, but in truth nature has done so
much for the scene that but little is required from art.

Oxwich Castle (one mile and a half from Penrice Village) rises
over woods near the village of Oxwich, to the south. The road
runs at the head of a salt-water lake and reclaimed salt marsh of
200 acres. *Objects of Interest* : The Norman Church, dedicated
to St. Illtyd, almost overhanging the shore—in a situation of
striking beauty ; the Parsonage House ; School, maintained by
Lady Mary Cole. A walk through the woods leads to the end of
the headland ; the view from a ruined outwork on ascending the
hill to the Castle, if the lights be good, stretches as far as Craig
y Llyn, at the head of the Vale of Neath.

EXCURSIONS TO THE WORM'S HEAD AND WESTERN COAST.

The Gower Inn is at present the only resting place for the
tourist in the Peninsula. The hardy pedestrian may obtain a
bed (a clean double-bedded garret) at the Mariners' Arms, Frog
Lane (Llanmadoc) ; but under ordinary circumstances the best
course is to make two excursions to the westward from the Gower
Inn ; each of which requires a day. 1. To Worm's Head ; 2.

To Webley Castle, Llanmadoc, &c.   There is, however, a minor
excursion to be performed to *Arthur's Stone*, the road to which
runs along the edge of

CEFYN BRYN,

or in English, " the ridge of the mountain," the ascent to which
commences near Penmaen Church, two miles from the Gower
Inn.   The late T. M. Talbot, Esq., cut a road in the turf on the
summit of the long upland ridge, for a distance of nearly four
miles, along which a carriage may be driven.   The position of
this hill, in the centre of the peninsula, surrounded by the Bristol
Channel and the estuary of the Burry river, commanding delicious
home views and the whole of Gower, and under favourable circumstances a vast prospect on all sides of the horizon (we have seen
Ilfracombe, under a refracted light, with marvellous distinctness),
renders it one of the most enchanting eminences that we can
call to recollection.   We have elsewhere spoken of its Druidical
antiquities.   Cefyn Bryn being crown land, is a free common.

In the grounds of Stouthall, near Reynoldstone, five miles from
the Gower Inn, is one of the largest Caves in the kingdom, in the
limestone rock.   It was accidentally discovered, and is capable of
containing 2,000 persons.

There are two roads to the Worm's Head.   The best plan is
to go through Penrice Park (four miles from the Gower Inn) to
Porteynon, a picturesque fishing village and bay, about two miles
on, with curious rock scenery.   The pedestrian should now
enquire for the path along the coast, beginning at Overton, which
runs on the summit of the cliffs, and is occasionally broken by
wild rock scenes and coves, once the haunt of hordes of smugglers.

THE BONE CAVES OF PAVILAND,

two of the most remarkable caverns in Britain, are on the
coast near Pitton, a sea-shore hamlet to the east of Middletown
(Rhosilly).   They face the sea, like the Bacon and Mitchen Holes,
in the front of a lofty cliff of limestone, which rises more than 100
feet perpendicularly above their mouth, and slopes below them at
an angle of about forty degrees to the water's edge.   These caves
are altogether invisible from the land side, and are accessible only
at low water, except by a dangerous path along the face of a nearly

precipitous cliff. The following particulars have been condensed from Dr. Buckland's *Reliquiæ Diluvianæ* and other sources :—

THE GOAT'S HOLE. The existence of this cave had long been known to farmers in the vicinity, and the summer before Dr. Buckland visited it the surgeon and curate of Porteynon discovered two molar teeth of an elephant and a portion of a large curved tusk. This attracted the attention of Sir C. Cole, L. W. Dillwyn, Esq., and Miss Talbot, who subsequently visited the cave and brought away many bones. Dr. Buckland came here in January, 1823, with Mr. Dillwyn. The floor ascends rapidly, and is covered with a mass of diluvial loam of a reddish yellow colour, abundantly mixed with angular fragments of limestone, and broken calcareous spar, and interspersed with recent sea shells, and with teeth and bones of the following animals, viz., elephant, rhinoceros, bear, hyena, wolf, fox, horse, ox, deer of two or three species, water rats, sheep, birds, and man. Dr. Buckland also found fragments of charcoal, and a small flint, the edges of which had been chipped off, as if by striking a light. One portion of the elephant's tusk was nearly two feet long. The entire mass through which the bones were dispersed appeared to have been disturbed by ancient diggings, and the antediluvian remains thereby to have become mixed with recent bones and shells, common to the adjacent shore. At the interior extremity the recent shells and bones of birds are most abundant, and the earthy mass containing them is cemented to a firm brecchia by stalagmite, and this is almost the only point in the cave where stalagmite or stalactite occurs. The human remains consisted of nearly the entire left side of a female skeleton, hidden by only six inches of earth. The bones appeared not to have been disturbed by the previous operations, whatever they were, that had removed the other part of the skeleton. They were all of them stained superficially with a dark brick red colour, and enveloped by a coating of a kind of raddle, composed of red micaceous oxide of iron. Two handsful of small yellow shells of the *nerita littoralis*, and forty or fifty small ivory rods nearly cylindrical, and varying from a quarter of an inch to four inches in length, which had been much broken, were found in contact with the ribs. In another place were three fragments of the same ivory, which had been cut into forms which were often unmeaning. One resembled a human tongue, others skewers, others rings or armlets. A wolf's-toe was moulded into the form of a skewer. This cave had been used as a human habitation at some remote period. The circumstance of the remains of a British camp existing on the hill immediately above the cave, seems to throw much light on the character and date of the woman under consideration, ...the latter of which was probably anterior to or coeval with the Roman invasion of this country. In 1836, Mr. Francis and Mr. J. G. Jeffreys found among the rubbish on the floor of Goat's Hole, " a third *brass coin of Constantius II.*, together with a piece of fine *Roman terra Cotta*, and a number of Celtic weapons of flint " which are now in the museum of the Institution at Swansea. A coin of the Emperor Caurausius has also been discovered. A long cavernous aperture rises like a crooked chimney from the roof of this cave to the nearly vertical face of the rock above. In some lateral cavities in this tortuous ascent, bones of various birds and small animals, and shells, were found in brown earth a foot thick.

The *Second Cave* is about a hundred yards farther to the west. It is very similar to the first, in size, form, and position, and closed on every side with solid rock, excepting the mouth, which is large and open to the sea ; its body contracts gradually towards the inner extremity and upwards also towards the roof, where it terminates in a vein that is still filled with calcareous spar : the cave itself, in fact, seems to be merely an enlargement of this vein. The floor is about thirty feet above the sea, and being more horizontal than the Goat's Hole, and within reach of the highest storm waves, is strewed over entirely, to the depth of more than a foot, with a bed of small sea pebbles. Below these, Dr. Buckland found a bed of the same argillaceous loam and fragments of limestone as in the Goat's Hole, and a still more abundant accumulation of animal remains. He believes that the entire floor beneath the pebbles is covered with a continuous mass of these antediluvian relics ; and that both caves are residuary offshoots or branches of some larger cavern, that has been cut away by the denudation which formed the present cliffs, and whose main trunk is now no more. Their relative position is such that if both were prolonged towards the sea, they would soon meet and intersect each other. Dr. Buckland considers that the caves which occur in the vertical cliffs that form the submarine valley which is now the estuary of the Severn, are analogous to the caves found in the lofty and vertical cliffs that flank the inland valleys of the Avon at Clifton, and several places on the continent. He found no evidence to show that either of the caves at Paviland were occupied as antediluvian dens. Two brass Roman coins were found some years ago by the Rev. Mr. Davis, of Reynoldston, in the western cave. In the flat surface of the fields, a quarter of a mile distant from Paviland, is an open cavern, to which it is not possible to descend without a ladder.—There are many specimens from these and the caverns to the east of Oxwich Bay, in the collection at Penrice Castle, in the museum of the Institution at Swansea, and at Oxford.

At Sprit-sail Tor, near Llanmadoc, on the other side of the peninsula, is another *Cavern*, something like those at Paviland. Bones of hyenas, of a rhinoceros, a human lower jaw, and other remains, were found in it in the year 1839. Five large Bone Caverns have therefore been discovered in Gower.

At the village of Rhosilly, a bleak place exposed to the fury of the western blast, entertainment can be obtained for man and horse at the house (" the Ship") of William Beynon, one of the most intelligent guides we ever met with, who beguiles the way to the Worm's Head with a store of wild anecdotes.   The distance to Rhosilly from the Gower Inn, by the coast, cannot be less than 12 miles, and is fully 11 by the nearest road.   The Church of Rhosilly is a very rude structure of considerable length, lighted by four small windows protected by shutters.   There is a ruined church near the beach below.   The limestone trade gives employment to 50 men at Rhosilly, who net about 1s. a ton.   Mr. Talbot receives 2d. per ton royalty, which produces £150 a year from these rocks alone ; his revenue from this source along the Gower coast must be considerable.   Fewer accidents occur than might be anticipated, from the " dreadful" appearance of the occupation : men are often suspended over the edges of precipices several hundred feet high ; and on some parts of the coast, vast fragments are rolled to the beach, to the imminent danger of those beneath.

THE WORM'S HEAD.

We have twice visited this remarkable feature of the Bristol Channel under circumstances calculated to enhance or rather give full effect to its natural impressiveness,—a violent gale of wind from the north-west.   Then this stern outwork of the mainland, its jagged defences, and dreaded neighbour, Rhosilly Bay—rife with melancholy memorials—seem as it were to wrestle with the western wave—

>   ——" When all that sea—
> The terrible Atlantic, breasts its rocks
> In thundering conflict, the unearthly howl
> Might almost wake the dead!"

The name Worm's Head is said to be derived from the appearance of the rock from the westward, when in the eyes of seamen it appears like a snake of fabled sea-serpent dimensions, with its head erect, rising out of the deep.   The distance from Rhosilly to the extremity of the headland is two miles, but the excursion cannot be well accomplished under three hours.   At high water the headland forms two islands ; and it is necessary to regulate a

visit by the state of the tide, in order to avoid the risk of being
detained for many hours on the rock. The annexed sketch affords
a faint idea of the scene. You traverse a honeycombed and
slippery causeway which connects the first island with the main
land ; then another and much more difficult series, 400 yards long,
of pointed rocks of volcanic appearance and as sharp as needles,
ending in " *the Devil's Bridge*"—the force of the sea having rent
a fissure in a neck of rock—which in coarse weather especially,
demands a steady eye and careful step. The Head rises to a height
of 300 feet, on the north side perpendicularly, above the sea,
and is of singular conformation. It is perforated at its western
extremity by a cavern 300 yards (?) long, "as large as a church,"
into which, during a profound calm, William Beynon once rowed
a boat with three adventurous visitors—the only persons who had
ever beheld the interior within human memory, neither is there
any tradition of such an occurrence. Yet Leland (temp. Henry
VIII.), evidently refers to this cave in the following passage :—
" There is also a wonderfull hole at the Poynt of Worme Heade,
but few dare enter into it, and men fable there that a Dore,
withein the spatius Hole hathe be sene withe great Nayles on it :
but that that is spoken of Waters there reunynge undar the
ground is more lykely." (Fol. p. 106. Vol. VIII.)

The great curiosity of the Head is the " Blow-hole," a narrow
cleft about a foot long and three-quarters of an inch wide, on the
hill-side near the supposed extremity of the cavern. The noise
made by the wind through this aperture is astounding, in consequence of the waves rushing into the space below and driving up
the air. When there is a ground swell, previously to a gale, we
were assured that the sharp sound was heard at night seven miles
inland ; and the country people call the Blow-hole the " *Rhosilly
barometer*"—the indicator of storms.* The tide rises here at

* Giraldus Cambrensis speaks of a small cavity of this nature in Barry Island,
below Cardiff; but as nothing of the kind can be discovered there, we entertain
little doubt that he mistook Barry for the Worm's Head near the *Burry*. Giraldus describes the noise as "resembling that of blacksmiths at work, the blowing of bellows, strokes of hammers, grinding of tools, and roaring of furnaces,"
and adds that he could not discover the cause, as the noises were heard at high
and low water, being ignorant of course of the nature of the cavity beneath.

springs 33 feet, and we have seen it dash to the summit of the
Head.   One of the curiosities is a wild place called "Mr. Talbot's
Summer House."   The late Mr. Talbot, the owner of the headland and most of the adjoining coasts, took great interest in the
locality ; and observing that the herbage on this Head was of
extraordinary luxuriance and peculiar nature, annually sent a
flock of sheep to fatten there, a practice which is still kept up ;
the mutton is said to be the finest in the kingdom.   In 1845,
twenty-two of the sheep which had taken shelter on the causeway
were drowned by the rapid rush of the tide.   On the side of the
Head is a ruined sheepfold, which affords an anecdote of the
ingenuity of smugglers.   Rhosilly, during the late war, was a
busy smuggling station ; and soon after Mr. Talbot had constructed the wall to shelter his sheep, the smugglers with great
labour excavated a cellar below, which they filled with tubs of
spirits.   The local annals, which abound with smuggling adventures, tell of the break-up of these bold free-traders, owing to the
treachery of a comrade, and of the discovery of this and other
artfully constructed nests and a large number of tubs hidden
in sheaves in harvest time : most of these places can still be seen,
amongst them the cellar on the " far " Worm's Head.   We were
told by the veteran officer of the coast guard at the Mumbles,
whose jurisdiction extends along these shores, that in 1802, so
largely was smuggling carried on in Gower, that at Pwldie Cove
alone 1,800 tubs of nine gallons each were landed in the space of
nine days, and taken away by the country people in the most
daring manner, in open day.   A couple of tubs were slung on a
horse, on which a man was mounted, who urged the animal to a
fast pace.   At Rhosilly, it was a common practice for a smuggler
to run in under the shelter of the Worm's Head in the morning,
under the plea of shortness of water or provisions, when the
captain came ashore, quietly made arrangements as to signals,
stood off, and returned at night.

This headland and the adjoining coast have long been the terror
of seamen in coarse weather.   Many wrecks, some of the most
harrowing description, have taken place, including Indiamen
that have missed the English Channel.   In August, 1844, when

a dreadful storm, occasioned by a very sudden change of wind, ravaged the Bristol Channel, fourteen bodies were washed ashore here. Two coasters were driven on the Head almost at the same moment, whilst the sea was running mountains. The captain of one was thrown on the slope of turf, the waves dashed over him fifteen feet deep, and he was nearly engulphed by the under-tow ; but he crawled out of the reach of the next, and was saved, with one of the crew of another vessel. Another ship was soon after driven on shore more to the eastward. William Beynon was one day standing on the Head, when he saw a fine brig, which had been abandoned in the hurry of a collision at night, drifting towards him, with her sails set, without a soul on board. She struck gently—for the day was calm—on the black rocks below, and was secured almost uninjured—a lucky windfall for Rhosilly.

We have never felt more impressed by coast scenery—by THE SEA—than at the Worm's Head. The combination of the beautiful with the sublime—the grandeur of the objects—the wildness of the seclusion—fascinate the mind.

RHOSILLY BAY is backed by the lofty and beautiful range of hills called Rhosilly Downs, which with Llanmadoc Downs, at their northern extremity, form bold landmarks to the channel. It is known but to few mariners that just below the village of Rhosilly, within the inner headland, there is good shelter and holding ground in this bay, except in a north-west wind. Many a vessel has been lost in consequence of ignorance of this fact, which is not noted in the charts ; but some of the Trinity House authorities, on visiting the place in 1846, were made acquainted with it. The depth in the bay varies from two to five fathoms ; there is a sandy shelving bottom, but off the Worm's Head the sea is very deep. The distance from the latter to the *Burry Holmes Island*, which terminates the bay to the north, is three miles.

Wreck of a Spanish Galleon. Legends.—Great interest has for many years existed in Gower and the adjoining coasts relative to the wreck of a homeward-bound galleon in Rhosilly Bay, which appears to have taken place during the first half of the seventeenth century. The following particulars have been chiefly picked up on the spot. The vessel struck the sand during a storm, and the survivors, without stating the value of the cargo, soon sold the wreck to a Mr. Thomas, of Pitton, for a small sum. This person, unaware of the value of his purchase, suffered the vessel to become embedded in the sand; but an impression gradually arose that she was a "treasure ship." The Lord of the Manor ultimately advanced a claim; but according to a local legend, 150 years ago one of the Mansel family forcibly broke into the vessel and carried off great spoil. The ill-gotten gain led to misery; Mr. Mansel fled the country, and is said to have met with some sad fate abroad. The country people now believe that his spirit haunts the sands at night; and some affirm that he may be seen riding thereon in a black coach drawn by four grey horses. Some years ago, an old man from Llangennith, who had wandered on the sands in the dark, was almost terrified out of his senses by the apparition of Mr. Mansel in his spectre chariot.—About forty years ago, a quantity of dollars, of the date of 1625, were found amongst the sand near the wreck, on a day when the tide had receded unusually far; and the sands having drifted considerably, the wreck became visible, and more dollars, with pewter and iron, were dug up. The sands again closed, and it was not until 1833, when a fresh change took place, that anything more was found. Fourteen men from Faversham, divers and reputed smugglers, the crew of a craft lying in the Burry river, set to work on the wreck, which had become exposed. This excited the country people. Valuable plunder was soon obtained; at one time 300 men were occupied about the wreck, and 2,000 persons assembled to look on. Mr. Talbot, the Lord of the Manor, found it necessary in order to preserve the peace, which had been broken, to settle a boundary between the strangers and the Gowerians. The former worked within iron frames placed on the sand, and were therefore the most successful. Great quantities of dollars, and guns (the stocks of which were finely inlaid with silver), pistols, swords, cutlasses, cannon shot, musket balls, cinnamon, &c., were recovered. Soon after the sand shifted, and the vessel, which had been visible to the extent of 120 feet, once more disappeared. In January, 1834, she was again visible, when a very large quantity of Spanish dollars, chiefly bearing

date 1631, were secured; and coins were occasionally picked up
for eleven years afterwards. The late Mr. John Beynon, of
Pitton, a descendant of Mr. Thomas, set up a claim to the property in 1834, but having failed to prove the purchase of the
vessel by any written document, Mr. Talbot, as Lord of the
Manor, became interested, and generously permitted the people of
the district to profit by the discovery.—There is another local
legend about the wreck of a vessel, called the " Scanderoon
galley," in the Burry River.

A quarter of a mile from the Spanish galleon is the wreck of
the " City of Bristol" steam-packet, which was lost during the
night of the 18th of November, 1840. Our Rhosilly guide gave
us a vivid narrative of this unaccountable casualty, which is,
however, too long for our pages. The vessel struck during an
easterly gale on her voyage from Waterford, about six o'clock in
the evening, and all on board might easily have been saved, had
not the captain supposed that the vessel would get off the sands
when the tide again flowed. Twenty-six persons, six of whom
were passengers, perished; only two were saved. Mr. George
Lunell, the chairman of the Bristol Company, to which the ship
belonged, mentioned in a narrative of the transactions that took
place after this wreck, which he published at the time, the following
facts, which redound to the credit of the people of Gower. " With
gratitude I bear testimony to the honesty and high moral integrity
of all the inhabitants of the neighbourhood ; though every part
of the bay was strewn with broken fragments, and continued so
for six days and nights, though many of the people were poor,
and fuel was scarce and dear, not the smallest particle was taken ;
but on Wednesday last, after disposing in small lots of all the
timbers and planks that had come on shore, I told them that they
were welcome to what remained, and nothing could show more
strongly that it had not been previously taken up because not
valued, than that after thanking me, they immediately set about
gathering it up, and in less than two hours scarcely a vestige was
seen. From every one I received sympathy and kindness."

We resume our EXCURSION. Pedestrian tourists may proceed
over the Down—a magnificent walk—to the northern side of

Gower, visiting some Camps by the way.   At Llangennith, which stands inland at the south-western foot of Llanmadoc Hill, is a church dedicated to and originally founded by St. Cenydd, son of Gildas.   The existing structure, which is the largest in Gower, was connected with a Priory, founded by Robert de Bellomonte, Earl of Warwick.   Several ancient monuments are to be found in the chancel.   There was a cell to this Priory on Holmes Island, the ruins of which still exist.   The distance from Rhosilly to Llanmadoc (where the bone cavern should be visited) is fully seven miles ; and from Llanmadoc to Swansea fifteen miles.   At the entrance of the Burry River is a curious narrow sandy peninsula, called Whitford Point, which protects that estuary from the sea. On returning eastward, pass Landymor and Webley Castles to the right, and encampments beyond Llanridian.   The tourist who does not wish to return to the Gower Inn (the best route to which, for the pedestrian, is through the *Green Combe*) may proceed to Swansea by a good turnpike-road, on the left, which saves two or three miles.   The scenery on this side of Gower, up to Llanridian, is dreary ; from thence to Penclawdd, the coast improves greatly. Those who wish to proceed to Lloughor, must be particularly careful in making local enquiries.   We have now made a circuit of the Peninsula, and proceed to describe its antiquities.

DRUIDICAL ANTIQUITIES. **Arthur's Stone** is perhaps the most celebrated although not the most remarkable *Cromlech* in Wales. It was called " the Wonder of the World on Gower," and the lifting of the stone into its existing position is mentioned in the Triads " as one of three arduous undertakings accomplished in Britain, and still more than that, one of the three wonderful exertions demonstrative of human power "—the other two being Stonehenge, and Silbury Hill.*   This Silent Watcher stands near the north-west end of Cefyn Bryn Mountain—six miles from the Gower Inn—overlooking a vast extent of Wales, and the number of Druidical antiquities and *carneddau* in the immediate vicinity, show that it was a place of great importance.   The man

---

* In the Triads it is termed " the Stone of Sketty," from a place of that name, it is supposed, overlooking Swansea Bay. A Welsh proverb expressive of arduous undertakings, runs " Like the labour at the Stone of Sketty."

must be destitute of feeling, dead to the Past, who does not feel impressed by these rude monuments of a dim antiquity. Like Mr. Borrow, in Spain, we always gaze with "reverence and awe on these piles where the first colonists of Europe offered their worship to the unknown God." The temples of more refined heathens have almost all crumbled into dust ; "not so, the Druids' stone : there it stands on the hill of winds, as strong and as freshly new as the day, perhaps thirty centuries back, when it was raised by means that are a mystery."

Most of the published accounts of Arthur's Stone are very inaccurate. It is about 14 feet long, 7 feet 2 inches in depth, and about 6 feet and a half at its greatest breadth, but it has once been considerably broader, as some pieces have been broken off for millstones, for which they are unfitted, being composed of the common "pudding stone." On the west or perpendicular side, a large flat piece nearly 30 feet in circumference, and more than three feet thick, hollowed below, lies prostrate. It had, we heard, been partly broken off by wedges, but the idea was abandoned. The elements did the rest. About thirty years ago, the mass fell in the place where it now lies, after a severe frost and rapid thaw. The weight of Arthur's Stone has been variously estimated : it is not less and probably more than 25 tons. When carelessly viewed, the stone apparently rests on nine stones, or uprights ; a recent work of some authority makes the number of actual supporters twelve ; A. J. Kempe, Esq., in an article in the 23rd vol. of the *Archæologia*, (pp. 420-425) affirms that there are eight perpendicular supporters in contact with the superincumbent mass ; but it actually only rests on *four* stones, one of which is at the south-west end, the other three,—the smallest of the whole and on which nearly all the weight falls— are below the centre. A close examination excites a feeling of insecurity, as the end stone only slightly touches its gigantic head. The other five uprights could not, surely, be placed where they stand for show ? The Cromlech, which is about eleven feet and a half high, stands in a large basin, so to speak, of rough stones, including large fragments, the circumference of which is about eighty yards. All these are composed of the *lapis molaris* which abounds on Cefyn Bryn. The name implies that this was the work of King Arthur, of whose fabulous exploits there are many traditions in Wales. There was formerly a celebrated Holy Well under the stone. Mr. Kempe remarks—" As we know that Druids consecrated groves, rocks, caves, lakes, and fountains to their superstitions, there is little doubt but Arthur's Stone was erected over one of their sacred springs : it afterwards became a place of adoration and prayer ; and as the adoration of the Virgin began in the darker ages, to vie with, if not altogether eclipse that of the Saviour of Mankind, the fountain obtained the name [in Welsh] of Our Lady's Well." There was an old and absurd tradition in the neighbourhood that this fountain ebbed and flowed with the tide, which has been adopted by many topographical writers. There must have been a well here once, and there may be a spring now ; but the water that appears below the stone seems little else than an accumulation after heavy rains, and which is said to dry up in hot summers. There are, however, we are told, " several mineral springs in the parish (Reynoldstone) to which medicinal properties are ascribed ; of these the most celebrated is 'Holy Well' [another] on the slope of Cefyn Bryn, to which in former times miraculous efficacy was attributed ; numbers drank the water, and according to an ancient custom, threw in a pin as a tribute of their gratitude."

Numerous other remains of a remote age exist on Cefyn Bryn. To the west of Arthur's Stone is a vast tumulus of stones, about 70 yards in circumference. To the south of this, an oval amphitheatrical depression in the earth, of regular form, surrounded with small stones, may be seen ; with an entrance on the western side. There is another large tumulus to the north-west ; a large lozenge-shaped stone ; a small circle ; many *carneddau*. On the eastern slope of the hill on which Arthur's Stone stands are the remains of a rock circle, numerous *carneddau*, and a crescent-shaped elevation : we traced also for some distance on the east, what seemed to be a *sacra via*, or path leading to the great Cromlech.—At the eastern end of Cefyn Bryn, overlooking Penmaen, are four large heaps of stones, or *carneddau*, one of huge size, called the Beacon, and vestiges of two others.—On the right hand side of the road, in proceeding from Stouthall to Llandewy, there is a Druidical stone about half the size of Arthur's Stone, standing upright in a field. .

ANCIENT ENCAMPMENTS AND ENTRENCHMENTS abound in Gower. The most important are, 1. an entrenched Camp, originally British, subsequently Roman, on the north-eastern end of *Llanmadoc Hill*, over the village of that name. It is called by the people there, "the round O," that letter imperfectly describing the form of the largest or eastern entrenchment; but a ground plan, which we have taken, exhibits a species of praetorium, and triple ramparts, covering at least four acres. This must have been a very important station; it commanded the entrance to the Burry River, and overlooked Gower and part of Carmarthenshire.— 2. A large camp on *Rhosilly Down*, rather more than a mile from Rhosilly village.—3. Another camp on *Harsden Down.*—4. *Califer*, or *Cil Ivor Hill*, to the east of Llanridian; strongly intrenched, it is believed, by Ivor ap Cadivor, a chief of Morganwg, in 1110, when the English had not obtained firm hold of Gower. The name signifies "Ivor's retreat."—5. Vestiges of intrenchments on *Cefyn Bryn.*—6. *Manselfold*, a strong intrenchment, apparently erected as a protection to Webley Castle.—7. A *British camp* on the rocks above the Caves of Paviland.

ROMAN ANTIQUITIES. The keep of Castle Lloughor occupies the site of a Roman station on the *Via Julia*—the *Leucarum* of Antoninus. Many coins and other antiquities have been found in the neighbourhood. At the Pengwern limestone quarries, near Lythrid (in the neighbourhood of the Gower Inn), upwards of 200 small silver coins of the Roman Emperors, from Nero to Marcus Aurelius, were discovered in the year 1823; and several brass and silver Roman coins have been found at and near Oystermouth.

CASTLES. The chief fortifications are the castles of Swansea, Oystermouth, Pennard, Penrice, Oxwich, Landymor (or Bovehill), Webley, and Lloughor; and there are slight traces at Llandewy, where there are earthworks, and at Scurlage Castle, a mile beyond Llandewy. The Normans and Flemings could not have kept their ground against the highlanders on the north, without this chain of defences. There is *no allusion* to any of the Gower Castles, except

Swansea, in the Essay in the *Cymmrodorion Transactions*, from
which we have elsewhere quoted.

Oystermouth Castle is one of the most majestic Norman
fortresses in the Principality, although but little appreciated until
very recently.   The structure, which stands upon a picturesque
eminence near the Mumbles, was so much hidden by ivy that its
outlines were hardly distinguishable — a mere shapeless mass of
ruin ; and the interior was also so much filled with rubbish as to
destroy its character.   In the year 1843, Mr. Francis, of Swansea,
who thoroughly appreciated the place, induced the Duke of Beaufort, to whom it belongs, to expend a small sum in repairs and
restorations.   It is said that only £200 has been expended, and
although more might be judiciously laid out, still the work of
dilapidation has been arrested, and a very fine example of medieval
military architecture disclosed.   Mr. Francis, under whose superintendence the restoration has been effected, has proved that a
large outlay is not required in cases of this kind—a valuable fact.

The foundation of Oystermouth Castle has been ascribed both
to Henry Beaumont, Earl of Warwick—the conqueror of Gower
—and to Richard de Granville, one of Fitzhamon's knights, and
the founder of the Castle and Abbey of Neath.   Before the invention of artillery this fortress must have been of great strength.
The north side is the most stately, and is pierced with more
windows than is common ; a lofty line of ramparts, with loops,
but destitute of bastions, is carried along the edge of the rock
that composes the site and influences the form of the structure,
throughout the west and south side, to the grand entrance at the
south-east end, which was strongly defended by towers and portcullises.   The chapel, the walls of which are of great thickness,
but which is the most elegant feature of the ruin, stands at the
north-east end, and is of later date than any of the other parts.
The mullions and tracery of the windows (which were until lately
walled up), have been restored ; and in the interior a piscina and
some frescoes have been brought to light in the upper part of the
south wall.   Topographers have hitherto called the chapel "the
keep."   The stately hall—an immense kitchen—and a guard
room, the roof of which is supported by a single pillar, styled by

the guide "the whipping post,"—have been also divested of rubbish and rendered accessible during the recent repairs ; the kitchen was choked with rubbish six feet deep.　There are few ruins more graceful and yet more commanding in effect than Oystermouth Castle ; it is one of those places which the oftener you view or inspect it, the more it interests you.—A guide, who lives at Norton, is in attendance at the gateway to conduct visitors over the ruin.

𝔓𝔢𝔫𝔫𝔞𝔯𝔡 𝔠𝔞𝔰𝔱𝔩𝔢 is romantically situated on a rock, at the edge of an elevated region of sandhills, overlooking a wild " pill," and the fine scenery of Oxwich Bay.　It is a rude British structure of considerable magnitude, and has been slightly altered by the Normans.　Its history is a blank.　The country people aver that it was raised in one night by enchantment, and that the neigh-bourhood was overwhelmed with sand, blown over from Ireland, in the same short space of time !　Perhaps the disaster occurred when Kenfig was destroyed.　In the fifteenth and sixteenth cen-turies, the coast of this county, and of North Cornwall, suffered much from an accumulation of sand, and in 1553, an Act was passed " touching the sea-sands in Glamorganshire."　Traces of a church can be discovered near Pennard Castle, and foundations of buildings in other parts of the sandhills; a hamlet near is called the South-gate, and an adjoining farm the North-town.—The *Draba aizoides*, a very rare plant, found nowhere else in Britain, grows on the walls of this castle, and on high cliffs and inac-cessible places on the coast from Pennard to Worm's Head.　The discovery is of rather late date.

𝔓𝔢𝔫𝔯𝔦𝔠𝔢 𝔠𝔞𝔰𝔱𝔩𝔢 occupies a rock in Penrice Park, and possesses a good Norman entrance.　This fine ruin is much hidden by ivy, and converted into stables and a laundry !　We believe that it is of British origin, but the chief portion was probably built by the Earl of Warwick, the great castle-builder of these parts.　The Mansels became the possessors of the property in the reign of Henry V.　In 1750, the estates of the family in this district passed, in default of heirs male, "to the second son of Mary, youngest daughter of Sir Thomas, afterwards Lord Mansel, who married John Ivery Talbot, Esq., of Lacock Abbey, Wiltshire."

𝕺𝖗𝖜𝖎𝖈𝖍 𝕮𝖆𝖘𝖙𝖑𝖊 apppears to be almost wholly unknown to topographers. Even the usually accurate Malkin, from whose book a dozen other works have been vamped, states that " a fine Gothic window is nearly all that remains of Oxwich Castle." We were, therefore, agreeably surprised to find a structure of considerable extent, and great interest ; one of the best examples of the transition from the castle to the castellated mansion. We

give a sketch of the eastern elevation of the tower, which is of keep-like dimensions, divided into six stories, and lighted on three sides by numerous round-headed windows, irregularly placed. There are the remains of only two fire places visible in the interior. The adjoining state apartments were sumptuous, and are externally in tolerable preservation. On the south side of the court-yard is a range of ancient buildings, now occupied as a farm house, of interesting character : the entrance to the court-yard is under a fine Tudor doorway, over which is carved the arms of the Mansels, in very perfect preservation, with the initials R. M. The north side of the court-yard has been destroyed. The ruins, like Mr. Talbot's other castles, are in a sad state.—In the chancel of Oxwich church is an altar tomb, with the recumbent effigies of a knight and lady, said to be those of the founder of the castle and his wife.—There is a ruined outpost, probably of an earlier castle on an adjoining rock.

Landymor Castle (called by the country people Bovehill from the farm in which it is situated), stands on the side of a hill, overlooking a little valley and hamlet near Cheriton. The remains chiefly consist of a rude curtain wall, but foundations are to be traced as far as a bold rock which overlooks the Burry, which prove that the edifice must once have been of an important character. The inscription on the monumental brass in Swansea church shows that the Duke of Norfolk conveyed this castle and manor to Sir Hugh Johnys in the first half of the fifteenth century. On the death of Sir Hugh, which took place before 1461, John, third Duke of Norfolk, was the owner. It then passed into the hands of the Earl of Pembroke, who sold it with two or three other manors to one of the Mansels, an ancestor of Mr. Talbot, the present possessor.

Webley Castle stands about a mile to the east of Landymor, and is, next to Oystermouth, the most interesting Norman structure in Gower. The late Mr. Rees Jones was of opinion that this and Landymor castles " were built to protect the country from any invasion which might be made on it through the only passes into Gower on this side, from the river Lloughor." This castle, like Oxwich, is hardly mentioned by any topographer. It is said to have belonged to the De la Beres, from whom it came into the hands of Lord Mansel. A small outlay would preserve this elegant and finely-situated ruin from impending destruction. The castle has been battered, and to a considerable extent destroyed or injured, on the land or south side. Many balls and an arrow-head have been found in the " leaguer " field near.

Lloughor Castle, or Castell Llychwr—the Roman *Leucarum* —which consists of little more than the shell of a small keep, occupies a mound in a village picturesquely seated on the shore of the Burry. This place was the scene of many terrible struggles between the Welsh and their invaders. Some writers say that it was once called *Tre Avane* (Beaver,) from the number of Beavers which were found in the neighbouring rivers.

CARMARTHENSHIRE.

The history of Carmarthenshire is full of picturesque materials.
The ancient princes of South Wales made a noble and successful
stand against Norman aggression ; for although superior in refined
" arts of war," the haughty conquerors of Glamorgan and part
of Pembroke were baffled by the bull-dog courage, skill in strategy,
and activity of their Welsh foes, who were adepts in Guerilla
warfare, had inaccessible hills at their back, and were anything
but despisable soldiers in the open field.   England was never able
to maintain a firm hold of this portion of Wales until the commencement of the sixteenth century, shortly before which Henry
VII. owed his crown to the assistance of the celebrated Sir Rhys
ap Thomas, a Carmarthenshire man, who is said to have slain the
" hump-backed tyrant " on the field of Bosworth.   The people
of this county have to a certain extent maintained their ancient
" isolation " from their neighbours on the east and west ; national
prejudices, old customs, linger ; the manners of the peasantry are
not so pleasing as in the " English" counties of Wales, and
farming is not so well understood, although much good has been
done by the establishment of Agricultural Societies, which are
well supported.   Vast tracts of land lie waste, or yield a niggardly
produce, which might be easily fertilized by efficient draining.
The county forms part of the great coal field of South Wales, and
contains a variety of mineral productions, of which the chief are
bituminous and stone coal, and iron stone.   The soils in the clay
and grauwacké slate and coal tracts are for the most part of a
rather poor quality ; but in the valleys there is much good land,
especially in the neighbourhood of the sea, and the banks of the
long vales of the Towy and the Tâf are usually very fertile.   The
small of the stone coal, which is the chief mineral of the county,
is called culm, and when mixed with clay, forms, when dried, in
the shape of balls, the principal fuel of the inhabitants.   The
northern outcrop of carboniferous limestone which surrounds the
South Wales coal field crosses the county in a waving line east
and west, appears along the coast at the northern end of Carmarthen Bay, and divides the coal field into two sections.   This

limestone forms valuable manure, and is easily burnt with culm. There is a small strip of old red sandstone which bounds the coal and limestone districts on the north, widening as it approaches Brecknockshire, which is mainly composed of it.

The antiquarian has a wide field for observation in Carmarthenshire, which has been imperfectly explored. The chief Druidical antiquities that have been hitherto discovered are in the parishes of Lanboidy, Convil in Elvet, Eglws Newydd, and Penboyr. Many traces of the Romans have been found, including very early coins. The *Via Julia Maritima* ran through the county, part of *Dimetia,* passing Llanelly and Carmarthen—the route selected for the South Wales Railway. Two other Roman roads joined the *Maritima* at Carmarthen : the *Via Julia Montana* (or superior) which ran down the Vale of the Towy ; and the *Via Occidentalis* (one of the Welsh *Sarn Helen's)* the course of which may be traced distinctly in several parts of the parish of *Llanvair-ar-y-Bryn* towards Llanio *(Loventium,* in Cardiganshire.) There are the ruins of twelve castles in the county, two abbeys, Talley and Whitland, and three small religious houses.

Carmarthenshire is encircled with mountains on its northern and eastern frontiers, and the greater part of its surface is hilly. The Black Mountains on the east are the loftiest and boldest ; but they are often dreary and rarely sublime. The Carmarthenshire Van is the third mountain in South Wales. The irregular chain which stretches into Pembrokeshire on the northern side, overlooking part of the Vale of the Tivy, is an extension of the vast group which forms a " sea " of hill tops to the north of Llandovery, running upwards through Cardiganshire towards Plinlimmon.

There are many rivers and torrents flashing through deep glens. The principal is the Towy, which rises in a large morass in the wilds of Cardiganshire, near the Brecknock border, enters Carmarthenshire, near Ystradffin, and in its course through the centre of the county to Carmarthen embraces many tributaries, the chief of which are the Dulais, the Cothy (25 miles long), the Gwilly, the Brân, the Sawddy, and the Cennen. The other chief rivers are the Tâf or Tave (28 miles long, with considerable tributaries), the Lloughor, the Gwendraeth Vawr, and, last not least, the Tivy, which forms the northern boundary of the county, from Lampeter to a point about-half-way between Newcastle-Emlyn and Cardigan. Most of the Carmarthenshire rivers abound with salmon, sewin—for both which the Towy is celebrated—trout, eels, &c.

Population in 1801, 67,317; in 1831, 100,740; in 1841, 106,326. Parliamentary representation: two members for the county; one for Carmarthen and Llanelly. Number of parishes (in diocese of St. David's), 76. Area, 974 square miles, 623,360 acres. Assizes held at Carmarthen. Educational statistics in 1847: 179 day schools, attended by 7,191 scholars; number of scholars in Church Sunday schools, 2,777; in Dissenting Sunday schools, 24,371.

Carmarthenshire, although the largest of the Welsh counties, possesses an insignificant coast line compared with its neighbours. The sea-shore scenery from the Towy eastward along the northern side of the Burry River, chiefly consists of sandhills; but it improves much towards the westward, the coast being deeply indented by the rivers Towy and Tâf; and as you advance, headlands, wooded dingles, and distant villages, give animation to the prospect.

CARMARTHEN BAY. A noble bay, the largest in this channel, with good anchorage, and an important shelter for shipping near the westerly extremity, in Caldy Island, which forms a natural breakwater—a refuge from all but easterly winds. The width between the Worm's Head and Giltar Point, near Tenby, is about fifteen nautical miles, and much exceeds the depth, which, to the entrance of the Carmarthen River, is about half that distance. The sea abounds with most varieties of fish found on our shores; but the fishery has, until of late years, been strangely neglected. At Carmarthen, in other respects one of the cheapest places in Wales, fish, until the year 1846, when the inhabitants started a joint stock fishing company for their own supply, was scarce and dear. Within the sweep of this bay are the ports of Tenby, Saundersfoot, Carmarthen, and Llanelly. The north-eastern portion consists of an extensive flat and a dangerous sand bank, called Cefyn Sidan, stretches for about six miles to the east of the Towy, the entrance to which river is impeded by a bar, over which there is 14 feet of water at half-flood.

THE BURRY RIVER. This estuary, which should be seen when the tide is in, is three miles wide at its entrance at Whitford Point, but the southern or principal channel for shipping, which is well buoyed, is not more than three-quarters of a mile wide. There is, on Burry Bar, a depth of six feet at low spring ebbs ; ordinary spring tides rise about 30 feet perpendicular—ordinary neaps about 12 or 14 feet. Pont ar Dulais, the head of the estuary, is 14 miles from Whitford ; and there is, in springs, depth of water for vessels of 200 or 300 tons as far as Lloughor.

WRECKING.

[In our first edition we gave some details relative to wrecking on the coast of Carmarthenshire, the accuracy of which has been impugned by an intelligent Welsh newspaper, the *Carmarthen Journal*, and also in a private communication with which we have been favoured. We have therefore felt it our duty to institute some further inquiries into the subject, the replies to which substantially confirm our statements, but our correspondents mention that a better feeling has sprung up amongst the sea-shore people ; that the population along the coast has increased considerably; and that the practice of lighting fires to entrap vessels has ceased for years. One correspondent, well acquainted with the coast, states that on the occasion of the second wreck on the Cefyn Sidan Sands which we describe, he saw people at middle day waiting with sacks to secure whatever might be cast ashore. These persons were no doubt much more active *at night*. Our remarks appear to have been somewhat misinterpreted: we meant them to apply to a certain class of the coast population—a class that exists in great force on the shores of Cornwall and North Devon, where wrecking is as lightly thought of as smuggling. We have no doubt that many persons on the Carmarthenshire coast have kindly extended succour to the shipwrecked, and guarded property cast ashore: a correspondent mentions (March, 1848), that " there are not people more ready to render assistance to vessels in distress than the people of Kidwelly and the Ferryside. On the occasion of the last wreck that occurred on Cefyn Sidan sands, the boatmen of the Ferryside were out all night in the bay in an open boat endeavouring to reach the wreck, and did eventually save the crew, and that without fee or reward, and in every instance within my recollection the same conduct has been pursued." We may add that we resided on the coast of South Wales when the wreck of the French West Indiaman that we have described took place ; and that the circumstances were notorious at the time.]

Q

The Cefyn Sidan Sands have been fatal to many a mariner. Ships sometimes bump upon them and get off; but some noble vessels, which have either got out of their reckoning or run into this bay for shelter, have here met with destruction. In November, 1828, a large French West Indiaman, from Martinique, struck on these sands, and went to pieces. Amongst the passengers was a niece of Josephine Buonaparte, whose fingers had been cut off to secure some rings. A very rich booty fell into the hands of the wreckers, who set all authority at defiance. An English vessel of 700 tons was lost nearly at the same place in 1843, under equally melancholy circumstances. We have been told that several of the bodies were still warm—almost breathing—when first cast ashore, but that no attempt was made to reanimate them. The captain had received £1,775 for freight, which the wreckers are said to have secured.

> " What knells for breaking hearts these waves have tolled !
> Eternal partings sob in this low roar."

The infamous system of exhibiting *false* lights used to be most ingeniously carried out on dark and stormy nights by the most abandoned class of wreckers : a horse, with two large lanterns provided with reflectors, was driven at a trot along the summit of the cliffs or high sandhills, so as to produce the effect of *a ship's light in motion* ; and thus lure perplexed vessels towards the shore. Our informant, who possesses an extensive acquaintance with the local shipping trade, informed us that this system has often succeeded. Another which has been practised here was termed " staking a man." After a wreck had occurred, those on the look out for plunder were often embarrassed with the extent of their riches, unable to carry off half they could wish. So when a number of dead bodies have been found upon the sand, it has been a common practice to take a body which there was not time to plunder and strip, and throw it into a pool, securing it to a stake which was carried for the purpose, by a rope, until an opportunity occurred of completing the " job." These were of course the practices of desperate wreckers, who had become thoroughly hardened by association and habit ; but there is another and a larger class on the Welsh—especially in eastern Glamorganshire—as well as on the English coasts of this channel, men who esteem it "no harm" to pick up property cast ashore, or even to plunder a vessel, looking upon these occurrences as "God-sends." The change that has been made in the law regarding wrecking* of late years does not appear to check the practice.

REBECCA.

The "Rebecca Insurrection" originated in Carmarthenshire, a circumstance which throws some light on the character of the people, who are true scions of the old stock. This outbreak, which commenced in 1843, and was at its height throughout 1844, is one of the most romantic incidents in our modern history, and appears rather to belong to the middle ages than the nineteenth century. For some months "Rebecca" pursued her lawless practices almost unchecked; a mob of about 600, nearly all of whom were mounted, used to assemble near St. Clear's, to the west of Carmarthen, under the guidance of a mysterious "tall man" and make nightly "frays" against the turnpike gates throughout the county, which were no sooner rebuilt than again destroyed. The proceedings were summary: "My children," asked the leader in Welsh, "this gate has no business here, has it!" This unnecessary question was of course answered with a shout, and in an incredibly short time the affrighted toll-keeper saw his dwelling a ruin, and his gates broken to pieces. Rewards were offered by the authorities in vain. Not a syllable of information was picked up which could be legally available—the whole of

* It is enacted by the 1st Victoria, c. 87, sec. 8, that " whoever shall plunder or steal any part of any ship or vessel which shall be in distress, or wrecked, stranded, or cast on shore, or any goods, merchandize, or articles of any kind belonging to such ship or vessel, on being convicted thereof shall be liable, at the discretion of the Court, to be transported beyond the seas for any term not exceeding 15 years nor less than 10 years, or to be imprisoned for any term not exceeding three years." Offences committed on the beach, in any creek or between high and low water-mark, may be dealt with as any other felony committed in a county; but in case the vessel should be surrounded with water, the felony is committed on the high seas, and therefore comes within the jurisdiction of the Court of Admiralty, in London.

the people seemed sworn to secresy. The contagion spread rapidly into the adjoining counties of Cardigan, Pembroke and Glamorgan : nearly the whole of South Wales was in a state bordering on insurrection ; and even when government sent detachments of " red-coats, " and higher rewards—more tempting baits—were offered to " traitors, " Rebecca kept her own counsel, and proceeded to more daring outrages. The military were harrassed nightly by false alarms ; Rebecca was like a will-o-th'-wisp, her followers spectre horsemen. At last, one of the " divisions " of the metropolitan police was sent to the aid of the soldiers. Their arrival evidently produced consternation amongst the insurgents, and some prisoners were made, but the only mode of preserving turnpike gates was by "garrisoning" them. When two morning newspapers sent "commissioners" down to investigate the nature of the alleged grievances, the leaders of the movement gained additional consequence. Matters gradually became more serious. The destruction of turnpike gates was succeeded by attacks on dwelling houses, by incendiarism, threats of murder—Rockite practices—including the murder of an old woman, a gate-keeper, at Hendy, under circumstances of great atrocity. An extravagant manifesto of "grievances" was put forth, almost revolutionary in its tone. No man slept safely in his bed. A riotous mob of many thousand persons on horse and foot, partly disciplined, entered Carmarthen in broad day, with the avowed intention of destroying the workhouse there—Rebecca waged war against Union Workhouses—of enacting the Frost or Chartist tragedy on a smaller scale. Had not a detachment of dragoons, which had made forced marches, galloped into the town in the midst of the meleé, it is difficult to say to what lengths the mob might have gone, after they had " tasted blood " by burning the workhouse. Some important prisoners were now made. Policemen and soldiers scoured the country, and we have heard stories of chases and escapes, more romantic than those of fiction.

A circumstance occurred in Cardiganshire which manifested, in a striking manner, the resolution of the Rebeccaites. A weir on the river Tivy, at Llechwryd, a few miles above Cardigan, had long been a bone of contention between the fishermen and people of the adjoining country, and the owner. It precluded salmon with which the river below swarmed, from ascending, and so inflicted an injury on a long line of country above. Rebecca in vain insisted on its removal. At four o'clock one morning, about 400 men, provided with crow-bars, pick-axes, and other instruments, assembled at the weir ; and in two hours demolished the whole of the strong massive erection, doing in that short time work that would have employed a considerable body of men for weeks under ordinary circumstances. They "worked with a will." The result of this act, for which, we believe, the owner obtained compensation from the county, has been most beneficial to the river : in the month of June, 1845, we heard when out on a fishing excursion that numbers of fine salmon were taken at and above Lampeter, many miles upwards.

This strange outbreak at length began to die away. The people gradually returned to their senses when they found that it was in vain to resist the strong arm of the law, and that there was a disposition to remedy proved abuses. Two of the ringleaders, who were found guilty and sentenced to transportation, made, when in Carmarthen gaol, full confessions, implicating many farmers and others in a respectable position. These men, who bore the names of *Shoni-scybor-fawr*, and *Dai-y-Cantwr*, mentioned an extraordinary circumstance, which can hardly be true, that it was the opinion—not of individuals—but of a large neighbourhood, that William Chambers, jun., Esq., of Llanelly, an active magistrate, *ought to be shot !*

The ignorance of the Rebeccaites was great ; and to the disclosures relative to the state of education in Wales, which were elicited by the inquiries made during the progress of the insurrection, the subsequent educational movement must be mainly attributed. We traversed the Rebecca country a few months after peace had been restored, and were assured that in the ruder districts a change had been effected in the character of the people, especially in Cardiganshire, which was likely to lead to beneficial results. Prejudices against the "foreigners" (English) had been broken down, and improved customs had sprung up.

EXCURSION FROM SWANSEA TO CARMARTHEN.

In the year 1833 a wooden bridge was constructed across the Burry at the ancient ferry of Lloughor, in consequence of which the stream of traffic from Swansea to the westward was mainly diverted from the old mail coach-road to Carmarthen by *Pont-ar-dulais* (a good fishing station) about five miles higher up. On crossing the bridge you enter Carmarthenshire, leave large copper works at Spitty on your right, and after a flat and dreary ride of five miles, reach a region of collieries, and arrive at

LLANELLY,

a thriving sea port, 11 miles from Swansea, the seat of copper and iron works, and the outlet of one of the most important coal districts in South Wales, which offers no attraction to the tourist, although a place of great antiquity. Its rise has been rapid. The Commissioners of the Burry Navigation, who are engaged in a Chancery suit with the Crown, recently gave the following sketch :—" In 1813, when the first Harbour Act was obtained, Llanelly was little better than an estuary, with a limited coal trade, and unsafe for loaded vessels exceeding 100 tons burthen to resort to. About that time a copper-work having been erected, a regular import trade of copper ore was established, which, with the prospect of an increased coal trade, induced the interests of the port to commence forming a harbour and docks of shelter, and to obtain an Act of Parliament, under the powers of which the commissioners formed a large breakwater to the west or sea-side of the docks, and proper rules and regulations were made for the government of pilots, buoyage, and layers. The trade increased in 1831 to 816 vessels, and 53,844 tons of exports and imports in that year. In 1840, to 1,592 vessels, and 115,792 tons ; and in 1845, to 2,061 vessels, and 140,990 tons." Vessels of 600 or 700 tons now regularly trade here ; and much coal is exported for steam purposes. The exports of coal from the harbour of Llanelly alone amounted in 1847 to 166,614 tons ; 28,370 tons of copper ore were imported, and 3,114 tons of copper exported in the same year. Out of 12,146 vessels that entered

the port between the years 1833 and 1843, only four were seriously
injured or lost.—The chimney of the Cambrian Copper Works,
231 feet high, is visible at Tenby and other places still more
distant. Population in 1841, 11,155.

About four miles from Llanelly the road to Kidwelly crosses
the lofty ridge called Pembrey Hill. The view from hence
embraces Gower, Carmarthen Bay, the Bristol Channel, and
extensive home views, particularly the wide vale of the Gwendraeth Vawr to the north-east. This ridge terminates in a low
promontory—hence the Welsh name *Pen-bre*—near the entrance
of the Burry River, at the edge of which is the commodious and
well sheltered artificial Harbour of BURRY PORT or PEMBREY
(three miles and a half from Llanelly), capable of holding eighty
sail of large coasters, and possessing an excellent depth of water.
It was constructed by a company in 1819, and a very large coal
trade was once carried on. A canal connects this place with
the Kidwelly and Llanelly Canal.

In consequence of the introduction of the iron trade on a large
scale in the Gwendraeth and other vales, Burry Port is likely to
become a place of some consequence. In the year 1846, 1,758
tons of pig-iron were shipped here. The following is a list of
the iron works connected with the port : the Gwendraeth, three
furnaces; the Trymsarm, two furnaces ; in Anman Vale, Mr.
Llewellyn's works contain six furnaces ; those of the Worcestershire Company three furnaces ; and there is also another new work
with two furnaces ; in all sixteen furnaces.

The road descends rapidly from Pembrey Hill to the flat
dreary region below, in the midst of which stands

KIDWELLY.

Distant from	Miles.	Distant from	Miles.
Carmarthen, by road	.. .. 10½	Llanelly 9	
Ferryside 5		Swansea 20	

Our first impressions of this old world place were strong. We
reached the hill on the Ferryside road that overlooks it, wearied
with travel, on a calm June evening. The slanting beams of the
fast-descending sun gave depth of shadow to an august feudal
castle, with " nodding towers " and ramparts apparently so

perfect that you *missed* the sentinels.   Below the structure nestled
a small and irregularly-built town in the midst of a vast marshy
flat, with a fine church and lofty spire—a sea-mark for many
miles.—We spied out the "Pelican," and entered a quaintly-
furnished parlour that had apparently seen better days, hung with
smoke-dried pictures—a place for Washington Irving to dream
in.   The town bore evident marks of decay.   There were many
old houses in the Flemish style, in ruins—a people that seemed
to have nothing to do but to gaze at the strangers.

There is an Old and a New Town, divided by the river Gwendraeth Vach, which was once navigable for vessels of burden;
but owing to the encroachment of sand, only a few small craft—
including occasional pleasure boats from Tenby—can now find
their way up the poor muddy creek that forms a streak in the
intervening salt marsh between the town and the sea outside.—
Kidwelly is said to have been once a place of commercial importance, but this must have been subsequently to the sixteenth
century.   Hear Leland : " The old town is prettily waullid and
hath hard by the waul a castel ; the old town is near all desolated,
but the castel is meatly well kept up."   The fortifications of the
town have chiefly disappeared, although tolerably perfect fifty
years ago.   In 1766 docks were constructed, and some time afterwards a canal ; then tin-works, which still exist.

The Church, a large cruciform structure, formerly attached to
a Benedictine priory, merits much more notice than we can
bestow upon it.   The transepts are almost in ruins, and the
edifice has suffered many other grievous dilapidations.   It was
dedicated to the Virgin Mary, a figure of whom stands over the
entrance.   There are also a monumental effigy of a priest—probably a prior—with an illegible inscription, and other antiquities.

Now to the Castle !   The person to whom the key is entrusted
lived out of the town, and although sent for, did not make his
appearance.   It was the grey of the evening.   As we walked
below the walls, and lamented the injuries sustained by the great
gateway—now blocked up—Dr. Johnson's observation to Boswell
came into our mind, that "one of the Castles in Wales would
contain all that he had seen in Scotland."   The situation of the

fortress was admirably chosen, the Gwendraeth forming a sort
of natural moat round two sides. We gazed upwards to the
graceful ruin of the Early English Chapel, which breaks the line
of defence on the east ; we admired the union of elegance with
massiveness—walls which seem to bid defiance to time, pierced
with light trefoil-headed windows. Then, the towers. There are
four round towers, each the size of a donjon, besides the enormous towers which flank the chief entrance. A half moon cast
an exquisite light over the stately ruin, as we stood at the northern end, where a modern gate, 25 feet high, has been placed to
shut out intruders. This obstacle excited our ardour. We scaled
it, and entered the court yard, the extent of which was not visible
through the gloom. Bats whizzed about, and two white owls,
disturbed by our presence, flapped across us, sailing up and down
in the moonshine over the ramparts, and whooping mournfully.
We went stealthily onward through this court into another, from
which it is divided by a tower and walls of great strength. The
hour—the death-like stillness—the solitude—the darksomeness
and depth—the fear of falling into some yawning dungeon (we
narrowly escaped one) were indescribably thrilling. We started.
Two large white objects moved from us, in the dim and spectral
light...bah ! they are only horses. What a moment for a superstitious man ! Another court ; divided, too, by towers and walls
more ponderous than those we had left behind. So the garrison
had three strings to their bow—a succession of defences of immense
strength. And, now regardless of danger, as if under the impulse
of a spell, we found our way up broken staircases and winding
passages—explored the interior of the great gateway towers,
lighted with loop-holes, through which the moon cast rays that
far surpassed the best effects of Cattermole. An hour passed
we knew not how. The increased elevation of the moon gave
distinctness to the outlines, which looked under that light gigantic
beyond anything we had ever recollected in military architecture.
—We once more scaled the gates, sauntered long on the pleasaunce on the northern side—once the resort of courtly dames
and high-born cavaliers—and departed with the conviction that
justice has not yet been done by pen or pencil to Kidwelly.

The history of such a fortress ought to be interesting, yet but little is known.

Three years after the conquest of Glamorgan, William de Londres invaded this district, built a castle of greath strength, and fortified the town with walls. At this time Rhys, Prince of South Wales, a youth, was in Ireland, and his mother, Gwellian, a true heroine, accompanied by her two younger sons, marched like another Catherine of Anjou on Kidwelly, near which, at a spot still called "the field of the grave of Gwellian," a fierce encounter took place between the Welsh and Norman troops. De Londres was victorious ; his fair foe fell with one of her sons, and the other was taken prisoner. One of the towers of Kidwelly Castle is still called Twr Gwellian. The castle is said by Powel to have been " rebuilt " in 1190, by Rhys ap Griffith, but we entertain no doubt that part of the original structure remains, and that the chapel and the greater portion of the existing ruins were added by Maurice de Londres, a descendant of the founder, into whose hands Kidwelly fell in the thirteenth century. After undergoing many sieges and vicissitudes, it became the property of the Duke of Lancaster by marriage, and was granted by Henry VII., who was entertained here, to Sir Rhys ap Thomas. On the forfeiture of Sir Rhys's grandson, the Vaughans of Golden Grove became the possessors, whose estates were left by the last male heir to the late Lord Cawdor. We respectfully urge Earl Cawdor to carefully preserve this fine national monument, the great entrance of which might be restored at a moderate cost.

FERRYSIDE. The road to this pretty little watering place is a good country lane, which runs near high land in front of a tract bounded by lofty sand-hills that stem the force of the sea—an extension of the Kidwelly flat to the entrance of the Carmarthen river. Ferryside has hitherto been only known to a few—it is the "bathing place" of the people of Carmarthen and the "interior," to whom it presents many recommendations in the beauty of its situation, the purity of its air, the extent of its sands, the number of its excursions, and last not least, its cheapness. There are no artificial excitements ; and all who consider

the pure and enjoyable influences of nature insipid ought not to
venture here.   This quiet retreat by the sea-side has been invaded
by the South Wales Railway, which has, in local estimation, at
the time we write, much injured it as a watering-place.   The view
of Llanstephan Castle, across the river, at full tide, ought to make
the fortune of Ferryside.   INN—The White Lion.

One of the great pursuits at Ferryside is cockle fishing.   Very
large quantities of cockles are taken on this coast ; and hundreds
of the country people go out far on the sands, and amongst brine
pools, with donkeys, in search of them.   The fish bury themselves in the sand, and are discovered by a small bubbling, occasioned by their breathing.   On the day before the steamer sails
for Bristol, 800 or 1,000 people are often seen on these and the
Llaugharne sands seeking for cockles.

Ferryside is not on the main road to Carmarthen, the nearest
way to which is by Llanstephan, across the ferry, from whence
the road runs ·near the western side of the river ; distance eight
miles.   There was, however, when we visited the place, a daily
tide boat from Carmarthen, commanded by one " Admiral Betty,"
a local character, whose Amazonian proportions would have
charmed the old Dutch painters, and who had been on the station nearly half a century.   The voyage is fifteen miles to Carmarthen Quay, and the scenery of the river Towy, along the eastern
bank of which the railway runs, is pleasing but nowhere grand.

CARMARTHEN.

Distant from				Miles.	Distant from				Miles.
Bristol, by Steam	..	..	..	138	Laugharne	..	..	..	12½
Brecon ..	..	..	..	49	Newcastle Emlyn	..	..	..	20
Cardigan	..	..	..	30	Pembroke	..	..	..	32½
Ferryside	..	..	..	9	Pater ..	..	..	..	33
Haverfordwest	..	..	..	32	Pontardulais ..	..	..	..	17
Kidwelly	..	..	..	10½	Swansea	..	..	..	26½
Llandilo Vawr	..	..	..	14¾	St. David's	..	..	..	47¼
Llandovery ..	..	..	..	29	St. Clear's	..	..	..	10
Lampeter	..	..	..	24	Tenby ..	..	..	..	26
Llanstephan ..	..	..	..	8					

VOYAGE BY STEAM.—A steamer from Bristol after landing

passengers, &c., at Tenby, usually goes on at once to Carmarthen (distance 30 miles, time three hours), but this depends upon tide and accidental circumstances, as it is sometimes necessary to remain at Tenby all night. The passage between Bristol and Carmarthen occupies fourteen or fifteen hours, including the stoppage. The vessel on its return calls again at Tenby, the run to which is a very charming one, thirteen miles river, and seventeen sea.

Carmarthen is very advantageously situated on irregular ground sloping to the river Towy, famed for salmon and sewin. The town was the *Maridunum* of the Romans, and *Caer-Merdin*, or Merlin's town of the Welsh, for it was the birth-place of that famous wizard and " prophet" in the fifth century. The Welsh princes dwelt here before the seat of royalty was removed to Dinevor, hence the town was considered the capital of all Wales, a distinction which was recognised after it was annexed to England as a Principality, the Exchequer and Mint being kept here. It was frequently attacked by the Normans, and also by the Princes of North Wales ; the Castle (which was built on the site of the Roman station) was often taken, sometimes besieged ineffectually ; the town was twice burnt, and its history for centuries presents a series of wild vicissitudes. The castle was dismantled by order of Parliament in 1648, and used as a prison ; and the chief portion that remained in 1787 was incorporated with a new county gaol, so that little is externally visible.

The " shells" of two priories are in existence, one of which was a cell to St. Augustine's, Bristol, and is tolerably perfect, particularly the gateway. The church of St. Peter, a structure of no architectural pretensions, ought to be visited for its monuments. The two recumbent figures on the north side of the chancel are monumental effigies of the great Sir Rhys ap Thomas and his lady, removed from the ancient priory church near at hand, now demolished, and which is said to have been their burial place. The gallant warrior is clothed in plate armour, with knightly insignia and heraldic honours ; but the dove at the feet of the gentle lady is a much more impressive emblem.

On the opposite side of the chancel is a grotesque female monumental figure, with a quaint and remarkable inscription :

> " A choice Elixar of Mortalitie,
>
> *   *   *   *   *
>
> Who by her loanes in spit of Aduerse fates,
> She did preserue Men's persons and Estates ;
> Would you then know who wen this good Woman
> Twas virtuous ANNE the Lady VAUGHAN."

The celebrated Sir Richard Steele is buried in a vault belonging to the Scurlock family, and the simple tablet which was erected here to his memory, in 1729, brings to mind many recollections. This eminent writer, after dissipating much of his fortune in the metropolis, retired to Wales for the purpose of passing the remainder of his days in literary ease, hoping by good management to partly retrieve his losses. Steele owed his property here to his wife, the only daughter and heiress of Jonathan Scurlock, Esq. ; and he appears to have lived partly at *Ty Gwyn* (the White House), the family seat, and at Carmarthen, at a house afterwards converted into the Ivy Bush Hotel, where he composed the comedy of "The Conscious Lovers," and other dramatic pieces and essays. His character was excellent, and he was greatly beloved.

A monument, which was erected to the memory of Sir Thomas Picton, at the western extremity of the town, on high ground, fell a few years ago into such a disgraceful state of dilapidation that it became necessary, in 1846, to pull it down. The base bore appropriate basso relievos, and supported a Doric column in the poor taste of Nash, at the top of which was a statue of the hero. A sum was subscribed to effect a restoration ; but after the old monument had been destroyed, the amount was found to be inadequate to erect anything more than an obelisk, which was completed in 1847. The gallant Picton was a native of and represented Carmarthen, and the Rev. Edward Picton has presented to the county an admirable likeness of his brother, by Sir M. A. Shee, which has been placed in the County Hall. The town also boasts of another military hero of equal renown, Sir William Nott, whose death here, after his return from the East, must be fresh

in recollection. About £1,300 was soon after subscribed for the
erection of a monument—a bronze statue on a granite pedestal—
the execution of which has been confided to Mr. Edward Davies,
a native of Carmarthenshire.

Great improvements have been made in Carmarthen, which is
about a mile in length, and half a mile in breadth ; some of the
streets, several of which are very narrow, have been partially
widened, and many good houses erected, but the pavements are
bad. The Guildhall is a well-designed modern structure. There
are commodious Markets. Amongst the institutions are a Free
Grammar School, founded by Dr. Owen, Bishop of St. David's,
in the seventeenth century ; a Presbyterian College, for the education of Dissenting ministers ; and an Infirmary. There are many
meeting-houses. Barracks enliven the dullness of the town, which
in winter is resorted to by several of the county families, so that
there is very good society. Ground was purchased in 1847 for
the erection of barracks for about 1,500 men, two miles from
Carmarthen, on the St. Clear's road.

The most important institution at Carmarthen is the Training
School for South Wales and Monmouthshire, established by the
Welsh Education Committee, a branch of the National Society.
Early in 1847, within a few months after the design had been
before the public, donations to the amount of about £3,000 had
been given to the Education Committee, and the annual subscriptions amounted to £2,500. It was resolved to found two institutions from this source, in North and South Wales. The foundation
of the latter was laid by the Bishop of St. David's on the 16th of
July, 1847, in the presence of 5,000 persons. Ten acres and a
quarter of ground have been purchased for the site ; and the
institution is designed to accommodate sixty students, a principal
and assistant masters. It includes a chapel, and practising or
Model Schools for the education of children. The estimate for the
cost of the buildings exceeded £8,000 ; and that for the annual
expenditure about £2,000. Education Boards, in connexion with
the Welsh Education Committee in London, have been formed in
the counties which are benefitted.

A Literary and Scientific Institution was established in 1846, at which lectures, which are well attended, are regularly given; classes have been formed for instruction.—At the meetings of the Carmarthenshire Agricultural Society, tenant farmers usually carry off the prizes.

The river remains in a state of nature, though capable of great improvement, and trade has been very much injured in consequence. Masters of ships are almost afraid of venturing up, the navigation is so seriously impeded by "dangerous banks and numerous sinuosities." The corporation have, however, lately had the river surveyed, and hopes are entertained that the natural advantages of the place will ultimately be fully developed. The quay extends for several hundred yards below the bridge; upwards of 50 vessels belong to the port.

The population between 1831 and 1841, declined from 9,995 to 9,526 persons; but there has since been a considerable increase. A few years ago there were a large number of unoccupied houses, but now there is great difficulty to meet with a house except in the worst situations in the town. The trade of Carmarthen is considerable, chiefly consisting of exports of agricultural produce, and imports of goods from Bristol and London: there are tin works. Markets, Wednesday and Saturday.

Carmarthen, in conjunction with Llanelly, returns one member to Parliament. The *Carmarthen Journal* and *Welshman* are published here. INNS—The Ivy Bush, and Boar's Head.

EXCURSIONS FROM CARMARTHEN.

CWM GWILLY—CARDIGAN.—The romantic defile of Cwm Gwilly, one of the finest in the Principality, has been altogether overlooked by writers on South Wales, in consequence of its being off the beaten track of tourists. The road which runs through it is, however, comparatively new; and we can promise those who wish to make an excursion of two or three days, in a country which abounds with varied scenery, very great gratification in a trip from Carmarthen to Cardigan. A mail coach starts daily from the Ivy Bush. You enter the pass of Cwm Gwilly at a point nearly opposite the Palace at Abergwilly, and ascend by the side of a playful mountain stream for many miles. Lofty hills rise

abruptly on either side of the narrow ravine, clothed with wood to
their summits, and often intersect each other at right angles.
In the parish of *Convil*, about seven miles from Carmarthen,
through which the road passes, there are many British antiquities,
including the fragments of one of the largest Cromlechs in Wales,
a remarkable earthwork called the Line, about 18 feet high and a
mile and a half long ; also a large British Camp. The ruin of the
first gate destroyed by Rebecca is passed in proceeding onward to
Newcastle-Emlyn, after which the road runs over wild mountain
tops, commanding prospects of great magnificence, extending to
the St. George's Channel beyond Cardigan. After this there is
a gradual descent to the picturesque town of NEWCASTLE-EMLYN,
where there is a small castle overhanging the Tivy, which was rebuilt by Sir Rhys ap Thomas. The river winds in a very singular
manner round the Castle Hill, and divides the town into two
parts ; the smallest portion, Atpar, is in Cardiganshire. INN—
The Salutation.

THE VALE OF THE TOWY,

Between Carmarthen and Llandilo Vawr—a distance of nearly
fifteen miles — abounds with beautiful scenery, and is famed in
song and story. A turnpike road runs on either side of the river ;
but the upper, or that to the north, is the most interesting.

Ty Gwyn, once the abode of Sir Richard Steele, stands near
the base of *Llangynyr Hill*, a little above Carmarthen, and is now
a farm house.   There is an exquisite prospect of the Vale of the
Towy from Llangynyr Church, which contains a monument to
the memory of Steele.   At *Abergwilly* (two miles) is the only
habitable episcopal palace of the Bishop of St. David's, sweetly
situated near the confluence of the Gwilly with the Towy.
MERLIN'S HILL, an eminence on the western side of a dell nearly
a mile and a half above the village of Abergwilly, is said to have
been the birthplace of the magician, and an opening in a rock
near the summit is styled *Merlin's chair*—the place from whence
he uttered his prophecies. The pedestrian tourist, on reaching
the hamlet of *Pont ar Cothy* (two miles further on), ought to walk
up the banks of that fine mountain stream the Cothy, in search
of the ruins of two castles of great antiquity ; the first situated

near the western bank of the river (two miles and a half up), the other about half a mile from the river on the eastern side, three miles higher up.   There is excellent angling in the Cothy, and its tributaries.   At a village called *Brechva*, 11 miles from Carmarthen, two fine brooks unite before joining the Cothy, in which, and in another brook higher up the mountains, there is an abundance of trout, although not of large size.   The artificial flies should be small.   The Towy now serpentises greatly for three or four miles.   A Tower erected by Sir William Paxton, to commemorate the death and services of the hero of Trafalgar, is a conspicuous object.   Further on to the right, on the main road, a short way beyond a little river, called the Dulais, *Dryslyn Castle* crowns an " insulated " green eminence near the western bank of the Towy, at a spot where the vale expands. The view from this hill stretches for nearly ten miles over a lovely country ; and the ruined fortress is very picturesque at a distance.   *Grongar Hill* rises at a little distance beyond Dryslyn to the eastward.

> " Grongar, in whose silent shade,
> For the modest Muses made,
> So oft I have, the evening still,
> At the fountain of a rill,
> Sat upon a flowery bed,
> With my hand beneath my head ;
> While strayed my eyes o'er Towy's flood,
> Over mead and over wood,
> From house to house, from hill to hill,
> Till contemplation had her fill."

It is said that the hawthorn under which Dyer* wrote the beautiful poem, of which these lines form a part, still exists here.   Traces of a Roman camp, thus quaintly described by Leland, are visible from the summit of this charming eminence :—" There is, within half a myle of Drislan Castel on Tewe, a myghtye campe of men

---

* Dyer was born in 1700, and was the second son of Robert Dyer, an eminent solicitor, at Aberglassney, near Llandilo Vawr.   He entered into holy orders rather late in life.

of Warre, with four or five diches, and an area in the middle."—
Golden Grove, on the opposite side of the river, is one of the chief
seats of the Earl of Cawdor.   During the civil troubles in Charles
the First's reign, the good Jeremy Taylor took refuge in an old
mansion that stood here until Golden Grove was built, and wrote
some of his most celebrated works ; this great divine was, however, much persecuted during Cromwell's day.   The beautiful
park of DYNEVOR is the great object of interest to the stranger on
approaching Llandilo Vawr, and is certainly one of the sweetest
places in Wales.   The boundary wall of the Park adjoins the
town, and several hours may be spent in the ruins of the ancient
castle, and in exploring the beauties of the scenery within the
grounds, which command some exceedingly exquisite distant
prospects.   According to Gilpin there are " few places where a
painter might study the inequalities of surface to more advantage."   Spenser sings of the " woody hills of Dynevor."   The
castle stands on a lofty eminence, and is more interesting from its
associations than its intrinsic beauty ; the chief features of the ruin
are a massive keep, an apartment called the Ladies' Dressing
Room, and a subterraneous passage.   The original form of the fortifications was circular ; and the natural strength of the position
was increased by a double moat.   The present castle replaced one of
greater antiquity, which was destroyed near the end of the twelfth
century ; and it was inhabited down to the year 1760, when a fire
destroyed all that was combustible.   This was the chief residence
from the year 877 of the Princes of South Wales ; Henry VII.
granted it to Sir Rhys ap Thomas, who was of regal descent.—
The modern mansion of Lord Dynevor, a large quadrangular
structure, is approached by an avenue of fine oaks and chesnuts,
at a considerable distance from the castle.   It contains, amongst
other objects of interest, two curious decorated chairs, which are
said to have been used by Sir Rhys ap Thomas, and are good
examples of furniture of the Tudor era.   The park is happily and
peculiarly situated, for the mountains in the neighbourhood cross
the country at right angles, and bound three vales, which each
possess a distinct character.   Grongar Hill, Dryslyn Castle,

Golden Grove, and Middleton Hall, can all be seen from the castle.

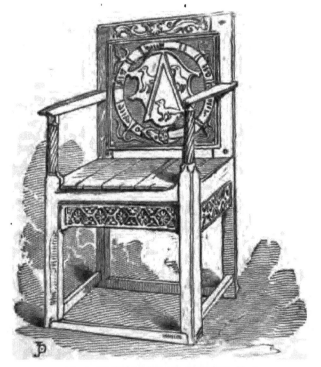

CHAIR OF SIR RHYS AP THOMAS, K. G.

LLANDILO VAWR.

Distant from				Miles.	Distant from				Miles.
Brecon	..	..	..	.. 35	Langadock	..	..	..	.. 7½
Carmarthen	..	..	..	.. 15	Pontardulais	..	..	..	.. 14
Llandovery	..	..	..	.. 14	Swansea..	..	..	..	.. 23
Lampeter	..	..	..	.. 17	Talley Abbey	..	..	..	.. 8

Llandilo, a small market town picturesquely situated on an eminence near the banks of the Towy, is a good central point for excursions. A great battle was fought in the vicinity in 1281, when the castle fell into the hands of Edward I. It was subsequently retaken for a short period.—The church, which is dedi-

R 2

cated to the celebrated British saint Teilo (whose baptistery, a well, may be seen in the churchyard) is a very ancient structure, with two of the lowest aisles in the kingdom. The parish is thirteen miles long and eight broad ; there were formerly four chapels of ease annexed to it, one of which exists at Llauduvaen, where there is a curious open quadrangular baptistery ; a new church was erected at Cwmaman in 1841. Population of the parish, 5,471 ; of the town, 1,313. Market, Saturday. INNS—The Cawdor Arms ; the King's Head.

Carreg or Caer Cennen Castle stands on an almost inaccessible rocky steep, amidst the Black Mountains, about three miles and a half from Llandilo. The road is steep and fatiguing. It is the beau ideal of the stronghold of a mountain chief—of a freebooter, who trusting to the strength of his position, might levy black mail on his neighbours with impunity. There are few castles so remarkable and so impressive. The ruins are rather extensive, and of a quadrangular form, enclosing a court, and include four large towers of rude character. Great skill was displayed in constructing the fortifications. The most curious feature is a well, or means of procuring water, access to which is first obtained by a narrow arched passage on the northern side, which leads to a gallery cut in the solid rock about 50 yards in length, from 3 to 12 broad, and from 4 to 10 high, at the lower end of which is a basin, about 4 feet deep, containing very little water.

The fortress was originally founded at a remote period, but has evidently been altered after the Normans introduced an improved style of military architecture.* It was given to the English early in the thirteenth century by the mother of a Welsh chief named Rhys Vechan, to gratify a spirit of revenge for some injury she had sustained from him ; but soon recaptured by the rightful owner. At the end of the following century the castle became a

---

* *Welsh Castles.* When there are no Portcullises, and the windows approach nearly to the Roman Curve, and are constructed of thinly-laminated stone walls, very rude in detail, and with few windows, no doubt can exist that the castle was antecedent to the Norman period, or built by the Welsh.

stronghold of robbers, who were ultimately extirpated by the efforts of the people of the county.

Many *Roman* coins (hence *Caer ?*), and a stone hatchet of British origin, have been found here; and two or three miles up the valley, near the source of the little river Cennen, there are a number of excavations, covered in the interior with fine grass, which are supposed to have been *ancient British habitations*.

LLANGADOCK, a decayed town on the mail-road between Llandilo and Llandovery, was once a place of importance defended by a castle, of which not a vestige exists excepting the mound on which it stood. It is prettily situated between the rivers Sawddy and Bran, near their confluence with the Towy. The church, dedicated to St. Cadog, is a venerable structure. On a hill called *Tri Chrûg*, or the "Three Hillocks," seen to the south-east of Llangadock, are three large *carneddau*, near which are striking vestiges of a *British Camp*, called *Garn gôch*.

There is a good deal of pleasing scenery on the road from Llandilo to *Pontardulais*, an inn and excellent fishing station, situated at the confluence of the rivers Llychwr and Dulais, the former of which takes its rise in the Black Mountains, and forms a partial boundary line between the counties of Glamorgan and Carmarthen. Sewin ascend the river from the sea in great numbers during the summer season.—At *Llandebie*, five miles from Llandilo, there is a Waterfall on the Llychwr, called Glynhir, in the grounds of a gentleman, on the right of the road to Pontardulais. A road leads from Llandebie to Carreg Cennen Castle, which is seen to the greatest advantage from this side; so that that structure could be visited on the journey *to* Llandilo.

An EXCURSION may be made from Llandilo up the *Vale of the Dulais*, to the ruins of Talley Abbey (eight miles). The scenery is pleasing. *Taliaris*, the fine mansion on the left, about half way, is the seat of William Peel, Esq., and formerly belonged to the Gwynnes. The beautiful seat and demesne near the abbey, distinguished by an avenue, is *Rhydodyn*, the property of Sir James Hamlyn Williams, Bart.

Talley Abbey stands in an exquisite situation, near two pools about fifty acres in extent, whence its Welsh name, Tal-y-Lly-chau, or " the Head of the Lakes." It was founded by Rhys ap Gruffydd, Prince of South Wales, who died in 1197, for Præmon-stratensian Canons. Few structures have suffered more from the ravages of man and time ; but sufficient remains to reward the lover of antiquity. We learn that " the Church, dedicated to St. Michael, having fallen into decay, was rebuilt in the *Grecian* style, in 1773, at the expense of the inhabitants, *principally from the ruins of the ancient Abbey*, the nave of which formed the old church, and of which there are still some remains in the burial ground, consisting of half of the tower, and other considerable portions." Talley was very richly endowed ; when Henry VII. landed in Wales its Abbot was one of his most influential friends. The value at the dissolution was £153 1s. 4d.—The river that runs near the ruin is a branch of the Cothy.

From hence, the tourist may proceed to PUMSANT, the best *Fishing Station* in this part of Wales, where there is an inn. The Cothy, which rises a few miles to the north, and which is joined here by a smaller river, the Twrch, is an excellent trout stream.

CAYO, or Conwil-Gaio, the mountain parish in which Pumsant is situated, possesses high claims to attention in an antiquarian and picturesque point of view. A Roman station of considerable importance, called by some old writers, *Caer Gaio*, appears to have been planted at Dolaucothy, in connection with mining operations, which were carried on extensively, as the remarkable caves, called *Gogofau*, attest. J. Johnes, Esq., of Dolaucothy, to whom the property here belongs, has in his possession many Roman relics dug up in the neighbourhood, amongst which are a rough stone with an amethyst in the middle, whereon is a figure of Diana, &c. Mr. Johnes also possesses a *Torch Aur* or golden chain, which was found here. Tradition points to a large town which was erected in this spot by the Romans, chiefly of brick, from whence it has been called Y *drêv Goch yn Neheubarth*, or the " Red Town in South Wales." Many red bricks and the remains of a bath have been found by the peasantry. Two monumental stones stood at a place called *Pant y Polion*, one of which is

supposed to have been erected to commemorate the interment
of a *Polin* or *Paulinus*, a British saint of the sixth century ; it
is still preserved, and bears the following inscription :—*Ser-
vatur fidei, patriæque semper amator, Hic Paulinus iacit, cultor
pientissimus æqui.*—Cayo church is of considerable dimensions,
and is supposed to have been attached to a monastic institution.—
It has been well ascertained that the Romans had lead workings
in Wales, but Mr. Robert Hunt, in a recent practical lecture on
mining, is of opinion that they searched here for gold rather
than lead. " The old workings called Gogofau," he observes,
" were however rather quarrying than mining—the material being
obtained in open caverns, with levels run a short distance into the
lodes, which consisted of lead, mixed with a very small portion
of gold." There are several remarkable and romantic traditions
connected with these ancient caverns.

Lampeter is about ten miles to the north-west of Pumsant.
The pedestrian should take the road over the mountain to the
right, when he arrives at the head of a lofty pass, and from whence
he obtains a fine and extensive view of the hill country of Cardiganshire, over which faintly loom the mountains of North Wales.
From the same place a panoramic prospect may also be obtained
of the vans of Carmarthenshire and the Brecknockshire beacons.
If, instead of proceeding into Cardiganshire, the pedestrian should
wish to remain in Carmarthenshire to explore the beauties of the
upper part of the Vale of Towy, he should leave Pumsant and
proceed along *the old road* through the village of *Conwil Gaio*
towards *Porth-y-Rhyd ;* and, after a walk of nearly ten miles, he
will reach the town of

LLANDOVERY.

Distant from				Miles.	Distant from				Miles.
Builth ..	..	..	..	.. 23	Llangadock ..	..	..	..	6
Brecon ..	..	..	..	.. 21	Llandilo Vawr	..	..	.. 12
Lampeter	..	..	..	.. 20	Pumsant	..	..	..	.. 10
Llanwrtyd Wells	..	..	.. 12	Trecastle ...	..	..	..	9

On a slight eminence where the church of Llanfairarybryn now
stands, about a quarter of a mile from the town, there was a

Roman station of considerable importance ; leading towards which
may still be traced in the neighbourhood the remains of four
Roman roads.   Pieces of Roman brick and pottery are frequently
turned up in the churchyard and the adjoining gardens ; Roman
coins have also been found near the station.   Between two and
three miles to the north of this Roman station may be seen the area
of a large *British Camp*, on the summit of a hill called *Penygaer*.

In the town of Llandovery there are on a mound, near the Castle
Inn, the remains of an old castle, which owes its origin to the
Norman Lords Marchers, in the early part of the twelfth century.
It was long a bone of contention between the Welsh and English,
and sometimes proved a tower of strength to its possessors, when
other more important and larger fortifications had been taken by
the besiegers.   This castle was in ruins in the time of Queen
Elizabeth, but the walls have within the last century suffered more
from the rapacious vandalism of innkeepers, who added to or
rebuilt the Castle Inn, than they previously did from the ravages
of war or the destructive effects of time.   The present remains
consist of portions of the keep, the walls of which are of immense
thickness and strength.

The town appears to have risen under the protection of the
castle.   Its situation in the upper part of the vale of Towy, near
the junction of the small streams Brân and Gwydderig, is extremely
pleasant and picturesque ; most of the hills which surround it
amphitheatrically being clothed with luxuriant woods.   A small
stream now covered over runs through the town, and forms an
admirable natural sewer ; and the salubrity of the place is further
increased by an abundance of the very purest spring water, which
filters through an alluvial deposit of gravel.

Llandovery is well known all over the Principality as having
been the residence of the celebrated Vicar Prichard, whose Welsh
Poems, written temp. James I. and Charles I., have been ever
since held in such high reputation amongst his countrymen, that
they are estimated next to the Holy Scriptures.   The house in
which the Vicar resided was built by him in 1620, and stands
near the end of the street leading to Trecastle.

A Welsh Educational Institution has been founded here by Thomas Phillips, Esq., of Brunswick Square, London, who had previously enriched St. David's College, Lampeter, with scholarships and part of its library, and who was 88 years of age when the school was finished. It was opened on the 1st of March, 1848, under the superintendence of the Venerable Archdeacon Williams, M.A., F.R.S.E., late Rector of the Edinburgh Academy. The object of the founder, who has placed the school under the control of five trustees, is to " benefit the rising generation in South Wales, to bring out, encourage, and cultivate their native talents, " and, as far as can be done, to give a complete education on moderate terms to those willing students who hitherto have not been enabled to receive an accurate course of instruction in classical and mathematical knowledge, without travelling in search of it beyond the bounds of the Principality. The education of twenty free scholars, natives of the dioceses of St. David's and Llandaff, has been provided for by the founder, as the reward of conjoined capacity, diligence, and accurate knowledge. The pupils are expected to devote a certain portion of their time to the accurate study of the Welsh language and literature, and are taught to recognize its great etymological value in connexion with the study not only of the learned languages, but with all the dialects of Western Europe. The terms for tuition are eight to twelve guineas per annum ; board and lodging to be had on very reasonable terms in the town and in its vicinity.

Llandovery is honourably distinguished by the press of Mr. William Rees, who has produced many of the most celebrated works connected with Welsh literature and antiquities. INNS— The Castle, the Clarence, and the Lamb.

The fishing in this neighbourhood up the Towy was at one time somewhat injured by the lead works of Rhandirmwyn ; this, however, is not now the case, but of late years the fishing has suffered more from the shallowness of the water, and the free liberty allowed to anglers of all grades. The rivers Brân and Gwydderig afford some good fishing. There is better sport to be had very early in the season in the Gwydderig (which may be fished up for about four miles and a half), than in the other streams. The Brân, which follows next, may be fished about nine miles, and is earlier than the Towy ; the latter has, however, the best fishing grounds. Trout fishing commences in March and finishes in October ; the best months are April and September. About the end of May the sewin appear in the river, and are in full perfection in June and July. August is the salmon month ; but old fish are sometimes caught with the fly in March, weighing upwards of 20lbs. Flat fish and eels are also taken by ground fishing. A small stream called Gwenlais falls into the Towy, about three miles up, and good sport may be had even in this brook for about two miles along its course. The Dulais, another brook that runs through the pass of Cwm Dwr, and falls into the Towy below Llanwrda, has about five miles of good fishing. Local flies and local information may be had of Mr. Evan Davies, a well-known fisherman, at Llandovery.

The road to Trecastle is carried up the Gwydderig river through the very romantic Pass of *Cwm Dwr*. Another Pass of the same name and of equal beauty is traversed by the new road to Lampeter, which, on leaving Llandovery, crosses the Towy over an elegant suspension bridge, 225 feet span, and enters the Pass at Llanwrda, about four miles lower down the vale of Towy. The summer coach from Brecon to Aberystwyth runs through both these beautiful passes.

THE CARMARTHENSHIRE VAN.

An excursion may be made from Llandovery to this mountain (*Bannau Sir Gaer*), one of the highest in South Wales (2,596 feet). The distance exceeds ten miles, and the walk offers great temptations to the fisherman. *Llyn Van Vach*, the smallest of two lakes that are to be found in these uplands, is full of trout, and occupies a deep hollow, a quarter of a mile long, at the foot of the vast rocky steep of the mountain. When there is an east, north-east, or north breeze, extraordinary sport may be obtained. South or west winds, unless very high, do not ruffle the lake, in consequence of the height of the mountain above those sides. The stream which runs out of the lake also affords excellent sport. It is called the Sawthe (Sawddy), and empties itself into the Towy below the town of Llangadock. The other lake does not contain

any fish ; there is something peculiar in its waters. The view
from the summit of the Van, which is separated by a narrow chasm
from another mountain in Brecknockshire, of similar character
but somewhat greater elevation, is of course exceedingly extensive.
The two mountains are usually called the " Carmarthenshire
Beacons," to distinguish them from the " Brecknockshire Beacons." These Beacons reckon next to the Brecknockshire in
height amongst the South Wallian hills. [See TRECASTLE.]

THE MOUNTAIN DISTRICT

To the north of Llandovery is known to comparatively few
persons, owing to there being no road through it ; but those who
have encountered the difficulties which it presents—explored its
Gorges (we have heard it styled " the land of the Gorges ")—
unite in opinion that it is one of the finest parts of Wales. The
outlines of the mountains are exceedingly graceful,—have a peculiarly dreamy look. We advise those who wish to traverse this
region to consult the Ordnance map, and make careful local
enquiries. These mountains are occasionally crossed in proceeding from Llandovery to Llanddewi Brevi and Tregaron, but it is
a very difficult matter to keep or find the path.

In going to Llanddewi Brevi the safest plan is to proceed
through the village of *Cilycwm*, (not far from which there is a lead
mining district, called Rhandirmwyn, where 180 men and 30
women and boys are employed), and pass near the mansion of
Neuaddfawr onward, leaving the lead mines on the right, and following the river Towy, until the entrance of Cwm Gwenffrwd, or
the dingle of the river Gwenffrwd, along which river an excellent
country road leads round the Mallaen Mountain towards the river
Cothy, up which river the tourist must proceed along a rugged
road near an almost unfathomable pool in the Cothy, called
" *Pwll Uffern*," or the Pool of Hell ; from this road some remarkable Cairns, called *Crugiau 'Ladys*, may be seen on the summit
of the mountain. After passing on about a mile and a half, the
small farm-house of Nantyrast is reached. At this place a guide
had better be obtained, to conduct the tourist across the bogs that
intercept the faint track of a road to the mountain near Llanddewi Brevi.

If Tregaron should be the point which the tourist wishes to reach, he must, instead of turning up Cwm Gwenffrwd, proceed up the Towy towards TWM SION CATTI's CAVE and YSTRADFFIN, which are ten miles from Llandovery, a route which we very strongly recommend.   Dr. Downes, the author of the " Mountain Decameron," describes this scene as " the most singular and even sublime congregation of mountains, with their waters and rocks in either Wales......The whole river forms a cataract down the ledges of rock which form one *whole* side of this pyramidal mountain, all the rest of it being hanging woods, or many coloured crags......Savage as the whole aspect is, of so many mountain heads and *four* meeting rivers, all is as sweet and pastoral as can be......High in the rock above the fall yawns a hole, hardly a cavern, where once lurked a famous freebooter of Wales, Twm Sion Catti, saith tradition.''   The mountain mentioned by Dr. Downes is called *Dinas*, and was an ancient Welsh stronghold.   " The entrance to this cave," says Mrs. Bowen, in a note to a charming descriptive poem on *Ystradffin*, published in 1839, ''is through a narrow aperture formed of two immense slate rocks, which face each other, and the space between them is narrower at the bottom than at the top, so that the passage can only be entered *sideways*, with the figure inclined, according to the slanting of the rock."   The history of Twm Sion [Shone] Catti, *alias* Thomas Jones, Esq., is very romantic.   He was a natural son of John ap David Moethe, by Catherine, natural daughter of Meredydd ap Ieuan ap Robert, grandfather of Sir John Wynne, of Gwydir, (see *The Heraldic Visitations of Wales*, by Lewys Dwnn, published by the Welsh MSS. Society,) and is said to have died in 1630, at the age of sixty-one.   In early life " he was a notorious freebooter and highwayman "—levied *black mail* on the country within reach of his mountain abode, with the aid of a small band of followers.   He soon reformed, married a rich heiress, was then created a justice of the peace for Brecon, and ultimately became sheriff of that county and Carmarthenshire. " He was," observes Sir S. R. Meyrick, " esteemed as an eminent antiquarian and poet, but is more known for the tricks attributed to him as a robber.''

Lord Cawdor is the owner of the immense estate of Ystradffin, and has much improved the road towards it. Some large lead mines exist on his property. At Nantymwyn, three miles lower down the river Towy, there are traces of these mines having been worked by the *Romans*. After enjoying the scenery about Ystradffin, the tourist must enter the Gorge of the *Doethiau*, and proceed along its side to its source, and thence across the mountains to Tregaron, unless tempted to turn aside into the Gorge of the *Pyscottwr* (the Fisherman), which empties itself into the Doethiau, about two miles from Twm Sion Catti's Cave. Both these rivers abound with fish.

In order to reach the Teivy lakes, near Strata Florida, it is better to proceed up the Towy from Ystradffin by *Trawsnant*, and on to the junction of Towy Vechan, about ten miles from Ystradffin, along which proceed to near its source, and thence across the Pass of *Bwlch Rhyd y Meirch*, and follow the narrow road to Strata Florida and Pont rhyd Vendigaid. This route is the shortest from Llandovery to the upper end of the Vale of Teivy, and is perhaps the most interesting to the angler and the lover of nature in her wildest garb.

––––––––––

We return to the southern part of the county.

𝕷𝖑𝖆𝖓𝖘𝖙𝖊𝖕𝖍𝖆𝖓 𝕮𝖆𝖘𝖙𝖑𝖊 overlooks the sea from a very picturesque promontory opposite Ferryside, and has long been a favourite subject with artists. All the concomitants of a fine landscape exist here. The colours, especially, are perfect ; and as a sunset view, when the tide is coming in, nothing can be imagined more exquisite of the kind. The outer walls of the castle are nearly entire, and of large extent, but the building is a mere shell. It was founded by a Welsh chieftain, taken by the Normans and Flemings in 1138, and recovered by Meredydd and Cade, two of the sons of Gryffyth ap Rhys, Prince of South Wales, in 1143. The Normans made great efforts to recover it, but were unsuccessful for many years. On the first occasion after the Welsh regained possession, " Meredydd suffered the Normans to complete the preparations for the attack ; the scaling ladders were fixed and manned ; but just as the assailants were gaining the battlements, he caused certain engines so to bear upon the enemy that they were precipitated to the ground."—The village of Llanstephan, where is a humble inn, stands in a graceful wooded hollow, a little way above the castle. There is a modern mansion and park here. The distance to Ferryside is a mile at high water. —A road, two miles and a third long, leads across the peninsula to a ferry opposite

LAUGHARNE,

which stands at the edge of the long tidal estuary of the Tâf—a vast expanse of sand at low water. The contrast is striking. A large Norman castle, which was besieged by Cromwell for three weeks, is the chief attraction of the place to a passer-by. The interior of the structure has been partly laid out as a garden and much spoiled; it is difficult to gain access. The town, which is also a miniature sea-port, chiefly consists of a long and well-built street, and contains about 1,400 persons. It has long been celebrated as a retreat for families who fix upon Wales as a residence from motives of economy; the price of provisions is low, and the sheltered nature of the site renders the place a desirable one for persons of delicate health. Until the commencement of this century Laugharne was divided into Welsh and English portions, and the people did not mix with each other. The church is of considerable size. Dr. Josiah Tucker, Dean of Gloucester, an eminent divine, was born in this parish, A. D. 1712.—The soil in the neighbourhood is good.—There are a variety of shells on the sands.—*Roche's Castle*, an old building about a mile from the town, is said to have been a monastic establishment.

Those who wish to enjoy a succession of beautiful scenery, should follow the coast road to Amroth Castle, which is within the borders of Pembrokeshire, and from thence proceed to Tenby.

The villages in this part of the country are pretty. About five miles from Laugharne is a natural curiosity, an excavation called " The Green Bridge of Wales," into which a small stream sinks.

St. Clare or St. Clear's, the head quarters of Rebecca, a small straggling town and port, once the seat of a Castle and Priory, now destroyed, stands about three miles to the north of

Llaugharne, and ten from Carmarthen.   A tumulus marks the
site of the Castle keep, which was once the regular place of meeting of a great assemblage of Welsh bards.   A pious lady named
Clara, afterwards canonised, is said to have founded a church
here in the fifth century.   The town stands at the confluence of
the Gynin with the Táf; and vessels of 60 or 80 tons can come
up to the quay.   There is a comfortable inn.   Some good fishing
may be obtained in these rivers.

In the churchyard at LLANVIHANGEL ABER
COWIN, about two miles form St. Clear's, *on
the opposite side of the estuary*, are three
remarkable tombs, to which the peasantry
attach great sanctity, said to be the sepul-
chres of holy palmers, " who wandered
thither in poverty and distress, and when about
to perish for want, slew each other, the last
survivor burying himself in one of the graves
which they had prepared, and pulling the
stone over, left it ill-adjusted in an oblique .
posture."   The peninsula of Lanvihangel
is, according to local belief, free from vene-
mous reptiles or toads, except when the
tomb-stones are overrun with weeds.—The
Cowin, which runs almost due north for
about fifteen miles, is a capital stream for
fishing.—We subjoin an engraving of one of
of the tombs from a sketch by Mr. J. O.
Westwood.

An EXCURSION may be made from Laugharne—and from Carmarthen, when the South Wales Railway is opened—to

Whitland Abbey, distant from the former place about eight
miles, and from the latter thirteen miles.   The site of *Ty Gwyn
ar Tav* (the White House on Tave), was skilfully chosen.   A deep
sequestered glen, environed by steep wooded hills, and watered
by a clear and rapid stream, was a spot peculiarly favourable for
religious seclusion : but little else than a shadow now remains of
the peaceful abode of the White Monks.   A manuscript account

of this abbey has been kindly placed in our hands, from which
and other sources we glean the following particulars. The founder
of *Alba Landa* was Paulinus, a pupil of St. Illtyd, at Lantwit;
and in the fifth and sixth centuries the place acquired some
celebrity. This fact has escaped the attention of the compiler
of the prize essay on Welsh religious houses, in Volume IV.
of the *Cymmrodorion Trans.*, who assigns the foundation of the
establishment here to Bernard, first Norman Bishop of St.
David's, in 1143. The fact is that the collegiate body at
Whitland, attached to the British church, was superseded by
Norman Cistercian monks. Only eight of the brethren remained
at the Reformation, when the yearly value was £153 17s. 2d.
The primitive British monasteries, or rather colleges, in Wales
differed materially from those introduced after the commencement
of the Norman era. A more rigid rule was formerly enforced;
the members laboured with their own hands for subsistence, and
were diligent in works of charity.—" Prince Howel Dda, who
had temporarily united the three provinces of Wales under his
dominion, assembled the bishops, clergy, and principal chiefs, at
Ty Gwyn, for the purpose of revising and consolidating the Welsh
laws.". This great Cambrian legislator, who passed much of his
time here, in the tenth century erected a large building of white
timber or wattles for the reception of this national council; and
his code, which was abrogated A. D. 1282, is still in existence, and
known by the name of Howel the Good's Laws. Whitland Abbey
is now the property of the Hon. W. H. Yelverton, who has erected
a modern mansion, and in 1837 made an interesting discovery.
A pond in a farm yard, occupying part of the site of the abbey,
was drained out, when the bases of several clustered pillars of the
church were revealed; westward of which foundations of cloisters
and monastic cells, a doorway, encaustic tiles, and several other
architectural fragments, were also brought to light. The style is
that of the twelfth century. On the walls of the farm-house is
a tablet of stone, on which are sculptured the armorial bearings
of Henry VII.—An iron forge, driven by water from a reservoir
formed out of the abbey fish-ponds, was carried on here for many
years, but is now in ruins.

Druidical Antiquities. Several interesting British antiquities exist in the parish of Llanboidy, about five miles from Whitland. On the summit of a hill overlooking a beautiful valley, in the grounds of Kilhernin, is a. *Cromlech* in fine preservation. The table-stone is about 30 feet in circumference, and three feet thick, and is supported by four large stones. An extensive camp may be traced at Bronyskawen, in which two hundred Roman coins, including several of the most ancient ever found in Britain, were discovered in the seventeenth century by some boys, in two leaden boxes. One was of Domitian's reign, A.D. 91. A circular Druidical temple, called "Buarth Arthur," about 60 feet in diameter, stands on a hill in this parish, near the banks of the Cleddy; about fifteen upright stones remain, some of which are seven feet high, and there are fragments of an avenue, 200 yards from which three very large stones are placed.

PEMBROKESHIRE

Is the Cornwall of the Principality. Its position—its stern and precipitous coast, deeply indented by Atlantic storms—the mildness of its climate—its scenery—bear out this parallel; but there is one remarkable difference—the character of the people. Pembrokeshire has been called "Little England beyond Wales;" Cornwall—a great refuge of the ancient Britons—is in many respects essentially Welsh. Mr. Malkin styles Pembroke "partly Dutch, partly English, partly Welsh," a description which tersely conveys a true idea of its peculiarities and history. Up to the Norman period the latter is uninteresting. Early in the reign of William Rufus, William de Tours, a Norman knight, who had obtained a lordship in North Devon, sailed with an expedition to the western coast of Wales, landed at Fishguard, and easily succeeded in making a conquest of the country between that place and Newport, at which he erected a castle. His son married a daughter of Prince Rhys ap Gryffydd. Another Norman knight sailed up Milford Haven, A.D. 1092, and settled at Pembroke, where he built a castle. The Welsh soon attempted to dislodge the invaders, but were repelled. In 1106, the largest portion of the colony of Flemings who were sent to colonise part of South Wales chiefly settled in the peninsula to the west of Tenby, which is called the Hundred of Castle Martin, and in the Haverfordwest district. These auxiliaries were strengthened in 1113 by more of their countrymen, who had been driven out of the Low Countries by a second inundation, and also by a reinforcement of Flemish mercenary troops, who had followed the fortunes of Stephen; so that the Normans were enabled to keep their ground without much difficulty, although there were a series of skirmishes between the Welsh and the "foreigners" for two or three centuries. Giraldus Cambrensis speaks in glowing terms of the warlike and enterprising character of the Flemings, who were as distinguished for their proficiency in the arts of peace as of war —skilful architects, good farmers, and dexterous in the manufacture of wool.—When Henry VII., then Earl of Richmond, landed at Dale, near the entrance of Milford Haven, Sir Rhys ap Thomas met the royal adventurer with a large armament. Lastly, the county was invaded by a modern French force in 1797, not far from the spot where William de Tours effected a landing seven hundred years before.

The grand Roman road, *Via Julia Maritima*, ran through the county from Carmarthenshire in a straight line westward to *Menapia*, near St. David's. Sir R. C. Hoare fixes the central station, *Ad Vigesinum*, at Castell Flemish, two or three miles E.N.E. of Ambleston Church. Remains of a Roman camp, near which was a bath, may be seen at Ford village, a little to the west. Traces of a branch road from *Loventium*, crossing the Preselly mountains, have been found; and it is believed that a road ran from Menapia to Dale near the entrance of Milford Haven, part of which, a paved way, has been discovered near the Newgale Sands in St. Bride's Bay.

In Druidical remains Pembrokeshire ranks first, and in military antiquities second, amongst the South Wallian counties. There were more religious houses than in any of the other counties, but none are remarkable, except St. David's. Ruined mansions, half hidden by ivy, are frequently met with. The Flemings built many houses of mud; and the practice of constructing cottages of this material has been extensively followed by their descendants, who adhere to large round wattle chimneys.

The coast—which embraces Milford Haven, the finest natural harbour in Europe—is double the length of the inland boundary line. The surface of the country is undulating, often resembling the long or Bay of Biscay swell of the ocean; and it is not until you approach the northern part, which is intersected by the Preselly mountains, an extension of the upland chain of South Wales, that the country assumes a bold character. But it has many sweet pastoral vales, with the lofty gray towers of rude Norman churches, pointing to Heaven; farm-houses on green knolls; seats of the lords of the soil nestling amidst trees.

The rivers and brooks of Pembrokeshire are very numerous, but only four are of any consequence—the Western and Eastern Cleddy (which unite five miles below Haverfordwest), the Nevern (Newport), and the Gwaun or Gwain (Fishguard); salmon, sewin, and trout abound. The Teivy forms part of the northern boundary. There are two small lakes near Lanychair Church, three miles from Fishguard.

Few parts of Britain offer finer studies for the geologist. "If a line be drawn through the centre of the county from east to west, we find the stratified rocks north of that line composed of slate, grit, and shale; to the south the older rocks are surmounted by the Silurian rocks, old red sandstone, carboniferous limestone, and coal measures." The whole surface is greatly diversified by trap rocks bursting forth in many places, and altering the structure of the sedimentary deposits. The carboniferous limestone dips below the millstone grit, forming a girdle round it in the eastern district, but disappearing in the west. The great coal basin of South Wales runs across the county, gradually narrowing until it disappears in Ramsey Island; the coal is chiefly anthracite; some of the seams are three feet thick.

There is much variety in the quality of the soils; those on the limestone and old red sandstone formations are distinguished by great natural fertilíty ; but the coal country and slate district to the north are covered by cold inferior soil. Timber does not thrive under the exposure to violent south-westerly winds, a circumstance which gives a bleak appearance to many of the landscapes. Lord Cawdor, and some other wealthy landlords, have made great exertions to improve agriculture ; Farmers' Clubs and Agricultural Societies exist, and there is excellent farming in remote parts of the Cawdor estates. Land generally lets at a rather high rent ; and the extent of waste is unusually small. A peculiar and fine breed of cattle, called "Castle-martins," exists in the hundred of that name, and other parts of the county.

The manners of the people are generally pleasing, but the Flemish districts do not possess the primitive character of Gower. National peculiarities have been lost, although the countenances of the people often resemble those of their opposite neighbours. The costume of the female peasantry is peculiar and not unbecoming ; a tight stuff or cloth jacket, with short sleeves—like that which is often depicted by Flemish painters—with a rather short petticoat, and peaked black beaver hat. The wages of servants in this and the adjoining counties are very reasonable. English is almost universally spoken. The population of the county in 1801 was 56,280 ; in 1831, 81,425 ; in 1841, 88,044. Number of parishes, 148. Area, 575 square miles, or 368,000 acres. Coast-line, about 100 miles. Parliamentary representation: One member for the county, one for Haverfordwest, St. David's, Fishguard and Narberth ; and one for Pembroke, Tenby, Milford, and Weston. Assizes and Sessions are held at Haverfordwest.

The number of Day Schools in Pembrokeshire is 206, which are attended by 8,053 scholars, or nine out of every hundred of the population. There are 223 Sunday Schools, attended by 3,403 Church scholars, and 14,013 Dissenters. . The preponderance of Dissenting *Sunday Schools* in the counties of Pembroke, Carmarthen, and Glamorgan over the Church Schools is in the ratio of 5 to 1 ; but Commissioners report that 77.8 per cent. of of the Education in *Day Schools* in those counties, is given "either in connexion with the Established Church, or by private and independent teachers." We shall commence our Itinerary at

TENBY.

Distant from				Miles.	Distant from				Miles.
Amroth Castle	..	..	..	7	Manorbeer Castle	..	..	..	6
Carmarthen	..	..	..	26	Narberth	..	..	..	10
Carew Castle	..	..	..	5	Orielton	..	..	..	14
Giltar Point	..	..	..	2½	Penally..	..	..	..	2½
Gumfreston	..	4.	..	2½	Picton Castle	..	..	..	19
Haverfordwest, by Narberth			..	21	Pembroke	..	..	..	10
Knightstone	..	..	..	3	Pater Dock	..	..	..	12
Llanstephan Castle	..	..	..	19	Saundersfoot	..	..	..	3½
Laugharne	..	..	..	16	Stackpole Court	..	..	..	15
Lamphey Palace	..	..	..	8	Slebech	..	..	..	17
Lidstep..	..	..	..	4	St. David's	..	..	..	36
London, by Steam-boat, and Great					Stack Rocks	..	..	..	19
Western Railway		..	..	227	Trefloyn	..	..	..	2

VOYAGE BY STEAM. The distance from Bristol is 108 miles, and the *average* passage used to be eleven hours ; but by the largest steamer on the station the voyage is usually performed in a much shorter period. We give the days of sailing in our steam-packet table.

Except under adverse circumstances, the Tenby boats run along the Gower coast, which—especially the Worm's Head—is seen to great advantage from the sea. About three quarters of a mile to the west of Porteynon Point the steamer passes the easterly buoy of the Helwick Sands, a long bank, divided in the middle by a shallow " swashway," which extends about four miles to the westward of the Worm's Head, where there is another buoy. On the 1st October, 1846, a light ship with a bright revolving light was moored near the latter point. We heard a curious legend at Rhosilly, in Gower, about these sands, which affords, at all events, a proof that the sea has made great inroads on this coast —much greater probably than those mentioned at p. 142. Our informant called the Helwicks, " *the old Highroad to Bristol*," affirming that at a remote period there was, according to popular tradition, dry land there !—Lundy Island now rises at a distance of 25 miles on the south-west, and Carmarthen Bay opens its

arms. The run, about 13 miles, across the bay, is generally
performed as the evening is setting in.   The Pembrokeshire coast
gradually begins to loom out, and as the sun sinks below the
breezy blue sea-sky, the dark headlands to the westward assume
distinct forms.   The presence of that beautiful little sea-bird the
Eligug, flitting across the waves like an arrow towards its rocky
home, betokens land.   Presently, three Lights—Lundy, Caldy,
and the Helwick—rise like evening stars.   The beacon light of
Hope to the anxious and storm-tossed mariner—the sailor's friend
—a lighthouse is to us, when viewed under any circumstances, an
object of no ordinary interest ; but when it lifts its head over the
sea, like some warning spirit amidst the gloom of night, what
object is more *real* or suggestive ?

> " —— but for yon light
> I had begun to dream this weary night
> For us, would have no morn. In greatest need,
> When through life's sea man's erring bark is driven,
> Thus doth the beacon Hope, with friendly gleam,
> Speak peace unto his soul."

Sweet romantic Tenby—gem of Channel watering places ! Who
can ever forget the first impression of that gentle bay—that sin-
gularly-situated congregation of dwellings—with their guardian
spire ascending into the sky—crowning a peninsulated steep, protected by islands from the raging of the sea without, and blending
the stern characteristics of the old walled town with the luxuries
of modern life ! What can be more picturesque in form or in
colouring than the gladsome bay between the deep purple headland of Monkstone, and the rocky point of the Castle Hill, set in
a green sea of delicious purity ?

But, we are alongside the pier ; reflection ceases ; the struggle
for luggage begins ; the crowd thickens ; there are warm greet-
ings—many pleasant recognitions ; we step ashore, and unless we
have friends to meet us, proceed to take our ease at our inn, the
floors of which seem so strangely affected with a heaving motion,
that when we suddenly wake up after having enjoyed a pleasant
sea repast with a true salt-water zest, we fancy for a moment
that we must have got back again into "the saloon."

Daylight always tests places, first seen of an evening, severely. But Tenby need not fear a scrutiny. Its principal thoroughfares are patterns of cleanliness ; every thing wears a cheerful look ; the terraces would not shame watering places of very high pretensions ; and although some of the back streets might be kept neater, the visitor is so charmed by quaint Flemish chimneys, or old gateways, or lines of walls with bastion towers, looking as grim as they did when they first reared their heads against the stout Welshmen, that he is not disposed to be critical.

The Welsh name of Tenby, *Dynbych y Pyscoed*, " the place or precipice of fishes," leads us to believe that it was a fishing town at the period of the Flemish invasion. These shrewd and hardy settlers appear to have been smitten with the natural advantages which it possesses ; a strong detachment soon pitched their tents here, and with the aid of Norman allies, built strong walls and a castle, the situation of which must once have been impregnable, except in case of surprise. A surprise—in revenge for a shameful outrage—did occur in the year 1150, when the town was "spoiled" and burnt, the fortifications ruined, and the garrison put to the sword, by the Welsh. William de la Grace, Earl of Pembroke, who had married Isabel, daughter of Strongbow, commenced the work of restoration, which was steadily proceeded with by his five sons, all Earls of Pembroke in succession, and who founded religious and charitable institutions here. The town and port throve greatly, became celebrated for woollen manufactures, and a considerable trade was kept up with foreign parts. The Earl of Richmond, afterwards Henry VII., sought shelter at Tenby with his mother, after being besieged in Pembroke Castle, and were lodged by Thomas White, then Mayor, a wealthy wine-merchant, whose monument is now one of the most interesting features of Tenby Church, and whose mansion, under which were immense vaults, was in existence in the year 1805. White provided a vessel for the royal fugitive, which conveyed him safely to Brittany, a service for which he was afterwards rewarded with a grant for life of the king's lands around the town. Tenby was strengthened at the time of the Spanish Armada ; and an inscription on a stone, "A. 1588, E. R. 30." is still to be seen in the walls near the

south gate, beneath the battlement. From this period the place
gradually declined, but it was an important stronghold in the civil
wars. " On the 7th of March, 1644, Colonel Rowland Laugharne
proceeded to attack Tenbigh, where Commissary Gwyn was
governor, and made a resolute defence ; but after three days
battery, a great part of the town being beaten down, it was taken
by storm, but not many killed." Three years afterwards, when
Cromwell went with an army into South Wales, Tenby, in which
a large number of country gentlemen had sought refuge with
their families, stood a longer siege. "The reducement of Wales,"
says Cromwell, in a letter copied by Mr. Fenton, " is more
difficult than expected, the towns and castles of Pembroke and
Tenby being equal to any in England, and well provided of all
things." From this period little is known of its history ; but
near the close of the last century we learn that it " was almost
entirely deserted, except by the poorer classes, and a few
respectable tradesmen." The town appears to have acquired a
rather sudden reputation ; for within the first fifteen or twenty
years of the present century it assumed the rank of a " fashionable " watering place. War was waged against the old houses,
and most of the curious and interesting examples of the peculiar
style of architecture used by the Flemings were recklessly
destroyed ; even an ancient chapel on the Quay, dedicated to St.
Julian, shared the common fate. A quarto volume of etchings
was published in 1812, by Mr. Charles Norris, which fortunately
perpetuates the memory of old Tenby.

A considerable part of the fortifications of Tenby is still
preserved. The south wall, which is strengthened by circular
bastions and two square towers, is very perfect in many parts,
and its termination on the lofty cliffs which bound the south
sands conveys the idea of great strength. From thence the
fortifications were carried along the rocks to the *Castle Hill*, but
only fragments remain. The tower on the summit of the Castle
Hill derives consequence merely from its situation ; part of the
buildings, on ascending the hill, are supposed by some to have
been storehouses ; but on the north of the great entrance to the
ruins, the remains of a hall, one hundred feet long by twenty

wide, and other large state apartments, may be traced, which leave no doubt that this was a superb baronial residence. The *South Gate*, of four arches, is in good preservation, and was defended by a portcullis. A walk, which is neatly kept and sheltered by trees, runs outside the walls from the end of the Lion Hotel to the South Gate.

The CASTLE HILL affords an enchanting lounge. The view embraces the whole of Carmarthen Bay, over which, to the north, may be seen in very clear weather the summit of the Carmarthenshire Van ; close at hand is the picturesque perforated rock called St. Catherine's Island, on the summit of which are slight remains of a chapel dedicated to the patron saint of the woollen trade. Beyond, is a view of Caldy and St. Margaret's Islands, terminated by Giltar Point.—The Preventive Service have a station on the Castle Hill.

The *Beacon*, which is seen in the bay to the eastward, is moored over the *Woolhouse Rocks*, a small reef covered at two hours' flood. The ball at the top is designed for shipwrecked seamen, and will contain eight persons.

The CHURCH. The first church erected at Tenby was burnt by the Welsh, and the founder of the present structure, which has been altered and extended at various periods, was Warren de Monchensy, Earl of Pembroke. Three chantry priests were appointed to officiate in it,. one at the altar of Jesus, another at the altar of St. Anne, and a third at the " Rood of Grace," for the maintenance of which services, lands near the town, now the property of the corporation, were settled on the church, which is dedicated to St. Mary. The exterior, except the doorways, is not remarkable : its chief feature is a tower and spire of stone, 152 feet high, painted white to give it additional prominence as a land-mark. The body of the church, which is 146 feet long and 88 wide, consists of a nave, north and south aisles, and a chancel leading to a very lofty altar, approached by *eleven* steps of Purbeck stone. On entering, the eye is first struck by the beauty of the wooden roof, which is divided into compartments enriched by many curious and interesting bosses, and rests on large corbel figures ; from these you look onwards to the chancel, shrouded in the dim religious light of stained glass, and you confess that you have seldom seen a vista fuller of charming architectural effects, or which awakens more solemn ideas.

In the autumn of 1847, the inhabitants subscribed about £400 in addition to a rate of eighteen-pence in the pound, for the purpose of new roofing and "repairing" the church. Mr. Tuder furnished £150 for the construction of a cornice round the gable and eaves of the church ; and Miss Tuder gave a sufficient sum for the opening and restoration of the arches and window under the steeple, which were hidden by a loft erected for the convenience of the ringers. A cannon ball which had penetrated a piece of oak in the roof of the north aisle was lately found.

Tenby Church is richer in monumental effigies than any church in Wales, except the cathedrals.

The altar tomb of the White family, celebrated in the history of Tenby, is one of the best examples of its class. There are recumbent effigies of the brothers John and Thomas White, habited in the robes and caps of their time, and bearing heavy purses ; the south side of the tomb is divided into eight compartments, each of which is designed to commemorate members of the same family, and form in combination a series of remarkable groups. This tomb was *exposed to the rain* for a whole winter nearly fifty years ago, which obliterated a great part of the legends carved on it in soft stone. In an arch opposite is another altar tomb from which a brass has been abstracted ; the forms however of a mitre and a crozier remain, from whence it is supposed that it was the burial place of Tully, Bishop of St. David's, who was interred in the church, but a representation of an emaciated figure in a winding sheet, which stands in the north wall, is also believed to relate to this prelate. Amongst the other monuments is one of considerable antiquity, with an interesting inscription, to the memory of a benevolent tradesman named William Risan ; and another, in the massive style of James the First's era, to the memory of Thomas ap Rhys, of Scotsborough, near Tenby, and his wife, containing in addition a group of their family. Those who have read the *Legend of Dunraven* [*ante* p. 144] will take an interest in an inscription on a stone in the north aisle, which was first brought to light by Mr. Fenton about forty years ago, and records the death of *Walter Vaughan*, of Dunraven, who appears to have retired to Tenby, then a secluded spot, and to have died on the 4th of January, 1637.

The keys of the church may be had of the sexton, or of the organist.

A Carmelite College, dedicated to St. Mary, was founded at Tenby A.D. 1399, and it is believed that the doorways in the wall opposite the west end of the church were entrances to it, although of later date. Some other very beautiful doorways connected with this college may be traced.—Two shields containing the arms of Henry VII. as Earl of Richmond and King of England, decorate a low arch of an interesting old building on one side of the churchyard.

There are three Dissenting Chapels : The Wesleyan, in High Street; the Independent, in Frog Street; and the Baptist's, in the South Parade. A second Baptist Chapel was shut up and sold in 1847.

The form of Tenby is influenced by the peculiarity of its site. A curving street runs almost from the pier to the opposite end of the town ; that portion of it called High Street contains many excellent shops, and is carried along the edge of the rocks that bound the North Sands. The hotels and some of the principal lodgings are situated here ; the fine terrace called "Croft," where some of the best lodgings are also to be found, is of comparatively recent origin, as is Lexden Terrace, another fine row of lodging-houses built in 1845, which command a view over the South Sands. On the retired side of the town (the south) are many other excellent lodgings in Marine Terrace, Paragon Buildings, the Rock Houses, and Rock Terrace, from all of which easy access to the sands can be obtained by steps cut in the rocks, &c. The minor or back streets are very oddly laid out, and often perplex a stranger. On the average, the charges for lodgings are not extravagant; and in some cases are very moderate.

Tenby commands two distinct marine views, and two beaches, which are both well provided with bathing machines. The North Sands are the most sheltered ; but the South Sands are the most agreeable and popular. Finer sea-bathing cannot be found : you have four concomitants, — a sea of perfect purity, firm gently-shelving sands, pure air, and good attendance. During high springs the tides sometimes rise 35 feet.

The BATHS, near the Castle Hill, were built by the late Sir W. Paxton C. Cook Wells, Esq., is now the owner. The arrangements are very complete. Prices : Single bath, 2s. 6d., subscription to be paid in advance; ten baths, £1 1s. ; shower bath, 1s. 6d. ; cold bath, 1s. 6d. ; vapour bath, 4s.

Amusements. An Assembly Room, of moderate pretensions, adjoins the Baths. In the summer season, promenade and full dress Balls are regularly held ; Master of the Ceremonies, W. B. Williams, Esq.—Races, which occupy two days, and afford good sport, take place in the middle of August, on level ground to the west of the town, belonging to C. Matthias, Esq., of Lamphey Court; and Races sometimes come off on the South Sands. There are Race Balls.—A miniature Theatre is opened during part of the season, near the South Parade. — There are two Billiard Rooms, also a Cricket Club. — A good Library and Reading Room is to be met with in the High Street, opposite the Church ; near which is the Post Office.

Tenby boasts of a Dispensary, a Clothing Club, and other charities; and possesses a National School, situated on the Castle Hill, and an excellent Infant School. All these institutions are supported by subscriptions and donations.

A Literary and Scientific Society was established on the 29th of September, 1847, and was opened by Dr. Wilbraham Falconer, who gave a highly interesting address on the occasion, which was published at the request of the members. The society's rooms—which include a well-supplied reading-room—are situated in Cresswell Street, near the Paragon. Dr. Falconer strongly urged the formation of a Museum "for the purpose of illustrating the geology, mineralogy, natural history,* and archæology, of the neighbourhood of Tenby and of Pembrokeshire."

_* *Natural History.*—"The Natural History of our neighbourhood, and, indeed of the whole of Pembrokeshire, is yet almost wholly uninvestigated, and the marine productions of our bay but very imperfectly understood; indeed, until within the last seven or eight years, the geology of this district, rich as it has proved to be in minerals, and fossil remains, [particularly plants, near the coal measures] had not been carefully examined or described. Pembrokeshire is one out of a few counties of Wales, the botany of which has never been thoroughly studied; and there are very good reasons for believing that it abounds with plants of the most interesting kinds to the botanist. Some distinguished naturalists who have, during the last five years, visited Tenby, have

The entrance to the Market is in the High Street, and there is usually an excellent supply of provisions, especially on Saturday, the principal market day, when many country butchers come in. The prices are a good deal lower than in England. Poultry to the value of £100 weekly is now sent to Bristol by steam ; this trade has entirely sprung up within the last ten or twelve years.

A new Fish Market was opened in 1847 at the end of Belle Vue, near the top of Quay Hill, and can be reached by a cross street which turns from High Street opposite the church to Belle Vue. The supply of fish is always abundant, and includes turbot, dorey, brill, halibut, soles, whiting, plaice, gurnet, grey mullet, and sometimes the delicious red mullet. The mackarel season generally commences towards the end of July ; herrings have not been very plentiful of late years ; in winter cod are caught in such numbers that a fish weighing 25lbs. is sometimes sold for a shilling. The oysters, although of large size, are good ; and the small Milford oyster is often hawked about. There are also lobsters, prawns, and shrimps.

The Tenby people were not alive until recently to the importance of their fisheries. They saw every year a fleet of about twenty fishing smacks arrive from Brixham in the English Channel at the end of April, and remain until September, during which they generally reaped a rich harvest. In 1842, there was only a single fishing smack belonging to Tenby, but several have been built since. The Brixham smacks form a club, with an agent at Bristol, to which port large quantities of fish are sent by steam. The trawl net is usually dragged from four to six hours, the crew (a master, a man, and two apprentices) taking regular turns or "watches." The value of one of these smacks, including nets, is about £500, and the crew are paid £15 per month. In former days, before the fishermen went on their hazardous occupation,

dredged a few times our bay, and the results in good, and some rare, marine specimens, have far exceeded their expectations." Mr. Watson, in his *New Botanical Guide*, observes of South Wales, that "there is probably no other part of Britain in which half-a-dozen counties together are so little known, botanically"; and we are glad to see that Dr. Falconer has published a small work, which will be very useful to residents and visitors, entitled "Contributions towards a catalogue of Plants indigenous to the neighbourhood of Tenby.

they assembled every morning in St. Julian's Chapel on the pier, when prayers were offered up by a priest " for safety to themselves and success to their undertakings. "

Tenby is an excellent and very cheap *winter residence ;* and many persons of small fortune reside here during that period.

Population in 1841, 2,803 ; since which time the town has increased considerably.

HOTELS—The White Lion, and the Cobourg, both in High Street. Amongst the other Inns may be mentioned the Albion, near the Pier, the White Hart, and the Commercial Tavern.—The agent to the Bristol Steam Company is Mr. Morgan.

WALKS AND EXCURSIONS. — Few places command a greater variety of Excursions and Walks than Tenby. It is a common mistake to estimate a watering place by its individual merits— the proper rule is to combine these *with the neighbourhood.* There are four classes of Excursions here : 1. Marine. 2. Walks. 3. Short trips (occupying a day or a few hours). 4. Distant.

Marine Excursions. Pleasure Boats may be hired at a fixed charge per hour, or by the day. Carmarthen Bay affords ample scope for sailing, and for deep-sea fishing. Amongst the distant excursions are *Llanstephan, Kidwelly,* and *Stackpole Quay ;* but the latter ought not to be attempted by ladies except under very favourable circumstances. There is a difficulty in landing anywhere on the western coast in consequence of the surf. *Caldy Island* affords a pleasant short excursion. [*See* ISLANDS.]

Walks. Along South Sands to Giltar Point ; there is a great variety of sea-weed and some shells on these sands ; return by Penally ; or first extend the ramble along the edge of the cliffs to a lofty promontory overlooking the romantic little bay of Lidstep ; there are curious depressions in the limestone which communicate with the sea, and we hardly know a more charming coast walk.— *Trefloyn,* a castellated mansion in ruins.—*The Hoyle's Mouth,* a curious cavern.—*Knightston* and *Scotsborough* (one mile and a half) ; the latter a large ruined mansion, once the residence of the Rhys family.—*Gumfreston,* with its church, and excellent chalybeate springs, which resemble those of Tunbridge, in Kent. —*St. Florence.*

Penally is one of the prettiest villages we have met with in our rambles, with a church and churchyard which are perfect gems. Altar tomb with two heads slightly raised, and cross beneath ; inscription, "William de Raynoor et Isemey sa femme." Ancient Cross. At least half a mile may be saved in walking to Penally by following a path across the Burrows or Sand Hills. The ruined tower is said to have been once a windmill.

SAUNDERSFOOT. A thriving coal port, picturesquely situated in a sheltered part of Carmarthen Bay, where there are excellent sands. The harbour, which belongs to a company formed in 1829, is artificial, protected by piers, and connected with tramways which lead to extensive collieries. The "Tenby, Saundersfoot, and South Wales Railway" Company, which has power to purchase all the works, mean to make important improvements. The anthracite coal-field in this vicinity contains 95 per cent. of carbon, and there is an abundance of iron and limestone.—Beyond Saundersfoot are *Hean Castle*, at which is a modern residence, inhabited by Mr. Stokes, and *Amroth Castle*, once a Norman feudal abode, and now a splendid, although uninhabited, modern mansion, exquisitely situated. The sea has made great inroads on the land in this part of the bay.

EXCURSIONS.—1. To *Manorbeer* and *Carew Castles*. 2. To *Pater* and *Milford Haven*. 3. To the *Stack Rocks* and *St. Gowan's Head*. 4. To *Lawhaden Castle*, *Slebech*, and *Picton Castle*. Each may occupy a day.

Manorbeer Castle.

The carriage road from Tenby runs through Penally, and near the sea coast. A more romantic place than Manorbeer, or "the manor of the lords," hardly exists. The village chiefly consists of decayed Flemish houses of great antiquity ; and the castle is set in a framework of hills, overlooking a delicious little cool sandy haven, and a wild and broken coast terminated by St. Gowan's Head. "The Castle remains," accurately observes Mr. Fenton, "the most perfect model of an old Norman baron's residence, with all its appendages, church, mill, dove-house, ponds, park, and grove still to be traced, and the houses of his vassals at such a distance as to be within call." The structure is the most entire in Wales, "for its fate has been singular,

having never experienced the ravages of enemies;" and it "ceased
to be inhabited ere the feudal age was passed," and has therefore not suffered from innovations.   The stone roofs of many of
the buildings are perfect—a rare circumstance ; and the chimneys

and other features show that a Flemish architect must have been
employed.—The founder is believed to have been a follower of
Arnulph de Montgomery—a Norman knight named William de

Barri, who strengthened his position by an alliance with a Welsh princess. Here, in the year 1146, was born the eminent ecclesiastic Giraldus de Barri, surnamed Cambrensis, who accompanied Archbishop Baldwin round Wales, to preach the Crusades, and whose Itinerary, which has been translated by Sir Richard Colt Hoare, forms a most valuable contribution to medieval antiquities and history. He has given an interesting description of his birthplace, which he styles " the most delightful part of Pembroke ; " and which was at that time full of orchards, vineyards, and hazel groves. Some think that Giraldus was buried in Manorbeer Church, where there is an effigy that is ascribed to him ; but Sir R. Colt Hoare entertained no doubt that Giraldus was interred at St. David's. The manor—the tenure of land in which is copyhold—and castle, passed from the de Barri's early in the reign of Henry IV., when they were bestowed on John de Windsor, from whom they reverted to the Crown, and were then purchased by Thomas Owain, of Trellwyn, from whose family they passed by marriage into that of Lord Milford, the present possessor.

On the slope of a steep hill, protected by the castle, is a rude and massive Norman church, with one of the graceful slender towers which distinguish many of the parish churches of Pembrokeshire. It contains an effigy of a Crusader chiefly in ring armour, with a shield charged with the arms of the de Barri's. In 1847, a hideous gallery of painted deal, which filled up the west end of the nave, was removed ; and open seats of oak substituted, at the expense of Mr. E. Wilson, of Lydstep House, who also provided means for the removal of a square sash window at the west end, for which a three-light Early English window has been substituted. The ruins of a chantry or small collegiate structure may be seen near the south side of the church.—From Manorbeer we proceed up a hill to the left, which leads across the Ridgeway to

Carew Castle,

another princely relic of antiquity. On the left hand side of the road, in approaching the village of Carew, is a lofty ancient Cross of great beauty, which we have here pictured. Mr. J. O. Westwood, who considers it one of the finest examples of this kind of monument he has ever been able to discover, conjectures that

T

its date may be referred to the eleventh century. Carew (pronounced Carey) Castle, originally *Caerau*, was one of the demesnes

of the Prince of South Wales, and
passed with seven others into the
hands of Gerald de Windsor, appointed
lieutenant of these parts by Henry I.,
on his marriage with Nesta, daughter of Rhys ap Tewdwr, who was
afterwards carried off by force, at
night, by Owain, a Welsh lord. In
the latter half of the fifteenth century, Sir Edmund Carew, one of his
descendants, mortgaged the Castle
to Sir Rhys ap Thomas, who made
it during the latter part of his life
his chief residence, and entirely rebuilt the north-east side, adding the
sumptuous series of state apartments,
which are now its distinguishing feature.   The Carew family regained
the castle and estates in the reign of Henry VIII. ; the present
owner lives in Somersetshire.   Sir Rhys ap Thomas, who resided
here in the style of a Prince, entertained Henry VII. on his
march to Bosworth Field ; but the chief incident in the history
of Carew, is a tournament which was given by Sir Rhys on St.
George's Day, in honour of his being created Knight of the Garter.
A very minute and graphic account of this festival—which was
attended by six hundred of the nobility and gentry of South Wales,
and lasted a week—is preserved.

The castle stands on a gentle elevation above a creek of Milford
Haven, and is of quadrangular form.   On the south-west side
it was battered severely by Cromwell's troops, to whom it was
surrendered after a sharp siege, before Pembroke fell.   Several
hours may be agreeably spent in examining the details.   Secret
passages in the walls, and other contrivances, are now laid open,
including curious dungeons ; but the state apartments and the
chapel will perhaps interest visitors the most.   These apartments

are of large extent ; the great hall measures 102 feet by 20 ; and externally there have been few designs more graceful than this range, two stories in height, lighted by lofty square-headed windows, the mullions and transoms of which are nearly perfect. —Near the entrance is a room 80 feet by 30 ; the arms over the gateway, on the west, are those of England, the Duke of Lancaster, and the Carews.—The person who keeps the key of the castle lives in a white-washed cottage opposite to the entrance.

The chancel of Carew Church is paved with encaustic tiles commemorative of Bishops of St. David's and the family of Sir Rhys ap Thomas ; there are several interesting ancient monumental effigies, chiefly of members of the Carew family.

EXCURSION TO ST. DAVID'S.

The construction of the South Wales Railway will render the accomplishment of the first or longest half of the journey from Tenby to St. David's, viz., to Haverfordwest, a very easy matter. Hitherto the best course has been to hire a car to the latter town, and from thence proceed on foot (if the tourist happens to be a pedestrian), so as to get into St. David's just after sunset.

At the thriving town of NARBERTH, which occupies an eminence a little to the east of the Eastern Cleddau river, there is a Norman Castle, which Leland styles "a praty pile of old Sir Rees" (Sir Rhys ap Thomas). This fortress was much injured in Cromwell's day, but it was inhabited in 1657, when it formed a portion of the vast possessions of the Barlows of Slebech. The Baron de Rutzen has built a market-house, and made other improvements at Narberth. INN—The Rutzen Arms. *Lampeter Church*, in this neighbourhood, is a very interesting structure.

Templeton, a mile from Narberth, a favourite hunting place of the Knights Templars of Slebech, contains a number of ancient cottages and some ruins. A large triangular *British Entrenchment* may be traced on the eastern verge of Canaston Wood.

𝕷𝖆𝖜𝖍𝖆𝖉𝖊𝖓 𝕮𝖆𝖘𝖙𝖑𝖊 is seen on a picturesque elevation, on the right of the road to Haverfordwest, about three miles from Narberth, the scenery from which town is frequently very beautiful. This structure, which possesses a most majestic entrance, was for

some centuries one of the principal residences of the Bishops of
St. David's. Bishop Barlow stripped Lawhaden and the palace
of St. David's of their leaden roofs, "as well as all his other
palaces of everything that could be converted into immediate
profit, to furnish him, by the dilapidation he himself had occasioned, with the plea of removing the see to Carmarthen, or at
least for contracting the episcopal establishment." Bishop Mil-
bourne, A.D. 1616, completed the work of destruction.—The village
of Lawhaden stands on the summit of a high ridge, overlooking
the river Cleddau, and is an excellent fishing station.

Three or four miles further on the road passes through the
demesne of *Slebech*, one of the finest estates in Pembrokeshire.
A commandery of the Knights of St. John of Jerusalem was
founded here, but their abode was chiefly destroyed in the civil
war, and the church, which contains recumbent effigies, forms
almost their sole memorial. In Slebech Hall, which stands near
the banks of the Cleddau river, is a massive sword, used at the
installation of the knights of St. John. The Baron Rutzen, the
present owner of this property, married a daughter of the late
Nathaniel Phillips, Esq., to whom the estate was left. The
Countess of Lichfield is her sister.—A new Church, which forms
a prominent object on the side of the turnpike road, was consecrated at Slebech in 1847. It is said to have cost nearly £15,000,
£10,000 of which sum was munificently presented by the Baron
and Baroness de Rutzen.

Picton Castle, the seat of Lord Milford (recently Sir R.
Bulkeley Phillips, Bart.) adjoins Slebech. Here, amidst ancestral
woods, is an ancient castle, still substantially the edifice founded
by William de Picton, a Norman knight, in the reign of William
Rufus. Probably no other structure in Britain of equal antiquity
has been so well preserved, and *continuously inhabited* by a regular
succession of the lords of the place. The castle was held for
King Charles by Sir Richard Phillips, and closely besieged, but
sustained little injury. The late Lord Milford made additions at
the west end, which are injurious in an architectural sense.—The
park possesses many attractions; the gardens are extensive; and
there is a beautiful walk to Slebech, near an ancient encampment

called *Castle Lake.* Picton commands a prospect of the confluence of two rivers, down the upper part of *Milford Haven :* and
the most striking approach in a landscape point of view is from a
ferry opposite Landshipping Quay, from whence there is a walk
through the woods.

HAVERFORDWEST.

Distant from				Miles	Distant from				Miles.
Broadhaven ..	..	..	..	6	Narberth	..	..	..	11
Cardigan	..	..	..	26	Picton Castle	..	..	..	5
Carmarthen, by St. Clears..			..	33	Pembroke	..	..	..	11
Fishguard	..	..	..	14	St. David's	..	..	..	15½
Milford	..	..	..	7½	Tenby, by Narberth ..		..	..	21

This town, which is the capital of the county, stands on a hill
overlooking a valley watered by the river Cleddau, and is an odd
mixture of modern houses with old zigzag streets. There are
very cheap and abundantly-supplied markets—especially famed
for the quality of the mutton—on Tuesday and Saturday, and
many persons have selected Haverfordwest or the neighbourhood
as a residence on grounds of economy.

Haverfordwest was one of the chief stations in the province of
Ros, which was peopled by the Flemings; and the town was burnt
to the castle gate by Prince Llewellyn A.D. 1220.

The Keep of the Castle, founded by Gilbert de Clare, has been
converted into the County Gaol ; and at the end of a parade or
public walk on an elevation over the river are the remains of a
Priory of Black Canons.—There are three churches, the chief of
which, *St. Mary's,* at the upper end of High Street, is a fine old
structure, which was most judiciously restored in 1844. The
carved roof, and clustered columns with grotesque capitals, are
much admired. Amongst the sepulchral memorials are a rude
stone effigy and some monuments of the Milford family.

A Literary and Scientific Association was established in the
spring of 1847, and was soon joined by about 150 members. A
good library and reading-room are attached, and lectures are
delivered during the winter season. The people of Haverfordwest
may vie in point of intelligence with any town in Wales. A county
paper, the *Pembrokeshire Herald,* was established in 1845.

There is only water for vessels of small burthen up to the town. One of the Bristol and Tenby steamers trades to Haverfordwest ; distance from Tenby by water 46 miles ; from Milford 14 miles.

The Assizes for the County are held at the Guildhall. Races take place in the autumn, and a pack of Fox Hounds is kept. The annual meetings of the Pembrokeshire Agricultural Society are held here in a new show yard or cattle market, of two acres, at the top of Barn Street, surrounded by a high wall, and fitted up at a cost of £400. The population in 1841 was 4,965, and in 1847 about 6,000. The Haverfordwest Poor Law Union comprises 63 parishes and townships ! INN—The Castle.

An omnibus runs to and from St. David's in the summer, every Tuesday, Thursday, and Saturday ; and a coach has, we believe, been started to Cardigan and Aberayron.

The road from Haverfordwest to St. David's is very tame for four or five miles, when suddenly a magnificent view of St. Bride's Bay, with its coasts and islands, opens before you. **Roch Castle**, or the Castle on the Rock, is a fine object on the right, and is much larger than it appears at a distance. The founder was Adam de Rupe, who also built Pill Priory. It was taken, burnt, and dismantled in the civil wars, when it was garrisoned for the king ; previously to which it had undergone considerable changes to render it fitter for a dwelling. Cromwell is said to have directed the assault, and to have been struck on his helmet by a javelin.

You now descend a steep hill to the *Newgale Sands* and pebble ridge, which extend for nearly two miles. Mr. Fenton states that "there is a tradition that a great part of this immense tract of sea, St. Bride's Bay, was land." The rock scenery to the west of Newgale, towards Solva, is of singular outline.

A little to the left of the road, about two miles further on, is an artificial mound called Pointz Castle, supposed to be the site of a Roman Watch Tower. The descent to the long narrow inlet or Valley of SOLVA is very beautiful, especially if the tide be in. Solva is one of the oddest little ports imaginable, with an entrance protected by rocks.

The country becomes more and more desolate as the traveller

advances westward.   " The land about this remote angle of the
sea is rocky, barren, and fruitless ; it is neither clothed with
woods, distinguished by rivers, nor beautified with meadows, but
constantly exposed to storms and tempests. "   This picture,
which was painted by Giraldus more than six centuries and a half
ago, is still applicable to a great extent ; for although the soil is
not fruitless it is poor, and the rude masses of primitive rocks that
frequently '' crop out '' give additional wildness to the scenery.
The effect of St. David's Head on the western horizon is grand
and singular.   On the north, the long and graceful line of Preselly
Mountains, affords relief to the wearied sight.—The mean street
which forms the " city '' of

St. David's

harmonises with the surrounding scenery.   We first entered it in
the hush of a glorious evening in July, about an hour after sunset.   We looked in vain, as we walked leisurely along, for any
signs of the Cathedral.   An old Cross beckoned us—so to speak—
onwards.   Suddenly we caught a glimpse of the pinnacles of a
solemn gray tower, and after walking a few steps to the inner
edge of the imposing Tower Gate which protects the Close, we
beheld, through the dim trembling light, the aged Cathedral, the
exquisite ruins of the Bishop's Palace and other ecclesiastical
edifices, reposing calmly, in what appeared to be a profound
hollow.   It seemed a realization of an abode of Peace.

But the religious establishment of St. David's leaves an impression, under broad daylight, which cannot easily be effaced.
When we saw it, there was much to admire, much to offend.   The
state of neglect is which the place had been left jarred harshly on
the feelings, and produced an impression of melancholy.

In this austere solitude, near the Roman *Menapia* (the terminus
of the *Via Julia*)—the very site of which is now doubtful—the
patron saint of Wales, " one of the greatest lights that the
Church ever enjoyed," founded a monastery towards the close of
the fifth century.   David subsequently succeeded Dubritius as
Archbishop of Caerleon, and partly in consequence of his venera-
tion for St. Patrick, partly on account of his love for retirement,
removed the metropolitan see hither.   St. David's "now a suffragan

itself, once numbered seven suffragans within its pale, viz., Worcester, Hereford, Llandaff, Bangor, St. Asaph, Llanbadarn, and Margam, all which, as such, gave meeting to Austin and his associates for composing some differences between the old and new Christians." Twenty-six prelates held the mitre here in succession ; and the see lost its metropolitan rank in the days of Archbishop Sampsom, who retired to Dol in Brittany, where he became involved in an useless dispute as to authority with the Archbishop of Tours.

The Cathedral. " In the year 1176," says Browne Willis, " when Peter de Leia became Bishop of the see, the cathedral had been so much ruined by the incursions of the Danes and other pirates, that it was thought right to take it down and rebuild it. " The character of the chief portion of the existing structure, which is dedicated to St. David and St. Andrew, leads to the inference that Bishop de Leia carried out much of the work during his lifetime. The plan is cruciform, and the dimensions are as follow : length from east to west, within, 290 feet ; of the nave, 124 ; of the choir and space beyond it, 80 : transept, 120 ; breadth of body and aisles, 76 ; height of the body, 46 ; and of the tower, 127 feet. The Lady Chapel is in ruins.—The nave possesses a fine roof of Irish oak, and is divided from the aisles by six Norman arches with bold mouldings, resting on massive columns. A clerestory, the windows of which " are deeply recessed within semicircular arches richly decorated with late Norman mouldings delicately carved," rises above a very indifferent triforium. The effect of this nave, which was for many years used as a parish church, is very impressive, and a great alteration for the better was made in 1844 by the removal of pews which formerly disfigured it, on the completion and restoration of the South Transept for a like purpose. The choir is lofty, but short, and chiefly occupies the space under the central tower. The Bishop's throne, and the stalls with grotesque carvings, deserve special mention. Beyond the choir is Bishop Vaughan's Chapel, an elegant building in the latest pointed style, with a vaulted roof of fan tracery. An avenue leads to the Lady Chapel.

Some of the monuments, which include recumbent effigies of

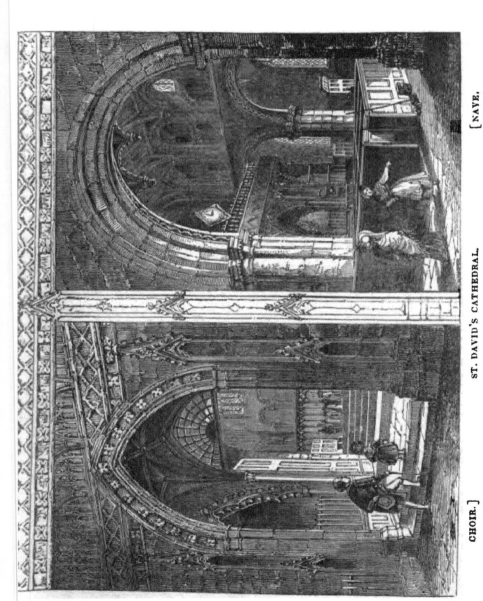

CHOIR.] ST. DAVID'S CATHEDRAL. [NAVE.

Bishops, are of high antiquity. The shrine of St. David (with recesses, where it is said that votaries used to deposit their offerings), the tomb of Edmund Tudor, Earl of Richmond, father of Henry VII., a figure of a priest in the southern aisle, said to represent Giraldus Cambrensis, who it is averred was buried here A. D. 1213, a monument of Rhys ap Gryffydd, Prince of South Wales, and of his son, Rhys Grug, are the most interesting. St. David's shrine was one of the most celebrated in the world. Multitudes of pilgrims of all ranks, including William I., Henry II., Edward I., and Queen Eleanor visited it ; princes came bare-footed.

There is a daily service. Since Dr. Connop Thirlwall was appointed to the see in 1840, laudable efforts have been made to cleanse the Augean stable which then existed at St. David's—we mean the material fabric. The diocese, under the new act, comprehends the counties of Pembroke, Cardigan, Carmarthen, and Radnor, with the exception of five parishes in the latter. The present excellent Bishop made himself a proficient in Welsh within a few months after his appointment to the see, and can perform every part of Divine Service, when necessary or desirable, in that language.

Considerable progress has been made with the work of restoration, which has hitherto been chiefly effected by the Dean and Chapter, but ought to be "made the object of a diocesan or national subscription." The chief works already completed, under the skilful superintendence of Mr. Butterfield, architect, of London, in addition to the restoration of the South Transept, are as follow : A large Decorated window has been inserted in the gable of the North Transept, hitherto blocked up. Two other Decorated windows, copied from an original example, have been placed in the aisles. A subscription has been raised among members of the University of Oxford, for the restoration of the rood screen and loft, which were long grievously disfigured by mean additions. The screen is a beautiful example of Decorated stone-work, and was the work of the famous Bishop Gower. "The entrance to the choir passes through the centre of the screen, under a stone ceiling of skeleton groining. The portion to the south of the entrance opens north, south, and west, by arches decorated with hanging tracery, and contains two tombs with groined roofs, divided by a traceried arch.   Each of these tombs, and a third to the north of the entrance, is surmounted by a recumbent effigy of an ecclesiastic....The interior was originally painted ; the crucifixion, the evangelistic symbols, and other sacred devices, being still visible." Light open gates of wrought iron have been substituted for ugly doors, which occupied the choir entrance ; and we believe that a new tile pavement has been laid down in front of it.   The Norman aisle, between the nave and the choir, which had been built up under the erroneous idea that it could not carry itself, has been opened.   When we visited the church, it appeared deplorably drained round the outside ; but we trust that this defect will be remedied.

St. Mary's College.   On the north of the cathedral are the ruins of a collegiate chantry, founded in the fourteenth century by Bishop Hoton, and John of Gaunt, Duke of Lancaster, for the maintenance of a master and seven fellows.

The Bishop's Palace is divided by the little river Alan from the foregoing, and even in its present state of miserable desolation is a most august structure.   The exterior is distinguished by a beautiful parapet built by Bishop Gower, in the style of Swansea Castle and Lamphey Court, consisting of a series of light arches, resting upon octagonal pillars with decorated capitals.   This elevation formed both an elegant screen to the roof, and a place of defence.   The plan of the palace was quadrangular, but only the south-east and south-west sides remain.   The former was appropriated to the residence of the Bishop, and contains a hall 67 feet long and 25 broad, entered by an elegant semi-octagonal arch.   Beyond this is a drawing-room and a chapel.   The kitchen, a curious structure, stood at the south-east end, beyond which is a superb range of buildings, containing a hall 96 feet long and 33 wide, entered by a beautiful porch, in which are mutilated statues of Edward III., and his Queen Phillipa.   This hall is erroneously styled " King John's," but it was not erected until many years after his reign.   The Bishop of St. David's had five other residences.—The Close is a mile round, and enclosed

by a wall ; and there are other antiquities of inferior interest in
addition to those we have described.

Inn—The Commercial, where a car may be obtained.

St. David's Head, the ancient *Octopitarum*, is a rugged gloomy
promontory of great height, three miles from " the city." The
convulsed scenery—the number of sunken rocks—the scattered
black islets which play with the white breakers for many miles—
are proofs of the effects of storms on this very exposed coast.
The Head was once a station of the Druids, of whom there are
many vestiges. In the clefts of the rocks a species of crystal
is found, which somewhat resembles the amethyst when first
obtained, and is called the " St. David's Diamond."

A Chapel dedicated to St. Justinian was built by Bishop
Vaughan for pilgrims who visited Ramsey Island, and who here
offered up prayers before embarking. Boats can enter a small
creek close at hand called Porthstinan, the distance from which
to the island is about half a league. [*See* Islands.]

———

The tourist who has proceeded to St. David's from Tenby, and
who wishes to return, may select either of two routes that we shall
describe ; but it is desirable, if time can be afforded, to follow the
western coast through Fishguard and Newport to Cardigan,
where the scenery of the Teivy offers great attractions. We shall,
to complete our itinerary, first take the latter course.

Those who have leisure and like to depart from beaten tracks,
will not only find some sublime and untouched rock scenery on
the coast between St. David's and Fishguard, which almost
throughout this side of Pembrokeshire exhibits very numerous
vestiges of earthworks thrown up by the Danes and other piratical invaders, but what is much more interesting, many fine
Druidical remains.

The coast recedes and forms a bay, part of which is called
Abermawr, from the confluence of a small river with the sea here—
protected to the north by a rugged promontory terminated by
Strumble Head. The sheltered position of Abermawr attracted
the attention of Mr. Brunel, after Fishguard had been abandoned
as the terminus of the South Wales Railway, and application was

made to Parliament in the session of 1848 to construct the terminus of the line here, at or near the boundary between the parishes of Mathry and Granston. There is a small creek at Abercastle, where a coasting trade has long been carried on in sloops ; "the force of the sea is here broken by a small island to the north-east, and by high lands embowing from the south-west, leaving a safe entrance, and forming a sheltered harbour." The island is accessible at low water.

At Long House, in the village of *Trevin*, above Abercastle, (supposed to be the grange of an episcopal palace, built by Bishop Martin, which once stood here, and of which a vault remains), is a large and perfect *Cromlech :* there are six supporters, only four of which are in contact with the covering or altar stone.—At *Treslanog*, about a mile beyond Mathry, on the right, are many Druidical vestiges, including a *Cromlech*, 14 feet long by 8 in breadth.—In the adjoining parish of *St. Nicholas* are two other *Cromlechs*, just above the village of *Trellys*, and at *Ffynnonddrudian*. From this wild parish you must enquire the best and nearest way to

FISHGUARD.

Distant from			Miles.	Distant from					Miles.
Cardigan by Newport	..	..	17½	Newport	..	..	..	..	7
Haverfordwest	..	..	14	St. David's	..	..	..	..	16

The supposed advantageous natural position of Fishguard as a point of embarkation for Ireland has for many years given it a certain degree of importance. "The extent of Fishguard Bay, from east to west, is about three miles, and from north to south, about a mile and three-quarters, and the general depth of the water is from 30 to 70 feet, according to the distance from the shore, which is bold all round. The quality of the bottom all over the bay is sand, mixed with mud a little below the surface, so that ships of the largest size may anchor in all parts of it, with south-east, southerly, and westerly winds, in perfect safety." The harbour is on the west side of the bay. Fishguard was an ancient British port and a seat of the Druids, and was occupied by the Romans. It is picturesquely situated near the mouth of the river Gwayn, and is divided into two parts, the Upper and

Lower Town. A number of vessels belong to the port, but the trade is unimportant. Population in 1841, 2,013.

The descent made by the French on the 20th of February, 1797, took place at Llanwrda, two miles and a half from Fishguard. About 1,400 ragamuffins landed under the command of General Tate, and surrendered on the following day, after committing several acts of plunder, to a force of militia and volunteers not half their own strength, under the command of Lord Cawdor.

There is a huge *Cromlech* in a field near Stonehall, in the parish of *St. Lawrence*, about six miles from Fishguard, a mile to the west of the Haverfordwest road.

Glyn Amnel, near Fishguard, is the seat of John Fenton, Esq., son of the lamented historian of the county.

NEWPORT stands near the extremity of a bay, at the mouth of the river Nevern. Very little is left of the Castle founded by William, son of Martin de Tours. The form of government conferred by a charter granted by this noble is still retained. A distant view of the town is much more inviting than a close inspection. Large quantities of slate are shipped here, several of the quarries being on the coast. There is excellent salmon fishing in the Nevern. Population of the town and parish 1751.— The distance from Newport to Cardigan is 10½ miles ; from Kilgerran 8 miles.

NEVERN is about two miles from Newport, and eight from Cardigan. Martin de Tours settled here, soon after he conquered the lordship of Kemmes ; and there are a few remains of his castle, Llanhyver, on an eminence to the west of the church. The parish, which is the largest in the county, stretching to the Percelly mountains, is romantic and diversified ; especially the scenery along the deep, wooded, and sometimes rocky course of the Nevern, (in Welsh, Niver, " a number," in allusion to the numerous streams that form this river). The Church, of which a fine engraving is given in Hoare's *Giraldus*, is a structure of some interest, founded by one of the early Norman lords of Kemmes, on the site of a British church built by St. Brynach—to whom it is still dedicated—in the sixth century. In the south side of the churchyard is a decorated *Cross* of great beauty, supe-

rior in the opinion of Mr. Fenton to that at Carew ; it is 13 feet
high, and 2 broad, and bears an illegible inscription.—Archbishop Baldwin, when on his mission with Giraldus, in favour of
the Crusades, preached, according to tradition, from a rock still
called *Craig yr Escob*, (the Bishop's rock), near a bridge over the
small river Duad, now styled *Pont Baldwyn*, a little way above
the village of College.   This fact is known to few.

Druidical Antiquities.   This is a land of primitive antiquities.
Two miles and a half north-east of Nevern Church, on Tre Icert

farm, is a *Cromlech*, supported by three upright stones, called *Llech y Drybedd*, pictured in the title of Fenton's *Pembrokeshire*, and which was mistaken by the late Sir S. Meyrick for the huge *Cromlech* of *Coeton Arthur*, or Arthur's Quoit, which stands on *Pentre Ivan* farm, two miles and a half to the *south*-east of Nevern Church, near the base of the fine hill, called Carn Englyn. This Cromlech once stood within a stone circle, 150 feet round. The subjoined engraving shows the character of this immense monument, which Sir R. C. Hoare considered the largest Druidical relic in Wales, but that gentleman appears not to have been aware of the Cromlech at St. Nicholas, Glamorganshire, (*ante* p. 133]. The top stone is 18 feet long and 9 broad ; the loftiest of the supporters is 8 feet high, the lowest 7 ; a person on horseback can ride under.

A huge recumbent stone may be seen in a neighbouring field ; and a correspondent of the *Archæologia Cambrensis* mentions the discovery of a curiously pitched way, called the *Causeway*, which tradition says formerly led to the Cromlech, from whence it is distant half a mile.—A very fine *Cromlech* stands in a field on the left of the road from Newport to Berry Hill, two miles west from Nevern Church. A curious *Druidical chamber* may be seen in a field adjoining the Fishguard road, about half a mile from Newport.

An excursion to the PERCELLY or PRESELE MOUNTAINS can be made either from Newport or Fishguard. This chain, which forms the most conspicuous feature in the scenery of the county, extends for nearly ten miles ; and the western summit, the *Vrenni Vawr*, commands an exceedingly fine prospect. *Cwm Cerwyn*, the central and highest summit, is 1,754 feet high ; the hill to the eastward is called *Moel Eryr*.

Kilgerran Castle, and St. Dogmael's Priory, are both just within Pembrokeshire, but as they are always included in an excursion to Cardigan, we have described them with that town.

We proceed to indicate the routes back from St. David's to Tenby. The pedestrian may avoid Haverfordwest, by following a road near the line of coast from Newgale Sands near the eastern

side of St. Bride's Bay, which runs by Nolton, Haroldston, and
Robeston, to MILFORD. The Nolton stone is equal to Portland.
There is a charming little watering place at

BROADHAVEN, six miles from Haverfordwest—much frequented
in summer—which commands a magnificent view of St. Bride's
Bay, from St. David's Head to St. Bride's, with the islands of
Skokam, South Bishop, and the port of Solva. It is celebrated
for the extent and hardness of its sands, and for the ocean purity
of its water, and is altogether one of the nicest places for a person
who wishes to live quietly and cheaply, in the kingdom. It is well
supplied with fish, and within an easy distance of Haverfordwest
Market. There are some beautiful rock scenery, and delightful
walks to the peninsula, beyond which *Skomer* and *Skokam* islands
rise out of the deep.

MILFORD

Is prettily situated on a sloping point of land, about six miles
from the entrance of the Haven to which it gives its name. It
rose into importance towards the close of the last century, the
Hon. Mr. Greville, heir to Sir W. Hamilton, having obtained an
Act to establish docks, quays, and other improvements for the
purpose of forming a station for the mail packets for the south of
Ireland. A dock and slips for building ships of war were soon
constructed, and the place steadily increased until 1814, when
the government removed the royal dockyard and arsenal to Pater.
For many years afterwards, however, Milford continued to be the
Irish packet station; at length the removal of the Waterford
steamers to Hobbs' Point at Pater gave the finishing blow to
its prosperity. Many excellent houses are now untenanted, and
the half-deserted place, which is exceedingly healthy, offers great
advantages to families who wish to carry out economy. The neighbourhood of Milford is associated in the mind with *Cymbeline*.

Some fragments of the once cruciform church of Pill Priory
exist at the inner end of Hubberston Pill, near Milford.

MILFORD HAVEN ought to be viewed from the water. The hills
have generally a monotonous character from the land; but when
afloat the attention is distracted by a variety of objects which
enhance the scenery, and the noble character of the estuary can

be estimated. The lower and broadest portion of the haven runs in an easterly direction for about twelve miles; it then turns abruptly to the north, forming several beautiful reaches towards Haverfordwest, below which it has its origin in the junction of the East and West Cleddau Rivers. Some parts of the lower portion are nearly two miles wide; and the haven altogether comprise five bays, ten creeks, and thirteen roadsteads. " It may," states Mr. Norie, " be entered without a pilot, either by night or day, even with contrary winds, only taking the tide ; and vessels may, without either anchor or cable, run ashore within it with complete safety on a bed of soft ooze." On the western or St. Ann's Point, near the village of Dale, are two lighthouses, which were erected in 1800. Vast fleets are sometimes detained here. The spring tides rise 36, and neaps about 26 feet. Milford Haven was protected by small forts called block-houses in the reign of Henry VIII., several of which still exist. The Board of Ordnance intend to make extensive fortifications at certain points.

At Milford a boat can be hired for Pater or Pembroke.

Those tourists who return from St. David's by Haverfordwest should take the Pembroke road to the Ferry, distant about nine miles ; and ought to diverge to the left to see Benton Castle (about two miles above the Pembroke Ferry), which is beautifully situated on a small promontory of land extending into the Haven, for the protection of which it was no doubt erected.—Near the " fishing village" of *Llangwm*, on the coast above Benton Castle, there is a famous Oyster Fishery.—We cross the ferry to

PATER, originally Paterchurch, where there is a *Royal Dockyard*, at which many of the finest ships in the navy have been built. The government establishments cover eighty acres of ground surrounded by a high wall, and are frequently visited by parties from Tenby, to whom the multifarious objects within the yard are a source of great attraction. There are twelve slips for ship-building, covered with iron roofs, and a launch is an event which draws thousands of spectators from distant places, Tenby included, of course. The jetty at Hobbs' Point, for Irish packets, stands a few hundred yards to the eastward, and there is a splendid Hotel, which was built by the government. The

U

fortifications connected with Pembroke Dockyard have been materially strengthened. Barracks on a large scale, an imperfect octagon, which includes an area of more than 6,000 square yards, have recently been completed under the superintendence of Capt. Farris, R. E., and strongly fortified with bastions, a wide and deep ditch, and loops for small arms. A new church was completed in 1848.—The population of Pater exceeds 4,000.

PEMBROKE.

Distant from			Miles.	Distant from			Miles.
Carew Castle ..	..	..	.. 4	The Stack Rocks	..	..	.. 9
Carmarthen ..	..	..	.. 35	Stackpole Court	..	..	.. 5
Haverfordwest	..	..	.. 13½	Milford	..	..	.. 7
Manorbeer ..	..	..	.. 6	Pater	..	..	.. 2

Pembroke (originally called *Pen Bro*, a promontory) is well situated on a ridge of land, running nearly due east and west, so that it chiefly consists of one irregularly-built street, with but slight intersections. There are no manufactures, and several persons of small property have pitched their tents here. The population of the parishes of St. Mary and St. Michael, within part of which the town is comprehended, as well as Pater, amounted in 1841 to 6,665, but there is a populous suburb called Monkton, which contains a town and rural population of 1,462. Pembroke stands on a creek of Milford Haven, which is crossed by a bridge, from which the finest view of the Castle can be obtained. Very fine oysters are dredged up in great quantities in Crow Pool.

The CASTLE occupies a rocky eminence at the edge of the creek, and both in an architectural and historical point of view is a structure of very great interest. The rude fortress erected here by Arnulf de Montgomery passed into the hands of King Henry the First, who conferred the lordship—which was elevated to the rank of a county palatine—on the redoubtable Gilbert Strongbow, created Earl of Pembroke in 1109, who greatly strengthened and extended the fortifications, and rendered the castle a residence fit for a family holding royal jurisdiction. Several subsequent additions have evidently been made, and the castle is a fine combination of the Norman and the early transition styles. It would be strange if a stronghold like this had not sustained many sieges. We can only refer to the most memorable—that of the seventeenth century (A.D. 1648), when Cromwell was compelled to proceed into Wales, where the royalists, cheered by the defection of Colonels Laugharne, Powell, and Poyer from the Republican cause, were in great force. Laugharne made a hasty retreat after his defeat at St. Fagan's to Pembroke, where he and a large body of cavaliers determined to make an obstinate stand. The castle was deemed almost impregnable, and all the experience of Cromwell in strategy, as well as force, was required to subdue it. The beseiged were gradually reduced to great straights ; then the enemy got possession of their mills ; and finally Cromwell managed to. cut off their water, by planting artillery " so as to batter down a staircase leading into a cellar of one of the bastions, where was their principal supply." The cavern, with a copious spring, and the broken staircase, can still be traced. The brave hearts of the leaders at last failed, and the garrison surrendered on terms ; but the chief leaders were compelled to throw themselves on the mercy of Parliament. Laugharne, Powell, and Poyer were tried by a court martial, and being found guilty of treason, were at first condemned to death, but it was resolved to spare the lives of two. Three papers were proffered them, on two of which was written " Life given by God "; Poyer drew that which was blank, and was shot in Covent Garden in April, 1649.

The rock on which the estate stands is in most parts forty feet high, and was encompassed with water except on the town side, where there was a dry ditch, protected by a barbican. A lofty embattled wall, strengthened by numerous bastions, and having only one entrance to the land through a gateway of prodigious strength, enclosed an inner and an outer ward, into which the castle was divided. The former contained most of the state apartments, and the circular keep. This tower, which is divided into five stages, is 75 feet high, and 163 feet in circumference at the base, from whence it gradually diminishes, forms one of the most beautiful features of the ruin, and visitors are always directed to

ascend it in order to obtain the view from the vaulted summit,
and to examine the remarkable nature of the winding staircase.
The walls are fourteen feet thick.   The superb state apartments
over the "Wogan" in the exterior of the inner ward are evidently
of later date than the rest of the castle ; the chapel is included in
this series, near which is a small apartment in which it is said
that Henry VII. was born.   Leland, however, who lived near that
time, states that the monarch first saw the light in one of the
handsome rooms of the great gateway : " In the latter ward I
saw the chambre wher King Henry the VII. was borne, in knowledge whereof a' chymmeney is new made, with the armes and
badges of King Henry VII.''—A very steady head is required to
follow the guide safely through some parts of the ruins.   Do not
omit to walk round the exterior, and to visit the enormous tavern
called the Wogan, fronting the river, which is 75 feet long and
59 wide, and communicates with the castle above by a narrow
stair, and with the harbour by a sally-port.

Strongbow fortified the town with a lofty wall, bastions, and
three gates, which were perfect three centuries ago.—Pembroke
contains three churches, one of which, St. Michael's, is early
Norman.—The markets are held on Wednesday and Saturday.
INNS—The Green Dragon, the Golden Lion.—In the suburb of
Monkton are the remains of a Priory.

> EXCURSION TO LINNEYHEAD, AND THE WESTERN COAST.

The tourist, when at Pembroke, should make a circuit *round
the coast* of the Hundred of Castle Martin from *Linney Head* to St.
Gowan's Head, from whence the best course is to return through
Stackpole to Pembroke.   A car can be driven to Linney Head,
distant seven miles.   We shall now conduct the reader part of the
distance—viz., as far as the Stack Rocks, reserving a notice of
the remaining portion of the coast to the eastward, for a *separate
excursion from Tenby.*

The road commands some beautiful views of the Haven as you
proceed from Pembroke, and passes through a rich country, well
timbered, to *Orielton,* the deserted seat of Sir John Owen, Bart.,
M.P., once the scene of princely hospitality. A *Cromlech* is to be

found in Castle Martin parish, two or three miles to the westward.
At Linney is a large farm-house, the last evidence of "civilization"
for many miles. A remarkable reef of rocks called "The Pole"
stretches into the sea in Freshwater Bay, a little to the north of
Linney Head. Now we commence one of the most sublime coast
walks in the world. The geological formation of the rocks—the
extraordinary dislocations of the strata—would even on an unex-
posed coast impart much interest to the scenery; but here, where
the tidal current from the Atlantic rushes with the greatest force,
and first meets with opposition, it may be conceived that the
appearance of the cliffs must be deeply interesting. A greater
extent of carboniferous limestone is exposed to view along these
shores than in any part of Britain. Wide undulating downs,
covered with short velvet turf and thyme, run round the coast;
but it is desirable to keep the edge, although the fatigue is consequently considerably increased, or much of the enjoyment will be
lost. Multitudes of sea birds build, or rather deposit, their eggs
in the cliffs. After passing the *Head of Man*, a bold over-hang-
ing promontory beyond Linney, you reach a *Danish camp*—the
first of several—on the outer agger of which a small tumulus may
be seen. "Harold is said to have infested this coast, and to have
left rude monuments of his predatory victories thus inscribed:
Hic·Haroldus victor fuit." Many vessels have been wrecked on
a rock called "the Crow," which can be seen about half a mile
from the land, but is covered at four hours' flood. The stratification of the rocks becomes more remarkable as you proceed;
"stacks" are sometimes separated from the mainland, and singular funnel-shaped depressions occur, one of which, of enormous
size, about three miles from Linney, hitherto unnoticed, exists at
some distance from the sea, with which it communicates. At
Flimson, where there is a ruined *Chapel*, we met with the first
dwelling we had seen for several hours; and found to our dismay
that Lord Cawdor will not permit a single inn, however humble,
to be opened on his extensive estates in this peninsula. We met,
however, with one of the most hospitable receptions we ever experienced from Mr. Lewis, the worthy farmer who occupies Flimson.
Here, as we are on the very verge of the most attractive of the

Tenby trips, we must suddenly return to that town for the purpose of describing the

EXCURSION FROM TENBY TO THE STACK ROCKS, ST. GOWAN'S HEAD, ETC.

This is a long excursion, the distance to the Stacks through Pembroke being about 19 miles, and it will be inferred that it is necessary to take provisions.—The road from Tenby to Pembroke is carried for six miles along the *Ridgeway*, a narrow elevation, which runs nearly east and west—with a gradual descent on either side—set between the "maritime land" and a fine inland valley. The road gradually descends to the village of LAMPHEY, about two miles before reaching Pembroke, where there are interesting ruins of one of *Bishop Gower's Palaces*, near which stand the modern mansion and demesne of Mr. Matthias, of Lamphey Court. Lamphey Palace can be examined during a distinct excursion to Pembroke Castle and Dockyard.

The best course is to obtain a fresh car at Pembroke for St. Gowan's. There is a very steep ascent on leaving Pembroke, and after passing St. Petrox, the view from Windmill Hill is really magnificent. A wild legend connected with the memory of a lady named Jane Mansel, who was buried in St. Petrox Church, is related. The country people affirm that her spirit, in the form of a headless spectre, may be sometimes seen driving round the parish in a carriage, with a headless coachman and headless team. You leave the carriage near Flimson, and walk to the edge of the cliffs a little to the westward, when

The STACK ROCKS or Castles suddenly fascinate you. No language can adequately describe the singularity and wildness of this scene *during a part of the summer*. The lofty rocks, up the bases of which breakers incessantly leap, are covered with innumerable sea-birds of various tribes—a living mass of feathers. Multitudes of others sail gracefully about, or dip fleetly up and down ; white wings flicker in the sunshine ; young birds make their first efforts to fly ; whole flocks repose idly on the heaving sea. Besides this, every cranny in the horizontal strata of the neighbouring rocks is tenanted by some distinct tribe of these wild and solemn visitors, whose peculiar voices fill the air. Each fresh arrival on the

Stacks is hailed with plaintive cries ; and although the whole community seems to be in a state of confusion, yet in reality there is none.   The puffins or eligugs occupy one station ; the razor bills another ; the guillemots a third ; the herring gulls a fourth ; the kittiwakes a fifth, and so on.   The Puffin or Sea Parrot, here called the Eligug, is the most numerous summer visitant of these shores.   Two varieties, the Parrot Bill and the Hatchet Bill arrive early in May, when they deposit a single large egg ; and the Stacks are seen to the greatest advantage about the middle of or the third week in July, when all the young birds are full fledged and ready to fly.   The eligugs begin to depart about Lammas ; but although a bird of passage, they now and then return in the winter for a day or two during foggy weather.   Their food is a small silvery fish, about an inch or an inch and a half long, which abounds in these seas.   Men sometimes *climb the Great Stack* in pursuit of eggs and feathers—a fearful exploit ; Earl Cawdor has, however, given strict instructions that the birds shall not be molested in any way.

At a short distance from the Stacks, on the mainland, is a large Danish Camp, which occupies a neck of land, and in which is one of the greatest wonders of the coast, the *Caldron* or '' *Devil's Punch Bowl ;*'' a black chasm or depression in the rock, which sinks to the sea level. The waves boom below, and may be seen dashing angrily in through the gloom of this abyss of horrors.

We proceeded onwards, and on reaching a limekiln near the edge of the fine new road in the turf, which has been made along this coast for miles at the expense of Earl Cawdor, diverged to the edge of the cliffs and saw the extraordinary narrow cleft called *Bosherston Mere.* This aperture is funnel-shaped—a place for Eolus to sport in ; in storms the effect is sublime beyond conception.   The waves lash the sides of the cleft with a roar which is heard at a great distance ; a column of foam forty feet high is occasionally carried into the air. Sheep are sometimes drawn down by the current of wind. Even on a clear day the sound of the sea produces an emotion of awe. The cliffs near Bosherston Mere assume very striking forms.

About a quarter of a mile onward is an immense fissure in the cliffs, which takes every one by surprise, called the *Huntsman's Leap*, over which thrilling depth two hunters, according to tradition, were carried in full chase !

The geological formation of the coast now gradually changes for the worse in a picturesque point of view ; the strata are of vast thickness, and often disposed horizontally ; thus the variety produced by the fractures to the westward is partly lost. The scale of the scenery, however, rather increases than diminishes.

A horse block in the sward marks the position of ST. GOWAN'S CHAPEL, the romantic position of which may be conjectured from our engraving. The appearance of any house dedicated to religion in a spot so wild and lonely, naturally excites earnest interest. That humble but now silent belfry once poured forth its invitations to wearied sinners to join in prayer and praise to the great Creator of the noble works around—thanksgivings faintly heard, perhaps, amidst the raging of the elements without. The descent to this oratory is by steps placed in a broken path through the rocks, which, it is said, can never be counted twice alike. We counted fifty-four before the line was broken. The Chapel, which occupies the pass to the sea, being placed across it, measures only twenty feet by twelve, and the rude solid stone altar, and a niche for holy water, yet exist. The arched doorway in the east wall leads to a cleft or excavation in the rock, just sufficient to admit a middle-sized man in rather a crouching posture. " There are," says Mr. Fenton, " numerous superstitions annexed to this miraculous cell, such as that it first opened to afford shelter to a Saint closely pursued by his pagan persecutors, and after the chase was given up and the danger over, let him out again, never closing afterwards, and retaining a faint impression of the body it had once unfolded ; that ever since it is of so accommodating a nature as to admit the largest as well as the smallest man ; and that if you frame a wish whilst in it, and do not change your mind during the operation of turning about, you will certainly obtain it." Young ladies and gentlemen never omit to enter this wishing place.

A second round-headed door near the west end of the Chapel

leads, by a broken path and steps, to a SAINTED WELL, which is placed amidst convulsed rocks at no great distance above the sea. This well, which now contains but little water, was once the resort of pilgrims, who flocked hither from all parts of the Principality

to obtain relief from its waters, which were said to relieve crippled patients miraculously. Such persons left their crutches behind as a votive offering on the altar ; and mentions that on the occa-

sion of his visit, which occurred less than forty years ago, he
perceived one placed there.   The well has been injured by a class
of visitors who everywhere disgrace the British name.   Close
below is a large fragment of limestone, which with one or two
others leading to the sea, emits when struck a bell-like tone.
There is a legend that pirates once landed here and carried off
the chapel bell, and '' that the stones it rested on or touched ever
after miraculously uttered a bell sound.''   At the period when
the devotee who chose his dwelling here '' amidst the rocks and
caves of the earth,'' in the early ages of Christianity, concealment
was very desirable, as these coasts were frequently ravaged by
pirates ; and a more secluded place it is difficult to conceive.*

The coast forms an enclosed scene terminating in the large
headland of St. Gowan's.   It possesses true elements of sublimity.   Imagine the effect of this wild view in a storm !.

St. Gowan's Head, the most southerly point of Pembrokeshire,
stretches into the sea about half a mile to the eastward of the
chapel, and commands a marine view of extreme interest.   The
coast now recedes, forming a species of estuary called *Broad
Haven*, and small vessels are able to approach it at a little pill
called *Stackpole Quay*.

The usual course pursued in excursions is to return through
Bosherston village and STACKPOLE PARK, one of the prettiest
places both in a natural and artificial point of view in Wales.
Pedestrians, however, may save nearly three miles, *if the tide be
out*, first crossing the country from St. Gowan's Head to a farm-
house called *Trevallen*, where they can obtain directions ; it is
necessary to wade a shallow marine lagoon to get to the park.

The coast is deeply indented here in two places, and the lofty
banks of the lagoons, which are almost dry when the tide is out,
have been skilfully planted, so as to obtain great warmth of colour.
One of the tongues of land was converted by the Danes into a
strong camp.   Stackpole Park, from the nature of its site, commands much variety of scenery.   The Court, Lord Cawdor's

---

* St. Gowan is said to have been a nephew of King Arthur, and in early life
a Knight of the Round Table.   A tradition long existed that '' Sir Gawain''
was buried in this chapel.

mansion, stands on the site of a castle originally founded by Sir Elidur de Stackpole early in the eleventh century, and which stood a brisk siege in Cromwell's time. The house, which has two chief fronts, is placed on a terrace which commands a lake and a long vista, fringed by dark woods ; the mind is left to guess at the extent of the scene. There is a walk from the terrace steps, along the edge of the lake, on which are many swans and flocks of *tame* wildfowl. The gardens and pleasure grounds are extensive and most judiciously laid out ; the rose garden is a gem at the proper season. Amongst the timber is a fine cork tree. The park abounds with deer, and the preserves with game. Earl Cawdor behaves with great liberality to strangers, who are permitted to put a moderate number of horses in his stables. *Stackpole Village*, on the upper side of the park, is a picture of rural felicity. In *Cheriton Church*, near at hand, is a fine altar tomb, surmounted by a canopy, to the memory of Sir Elidur de Stackpole.

From hence the tourist proceeds by the carriage road to Pembroke ; but we have walked direct to Tenby, crossing the edge of Freshwater Bay on our route to the Ridgeway, which we struck about four and a half miles from our destination. The walk is an exceedingly arduous one.

CARDIGANSHIRE

Is the most primitive and the wildest county of South Wales. The blood of the old race flows without intermixture amongst its people : its hills, although often inferior in grandeur to those of its neighbours, seem more untamed and trackless.

The district formed part of the ancient *Dimetia*. The Romans had an important station at *Loventium* (Llanio isau), from whence a road ran north and south, which is called Sarn Helen or Helen's Causeway, from *Sarn Lleon* or the "Legionary Way." An extraordinary number of British fortifications and primitive antiquities are scattered over the surface of the country. It would weary one to count the number of camps, and carns, and tomens laid down in the Ordnance maps. The following seem to have been the principal fortifications :—Cardigan, Aberystwith, Ystrad-meiric, Lampeter, Llanrhysted, Cilcennin, Dinerth, Abereinon, Castell Gwalter, Castell Flemish, Moyddyn, Penwedie, Castell Cadwgan (Aberayron), Hên Castell (Cardigan), &c. For three centuries an almost incessant war raged between the Normans—whose chief castles were at Cardigan and Aberystwith—and the Welsh. Traces of a number of fortresses of lesser importance, chiefly Welsh, may be found; but the county is not at all remarkable for architectural antiquities.

There are only a few fragments left of the famous Abbey of Strata Florida; and little else than the shadows of the names remain of inferior religious houses which existed at Llandewi-Brefi, Cardigan, Llanrhysted, and Lampeter, to tell of the Past.

Cardiganshire possesses a long line of coast, but except near the entrance of the Teivy, and near Aberystwith, the sea-shore is rather tame ; which supports the tradition that Cardigan Bay was once dry ground—the " lowland hundred." There is but little level land in the interior, except in the valleys of the Teivy, Aëron, (the south-westerly portion may be called the " low country "), and Rheidol.

The chief portion of the county is mountainous—vast sweeping ranges of hills which bound the horizon apparently without a limit. At the Devil's Bridge, and in other parts of the northern district, one is reminded of Glamorganshire, in which profound depressions of the earth below the ordinary level form marked features. We shall describe the hill country more at large, in the proper place ; but we may remark that there is a dreary sameness about many of the upland regions—perhaps because the eye ranges over a series of flat-topped eminences on a level. Many of these hills are so barren, that in ancient times the people of the adjoining counties styled Cardigan " the devil's grandmother's jointure." In the last century we are told, that " a person who was endeavouring to sell a considerable estate by auction, after having explained the value of the property, the present rents, and future capacity of improvement, thus addressed the company : ' And, gentlemen, there are ten thousand acres lying ———, not mentioned in the particulars of the estate, which will be thrown into the bargain to the purchaser " ! It is said, we believe with truth, that a man might ride sixty miles ahead through a portion of Cardiganshire and the country stretching across Wales to the north-west, and hardly meet with a house, or a human being. Large tracts of land, now either partly or wholly unprofitable, are, however, susceptible of great improvement, by means of draining. The late Mr. Thomas Johnes, who was one of the greatest planters that this country has produced, set a noble example at Hafod, which has been followed by several other land-owners ; but there is a wide field open, and a profitable return might be made if districts now useless were planted with larch. In the vales of the Teivy and the Aëron, and some other neigh-bourhoods, there is tolerably good farming : but the great majority of the farmers are a perfectly primitive race—ancient Britons in practice as well as in form—men who depend mainly on cattle, sheep, and ponies. The cottages of the peasantry are proverbi-ally wretched, yet with their broken thatched roofs and thin streams of peat smoke curling in the mountain air, they often charm the wayfarer who is weary of the every-day world, and afford perfect " studies " for sketchers. A considerable quantity of oats and butter is exported.

Cardiganshire is the Lake-land of South Wales. We have explored or enumerated about twenty, which are elsewhere described. The county, as old Drayton poetically says, also "takes delight" in brooks and rivers. Of these, the queen is the Teivy, which rises in Llyn Teivy. Next, the Rheidol, one of Plinlimmon's progeny ; the Ystwith, which receives twenty-four tributaries before it flows into the salt water ; the Mynach, or " Monks' river " ; the Aëron, between the outlet of which and the Teivy, eighteen brooks fall into the sea ; the Dothie, and the Pyscottwr, tributaries of the Towy, which, with the Claerwen and the Elan, are also of Cardiganshire birth. The only other streams worth mentioning are the Berwyn, the Wirrai—between Aberayron and Aberystwith—and the Lery, north of the latter town.

Statistics : Population, in 1801, 42,956 ; in 1831, 64,780 ; in

1841, 68,766. ·Number of parishes, all in diocese of St. David's,
68. Area, 675 square miles. Parliamentary representation : One
member for the county, one for the united boroughs of Cardigan,
Aberystwith, Lampeter, and Atpar.—*Education : Day Schools*—
Church or National, 37, attended by 1,643 scholars ; private
schools, 49 ; British, 2 ; Dissenting, 2 ; Dame, 8 ; total in these
classes of schools, 2,242 ; general total, 3,885. *Sunday Schools :*
Number of Church scholars, 4,074 ; number of Dissenting scholars, 23,057. In Cardiganshire, Mr. Jelinger Symons computes
that 3,000 persons out of 68,766 speak English as their fireside
language.

The manufactures of the county are chiefly confined to woollens
and gloves for local consumption ; knitting affords an almost
constant occupation for the women and girls.

MINING.

The county is geologically included in the slate and shale
tract of South Wales, which belongs to the transition series, and
is destitute of organic remains. It possesses neither coal nor
limestone, but has for centuries been famous for its metal mines,
which were worked under royal patent in 1567. Sir Hugh Myd-
dleton drew the vast wealth required for the construction of the
New River, by which London was supplied with water in the first
half of the seventeenth century, from Cardiganshire ; and one of
his successors, Mr. Bushel, clothed the army of Charles I., and
lent that monarch £40,000 from the same source. For this
service, he had permission *to coin the metal* that he raised, and a
mint, which was ultimately removed to Shrewsbury, was for some
time in operation at Aberystwith. During a long period mining
was almost abandoned in Cardiganshire, but of late years a considerable capital has been invested in working lead and sulphate
of zinc. "The mines of this county are in three channels of
ground, running about 10° or 15° east of south, and west of
north, and are distant from each other from two to three miles."
(*Mining Journal.*) Many of them produce silver "varying in
quality in the different mines from 14 ozs. to 80 ozs. in the ton
of lead" ; Llanvair, between Llandewi Brefi and Lampeter, is
the richest, but is not rich in lead. About 100 ozs. of silver to

the ton have occasionally been procured in this mine, and the produce is worth £28 to £30 per ton. Copper ore is sometimes found in the county. We have taken some pains to obtain a correct list of the mines at work, in a line from north to south ; those that are said to be the most important are distinguished by *italics* :—Darren, Cwm Cwmsynlog, *Goginian, Bwlch Cwm Erfin, Rheidol Mines*, Nant y Cria, *Cwm Ystwith, Lisburne* (Frongoch, &c., and Level Vawr), Glog Vach, Escair Newyn, Bron Berllan, near Pontrhydvendigaid, Llwyn Malces, Bog Mine, *Llanvair*. The average value of the lead ore varies according to the state of the market, from £9 to £12 per ton. Wages to the amount of £1,200 per month are paid at the Lisburne mines alone ; and it is estimated that £60,000 per annum is spent in Aberystwith by the mining population. The wages of men vary from 10s. to 18s. per week. Most of the mine-agents, and a few of the miners, are Cornishmen. The progress of mining enterprise has been much checked by the excessive amount of royalty demanded by landlords, one-seventh being a common rate ; Col. Powell, of Nanteos, has lately set a good example by reducing the royalty to, we believe, one-tenth. Large sums have been lost in mining.

We enter Cardiganshire at

LAMPETER.

Distant from	Miles.	Distant from	Miles.
Aberystwith	.. 28	Llandovery	.. 20
Aberystwith, by Tregaron	.. 32	Llandilo Vawr	.. 18
Aberayron	.. 15	Newcastle Emlyn	.. 21
Carmarthen	.. 24	Pumsant	.. 9
Cardigan, by Newcastle ..	.. 31	Tregaron (new road) ..	.. 11
Llandewy Brevi, (old road)	.. 7		

We have indicated *(ante p.* 250) the route from Llandovery to Lampeter, which is a new road for part of the distance. A pedestrian may save a couple of miles by enquiring for the old roads.

The town of Lampeter, which stands near the Teivy, contains not a single object of interest except St. David's College, which was founded in 1822 by the late Bishop Burgess, and completed in 1827 for the reception of students in divinity, at a cost of £20,000, upwards of one-third of which was contributed by the Government and the Crown, and the rest produced by collections in the Diocese. The total annual receipts exceed £3,000. It is a most valuable institution, as young men destined for the Church, and who are unable to incur the expenses of a regular University education, are here enabled to obtain first-rate instruction at a very low rate. A few Englishmen avail themselves of the advantage, but unfortunately no degrees can be conferred. There are several scholarships. The structure, which is quadrangular, was erected from a design by Mr. Cockerell, and is calculated to accommodate about seventy students. There is a chapel and library, which includes 9,000 volumes left by the late Dr. Burgess. The present head of the College is the Very Rev. Dr. Llewellyn, Dean of St. David's. Students are obliged to reside four years before they can obtain a testimonial. The annual fees for tuition are 12 guineas per annum ; rent £5. There is a good grammar school at Lampeter, in connection with the College.

Lampeter is a favourite fishing station, especially for salmon, and an excursion may be made from it to Llandewy-Brevi, Llanio, Tregaron, and Strata Florida. INN—The Black Lion.

There is a well-supported and useful Agricultural Society here.

We shall make a circuit of the County, first following the line of the Teivy to Cardigan ; but it is desirable to mention that there are two roads from Lampeter to Aberystwith—besides the circuitous route by Tregaron—the pleasantest of which is by Aberayron.

The road from Lampeter to Newcastle-Emlyn (ante p. 240) chiefly runs through a dreary uncultivated region. Beyond Llandyssil (11½ miles) the scenery of the Teivy becomes very pleasing, but it is below Newcastle that the river displays its chief beauties. At *Kenarth*, a sweetly situated village, there is a celebrated salmon leap,* at which 100 salmon are sometimes taken in a

* It is well known that salmon overcome extraordinary obstacles in going up rivers to spawn. *Giraldus* thus describes their motions: they " bend their tail towards their mouth, and sometimes, in order to give a greater power to their leap, they press it with their mouths, and suddenly freeing themselves from this circular form, they spring with great force (like a bow let loose) from the bottom to the top, to the great astonishment of beholders." When Giraldus wrote, *beavers* inhabited the Teivy. Mention is made of the animal in the laws of Howel Dha.

SOUTH WALES,

NORTHERN DIVISION.

SCALE OF MILES

5 4 3 2 1 0   5   10

S.^T   G E O R

C H A N N

C

Strumble H.^d   Dinas H.^d   Newp

Penbrush P.^t   Llanwnda   Fishguard
Bay   Dinas

Pwllcrochen Bay   St Nicholas   FISHGUARD   LANI
                                          Llanstinan   Llanych
Castellcoch P.^t   Abermaur
                   Brawnston   Llanfair   Cas K.
Abereiddy B.   Llanrian   Castell Morris   E M   Morfil   Hol Hai
                                            B   Punch
St DAVIDS   Camp   E   St Edren   S.^t L   Ll Newgwla
HEAD   R
        Llanhowel   Llanrerthan

morning. On these occasions the price falls to 4½d. per lb., but it is usually 6d.—Newcastle Emlyn is situated in this parish, and as the church is 2¼ miles distant from that town, a new church, containing 500 sittings, 400 of which are free, has been erected there. On crossing Kenarth Bridge, we again enter Cardiganshire, the Teivy being the southern boundary of that county; about two miles onwards, on the south side of the river, Carmarthenshire ends and Pembrokeshire commences. The drive from Kenarth to Cardigan is one of the prettiest in South Wales; some of the scenery is of a high class. We recommend pedestrians, however, on reaching *Llechyrd* (three miles from Cardigan), to cross the bridge into Pembrokeshire, and follow the course of the river along the edge of the grounds of the romantic seat of Abel Lewis Gower, Esq., *Castle Maelgwyn*, the steep wooded banks of which rise to a great height.

Kilgerran Castle, a majestic ruin overhanging the Teivy, suddenly appears on opening a long and graceful reach—a river scene of extraordinary beauty.—There is an INN, the Red Lion, at the village of Kilgerran, which is a street, half a mile long. Extensive slate quarries, the produce of which is shipped at Cardigan, are worked in this parish.—The scenery here *should be viewed by water*; and the usual course is to take a boat and proceed with the tide from Cardigan, which is distant about three miles and a half. Sir R. C. Hoare—no mean judge—says, " I have never seen ruins more happily combined with rocks, wood, and water, a more pleasing composition, or a more captivating landscape, which is animated by the numerous coracles employed in catching salmon." Gilbert Strongbow is said to have been the original founder of this castle in 1109; but the chief portion of the present edifice is attributed to William, Earl of Pembroke, in the next century.—There is a rude path by the side of the river to Cardigan, and a turnpike road.

There are more *coracles (corgw)* employed on the Teivy than on any river that we have seen in Wales. The fishermen, as they wend their way to the stream with their boats on their backs, look at a distance like huge tortoises, or South Sea Islanders;

x

sometimes 100 coracles may be seen afloat together in the height of the salmon season. Most of our readers are of course aware that the coracle is the ancient British boat; its shape somewhat resembles the section of a walnut shell, the dimensions are about 5 feet by 4, and the weight when dry, from 30 to 50lbs. The material is strong basket-work, covered with hides or pitched canvass. Some dexterity is required to manage these tiny barks, which are propelled and steered with a paddle, and remind one of Shakspeare's witch,—" Thither in a *sieve* I'll sail."

CARDIGAN.

Distant from					Miles.	Distant from				Miles.
Aberayron	..	..	..	..	23	Lampeter	..	..	..	.. 21
Aberporth	..	..	..	..	6	Newcastle Emlyn	..	..	.. 10
Aberystwith	..	..	..	..	39	Newport	..	..	..	.. 10½
Fishguard, by Newport		..		..	17½	New Quay..	..	..	..	.. 21
Haverfordwest		..	..	..	26					

The sea-port town of Cardigan, or Aberteify, does not contain much to interest a stranger; but affords from the bridge across the river, which has expanded into a broad and stately stream, a very picturesque scene for an artist. Scarcely a vestige remains of the castle, founded by Gilbert de Clare, A. D. 1160, and which became one of the most celebrated in Wales. What does exist— two bastions, and part of a curtain wall—is hidden within the enclosure of a modern mansion which stands on a low rock, the site of the keep, close to the south side of the bridge. A strong camp, called Hên Castell, stands on the banks of the Teivy, near the town. The church, which is capable of containing 1,200 persons, is a fine old building, injured by modern innovations. " The Priory," a modern house, erected in the grounds which adjoin the church, is so called because it occupies the site of a Benedictine house, a cell to Chertsey, once occupied by eleven black friars; it now belongs to the Rev. Robert Miles, son of the late P. J. Miles, Esq., of Bristol, who left large property here.

This is the county and assize town, and possesses the usual structures. The corporation and inhabitants have lately carried out several improvements. A free grammar school, founded in

1653, exists here; a Literary and Scientific Institution, at which
there are discussion classes, has lately been established. The
Angel Inn was purchased by Government in 1847, for the construction of new barracks.

The trade of the port is cramped by a dangerous bar, over
which at high spring tides there are 22 feet of water, and sometimes at low tides only 6 feet : the average of neaps is 11 feet.
Ships of 400 tons occasionally come up to the bridge, but the trade
is chiefly confined to vessels between 20 and 100 tons. Nearly
300 vessels, employing more than 1,000 men, are registered at
this port, the jurisdiction of which extends from a point four miles
below Fishguard, to one just above Aberayron, 24 miles to the
north. A steamer is much required. The salmon fishery is very
productive, and there is also a good herring fishery. Population
of the town, 2,925. INNS—The Black Lion, and the White Hart.

The ruins of St. Dogmael's Priory, founded by Martin de
Tours, about a mile and a half from Cardigan, now partly surrounded by a straggling " fishing " village, adjoining the left
bank of the Teivy, are worth visiting. There is but little left of
the old priory except part of the northern transept ; a portion
of the building has been used to construct the adjoining parish
church, which stands in a wooded nook. This must once have
been one of the most charming retreats in Wales. Subscriptions
were entered into in 1848 for the erection of a new church.

An excursion should also be made to the entrance of the
Estuary of the Teivy (distance 3½ miles), where there are very fine
rock scenery and vast caves. Chief objects : Cardigan Head ;
Cardigan Island ; on a very clear day, Bardsey Isle can be seen.

We proceed northwards up the coast.

ABERPORTH, at the mouth of the river Howny, is a thriving
little port, into which much coal, culm, and limestone is brought.
Cribach Road affords good shelter for shipping. A herring fishery
is carried on, and porpoises and sea-calves abound along the coast,
which is rocky, and shelters many foxes. The coast of Ireland
may be seen from a high hill in the parish. Plâs, belonging to the
Morgan family, is an ancient cruciform seat. Many persons resort
to Aberporth in summer for sea-bathing.—We either regain the

main northern road, or follow a parish road which intervenes
between that and the sea, to

. NEW QUAY, a port of some consequence, which stands on the
verge of a bay, well sheltered from westerly winds, within New
Quay Head, in the parish of Llanllwchairn, containing 1,475
persons.   The church is Early English.   There are vestiges of
an earthwork, called Pen-castell.   Ship-building is extensively
carried on ; in 1848, upwards of a hundred vessels belonged to
the place ; there are usually ten schooners on the stocks, some of
which are of nearly 200 tons burden ; this trade has arisen within
about twenty years.   A good road was made to Aberayron in
1836.   The fishery on the coast, particularly for soles, turbot,
and oysters, is very productive.   Very fine stone, blocks of which
have been cut to a length of 30 feet, is worked near the port.
New Quay has become a summer " bathing-place," and comfortable lodgings may be obtained.   The church at *Llanina*, the
adjoining parish, is dedicated to St. Ina, King of the West Saxons.
We proceed to

ABERAYRON.

Distant from				Miles.	Distant from				Miles.
Aberystwith	..	..	..	.. 16	Lampeter	..	..	..	.. 13
Cardigan	..	..	..	.. 23	New Quay	..	..	..	.. 4

Aberayron or Aberaëron, ranks second amongst Cardiganshire
watering-places, and is much frequented in summer.   Two piers,
enclosing a small harbour, were erected here in 1807 by the Rev.
Alban Gwynne ; one of which (the western) has since been extended 100 yards by A. T. J. Gwynne, Esq., who is the proprietor
of the town and adjoining estate, and has granted many building
leases on liberal terms.   Mr. Gwynne's residence, *Mynach-dy*, is
supposed to stand on the site of a monastery ; there are tumuli in
the grounds.   A circular camp, constructed by Cadwgan ap
Bleddyn, A. D. 1148, stands on the sea-shore.—In consequence of
the central situation of Aberayron, the county sessions are now
held there, a building having been erected for the purpose.   About
40 vessels belong to the port, near the entrance of which there is
a bar, dry at low water.   INN—The Feathers.   The *Collegian*
coach from Brecon runs through Aberayron in the summer.—The

ABERYSTWITH.

scenery of the wooded *Vale of the Ayron*, for four or five miles inland, is extremely pleasing ; on the north, the Talsarn mountain gives character to the country. The Ayron is said to be a good trout and salmon stream.

The road from hence to Aberystwith runs close to the coast, but is dreary.

ABERYSTWITH.

Distant from			Miles.	Distant from			Miles.
Aberdovey, across the Sands		..	11	Lampeter, by Aberayron	..	..	29
Aberayron	..	..	16	Llanddewy Brevi	..	..	24
Barmouth	..	..	45	Llanvihangel Genau'r Glyn, nearly			5
Barmouth (by Sands)	..	..	27	Machynlleth	..	..	18
Borth	.. ..	..	7	Mallwyd	..	..	28¼
Borth, by Llangorwen	..	..	5	Plinlimmon	..	..	16
Bedd Taliesin	..	..	9	Pontrhydvendigaid	..	..	15
Carnarvon (by Sands)	..	..	72	Rhayader, by Devil's Bridge	..	31
Devil's Bridge..	..	..	12	Rhayader, by New Road	..	..	33
Dolgelly	..	..	33	Shrewsbury	..	..	75
Dyffryn Castle Inn ..	..	..	14	Tal-y-Llyn	..	..	28
Hafod ..	..	..	16½	Tregaron	..	..	21
London, by Gloucester	..	..	210	Towyn, across the Dovey	..	..	15
Llanbadarn Vawr	..	..	1¼	Strata Florida Abbey	..	..	16

When the rage for bathing-places began to spring up towards the close of the last century, persons of taste directed their eyes to the western coast of Wales, where they found a town previously known but to a few, seated on the margin of a magnificent bay—at the confluence of two gladsome streams—with a green sea tumbling on a fine beach—a store of pebbles which afforded constant amusement—cheap living—and a pleasant neighbourhood backed by breezy mountains. The place was then perfectly primitive ; the harbour almost "sanded up," and the appearance of a ship, or even a distant sail, was an event. Visitors soon gave a good name to Aberystwith, a coach from Shrewsbury was started in 1805, and the town has gone on prospering until it has become the real capital of the county—an abode of health and good spirits sought by numbers every summer,—a "*fashionable watering-place.*" If the town were more easily accessible, its merits would be better known than they are ; there are neither railroads nor steam-boats, and coach travelling seems tedious to many in these days of rapid locomotion. Still, coach travelling

has its pleasures as well as its discomforts.   You are rewarded in
this case by much fine scenery, by pure air, and then you have
the charm of vivid contrast—the SEA rolling before you—the sea
on which you might sail to Cape Horn without touching land.
The mind, which has been confined within passes in the hills,
bounds elastically when you touch the shore—stand as it were
between two worlds—the " strong mountains" and the " great
deep."

Thirteen hundred years ago Cardigan Bay was a rich province
of ancient Wales—*Cantref-y-Gwaelod* the Lowland Hundred—
a sort of Welsh Flanders, defended by dykes and dams.   This
fair and fertile region, which contained sixteen towns, was sub-
merged A. D. 520, owing to the folly of a drunkard.   Ruins of
houses can, it is said, be discovered by those who put on their
spectacles during boating expeditions, quite " out to sea," and
the bottom chiefly consists of the decayed matter of a Forest.

Gilbert de Strongbow built a Castle at Aberystwith in 1109,
which seems to have been for centuries a mark for foes to aim at
—it was often taken and retaken, often burned.   A small town
soon nestled under the wing of the fortress, which gradually grew
in size and was walled.   Llewellyn, prince of North Wales, was
the possessor of the fortress early in the reign of Edward I.; the
latter rebuilt it A. D. 1277.   Owen Glendower carried it by storm
A. D. 1404, and kept it for three years, when he gave it up to Prince
Henry; Owen soon after retook the castle by stratagem, and the
English did not obtain final possession until A. D. 1408.   The
castle and fortifications were dismantled in 1647, when they were
torn from King Charles, who had a mint here.   The last remains
of the town walls, which were perfect in Leland's day, were
removed a few years ago.

We have followed the usual accounts in this summary of the
history of the fortifications; but a learned correspondent, (Mr.
John Hughes, of Lluestgwilym), has furnished us with the following valuable communication, in which we place full reliance :—

" From the description in the *Welsh Chronicles* it may be doubted
whether the Castle, built by Strongbow, occupied the *site* of the *present*
ruins. In one place (in these Chronicles) it is stated that the Castle was

built ' at the *mouth of the river Ystwyth*,' and in another that ' *it stood on the top of a high hill, the declivity of which reached the river Ystwyth over which there was a bridge.*' This description would seem to point to *Pendinas*, or to the opposite hill on the other side of the ' Ystwyth,' where the remains of a ' Castell' are now plainly to be seen. The first mention of the *Town* of Aberystwyth is made in reference to a quarrel between the sons of Prince Rhys ap Gryffydd, Justiciary of South Wales, commonly called the Lord Rhys, who died in 1196 ; and is to the effect that the Lord Rhys's son Gryffydd, succeeded his father in property and power, but which he was not able to retain long, for his brother Maelgwn, whom the father had disinherited, came suddenly upon him at Aberystwyth, in conjunction with Gwenwynwyn, the son of Owen Cyfeilioc, with a powerful force, and took the *Town and Castle.*"—Mr. Hughes adds, that he does not think it at all probable that Cromwell was here during the seige in 1647, as has been hitherto believed."

The ruins of the Castle stand on a rocky elevation washed by the sea, and afford a pleasing lounge, being nicely laid out with walks and seats which command enchanting prospects. The existing relics evince that this was a grand feudal stronghold; and we cannot too highly commend the efforts that have lately been judiciously made to preserve all that time and war have left. The castle well, which had been lost for many years, was not long since discovered. There is a slight semicircular sweep in the coast from the Castle Hill to Craiglais or Constitution Hill, a lofty promontory on the north, and here is naturally planted the *Marine Parade* or Crescent, a long range of excellent houses, chiefly lodgings, from whence the visitor can step at once upon the beach, sniff the sea-breeze through his windows, and hear the waves boom below. A range of other houses of some pretension succeeds, and lodgings " without a sea view " can be obtained in other parts of the town. Near the south end of the Marine Terrace is the Castle House, entered through a gateway, a " gothic " structure built for the late Sir Uvedale Price, of Foxley, by Nash.

A Church (St. Mary's) which stood somewhere in front of the Castle House—between that and the Castle point—was carried away by the sea about two centuries ago. It is supposed to have been a chapel belonging to the garrison, as there is no notice of any endowment belonging to it. A second Church (St. Michael's) was consecrated in 1787, as a Chapel of Ease, under Llanbadarn Vawr. It stood a little to the south of the present church and within the churchyard. This structure having become too small for the accommodation of the inhabitants, measures were taken for building a larger one, which was consecrated in 1833. It cost nearly £4,000, towards which the Commissioners for Building New Churches contributed £1,000, and the Society for Promoting the Rebuilding and Enlargement of Churches and Chapels £400. It is now a perpetual curacy, and independent of the mother church; but the vicar of the latter has the right of presentation to it. Old St. Michael's was taken down in 1836. The Welsh service is at present performed at the school-house, which has been licensed for the purpose, and adjoins the churchyard. There is an English service in the new church, at eleven and six ; 529 of the sittings are free, and visitors are accustomed to use them—an excellent arrangement ; kneelings ought to be provided.

The Wesleyans, Calvinistic Methodists, Baptists, and Independents, each have Chapels. A Roman Catholic Mission has lately been formed, and the Theatre is about to be converted into a Roman Catholic Chapel.

Amongst the Institutions are an Infirmary ; and a Deaf and Dumb Asylum for North and South Wales, established by subscription in 1847, which is well supported. It contains about twelve inmates. There are grammar and national schools.—A new Town Hall, in the Ionic style, has been erected, chiefly with funds furnished by the corporation ; aid to the extent of £800 was promised from the county rate, but the county magistrates coupled the grant with a condition as to ownership and control, to which the borough magistrates could not accede. One object which the projectors of this edifice had in view was to secure one of the assize fixtures every year, and a portion of the sessions business.

Bathing. The sea is perfectly uncontaminated on the pebble beach, and the bathing machines and Marine Baths are well conducted. The latter are admirably situated on a rock near the north end of the Marine Parade. The Baths of Mr. John Lewis, 14, Marine Terrace, are excellent. Prices moderate.

A Chalybeate spring, which resembles that at Tunbridge, and

is highly esteemed, was discovered in 1779, close to the town, near the walk that runs by Plas Crûg to Llanbadarn Vawr. A small building has been erected over it. It is desirable to obtain medical advice before commencing a course of this water, the usual time for taking which is eight in the morning, and again between breakfast and dinner; the quantity must depend on age and circumstances. There are other springs which possess a ferruginous impregnation in the vicinity; traces of sulphur have been found at Penglais.

Amusements. The Public Rooms, which stand near one side of the Castle Hill, were erected in 1820, in the Grecian style, on ground given by W. E. Powell, Esq., of Nanteos, and include an assembly and promenade room 45 feet by 24 feet, and card, reading, and billiard rooms. Balls are held during the season between July and October; the Race Balls are very brilliant. The Stewards perform the duties of a "Master of the Ceremonies."— The Races, which last two days, are held in September, in the grounds of Pryse Pryse, Esq., M.P., at Gogerddan (Gogerthan), about three miles from the town. Cricket and Archery are favourite amusements. There is an efficient Public Band.

The Public Libraries are—Mr. Cox's, Bookseller, Pier Street; Mr. Careswell's, at the Assembly Rooms, Church Street; Mr. Cranston's, Church Street.—The Post-office is in Pier Street.

The beach is celebrated for its pebbles—to the great horror of over-loaded coachmen, post-boys, and porters—which are a constant resource to loungers, and a source of profit to local lapidaries. Cornelians, jaspers, crystals, agates, pudding-stones, trapstones, moccos, &c., abound, many of which are very beautiful.—There are always *Pleasure Boats* on the beach, which can be engaged for marine excursions or deep-sea fishing.

The lead mines have destroyed the fishing in the Ystwith, and also in the Rheidol below a point, a few miles above the town, where the lead-water from Goginian joins the river. Tolerable fishing is to be obtained in the Rheidol, farther up.

Aberystwith occupies a gentle eminence, so that the ground slopes from the centre. The Rheidol, which is crossed by a bridge of five arches, flows next to it, expanding so as to form a sort of inner harbour where it is joined by the Ystwith, and the two streams, thus united close to the sea, flow out through the opening at the pier head. Most important improvements have been effected in the harbour, which has been deepened upwards of three feet; and vessels of considerable burden can now enter at spring tides. Shipping to the extent of about 9,000 tons belong to the port, and there is generally a tolerable array of masts alongside the pier. The Duke of Newcastle contributed £1,000, and the members for the county and borough £500 each, towards the harbour improvement. There is considerable trade, both inwards and outwards, which has been much increased by the re-establishment of the mines.

The Workhouse for the Aberystwith Union, which comprises no less than thirty parishes and townships, stands near the north turnpike gate.

The markets take place on Monday and Saturday. That for fish, poultry, butter, cheese, &c., is chiefly held in an area under the Town Hall; the butchers occupy a new Market-house 104 feet in length, in the street leading to the Castle ruins; there is also a Corn Market. The supplies from the surrounding country are very extensive, and prices reasonable.—Population in 1841, 4,916.

Aberystwith, like Swansea, is a borough by prescription (the Charter, which was granted by Henry VIII. " to the burgesses of the town of Llanbadarn" having been lost). Under the Municipal Corporation Reform Act, Aberystwith is placed in Schedule A: has a mayor, 4 aldermen, and 12 councillors.

Upwards of £15,000 have been laid out within a few years in improvements at the harbour, without burdening the inhabitants with rates; and more than £6,000 on different improvements in the town.

HOTELS—The Belle Vue, on the Marine Parade, fronting the sea; the Gogerddan Arms, well situated in the centre of the town.

Principal Public Conveyances. The *Gloucester Mail*, through Hereford, Kington, and Rhayader. The *Shrewsbury Mail*, through Machynlleth and Mallwyd. In the summer a coach runs to *Carnarvon*, through Dolgelly and Barmouth, and another to Ruabon

Station on the Chester Railway; the *Collegian* runs to Brecon through Aberayron and Lampeter; and there are also coaches to Shrewsbury, &c.

WALKS AND EXCURSIONS.—*Constitution Hill.* Ascend this bold headland, at the north of the Marine Parade, from the summit of which there is a view of immense extent, embracing in clear weather nearly the whole of Cardigan Bay. The three headlands to the south-west are New Quay, Cardigan, and Strumble. To the north, the Cader Idris group of the Merionethshire mountains first strikes the eye, which ranges upwards to Snowdonia, and follows the exquisite line of the Carnarvonshire coast—including the Rival Mountains—to its termination, at the end of which, Bardsey, like a fairy isle, floats in the deep. This coast frequently resembles the Dream Land which used to excite the hopes and the ardour of Columbus and the early voyagers. Aberystwith is a place of glorious sunsets on a restless oceanic horizon—of magical moon-light effects.—From Constitution Hill a path is cut in the turf, high above the sea, which may be followed to the Vale of Clarach. This is a charming *evening* walk.

Vale of the Rheidol. This walk must embrace Plas-crûg and Llanbadarn Vawr. The district is a favourite habitat of the gorse; and the richness of the colouring when it is in blossom—the delicious odour which scents the air—make up for defects in the landscape. *Plas-crûg* was in the last century a very perfect specimen of an early fortified house; but has undergone so many injurious changes that but little of the original structure is left. The present tower was erected about a century ago. The history of Plas-crûg has been wrongly given in all the publications that we have met with. Prince Gryffydd ap Rhys did *not* encamp here, as asserted, after his return from Ireland, before he attacked Aberystwith, but at *Glascrug*, about a mile to the *east* of Llanbadarn Church. Nor is it the place where Glendower ratified the treaty with the King of France; that was done at his *Castle of Llanbadarn*, which means the Castle of Aberystwith, called Llanbadarn in all the ancient charters. At the date of this treaty (1405) the castle was in possession of Glendower, and so continued for a long time afterwards. Plas-crûg might have been the residence of some person of distinction—a Manor House perhaps —but was never, in our opinion, a *Castle*.

Llanbadarn Vawr—the Great Church of St. Padarn—is one of the most ancient and interesting places in Wales. St. Padarn or Paternus, a pupil of Iltutus, founded a religious house here in the sixth century, which was converted into a See with a considerable territory, and subsequently annexed to St. David's. The Danes destroyed the edifice A. D. 987, and also another on the same spot in 1038; but the present church contains portions of the older structures. Gilbert Strongbow appears to have made a grant of the revenues of this place to the Abbey of St. Peter's, at Gloucester, in the year 1111; yet the ancient religious establishment was not broken up, and when Giraldus visited it in 1188, he complained of the laxity of discipline that had crept in, and of the abstraction of a large part of the revenues by the laymen of one family. About a century later the church was appropriated to the Abbey of Vale Royal, Cheshire. Llanbadarn is a cross church with a singularly-massive tower, and an unusual number of small round-headed windows, the heads of some of which have been slightly altered. The northern transept is the oldest portion of the structure; a perpendicular window, in the style of the fifteenth century, has been inserted in lieu of one of earlier date at the east end of the chancel. The nave is entered by a recessed doorway of great beauty at the south side, and is much the most impressive part of the church. Few churches have either suffered greater injury, or are more disfigured internally than Llanbadarn. Screens, of the date of the fifteenth century, which used to stand at the entrances of the chancel and one of the transepts, and the rood loft, which was perfect previously to 1820, have been swept away. A floor for the ringers, with rails, which some mistake for the rood loft, stands under the tower, which contains six bells. The chancel contains many monuments to members of the families of Nanteos and Gogerddan—including one by Flaxman to the memory of Harriet, daughter of Viscount Ashbrook, and lady of Pryse Pryse, Esq.; Lewis Morris, the eminent antiquarian, is buried here. There are two very early *Crosses* without inscriptions in the churchyard, one of which is called "Sampson's flail," after Bishop Sampson. Great hopes were entertained when the Cambrian Archæological Association held their meeting at Aberystwith in 1847, that an energetic effort would be made to raise funds for the repair and restoration of this church, but we are sorry to say that little has been done. We trust that these pages will meet the eye of the worthy vicar. There are no tithes belonging to the vicarage, however; the Chichester family swallow up all, to the extent of £2,400 a year, allowing the incumbent £20! —Service is performed in Welsh here at 10½ and 3½.—The parish of Llanbadarn extends for a distance of 15 miles, and is on an average 6 broad. Patron of the living (a discharged vicarage), the Bishop of St. David's. Two Chapels of Ease are annexed, at Yspytty Cenfyn (in Creuddyn Ucha) and Bangor, at Tŷ'n Llidiart.—Many encampments exist in the parish, some of which are near Aberystwith; near Craig Glais is a rock called Brŷn Diodde, "The mount of Suffering," once a place of execution.

Excursion to Llanvihangel Genau'r Glyn, Borth Sands, &c. The Machynlleth and Shrewsbury road runs for nearly a mile and a half up a steep hill, which commands a magnificent prospect over Wales; there is then a similar descent to the *Vale of Clarach*. *Gogerddan*, the ancient seat of Pryse Pryse, Esq., M.P., (three miles), is hidden by woods on the right, but the race-course in the park can be seen. (Two miles out of the town is an ivied cottage on the left of the road, the dwelling of "Nancy, the Blind Harper," at which tea, &c., can be obtained.) The chief objects in the Vale of the Clarach are *Llangorwen new Church*, and *Cwmcynfelin*, the seat of Mr. Williams. You now pass through a long straggling village called *Bow Street*, in which there is a rude inn called the "Cross Axes," and a little beyond the fourth milestone turn down the road to the left, along the picturesque vale of *Llanvihangel Genau'r Glyn*. The cruciform church, nestling amidst leaves, on the hill side, at the edge of a sweet dingle, is a charming object. The churchyard is thoroughly Welsh—straggles up a steep—a meet resting place for mountaineers. A rippling stream completes the soothing effect—the holy calm—of the place. Great care is bestowed on the graves, at one of which we saw two women weeping. The church is deformed by windows of the commonest sort.—

Ascend the dingle, and on the top of the hill on the left you will find one of the most perfect things of its kind—*Castell Gwalter*, or Walter's Castle ; a circular *camp*, the earthworks of which are almost uninjured.   It is affirmed that Walter l'Espec, a Norman baron, who seized lands in this district, erected a castle on this hill, and that it was destroyed A. D. 1135, by Owen Gwynedd and Cadwaladr his brother, sons of Grufydd ap Cynan, who also took Aberystwith Castle.   The present remains, however, appear to be those of an ancient hill-fort, or small camp.—We have walked back to Aberystwith from Castell Gwalter, by keeping a road over the hill to the left, then to the right, getting into the old road to Borth.—The usual plan, however, is to descend again to the main road to Borth, which partly runs along the river Lery.   *Borth* is a real salt-water place, with an "ancient and fish-like smell,"—a white street of mean houses on the strand, so close to the sea that they must be sometimes washed by high tides—with boats on the "hard," and nets drying in the sun.   The sea has made such great encroachments on the beach during the present century that Borth and Gors-Fochno, the adjoining marsh and turbary of 10,000 acres, seem in danger of sharing the fate of *Cantrev-y-Gwaelod*.   The sands stretch for about four miles, and the road to Aberdovey runs close to their edge.   There is a public-house at *Moel Ynys*, near the end, also one at Borth.   Large sand banks, the nature of which tends to confirm the legend of the inundation in the sixth century, stumps of trees being often found, are exposed at low water; the most remarkable, Sarn Gwallog, stretches for miles in a S. W. direction.   Previous enquiries relative to the state of the tide ought to be made by those who intend to cross the estuary over the sands to Aberdovey, which town stands near the foot of the south Merionethshire mountain group.

We recommend visitors, whether in carriages or on foot, to follow the old road from Borth to Aberystwith on returning.   It is hilly, but commands pleasing scenery, including the grounds Cwmcynfelin near the foot of Clarach Vale.   This road falls into the Machynlleth road, about a mile from Aberystwith.   Pedestrians ought to take the *coast path* which is seen on the right of Cwmcynfelin.

Bedd Taliesin and Stone Circles. The best plan is to go in the morning by the Shrewsbury mail, as far as a hamlet called Tre Taliesin, on the road side near Tre'rddol. The carn which is supposed to surround the grave of Taliesin—a most celebrated bard who flourished in the sixth century—is 130 feet in circumference, and the cistvaen, or grave, is formed of massive stones 8 feet long by 2½ wide. The chief covering stone is 5 feet 9 inches long. There is a tradition concerning this "bed" that "should any one sleep in it for one night, he would become either a poet or an idiot."*

Two or three miles up the mountain towards Plinlimmon there are two *Druidical Circles*, above Nant-y-nộd, one of which consists of 76 upright stones, and is 228 feet in circumference. A smaller circle, 90 feet round, stands higher up the mountain ;—on the top of *Moel-y-gaer* are remains of a British hill-fort.

Excursion to Plinlimmon. The great road to the eastward used to run by the Devil's Bridge ; but a new mail road, with fewer and much shorter hills, has been constructed through the mountains to Rhayader, which has greatly facilitated travelling. You meet with much beautiful scenery on ascending : seven miles up the vale are the *Goginian* lead mines, opposite to which there is a roadside inn, where the mail changes. *Pont Erwid* Inn—which was closed when we last saw it—about five miles on, a fishing station, commands a striking rock and waterfall scene. The effect of this scenery is *much* greater on proceeding *to* Aberystwith ; the road is cut through rocks and the picturesque vale, terminated by Aberystwith and the sea, bursts suddenly into sight. There is an exquisite scene for an artist on the road near Pont Erwid, a true Welsh bridge and other concomitants. About two miles beyond

* When the members of the Cambrian Archæological Association visited Bedd Taliesin and other remains of antiquity in the district in September, 1847, "the very rev. the Dean of Hereford, while standing at the brink of the grave, the turf being slippery, and the stones at the side giving way, fell in, and lay in the grave at full length. His very rev. brother the Dean of Bangor sympathising with him, said he should not remain there alone, and immediately leaped in, and took his station by the side of his brother dean, exclaiming, ' There lies the downright dean,' and pointing to himself, said, ' here lies the upright dean.' "—*Arch. Cambrensis.*

Pont Erwid is a good inn called *Duffrin Castle*. It is difficult to obtain a view of the highest point of Plinlimmon (2,463 feet), because the mountain virtually consists of a group of three blended together, which cover a large surface. Most persons take a guide, but the view from the summit does not compensate for the toil of the ascent. On *Pumlumon* (that is its true name) five rivers take their rise: the Severn, Wye, Rheidol, Ystwith, and Cleywedog. The source of the Severn, locally called "the Well," is a spring near the highest part of the south-eastern side of the mountain; that of the Wye is about two miles distant.

Vale of the Ystwith. Three roads meet at a turnpike gate to the south of the town; that on the left goes to the Devil's Bridge; that in the centre to Nanteos, Crosswood, Strata Florida, &c.; the third is the Aberayron road, but about a mile and a half on this a road diverges to the left up the Vale of the Ystwith by Llanilar [see below]. *Nanteos* is the seat of Colonel Powell, M.P. for the county; carriages are not now allowed to cross the park. *Crosswood*, nine miles from Aberystwith, on the left, is the seat of the Earl of Lisburne. Unless the tourist means to proceed to Strata Florida, the Vale of the Ystwith ought to be visited in *returning from the Devil's Bridge,* as elsewhere indicated.

EXCURSION TO THE DEVIL'S BRIDGE, HAFOD, &c.

The best and indeed the only method of making this excursion with advantage is to ascend the valley of the Rheidol, as far as the Devil's Bridge; thence after having seen the falls—and, if there be time, *Pont Bren*—to procure a fresh conveyance at the hotel, and visit Hafod, returning by the wild and beautiful valley of the Ystwith, *via* the new private road belonging to the Lisburne Mining Company, as far as Llanafan Bridge, and thence pass Crosswood Park, and Nanteos to Aberystwith. There is another road from Crosswood through Llanilar, one mile further round, but which avoids some very tedious hills. Both are pretty. *This route must by no means be reversed,* as the only entrance to the grounds at Hafod through which visitors are admitted is at the *upper lodge* on the approach from the Devil's Bridge.

The hilly road from Aberystwith to *Pont y Mynach*, or the Devil's Bridge, commands many wildly beautiful prospects. On the left, the river Rheidol runs through a valley, which gradually narrows and becomes more romantic until an abrupt turn brings the traveller suddenly in full view of the bridge scenery.

The Devil's Bridge has for the last century been one of the grand scenes of Welsh tourists ; but although all its elements are essentially picturesque—in outline, in colour, and in grouping—yet it looks flat under broad sunshine. A landscape, like a picture, requires a good light ; and those who arrive here under the glare of a morning or mid-day sun, or cold grey sky, and depart near a fine sunset, can hardly believe that the same scene could exhibit contrasts so great, if they did not see it with their own eyes. Then, the natural beauty, the grandeur of the parts of which the landscape is composed, is understood. The solemn wooded steeps and distant mountains have their due breadth of shadow ; the glen sinks to a profound depth ; the waterfalls flashing through savage rocks and trembling foliage become impressive.

The small and rapid Mynach rises in the mountains to the north-east, and is swollen, 1. by the Merin, which is formed by the junction of two streams that flow from Llyns Ivan issa and Ivan ucha ; 2. by the Rhuddnant and two brooks. Thus strengthened it forms a considerable torrent, flowing upwards of a mile through a deep rocky bed or chasm in the rocks overshadowed with wood, which at the last, on approaching the Devil's Bridge, is 114 feet deep. At this spot the ecclesiastics of Strata Florida, so saith tradition, threw across a bridge, a feat so marvellous in those days that the country people deemed it supernatural, and affirmed that his Satanic majesty had a hand in it—no compliment to the monks. The bridge is said to have been built A. D. 1087, but Strata Florida Abbey was not founded until 1164 ; Giraldus passed over it with Archbishop Baldwin when preaching the crusades in 1188, and it is very probable that the first date is erroneous. The original arch is 29 feet span ; and it became necessary, in 1753, to construct a more substantial one, which was done at the expense of the county ; but the old bridge was not removed, and can be seen at a depth of about 20 feet below.

Mr. John Hughes, of Lluestgwilym, Aberystwith, has favoured us with the following remarks, which throw a new and interesting light on the origin of the Devil's Bridge, and of the *Hospitia*, which have also been hitherto ascribed to the monks of Strata Florida :—

. "This bridge is by all tourists stated to have been erected by the monks of Strata Florida, but the assertion rests merely on conjecture. If it be assumed that it was built by any monks at all, I should be disposed to think that it was built by another order, *i. e.* by the *Knights Hospitallers*, and my reason for so thinking is this:—The chief, or at any rate one of the prominent objects of the order, as its name implies, was hospitality—to establish places of-rest and entertainment for the accommodation of pilgrims and travellers. Their patron saint was St. John the Baptist. It is a recorded and well authenticated fact, that at one time the whole of the parish of Yspytty-Ystrad Meyrick was their property. We find there a Chapel, dedicated to St. John; also *another* at Yspytty Ystwith, a few miles distant from it. These two are on the south side of the bridge ; on its *other* side, at a distance of about two miles, lies Yspytty Cenfin with another Chapel dedicated to St. John. Here we find three of these *Hospitia* within a short distance of each other, and at each a Chapel, dedicated to St. John, the Patron Saint of the Knights Hospitallers ; hence I infer that these three hospitia were established by this Order, and, as one of them is on a different side of the River Mynach to the others, that the bridge was put up by the Knights Hospitallers for facilitating the communication between the *Hospitia*, and not by the Cistercian order of Strata Florida, whose Patron Saint is, I believe, *St. Mary.* The position of the three hospitia of Strata Florida will be better understood through a glance at the Ordnance Survey."

The Falls of the Mynach. After crossing the bridge, visitors turn to the right and descend rather slippery rocks towards the river, in order to command a view of the scenery—(the best view of *the bridges* spanning a dark fissure, the depth of which can only be guessed at here). Several accidents have occurred at this spot—very narrow escapes. A few years ago, a lady's maid lost her footing whilst gazing at the abyss, and instantly fell ; but fortunately her dress acted like a parachute, and she was buoyed up in her descent to the gloomy pool beneath. Ropes were obtained, but the poor creature fell again, and was ultimately saved owing to the courage of a boy.

The road is regained, and the second descent ought to be made through a wood, a few yards from the bridge, to a rock, from which the four successive falls of the Mynach may be seen at once. The bottom of the lowest fall is 322 feet from the bridge, which is not visible, and the heights are as follow:—First fall, 18 feet ; second, 60 ; third, 20; and fourth fall, or great cataract, 110. In dry weather they disappoint; but, "when the waters are out," the scene is one of the finest of its kind in Wales. The woods near abound with nests of the *Formica Herculanea*, the largest British ants.

Ascend again, repass the bridge, and make another descent at the side of the falls to the *Robber's Cave*, at the jet of the lower fall, a place of about six feet deep. It is said—but the legend must refer to some other cave now forgotten—that in the fifteenth century this savage retreat was the abode of two men and a woman styled Plant Matt, or Matthew's children, who committed many depredations with impunity for years, but were ultimately traced and executed for a murder. Their father kept an inn at Tregaron. From this spot a further descent may be made down into the very bed of the river. The task is somewhat arduous, but when you gain a large flat rock that lies midway in the stream, the magnificence of the scene affords compensation.

The Fall of the Rheidol. The guides often make a complete circuit of the scenery, proceeding up the road for some distance, and turning to the left down a difficult wooded descent, to the *Fall of the Rheidol*, after viewing which the visitor is conducted along the bottom towards the junction of the Rheidol and the Mynach, from whence he ascends to view the Falls of the latter. Visitors, however, very often merely visit the Mynach Falls, and we therefore think it necessary to state that the Fall of the Rheidol embraces by far the finest portion of the scenery. The volume of water is fully as great as that of the Mynach Fall, which, although very superior in height, it surpasses in wild and solitary beauty. The cascades on the rivers cannot be seen at one view.

About two miles up the Rheidol is the " Parson's Bridge," or

Pont Bren, another grand river scene, which an eminent critic in landscape has pronounced "the perfection of the whole." Two trees are placed across a deep chasm, with a hand-rail on one side, below which the Rheidol foams angrily over remarkable rocks. A clergyman, who did duty at Yspytty Cenfaen Church (near the Llanidloes road), is said to have had this bridge constructed in the last century, to shorten his route from another church. There are Druidical remains in Yspytty churchyard.

The Hafod Arms Hotel at the Devil's Bridge is so placed as to command some of the finest points of the scenery. It was for several years almost closed; a new road was formed to Aberystwith from Rhayader by a different route, and the inn was fast going to decay, when the Duke of Newcastle purchased the Hafod estate, rebuilt this celebrated inn from his own designs in 1839, and it may now be ranked amongst the first establishments of the kind in Wales.

DISTANCES *from the Devil's Bridge :* Aberystwith, 12 miles; Rhayader, by old road 18,—by new road 23 ; Pont Bren, 2 ; Pont Erwid, 4 ; Duffryn Castle Inn, under Plinlimmon, 4½ ; Hafod, 4½ ; Strata Florida Abbey, by Yspytty Ystwith, 10.

HAFOD

Is about four miles distant from the Devil's Bridge. Tickets for viewing the grounds are to be procured *only* at the Hafod Arms ; during the progress of the present improvements admission to the House is not attainable. The road to Hafod is carried through a wild mountain district, commanding the darksome ravine of the Mynach, and running over the summit of the Cwmystwith Hill, from whence a tourist can pause and "drink in" a wide view of the mountains of North Wales and the Bay of Cardigan. You pass through a rude arch, descend a steep hill through larch plantations, and turning to the right enter the Hafod demesne. The scenery of this leafy region — the contrast between the bowered vale and the pale mountains that rise towards the blue vault of Heaven—the music of the Ystwith as it leaps joyfully onwards—the "deep dingles, and mighty wooded slopes" —are full of harmony. Suddenly you sweep in front of the finely-situated mansion, which is likely to become one of the most perfect residences of its kind in the hands of its munificent owner, Mr. Hoghton.

There are few places that have been more extolled, on which more florid and ridiculous epithets have been bestowed, than Hafod ; thus expectation is excited to a pitch which not unfrequently produces disappointment.   Yet it *is* a lovely spot,—

> " Embosomed in the silent hills . . .
> Where quiet sleeps, and care is calm,
> And all the air is breathing balm."—THOS. MILLER.

Hafod, " the Summer Residence," was originally the abode of a branch of the Herbert family, who embarked in mining adventures, and planted considerably.   Thomas Johnes, of Llanvair Clydoge, near Lampeter, married the sole heiress of the last William Herbert, who died in 1704.   One of his descendants, Thomas Johnes, M. P., and H. M. Lieut. for the county, built a new house, and made Hafod his principal residence in 1783, devoting himself to its embellishment and improvement.   Colonel Johnes unfortunately lived in an era of false taste, and the trashy Doric temples, Roman baths, mimic Stonehenges, pagoda bridges, monuments, and grottoes, with which the grounds were covered, and which excited the admiration of Mr. Cumberland and other literary tourists, have nearly crumbled into dust.   His plantations, however, remain, and form a more enduring and a worthy memorial of his taste and enterprise.   It is a mistake to suppose that Col. Johnes *created* the scenic effects of Hafod.   Since we wrote our first edition we have looked closely into the history of the estate, and find—we may instance a description given by a Mr. Paynter, who took the place from Colonel Johnes' father on a life lease— that, long previously to 1783, the woods of Hafod excited admiration ; and the appearance of the trees—some of the oaks are at least a century old—proves this.   Colonel Johnes, however, *did* plant on a great scale.   It is stated that in little more than five years, between the end of 1796 and the beginning of 1801, upwards of two millions of trees, including 1,200,000 larches, were set, and an enormous number of acorns sown.   For several years afterwards plantations were made at the rate of 200,000 trees annually ; at last poor Colonel Johnes got into difficulties, died at Exeter in 1816, and was buried at *Eglwys Newydd*. His house, with a superb library, including many valuable MSS., were burnt in 1807 ; but a new *gothic* mansion, from a design by Nash, was erected soon after. The fire led to a loss of £70,000 ; an insurance had only been effected for £20,000. Johnes, imitating Walpole, had a private printing press. The estate was long in Chancery after the death of Mr. Johnes, (the family became extinct on the death of his only child, a daughter, in 1811, and of his widow, in 1833), and in the latter year the Duke of Newcastle became the purchaser for £70,000. His Grace, after adding largely to the extent of the property, and expending upwards of £20,000 on the house and grounds, parted with the estate in 1845, including the whole of the woods, farming stock, furniture, library, &c., for £97,000, to Henry Hoghton, Esq., its present possessor, who has now made it his residence.

The Hafod estate, which extends for many miles, including vast sheep walks, consists of 14,850 acres, 1,390 acres of which are woodland. Its rental is about £2,000 a-year, but the timber must be very valuable. A new mansion is in course of erection on an extensive scale, from a design by Mr. Salvin, of London, in the irregular villa Italian style, with low projecting roofs, terraces, and a campanile.

A modern church (*Eglwys Newydd*) was erected within the grounds in 1803, at the expense of Colonel Johnes, on the site of an old edifice that had fallen to decay. It stands north-east and south-west, and contains a very beautiful monument to the memory of Miss Johnes, which ought to be seen.

The *Old Road* from the Devil's Bridge to Rhayader, although now rarely traversed, possesses many charms for those who love to plunge into a wild and solitudinous mountain district. The country consists of vast green hills, often covered with turf-like velvet. After passing through the hamlet of Brunant, where there is a small inn, you ascend the pass of *Cwm Ystwith* up a steep road, through striking scenery, to a region of mountain tops, which you traverse until you get within three or four miles of Rhayader, to which town there is a long and fatiguing descent.

We return from the Devil's Bridge and Hafod to Aberystwith.

EXCURSION, OR ROUTE, TO STRATA FLORIDA, THE TEIVY LAKES,
TREGARON, LLANDDEWY BREVI, AND LAMPETER.

We have already described the road along the Vale of the
Ystwith as far as *Pont Llanavan* (10 m). After ascending a steep
hill a mile long, a small hamlet, where there are a little woollen
mill and a flour mill, is reached. On diverging a few yards from
the road you overlook a deep solemn glen, and waterfalls, called
Pwll Caradoc, from a tradition that a prince of that name threw
himself headlong over, and was killed, after a severe defeat.
There is a monumental stone to his memory in Gwnnys churchyard, near at hand. If the brook be full, *descend* the steep.—At
Yspytty Ystrad Meyrick (13 miles) is a free grammar school,
called the Welsh College, founded in 1757 by Edward Richards,
a *rich* pastoral poet, who bestowed an endowment worth £237 8s.
per annum on it, and an exhibition to St. John's, Cambridge, for
the best Greek scholar. A cell belonging to Strata Florida existed
here—an ancient house called Mynachty is supposed to have been
the hospitium—and remains of a *Castle* party Welsh, partly Norman, stand on an eminence ; also a Roman entrenchment, on a
lofty hill a mile from the church, Pen-y-friwllwyd. We next
reach the village of

PONTRHYDVENDIGAID, "the Bridge of the Blessed Ford " (pronounced Pontrhydvendiget), where comfortable accommodation
may be obtained at a small inn. About a mile distant is

Strata Florida, or Ystrad Flûr **Abbey**, which stands near
the banks of the infant Teivy, in the midst of a comparatively
luxuriant vale, near mountains that almost overshadow it on
three sides.

In this deep and wild solitude, well calculated for religious meditation, and discipline of body and mind, a stately Abbey and
seminary of learning were founded A.D. 1164, by Rhys, son of
Griffith ap Rhys, Prince of South Wales. The community, who
were Cistercians, soon attained great celebrity, and acquired
extensive possessions. A large library was formed, which included
the national records from the earliest period, the works of the
Bards, and the genealogies of the Princes and other great families

of Wales. The monks compiled a valuable history of their
country down to the death of Llewellyn the Great.* Edward I.
ordered the Abbey to be burned A. D. 1295, after the death of
Llewellyn, because the Abbot failed to keep a promise that he would
bring the county of Cardigan into amity with the King. The
latter, however, afterwards gave £78 towards its restoration, on
condition that the monks cut down the thickets with which
the adjoining hills were then covered—and which had long afforded
safe harbour to the Welsh " guerillas "—as well as maintain the
highways. Leland furnishes the following picture of its appearance a short period before the Dissolution of Monasteries,
when the revenues (the territorial possessions were immense)
amounted to £122 6s. 8d. :—" The church of Strateflere is larg,
side ilid and crosse ilid. The fundation of the body of the church
was made to have bene 60 Foote lengger then it is now. By is
a large cloyster, the fratry and infirmitori be now mere ruines.
The Cœmeteri wherein the cunteri about doth buri is veri large
and meanely waullid with stoone. In it be xxxix great hue trees.
The base Court or camp afore the Abbay is veri fair and large. "
Old Leland then speaks of the remains of extensive woods in the
vicinity. It is said that the burying place covered 120 acres, and
a long list of eminent persons from all parts of Wales who were
interred here, including Davydd ap Gwilym, the celebrated bard,
has been preserved.* The churchyard is now reduced to small
dimensions, but leaden coffins have often been dug up at a distance : and only two or three yew and some box trees are left.

It appears from a print in *Buck's Views*, 1740, " that a considerable portion of the north transept with its pointed windows"
then existed. The most important feature of the remains, an
arch of extraordinary beauty, with part of the adjoining wall and

---

* " The earliest account of the Kings of Britain was brought from Britanny
in France, by Gualter, Archdeacon of Oxford, A. D. 1100. The M.S. was called
Brut y Brenhined, which brought down the history to A. D. 700. There was
a copy in the library of Mr. Davies, of Llanerch, in Denbighshire. Geoffry of
Monmouth's history is a free translation of this work. Caradoc, of Llancarvan,
took up the history where the author left it, and continued it to A. D. 1157."
Copies of Caradoc were preserved in Stata Florida and other archives.

a small window, now stand within the garden belonging to an old
farm-house.   The ornaments of this late Norman recessed arch
differ from those found on any other ancient specimen ; the co-
ordinate arches which compose it, are tied together by three
croziers on either side ; we copy the beautiful sculptured stone
over the centre.

The existing re-
mains—which in-
clude a fragment
about 40 feet high
—are of the transi-
tion style, between
Norman and Early
English.   An ela-
borate paper on
Strata   Florida,
written   by   the
Rev. G. Roberts,
which   clears   up
difficult points in
its history, was read at the first meeting of the Cambrian
Archæological Society at Aberystwith, in 1847, and has since
been published in a cheap form.   The members subsequently
visited the ruins ; previously to which some important excavations had been made—chiefly on the eastern side of what had
been the south aisle, and on the eastern side of the chancel.
These researches showed that "some of the building was composed of portions of an earlier structure."   Several interesting
tiles (many once cased the walls, in the style of paintings met
with in old missals) and fragments, including a piece of the
piscina of very early date, were found.   The dimensions were
ascertained to be nearly as follow :—Nave, from corner of transepts,
45 feet by 32 ; chancel, 45 feet by 28½.   An interesting crossed
tombstone was removed into the cemetery.   We hope that the
mass of ruin will be fully explored.—A mean church, which has
been constructed out of the ruins, stands within the Abbey
enclosure, in a churchyard of two acres.   In the Abbey farm-

house is a curious picture illustrative of Temptation, which no doubt belonged to the monks.

About two miles from the Abbey, adjoining the Tregaron road, the foundation of what appears to have been the church of *Hen Monachlog*, "the old Abbey," may be traced on a slight eminence between two brooks, one of which is called the *Flûr*. There was no doubt a small religious house here *before* Strata Florida was built in 1164. Mr. Roberts has recently found in the *Myvyrian Arch.* a chronological account of the day and year when the monks entered the "New Church," forty years after they came to Strata Florida. A barn at Hen Monachlog, mentioned by Sir S. Meyrick, as belonging to the monks, is of much more recent date.

THE HILL COUNTRY.

The mountain district which commences a few miles to the north of Llandovery, and stretches to Plinlimmon, forming an irregular oblong parallelogram, is one of the wildest and least known parts of Britain, and may be called the "great desert of Wales." The Ordnance maps are studded with the names of little else than hills, valleys, brooks, and rivers, with now and then a lonely farm-house. There are only two twin parish churches, *Llanddewi Abergwessin, Llanvihangel Abergwessing*, and *Capel Ystrad Fin*, a chapelry, in a district, by crow flight, about thirty miles long! A very few churches are scattered on its borders in the low country; but the people, on an average, must probably have to travel eight or ten miles to church or chapel on a Sunday.

On a fine spring or summer day—sunshine and cloud are indispensable lights—this region of hills and glens looks tameless ; fancy it wrapped in mist, as it is for many months in the year—or covered with deep snow—or at a time when the mountain torrents which, as an old writer says, "flete and rage upon stones," are angered by winter rains or thunder storms, and form tremendous floods, that carry all before them in the low lands, in an inconceivably short space of time. Fancy what you would do if you were lost in these wilds at night ; how providential would the barking of watchful sheep dogs in some solitary glen seem to the ear ! The country people know the roads—and there are some distinct rugged tracks along which carts and sledges may be driven well enough to market or fair, or with peat, across these hills, connecting distant towns together ;* roads which often follow the courses of rivers for miles, and which were originally formed, no doubt, to some extent by the good monks of Strata Florida, who opened their doors at nightfall to all weary guests. " The Pastures of thes hills, " says old Leland, " be fre to the Inhabitantes, as well as al montaine pasture longging to Strateflere Abbay."

The group forms part of four counties ; but Cardiganshire claims the largest one corner, *Cwmtoyddr*, belongs to Radnor. In old writings the hills are called *Maelienydd*; Giraldus calls them *Ellennith* ; the early English name is the most expressive—*Moruge*, or moors, *i. e.* " the heights of marshy places "; this, according to Leland, *(Collect.* vol. ii. p. *75),* is the meaning of the old Welsh word, *Ellennith.* These hills, probably the sides, were once covered to a great extent with wood, which Edward I. ordered the monks of Strata Florida to cut down, because it afforded harbour to his Welsh foes. Leland, about two centuries and a half afterwards, says, " Many Hilles thereabout hath bene well woddid, as evidently by old rotes apperith, but now in them is almost no woode." This he ascribes to three causes :—1. " The wood cut down was never copisid, and this hath bene a great cause of destruction of wood through Wales. " 2. To injury done by goats. 3. " Men for the nonys destroied the great Woddis, that the should not harbour Theves."

The farms are of vast extent : we have seen one which was more than six miles in length, the farmer's dwelling being at the extreme end, nearest the market town ; the shepherds and their families, who also look after black cattle and ponies, which are turned out to pasture about the middle or end of May, were stationed in three-aged farm-houses of the most primitive sort, two or three miles apart, buried near water-courses in the deep shadows of lonely *cwms,* into which sunbeams never penetrate throughout weary winters. The simple people rarely emerge into the every-

* Amongst these are roads from Strata Florida to Rhayader, from Tregaron to Rhayader, to Builth and to Llandovery, &c.

day world except at fairs. The farmer had six or seven thousand small ragged sheep—true mountain mutton—a number of which are snowed up in deep drifts and lost in winter, but they are wonderfully hardy. One of the adjoining hills bears the expressive name of *Drum yr eira*, "the Snowy Ridge." The peasantry live chiefly on oat-cakes, cheese, and buttermilk ; they have so faint an idea of growing corn or potatoes, *that we have seen heaps of manure placed in the middle of brooks, to be swept away by the first fresh of water !* Yet the soil is not really barren, as reputed ; but in many parts capable of growing good crops. These uplands furnish excellent pasturage in summer. Leland says, and the description still holds true—" The pastures of the montaynes of Cairdiganshire be so great that the hunderith part of it rottith the ground, and maketh sogges and quikke more by long continuaunce for lack of eting of hit." Most of the lowland farmers have some rights of pasturage on the highlands. It will be understood then that the hills are chiefly green, that there is but little heather.

A portion of these mountains is Crown land ; Colonel Powell, of Nanteos, has a vast tract which once belonged to Strata Florida. There are hardly any fences, or stone walls, a remarkable circumstance in Wales, where very great jealousy is displayed by landowners, respecting boundaries.

THE LAKES.

The *Llyns* of Cardiganshire chiefly lie on the wild hill tops, and few are distinguished for the beauty of their scenery ; yet there is an indescribable charm about these rude tarns, parents of many flashing streams which make the waste vocal with their melody. They are the eyes of the mountains ; and full of interest to those who love the most healthful, and to us, the most pleasurable sport in the world. Lake fishing is, however, a science of itself ; greater skill in manipulation, greater knowledge of flies, are requisite to ensure success, than in river fishing ; but when success does reward the patient angler, he is amply repaid. The trout in mountain lakes vary much in size and quality ; at two of our Cardiganshire Llyns (*Cerrig Llywdion*) a very skilful angler may sometimes take more than 300 small trout, weighing between 40 and

50 lbs. in a day! At others a man may "flog the water" from morning till night, and hardly catch anything. We proceed to "group" the lakes as they run from north to south, premising that the Ordnance maps, unless the angler have a guide, are indispensable in these hills.

Llyns Ivan issau and Ivan ucha (the *Llynodd Ieuan* of Ordnance survey). Two long narrow pools. Trout rather small. Distance, about 2 m. from Duffrin Castle Inn.

Lakes within reach of old Devil's Bridge and Rhayader road: Llyn Rhyddnant. Small pool, 1¼ m. to south of foregoing llyns.—*Llyn y Helygen*, small, 2½ m. from road; a brook from it joins the Elan. About a mile distant is *Llyn Gwyngy*, the source of the Gwyngy, a large tributary of the Elan; good trout.—*Llyns Cerrig Llwydion isaf* and *uchaf*, about 3 m. to S. of road, and 9 from Rhayader; a river called the Hirin flows from thence into the Elan; the first lake (that to the N.) is the largest. Trout very free, but small; best weather, a bright sky, and moderate breeze.—*Llyn Figen Felan*, in the heart of the hills, 2 m. W. from Cerrig Llwydion, said to be destitute of fish.

THE TEIVY GROUP: A mile and a half N. of Llyn Hir are *Llyns Fyrddin Vawr* and *Vach*, the former nearly three miles round; fish free but small.

Teivy Lakes. The best station for these five and the two foregoing lakes, as well as for Llyn Gynon, is Pontrhydvendigaid. Some take a guide, who ought to be acquainted with fishing; we can recommend David Davies. The road runs by Strata Florida, along the infant Teivy, which is crossed more than once. *Llyn Teivy* (4½ m.) is the nearest. Fish good, sometimes free and large. A strong breeze is essential, and a lowering day is better than a bright one for this group. Leland describes the scenery near the llyn graphically :—" Of all the pooles none stondeth in so rocky and stony soile as Tyve doth, that hath withyn him many stones. The ground al about Tyve, and a great mile towards Stratfler, is horrible with the sighte of bare stones, as Cregeryri mountains be." Leland only saw, from a place called "Cragnaulin Stone," four lakes, which he designates Llinynigin Velin (yellow quaking moor), Lacus Petrinus Llinnllabeder, and Llinyrydde: " These iiii Pooles long to the Abbat of Stratflere." On ascending a hill at the side of Llyn Teivy, portions of the other four lakes can be seen at one glance, as they lie near together. *Llyn Hir*, the " long pool," is the second lake; fish large, but rather shy. *Llyn Egnant*, the largest of the five, lies near; fish usually free, of moderate size, some large—an excellent lake. *Llyn Gorlan*, to S. of Llyn Hir, a small pool, with large trout, shy. In little *Llyn Gron*, from whence a brook runs into Egnant, there are no fish. These lakes are.

partly Crown property, partly belong to Lord Lisburne, and Col. Powell. They are not preserved.   Lord Lisburne has two boats.

Llyn Gynon (Gunnon).   The nearest way to this lake, which is fully three miles round, and the largest on these hills, is up a valley seen on the right, after leaving Strata Florida for Teivy Pool, through which a large brook runs from Llyn Egnant. *Llyn Gynon* swarms with fish, some of which are large, but most of those round the shore are small, yet still a nice and very free fish.   On a good day a basket may soon be filled. This and a small llyn, three quarters of a mile to the S., *Gorast*, belong to Col. Powell.

Maes Llyn.   On side of road between Pontrhydvendigaid and Tregaron. Very large fish ; preserved by Lord Lisburne.

TREGARON GROUP :—*Llyn Berwyn*, on a mountain beyond a very romantic pass, *Nant Berwyn*, 5 m. from Tregaron.   Ponies may be left at Dyffwys, a little farm-house, in a hollow by the brook, on left near head of the pass, about half a mile from the lake.   Many of the fish in this fine lake are amongst the most beautiful in Wales, of good, some of very large size, and moderately free. The fish are fond of a dark fly, with some tinsel. *Llyn Crugnant*, the origin of a large tributary of the river Berwyn, lies in the hills 2½ m. to the N.—*Llyn Ddu*, a somewhat larger lake, lies one mile due E. from Crugnant.

There are many wild fowl on the lakes.

––––––––

The river Teivy below Pontrhydvendigaid runs for several miles through a flat country—a vast peat bog, from which many hundreds draw their supplies of fuel.   A certain number of yards is allotted to each applicant ; a cottager can obtain as much of the most agreeable fuel in the world as he can burn in a year, including cutting, for less than a pound.   Coal is a very costly commodity in this county.   How providential is the distribution of fuel !

TREGARON, distant about six miles from the "Blessed Ford," is a primitive little place on the river Berwyn, with a well-attended Market on Tuesdays.   The Church, dedicated to St. Caron, a Welsh prince who was canonised in the third century, has a good tower ; there are monumental stones, said to be of the date of the sixth century, in the churchyard.   Twm Shone Catti [see p. 252] resided at Porth Fynnon, near the town, on the east.   Tregaron is an excellent fishing station—perhaps the best for the Teivy. Above the bridge, first rate sport may often be obtained in the "lanes" of water, when ruffled by a breeze ; and there is capital fishing ground below, for many miles. April is the best month for this fine river. Population of the parish, 2,573 ; of the town, 692. INN—The Talbot.—*Distance* to Lampeter by new road, 11 miles ; the road by Llanddewi Brevi is a mile shorter, but the former is much preferable for a carriage.

Llyn Berwyn has already been described. About two miles to the N. of it is a camp called *Castell Rhyfell ;* two large *carneddau* may be found about a mile more to the N. on lofty mountains, near which, close to an Ordnance mark, a remarkable British road called *Cwys yr Ychen Bannog*, or "The Furrow of the Bannog oxen," may be traced in a direction N. by W. for about a mile and a half. There are many *carneddau* on these hills.

Those who wish to enjoy a very long day in the wilds may cross to Llandovery, partly by the aid of a guide and partly by Ordnance map, either from Tregaron or Llanddewi Brevi [*see* LLANDOVERY]. About five miles from Llanddewi Brevi there is a farm-house on the mountains, which cannot be found without a guide, called *Blaen-twrch-uchaf*, at which refreshments can be obtained ; three or four miles may be saved by going this way, as compared with the distinct road from Llanddewi Brevi up the glen of the *Brenig*, and thence to the *Pyscottwr Vawr* and *Vach* rivers, down to *Ystrad Ffin.* The rude road from Tregaron joins that from Llanddewi on the mountains about five miles from the latter place.

Loventium. Faint traces of this important station[*] on the *Sarn Helen* may be seen at *Llanio isau*, a farm-house down a lane a little way to the left of the new Lampeter road, about 4½ miles from Tregaron. The ground is elevated on the portion called

---

[*] *Roman Remains.* " Roman stations are never found on high mountains, but generally on gentle eminences, having an open circuit of country about them. The form of camp when made by the Romans was always *rectangular,* sometimes square, sometimes oblong, with the corners generally rounded, a peculiarity of construction which that people adopted in their stone walls. Roman causeways are seldom found entire.....The *British Ridgeway,* which is still visible on some of the Welsh mountains, often misleads by its pavement, &c., but there is not that regularity of design, direct line, &c., which was the invariable system of the Roman engineer."—Sir R. C. HOARE.

Caer Castell.   Sir S. R. Meyrick mentions that three stones thus
inscribed were to be seen at this farm-house : "*Caii Artii Manibus*
(or memoriæ) *Ennius Primus.*"   "*Overioni.*"   "*Cohors Secunda
Augustæ.*"   "*Fecit Quinque passus.*" We could only discover that
with the last, which is used as a seat near the farm door, and
the inscription on which will soon be obliterated.   Coins and pottery have been found here.   There is a *Maen Hir* of great size in
a field on the other side of the road, half a mile off.   The *Sarn
Helen* runs due north for many miles.   A mile from Llanio isau
is *Pont Llanio*, a bridge over the Teivy, to

Llanddewi Brevi, one of the most celebrated places in the
history of the early British Church.   A Synod or Convocation
was held here A. D. 519, on the summons of Dubricius, Archbishop
of Caerleon, to consult on the best means of opposing and quell-
ing the Pelagian heresy, which was then making headway in
Wales.   St. David attended this assemblage, and the pious
Dubricius, weary of the world, resigned his archbishopric to
him, and retired to Bardsey Island.   There is an ancient stone
pillar—seven feet seven inches high and ten inches broad, with
an illegible inscription—close to the west end of the church,
called by the people of the place "*David's Staff,*" on which both
he and Dubricius are said to have leaned whilst preaching at the
synod.   A stone without an inscription may be seen opposite the
south door.   The church stands on a mound, which miraculously
rose, according to monkish tradition, when St. David preached.
This and other monkish fables, the most foolish of which relates
to the " Bannog oxen," are still rehearsed here.   The church is
dedicated to St. David, and was founded A. D. 1187 ; the nave
was rebuilt in 1834, and new pewed in 1848, and there is nothing
to excite interest except the chancel and tower ; the transepts are
destroyed.   The clerk told us that there is a " great congregation" and a hundred communicants, a fact which shows that
reverence for the ancient Church may still be found in Wales.
The situation of Llanddewi Brevi, at the entrance of a beautiful
mountain glen, the outlet of the river Brenig, is striking.—A Collegiate Church, for fourteen prebends belonging to St. David's,
was founded here A. D. 1187, and became a very celebrated sanc-

tuary; its ruins are called *Lluest Cantorion*, or the "Residence of the Chanters." Llanddewi Brevi is a place of the Past: one peoples the consecrated mound with an earnest group of early Christians—associates it with an Apostolic age. There is a small Inn, where tourists can be accommodated, called the "Voelallt Arms." *Voelallt* is an ancient Welsh mansion, nearly a mile up the glen.—Distance from Tregaron, by old road, three miles; by Pont Llanio, five miles.—At *Llanvair Clydoge*, half way between Llanddewi Brevi and Lampeter, are large silver-lead mines.

We regain the new Lampeter road. About 3½ miles from that town, the grounds and house of *Derry Ormond* attract attention. The conspicuous pillar on the hill was erected to the memory of the late possessor of the estate, Mr. Jones. There is a Roman Camp, called *Caer*, on the road side near. We have now made a complete circuit of the county.

RADNORSHIRE,

Once a portion of *Siluria*, and after its abandonment by the Romans, a petty Principality, is the least important county in Wales. The great families of Mortimer and de Breos soon gained a footing in it when the Norman era commenced, but there is nothing in its history, with the exception of circumstances connected with the last hours of Llewellyn the Great, of popular interest; no towns of consequence; and the scenery, although hilly or mountainous throughout, does not, with several most striking exceptions, present high attractions for the lover of the picturesque, although it impresses the mind with the peculiarity of its character. Radnor was not created a county until the reign of Henry VIII., and was once most celebrated for its forests, of which little else than the name remains; but modern planters have clothed the sides of many of the valleys with wood. Nearly two-thirds of the county are unenclosed—a vast proportion; much could be done by efficient draining. Few districts are more thoroughly pastoral than this region of large round green hills, suggestive of shepherd life.

z

The mineral productions are unimportant, most of the county being composed of grey wacké or clay slate, with a considerable tract of old red sandstone in the south-eastern side.   The county contains much, however, to interest the geologist.   "There is not perhaps in Great Britain," observes Sir R. I. Murchison, "a finer mass of altered·and crystalline limestone than that exhibited at Nash Scar, the principal cliff of which rises to the height of 200 or 300 feet above the adjoining valley of Knill and Presteign." The same limestone is seen in perfection at Old Radnor, where portions of the Silurian rocks can also be seen.   "The trap in the vicinity of Old Radnor occupies two parallel ridges : the eastern, three miles in length, comprising Stanner Rocks, Worsel Wood, and Hanter Hill ; and the western, called Old Radnor Hill, about half the length of the other.   The trap of the first ridge passes from a coarse crystalline hypersthene rock into fine-grained greenstone, and resembles the hypersthene rock of Coruisk in the Isle of Skye.   The mass of Old Radnor Hill is a dark green stone, but there is a peculiar conglomerate thrown off on the western flanks, having a base of grey and green felspar, enclosing pebbles of quartz, some of large size.   From this composition it may be inferred that a stream of compact felspar, or submarine lava, entangled in it the sand and pebbles of a former bed of the sea." Sir R. Murchison compares "the phenomena at Old Radnor to those of the Val di Fassa in the Tyrol, the latter, however, being on a much larger scale."   There are some important.Mineral Springs in the county, which "issue from the altered strata in junction with the trap rocks, and like the mineral springs in Brecknockshire, are supposed to owe their origin to the decomposition of iron pyrites and other mineral ingredients."

The antiquities are slight.   The British remains consist of a few camps and *carneddau.*   We have described those of the Roman age in our account of Llandrindod.   Many castles existed in the old time, yet only a few crumbling fragments are left, the chief of which are Llewellyn's hunting seat at Aberedw, slight ruins on an eminence two miles above Builth, Boothroyd on the Wye, and New Radnor.   There is only one religious house—Abbey Cwm

Hir. Offa's Dyke, the celebrated boundary constructed by Offa between his kingdom of Mercia and the territories of the Welsh princes, enters Radnorshire near Knighton, between which place and Presteign the turnpike road crosses it twice. The Dyke runs into Herefordshire near a hill called Berva Bank. It is in tolerably perfect condition on high unenclosed ground, but elsewhere has been almost destroyed.

The Wye forms the boundary between Radnor and Brecknock, from a point about two miles below Rhayader to Hay, and nearly all the other streams in the county fall into it. The most important or beautiful are the *Elan*, the *Ithon*, the *Edw*, the *Machwy*, the *Somergill*, the *Marteg*, and the *Clywedog* (a tributary of the Ithon). The Teme, which rises in the Kerry Hills, Montgomeryshire, divides the counties of Radnor and Salop. There are four lakes : Llanbychllyn, a mile and a half round, between Llanbadarn-y-Garreg and Llandewi-vach; Llyn Gwyn, near Rhayader ; Llyn-Llanillyn ; and Llyn Hindwell, near Old Radnor.

Statistics : Population, in 1801, 19,050 ; in 1831, 24,651 ; in 1841, 25,356. Number of parishes, partly in the diocese of St. David's, partly in that of Hereford, 53. Area, 426 square miles, nearly one-third less than Pembrokeshire, the next in point of size amongst the South Wallian counties. Parliamentary representation : One member for the county, one for the united boroughs of New Radnor, Presteign, Knighton, Rhayader, Kevenleece, and Cwmclas. Assizes held at Presteign.—*Education* : 28 Church or National Schools, with 1,014 scholars ; Adventure or private schools, 14, with 341 scholars ; Dame school, 1, with 26 scholars. No British or Dissenting Schools. —Sunday Schools : Church, 25, with 1,146 scholars; Dissenting, 28, with 1,163 scholars. Mr. Symons computes that 23,000 persons out of 25,356 speak English as their fire-side language ; Welsh is spoken in the district to the north and west of Rhayader.

We resume our Itinerary, proceeding eastward from Duffrin Castle Inn [*ante* p. 320]. The mail-coach road from Aberystwith to Gloucester runs for about ten miles through Montgomeryshire, passes *Llangurig*—a village situated near the point of junction with the Llanidloes road, at which there is an ancient and remarkable church—and enters Radnorshire about seven miles from Rhayader. We have described the character of the scenery of this interesting route in our notice of the Wye.

RHAYADER.

Distant from			Miles.	Distant from				Miles.
Aberystwith ..	..	..	.. 33	London *via* Gloucester	..		.. 191
Abbey Cwm Hir	..	..	.. 7	Hafod ..	..	..	..	.. 17
Builth ..	..	..	.. 14	Llandrindod ..	..	..	.. 11
Cwm Elan	..	..	.. 5	Llanidloes (old road)	..		.. 12
Devil's Bridge	..	..	.. 19	Penybont	..	..	..	·.. 10

Rhayader (*Rhaiadyr-gwy*, "the Fall of the Wye") is a "decayed" town, in medieval times of considerable extent, picturesquely situated near towering mountains. Four mean streets run at right angles from a very rude town hall in the centre, which *Nicholson*, in his *Welsh Guide*, styles "a very handsome building"! There was a castle which was destroyed temp. Charles I., the fosse of which can be traced ; the site of another castle is visible on the opposite side of the Wye. The church was rebuilt in 1733 : there is a free grammar school. A small manufacture of coarse woollens is carried on in the town ; and in the adjoining suburb of *Llansantfraid-cwm-toyddyr*, "the church of St. Bridget in the dingle of the two rivers," across the bridge, in which parish there is a remarkable barrow, called *Tomen-Sant-fraid* ; there are other tumuli in the vicinity. There are few better river scenes of the kind than the fall of the Wye over huge rocks into very deep pools at the bridge. Some delightful excursions may be made in the neighbourhood, which also offers great attractions to the angler, both for salmon and trout fishing. Llyns Cerrig Llwydion (nine miles) and other lakes are also within reach. Population, 742.—The parish of *Llansantfraid* is ten miles long and five broad, and stretches far into the mountains. Population, 883.—Market, Wednesday. INNS—The Red Lion (which is the best) and the Black Lion.

Llyn Gwyn, a large pool near the Devil's Bridge road, about two miles off, only contains carp and eels ; the "last trout" was caught thirty years ago. We confounded this lake with another in our first edition.

Abbey Cwm Hir stands in the hills about seven miles east by north from Rhayader. There is no road to it for carriages, the last three miles being mountain—partly an uncertain track. We have described it with Llandrindod, from which place it is easily accessible.

CWM ELAN.

The rapid Elan *(Anglicé* "the Roe,") makes an abrupt turn—a sweet river scene—a mile and a half from Rhayader, and joins the Wye about two miles below that town. A most romantic country soon opens, partly hidden by venerable woods, which also for a considerable distance hide the river. The portal of Cwm Llan is a grand mountain glen, on either side of which hills of the most exquisite character rise boldly. That on the right, *Cefyn Craig-y-Foel*, is a "study" of itself. The river tears below in a channel full of huge rocks and stones, that attest the severity of the storms and floods, which are so tremendous in winter, that many of the trees high up the river bank are barked eight feet up their trunks by masses of ice in their passage down. The suggestive alpine vale in the vista, apparently terminated by a wall of mountain, with a fine mansion, *Nant Gwyllt*, the residence of Mr. Lloyd, which stands in the foreground, is not *Cwm Elan*, as a stranger might suppose, but the Vale of a large and rapid stream, the *Claerwen*, which here forms an alliance with our heroine, the *Elan*. You turn suddenly to the right, after passing *Capel Nant Gwyllt*—

> " Now through the wood
> We steal, and mark the old and mossy oaks
> Imboss the mountain's slope ; or the wild ash,
> With rich, red clusters mantling; or the birch
> In lonely glens light-wavering ; till behold
> The rapid river shooting through the gloom
> Its lucid line along."

Here is the mansion of *Cwm Elan*. There is but one hill in Wales—that in the Pass of *Pont Aberglaslyn*, near Beddgelert—which approaches *Craig y Foel*, opposite Cwm Elan, in warmth and beauty of colour. It delights the eyes—we could look upon it for hours—but the whole scene is one which a poet or painter only can pourtray, and happily Lisle Bowles in his poem

of *Coombe Elian*, from which we have just quoted, has done
justice to it.

Many persons follow the romantic windings of the Elan into the
mountains, crossing a rude alpine bridge, and get into the old
Aberystwith road at *Pont ar Elan* (six miles from Rhayader)
after walking six or seven miles, and return to Rhayader by that
road, or go on to the Devil's Bridge—a hard day's journey.

Towards the end of the last century, Mr. Groves, a gentleman
from Wiltshire, purchased an estate of 10,000 acres at *Cwm Elan*,
which he wished to make a second Hafod.   He planted on a large
scale, and built a house in the bad taste of the time.   In other
respects Art has happily not injured Nature.   After his death the
estate passed through several hands ; the Duke of Newcastle
became its possessor, and sold it in 1843 to an English baronet,
who has since hardly seen his property—one of the gems of the
Principality.

We advise tourists as well as fishermen to ascend the valley of
the Claerwen, which has many tributaries in the distant green
mountains.

———

There are four great highroads in Radnorshire : 1. the mail
road, which runs through the centre of the county; 2. that from
New Radnor to Presteign and Knighton ; 3. the road from Rhayader to Builth ; 4. that from Builth to Newtown, which intersects
the first at right angles, running nearly due north and south.
Large portions of the old roads from Rhayader to Llanidloes, and
Rhayader to the Devil's Bridge are also included in the county.

We shall begin with the first.   At PENYBONT, in the parish of
Llanbadarn Vawr (10 miles from Rhayader and 11½ from Builth),
where a new iron bridge has been carried across the river Ithon,
the scenery is very pretty ; the extensive woods of Penybont
Hall, the residence of J. C. Severn, Esq., adjoin the road.   The
"Severn Arms Hotel" is a very comfortable house, in the Elizabethan style, built in 1840.   About two miles and a half further
on is LLANDEGLEY, where there is a much frequented *Spa*.   One
spring is a strong chalybeate, the other is powerfully impregnated
with sulphur.   The hamlet contains an excellent little Inn, "The

Burton Arms." On the north-east is the lofty group of mountains called Radnor Forest, one of which is 2,163 feet high. There is some fine rock scenery near Llandegley, from which beautiful spar can be obtained.

The scenery progressively improves as you proceed eastward, the road being carried through the hills, which are often of fine outline, and clothed with "hanging woods" of fir, larch, and other timber. The pass in which the church and hamlet of *Llanvihangel-nant-melan* stand is defended by a well-defined British camp, which is apparently one of a chain of similar forts ; a tumulus or mound may be seen in the vicinity. About a mile from the hamlet, at the side of the road to Builth (from Knighton) is *Llyn Llanillyn*, a pool three-quarters of a mile in circumference. A new church has been built in this parish after the model of Kilpeck Church, Herefordshire.

Water-break-its-Neck, one of the largest and most celebrated cascades in Wales, is to be found on a rocky hill side, a mile to the north-west of the mail-coach road, at a point about two miles to the west of New Radnor. The glen into which the waterfall dashes is truly Alpine ; and the scenery, which becomes very rugged and gloomy, assumes an amphitheatrical form. A small stream—very small in summer—descends a deep and narrow aperture ; and we have heard that a gentleman of the neighbourhood once achieved the very difficult feat of climbing to the top.

This, with the exception of Cwm Elan, is much the finest part of Radnorshire. A very precipitous bluff mountain near the road, not far from New Radnor, was a few years ago the scene of a very daring hunting exploit. A man, well mounted, rode in the excitement of the chase down the side of the hill at full speed, and reached the bottom safely !

NEW RADNOR, or *Maesyved*, "the imbibing meadow," once the capital of the county, and the seat of a border castle of great importance, built by the Mortimers, is now a mere village. The fortress was chiefly destroyed and the town burned in 1401 by Owen Glendower, who ordered the whole garrison, 60 in number, to be beheaded. In Leland's day the town had four gates ; the course of the walls may still be traced. The castle, of which little remains, stands on the top of a lofty eminence on the north-east, which commands a lovely view of the Vale of Radnor, Radnor Forest, and the rich country towards Presteign.   The river Somergill, said to be a good trout stream, pursues an under-ground course near this place—hence its Welsh name.

Harpton Court, on the right of the road, about two miles from New Radnor, is the seat of Sir Thomas Frankland Lewis, who has been the great planter of the district.

The STANNER ROCKS, which stand on the left of the road about three miles from New Radnor, form from their size and perpendi-cularity an exquisite landscape, and their clefts are full of wild flowers, whence the country people call the summit "the Devil's Garden."   Three miles from the Stanner Rocks is *Knill Court*, within the beautiful grounds of which, in an ivied church, the remains of Sir Samuel Romilly repose.   Enquire the way to Knill, at Walton turnpike gate on the mail road, three-quarters of a mile before you reach the Stanner Rocks, in proceeding from New Radnor.   Offa's Dyke winds over the summit of the hills of Knill Garraway and the Herrock, opposite Knill.

Three miles onward, to the right—not on the mail road—is OLD RADNOR, called *Pen-y-Craig*, from the site of its church on the summit of a rock.   The parish is hilly, populous, and of great extent (7,160 acres).   Charles I. passed the night at a house called "The Stones," which stands about half a mile to the west of the church, on the 6th of August, 1645.   We have already indicated the geological curiosities of Old Radnor.

The picturesquely situated market town of Kington, in Here-fordshire, is six miles from New Radnor, midway between which the counties join near a turnpike gate.

PRESTEIGN.

Distant from		Miles.	Distant from				Miles.
Builth by New Radnor	..	.. 20	Knighton	..	..	..	.. 7
Hereford	.. .. ..	.. 27	Leominster ..	..	..	.. 14
Kington	.. .. ..	.. 6½	New Radnor ..	..	..	.. 8

Presteign (*Llan Andras*, the church of St. Andrew), founded by Martin, Bishop of St. David's, in the thirteenth century, rose on the ruin of New Radnor, which lost its consequence when it ceased to be a border fortress, this town being much better situated as a market for agricultural produce. It is now the capital of the county, but is partly situated in Herefordshire, from which it is divided by the river Lugg, an excellent stream for grayling and trout. The church is rather a large structure, in the early Decorated and Perpendicular styles, with a square . tower at the west end ; some tapestry in good preservation, representing the entry of our Saviour into Jerusalem, may be seen over the altar. Amongst the structures are the Shire-hall, erected in 1829 for the assizes, &c., and the County Gaol. A free grammar school was founded by John Beddowes, a clothier, in 1565, with an endowment of £140 a year.

Presteign is a neat, cheerful, prettily-situated place, is the abode of many respectable families, and has the advantage of public walks in an elevated situation called " The Warden," nicely planted at the expense of the Earl of Oxford. Population, 2,217. Market, Saturday. INN — The "Radnorshire Arms." — Four miles distant, to the south, is Weobly, or *Wapley Encampment*, which occupies an irregular oval area of great extent, and is in every respect one of the finest and most perfect camps in Britain. It was originally British, subsequently Roman, and was occupied by Caractacus. The view from the summit stretches as far as May Hill, in Gloucestershire.

KNIGHTON (Tref-y-clawdd, or the town on the [Offa's] Dyke) is well situated on a hill above the river Teme, and may be considered the second place in the county. The regular roads from Builth, and from Kington, through Presteign, unite two miles and a half to the south of Knighton, and then form the high road to Shrewsbury, through this border town. About three miles off, a very large British *camp* can be traced on the top of a high hill. Population of the parish 1,404. Distance from New Radnor 10 miles.

———

The road from Builth to Newtown, in Montgomeryshire, which stands due north, runs for many miles close to the river Ithon, the scenery along which is in many parts very picturesque, and has been much improved by judicious planting. The Ithon, which pursues a snake-like course, is about 30 miles long, and joins the Wye four miles above Builth; it is first seen at Llanbadarn Vawr, beyond Llandrindod, where it makes an extraordinary bend to the south, and thence back to Penybont.

Penkerrig House (two miles)—a very beautiful seat, with a lake of six acres—and *Disserth Hall*, near the common, are passed in proceeding through the pretty country that intervenes between Builth and Llandrindod Common, a vast open expanse, about five miles in length. About half way across, amidst plantations on the right, we reach

LLANDRINDOD WELLS.

Distant from	Miles.	Distant from	Miles.
Abbey Cwm Hir	9½	Llanwrtyd (cross road)	15
Builth	7	Penybont	4½
Llanbadarn Vawr Church	2½	Penybont (cross road)	3
Llandegley Wells	7	Rhayader	11¼

The mineral waters at Llandrindod were locally celebrated so far back as 1670, and about the middle of the last century (1749) comfortable accommodations were provided for strangers in a large house, called Llandrindod Hall. The reputation of the place has ebbed and flowed, owing to various circumstances. Towards the close of the century the proprietor of the property pulled down the "Hall" from religious motives, the spa having unhappily become a resort of gamblers and libertines, and for a time Llandrindod was in the shade; but it soon rose again, and has for many years steadily maintained its reputation, which is based : 1. upon the great efficacy of its waters in complaints which we shall specify ; 2. upon the extreme salubrity of its situation. The common looks dreary to a passer-by, on a dull day ; but its elevation always ensures a breeze, almost in the hottest and calmest weather ; it commands magnificent distant mountain prospects ; its wild freedom fascinates ; and sportsmen can obtain liberty to fish and shoot. There is no lack of amusement in the season, when the boarding-house is full of company.

The chief establishment is called the *Pump House Inn*, the grounds surrounding which are tastefully laid out, all the ar-

·angements being contrived to promote the comfort and plea-
:ure of the visitors. This is now the only boarding-house here ;
·orty-four beds are made up, and the company assemble regularly
it meals at a *table d'hôte*. Terms per week, including the use of
:he waters, for board and lodging, £2 2*s.* ; ditto in commercial
·oom, £1 15*s.* For any period less than a week, per day, 7*s.*
Flys, cars, and ponies are kept. The season commences early in
May, and terminates in October.—At the *Rock House*, a comfortable place in the dingle below Llanerch Inn, which stands on
the side of the common a little above the Pump House, and also
at several farm-houses in the vicinity, lodgings can be obtained
by those who wish to provide their own provisions.—We copy,
with slight alterations, from Mr. Lewis's valuable work, the following account of the waters :—

" There are three different springs, called respectively the rock or chalybeate, the saline pump water, and the sulphureous spring; there is also
a spring called the eye water, supposed to be efficacious in diseases of the
eye. The rock, or *chalybeate* water, issues from a slaty rock, near the
boarding-house, to which it gives name : a gallon contains 57 grains of
muriate of lime, 48¾ grains of muriate of magnesia, 239 grains of muriate
of soda, three grains and two-fifths of carbonate of lime, one grain and a
third of silex, and nearly six grains and one-fifth of carboate of iron.
The *Saline* spring is within the grounds of the pump-house ; one gallon
of this water contains 67 grains of muriate of lime, 25 grains of muriate
of magnesia, 242 grains of muriate of soda, five grains and one-fifth of
vegetable matter, and three-fifths of a grain of carbonate of magnesia. The
Sulphureous spring is situated within 100 yards to the south of the saline
spring : one gallon of the water contains 54 grains of muriate of lime, 31
grains and two-fifths of muriate of magnesia, 216 grains and three-tenths
of muriate of soda, and six grains of vegetable matter : this water is best
adapted for artificial baths, but like the saline water, is also taken internally. The waters are recommended to be drunk in the morning, and
upon an empty stomach, in moderate quantities, and when used both
internally and externally, have been found very beneficial in numerous
chronic cases, among which may be enumerated, rheumatism, gout, inve-
terate ulcers, and scrofula. The saline and sulphureous springs are considered by medical men very efficacious in cases of diseased liver, indiges-
tion, gravel, cutaneous distempers, and general debility, whether arising
from sedentary habits, or from too free a use of vinous or spirituous
liquors. The rock water is only drunk in particular cases, and then after

a course of the former. The sulphur water is considered to be the best adapted to external applications, and is therefore sometimes used as a bath."—Medical advice should be obtained in the first instance, before using the waters. It is better to *begin* with small doses; suggestions as to quantities may be obtained on the spot. Some people can accustom themselves to drink sixteen or twenty half-pints in a morning! It is desirable not to walk or ride much after drinking the *sulphur* water.

The church, dedicated to the Holy Trinity—hence the name of the parish—is a small structure built in 1603. There are *British and Roman Antiquities* in the vicinity. Near the church, on the common, is an earthwork about 100 yards round, defended by a vallum with round angles. Above the hamlet of Howy, at the east end of the common, are remains of a nearly circular camp, 50 yards across, enclosed by an exterior vallum, with entrances only on the west and east; this has been wrongly conjectured to be a Roman circus. Traces of another camp, square, with two angles rounded, may be seen near. These camps, which are called in the *Archæologia*, " *Campi Æstivi*," are placed on the common near the line of an ancient paved way, which probably led from a station on the river Ithon, on Cwm farm, in the parish of *Llanvihangel-Helygen* or *Vach*. An old lead mine, with a narrow shaft said to be 300 feet deep, leading to a level about three-quarters of a mile long, may be seen near the church; it is ascribed to the Romans, but has been partially worked in more recent times. The *camp* at Llanvihangel-Helygen is square; the area, four acres, was surrounded by a massive stone wall and fosse, foundations of which and other works can still be traced.

Abbey Cwm Hir.

"Comehere, an Abbay of White Monkes, stondith betwixt ii great hills, in Mellenith, in a botom, wher runnith a litle brooke. It is vii miles of Knighton; the first fundation was made [A. D. 1143] by Cadwathelon ap Madok for lx monks. No chirch in Wales is seen of such length as the fundation of the walles ther begon doth show; but the third part of this worke was never finished." The once majestic Early English structure pithily described by Leland, and designed for sixty Cistercians, narrowly escaped destruction—the grange was burnt—in 1231, Henry II.

who came here with an army, having been enraged at an act of
treachery on the part of one of the monks, which had led to
the loss of Montgomery. A payment of 300 marks averted the
monarch's anger. In 1401, it *was* "spoiled and defaced" by
the Welsh Oliver Cromwell, Owen Glendower, then stationed at
the head of an army on Plinlimmon, who sent a detachment of
300 men to wreak vengeance on the ecclesiastics, because they
were friendly to the English. The church, which was dedicated
to St. Mary, appears to have been only partially restored, and
the community at the Dissolution, when the revenues were only
£28 17*s*. 4*d*., had dwindled to three. The screen and font were
removed to Newtown Church, in Montgomeryshire, and some of
the clustered columns and arches, and the wooden roof, which is
elaborately decorated with 34 large pendant corbels, were taken
to Llanidloes Church.

About a mile and a quarter beyond the cross gate, near Llanbadarn Vawr Church, a road turns to the left which soon brings
you near the side of the *Clywedog*, a tributary of the Ithon,
which runs through very pleasing scenery, and which is preserved
for four miles below the abbey. A mile and a half from Cwm Hir,
Thomas Phillips, Esq., the owner of the abbey estate, has erected
(1848) an iron bridge across the river, and made a new road,
which have rendered the ruins, to which there was previously only
a narrow lane, easily accessible for carriages. A more secluded
spot—one more shut out from "the world"—than this, was never
chosen for devout meditation. A beautiful hill, called the Sugar
Loaf, encloses the glen at one end; and two gracefully-wooded
hills, of considerable height, called the Great and Little Parks,
overshadow it on the north. Picture not to yourselves pillared
aisles, and airy tracery, canopy, niche, or slender lancet—there
have been modern spoilers at work as well as medieval, who
have not left even a corbel head to tell the story of the past.
Look at the adjoining mansion, if you dare penetrate the foliage
which screens it from the plundered abbey—the mansion built
(1816) "out of the ruins"—and there you will find corbels and
other carved work which have been broken down by axes and
hammers. Still there is something left for the curious to gaze at.

Mr. Wilson—who possessed the property before Mr. Phillips—cleared out the area of the unfinished church, which is 238 feet long by 64 broad. The bases of two doorways—at the terminations of aisles—were discovered at the east end, and appear to have been deeply recessed and of great beauty ; triple clustered shafts decorated the angles, between which were a series of four shafts ; it is inferred, from some vestiges, that doorways of a similar character existed on the north-east side of the church. A portion of the east wall is 14 feet high ; the south side of the church, part of the ruin of which rises 21 feet, is much the most perfect ; you can trace the places from whence the arches sprung ; there is a plain doorway near the east end on this side. The bases of three of the twelve elegant clustered columns which once divided the nave from the aisles have been found, and fragments of the shafts ; the bases form nearly a square, and the flutings show that the pillars had eight clustered shafts ; one base is perfect. The religious establishment, including the cloister, appears to have covered at least an acre of ground ; and to have been defended by an earth-work which was carried across the valley at some distance on the east. The fishpond, which is full of trout, is still kept up, as well as a large pool on the mountains that formerly supplied the brethren plentifully on fast days. A mean Church stands at the road side not far from the ruin, in which we discovered an interesting incised monumental stone, which was found in the abbey, and built into the wall here. It bears a cross, and rude inscription.—Soon after the Reformation, the abbey and its broad acres came into the hands of the Fowlers, one of the most ancient families in Wales, which became extinct on the male side by the death of Sir Hans Fowler, Bart., without issue, in 1773. The estate has subsequently passed through many hands.—There is a small Inn opposite the church.

———

We have indicated the characteristics of the Valley of the Wye, from Rhayader to Glasbury—lingered at Aberedw and Pwll Dû—in our tour of that romantic river ; and must cross Builth bridge, from the little church of Llanelwedd, to the sister county of Brecon.

BRECKNOCKSHIRE.

"The *character* of Brecknockshire," observes an accurate but almost unknown critic in landscape, "is strongly marked by a *mixture* of sublimity and cultivation. It is distinguished from Glamorganshire by more level and extensive valleys, and more continuous and lofty mountain tracts ; neither are the changes of scene so sudden, unexpected, and frequent.'' We can add little to this outline. The ancient name of the county, Garthmadrin or the Fox-hold, is suggestive. The Highland country to the south of Brecon is the finest in South Wales. Old Michael Drayton describes the Beacon, the central point, as

—— "stern, and full of dread,"—

covered with a "helm of clouds."

The Romans do not appear to have gained possession of this district, part of *Siluria*, until after the defeat of Caractacus. The *Via Julia Montana*, a branch of the maritime road, ran through Brecknockshire from east to west ; the remains of two important stations on it still exist, as well as other relics of the conquerors of the world. Most of these works were probably constructed during the era of Ostorius. A Welsh prince called Brychan, who lived in the fifth century, gave his name to the district. Soon after Fitzhamon conquered Glamorgan, Bleddyn, lord of Brecknock, was overthrown and slain in a great battle, A. D. 1088, by Bernard Newmarch, a Norman baron of high degree, who thus obtained possession of a large part of this old Welsh lordship, but it was not until the fall of Llewellyn, two centuries later, that the mountain chiefs were subdued. Owen Glendower did much mischief to the towns and castles. Part of the district was included in the Marches or borders, but Brecon was not created a county until the union of England and Wales in 1534. We have indicated the principal British and Roman remains in our Itinerary, and also the architectural antiquities, which include two religious houses and nine castles, none of which are now of much interest.

Geological Features. The central and south-eastern districts consist of the old red sandstone, which has been proved by Sir R. I. Murchison to be divisible into three sub-formations : "a lower zone of tile stones ; a central portion of marls, concretionary limestones, sandstones, &c. ; the upper portion of sandstone and conglomerate. This upper portion, occupying the summits of the Vans (Beacons) and other lofty mountains, between Brecknock and Abergavenny, is by its inclination carried under the whole of the great productive South Wales coal-field." The coal and iron tract comprises a narrow district along the whole southern side of the county. The western side is distinguished by greywacke slates : the transition rocks are singularly devoid of limestone. " One of the most remarkable features in the geology of Brecknockshire is a peninsula of transition rocks, which is thrown up from north-east to south-west, ranging from Erwood on the Wye to the rocky promontory of Corn y Fan, five miles north of Brecon."

Few counties exhibit a greater diversity of soil than this healthy district ; the best land is in the hundreds of Crickhowel and Talgarth, and the farm-houses throughout the county, owing to the exertions of the Brecon Agricultural Society, are better than in most other parts of Wales. The Hereford cattle have superseded the old Welsh black breed in this county, and also in Carmarthenshire; this has only lately taken place in the latter, at the agricultural exhibitions of which hardly any cattle but Herefords are shown.

The southern part of Brecknockshire is very wild and elevated. First, there is the eastern Black Mountain group, amidst which *Pen Cader* (2,545 feet) reigns supreme. The *Brecknock Beacons* (2,862), which are only 52 feet lower than Cader Idris, in North Wales, rise majestically about 13 miles to the south-westward. *Mount Capellante* (2,394) then lifts its head ; finally the *Brecknockshire* (or Trecastle) *Van* (2,594), which forms the eastern end of the Carmarthenshire Van, completes this semicircular range of hill-kings. The long barren chain, called *Mynydd Epynt*, stretches across the county in a north-easterly direction between Trecastle and Builth, opposite to which is the great region of hills that we have described with Cardiganshire, a portion of which, including their highest summit, *Drygarn* (2,071), is in Brecknockshire. One-half of the boundary of the county is clearly defined by rivers·

First, the Towy on the west; the Claerwen; then the Elan, which joins the Wye below Rhayader, from which point the latter forms the entire boundary to Hay.—The *rivers* are very numerous, each large stream possessing many tributaries. In addition to those enumerated, are the Usk, which rises in the Carmarthenshire Beacon, six miles from Trecastle; the Honddû, which has its source in Drum-dhu, and joins the Usk at Brecon; the Irvon, which rises in Bryn-garw, at the north-western extremity of the county, and falls into the Wye near Builth; the Yskir, the Taff, the Tarell, the Tawe, and the group of rivers and waterfalls at the head of the Vale of Neath. [*See ante* p. 171.] There are several lakes: *Llyn Savaddon*, which is the largest in South Wales; *Pwll Bivery*—near *Capel Calwen*, a parish to the southwest of Mount Capellante—adjoining the road between Trecastle and Ystradgunlais; *Llyn Van Vawr*, under the steep of the Brecknockshire Van, about four miles from Bivery. Lastly, *Llyn Carw*. [*See* LLANWRTYD.]

Statistics: Population in 1801, 31,633; in 1831, 47,763; in 1841, 55,603. Number of parishes, all in diocese of St. David's, 66. Area, 754 square miles (the county ranks third in South Wales in point of size). Parliamentary representation: One member for the county, one for Brecon. Assizes and Sessions held at Brecon. *Education*: Church or National schools 38, with 1,873 scholars; private schools 33, with 1,249 scholars; British 5, with 443 scholars; Dissenting 2, with 79 scholars; Dame 18, with 341 scholars. Total, 3,985. Sunday schools: Church 40, with 2,409 scholars; Dissenting 141, with 11,245 scholars. Mr. Symons computes that 23,500 persons out of 55,603 speak English as their fireside language; the county therefore retains its Welsh character.

A canal, suited to barges of 25 tons burden, was constructed between Brecon and Abergavenny in 1811, at a cost of £170,000. A tramway connects Brecon with Hereford, through Talgarth and Hay. There are other tramways, the largest of which runs from the head of the Swansea canal at Ystradgunlais to Devynock, near the mail road a few miles east of Trecastle, and is a means of conveying coal for a wide district.

A A

BUILTH.

Distant from				Miles.	Distant from			Miles.
Aberedw	..	..	..	4½	London, by Great Western Railway,			
Brecon..	..	..	..	16	via Gloucester and Hereford		..	178
Glasbury	..	..	..	15	Newtown	.. .. ..	..	32
Llanwrtyd Wells	..	..	..	14	Presteign, by New Radnor		..	20
Llandovery	..	..	..	23	Radnor (New)	.. ..	..	12
Llandrindod	..	..	..	7	Rhayader	.. .. ..	..	14

The name of Builth calls up impressions of a romantic river, and beautiful scenery. The rude town—which is a grand central point in this part of Wales—possesses character ; and there are many attractions in the neighbourhood for the lover of the picturesque, the fisherman, and the valetudinarian. The view from the long bridge of six arches which spans the Wye, especially if the day be bright—the scene is much enhanced by sunshine—is perfect of its kind.

The Welsh name of Builth, *Buallt*, is said to be derived from *Bu*, an ox, *Allt*, " a wooded eminence." In ancient documents it is styled *Llanvair-yr-Muallt*; this was evidently a great grazing country. Some writers have fixed the Roman station *Bullœum Silurum* of Ptolemy here, but the fact is unsupported by antiquities; might it not have been at *Llanvihangel-Helygen* (see p. 348) on the road from *Deva* (Chester) to *Bannium?* Philip de Breos, a follower of Bernard Newmarch, is styled, in an early record, " Lord of Builth, which he obtained by conquest." He no doubt strengthened and enlarged the castle, the foundations of which, including some very strong earthworks, exist at the east end of the town. The keep stood on the lofty moated mound in the centre, which is fifty yards in circumference ; the state apartments and offices were on the south-west side, to which there was a branch from the inner moat. Sir Roger Mortimer held it for the English Crown, A. D. 1260, but it was taken by Prince Llewellyn ap Gruffydd, who held it until his death, when the garrison betrayed him. The loss of this fortress was considered of very great importance, and Mortimer was tried for it, but acquitted. The story of Llewellyn's end has been frequently told, but like other memorable events it never palls on the mind.

The accounts that have been given by Welsh and other historians
and topographers are so conflicting, that it is no easy matter to
thread the maze.   In the year 1282, the forces of Edward I. had
entered North Wales at various points, and Llewellyn—the last
Prince of Wales who held regal power, and its greatest patriot—
deemed it necessary to make a rapid journey to the south, at the
head of a small army, in order to obtain auxiliaries, as well as to
harass the enemy, then in force in Cardiganshire, as he marched
onwards.   He left the greater part of his troops in that county,
which he subdued, and proceeded towards his castle, or hunting
seat at Aberedw—where he had a garrison—with a small retinue,
part of whom he posted at a bridge across the Irvon, in a dingle
above Builth.   The English had intelligence of his movements,
and a considerable force from Herefordshire, commanded by
Edward Mortimer, marched up the opposite side of the Wye,
intending to cross that river at a place called *Cefyn twm bach*,
"Little Tom's Ferry," and surprise the monarch at Aberedw;
also to send a smaller force forward to seize the bridge at Builth,
and afterwards overwhelm Llewellyn's detachment.   The Prince
perceived the movement, and determined to make an effort to
rejoin his retainers, but first to try the fidelity of the garrison
that occupied Builth Castle, which had been strongly suspected.
The snow was on the ground, so he had the shoes of his horse
reversed, a fact which was soon betrayed to Mortimer by a
traitorous blacksmith, and he succeeded in crossing Builth bridge,
and in holding a parley with the troops in the castle, before the
enemy came up.   Assistance was flatly denied by the "traitors
of Builth," as they have ever since been called; and the Prince
rode forward towards the dell where he had left his faithful
followers.   The English were, however, before him; and although
the Welsh defended their post with obstinate gallantry, they were
overpowered by superior numbers.   Llewellyn, who was almost
unarmed, got amongst his foes during the *mêlée*, and was slain
with a spear by Adam Francton, a common soldier, who was
not at the time aware of Llewellyn's rank, but discovered it on
returning from the pursuit of the Welsh, and then cut off the
head of his victim and sent it to King Edward.   The dell is called

A A 2

"*Cwm Llewellyn*," or Llewellyn's dingle, to this day. The body
of the prince was afterwards dragged to a spot where the road
from Builth (distant two miles and a half) divides—one branch
leading to Llanavan Vawr, the other to Llanavan Vechan and
Llangammarch; two cross roads meet here besides. Here it was
interred in a place which has ever since been denominated *Cefyn-
y-bedd*, or Cefyn-y-bedd Llewellyn—"the ridge of Llewellyn's
grave."

Cwm Llewellyn may be seen a little to the left of the main road,
beyond the place where the roads meet. A peasant working in a
field hard by told us that the dingle and valley below were covered
with broom at the time Llewellyn died, that he was literally killed
with a broom-stick whilst lying wounded on the ground, and that
no broom has ever grown in the vicinity since! The man related
this with an air which evinced his belief in the ancient local
tradition.

Builth was chiefly destroyed by fire in 1692, but a number of
houses exist of older date. The body of the church was rebuilt
in 1793; the tower is ancient. The romantic parish of *Llan-
dewi-y-Cwm*, about two miles distant to the south, is annexed to
this parish; and we recommend those who have time to spare to
walk to the new church that has just been erected there; there
are a small village on a hill, deep glens, and exquisite woodland bits.

The town is much benefitted in summer by the resort of valetudinarians, who lodge here and walk to PARK WELLS, a spa, which
stands amidst pretty woods, about a mile from the town, by the
road across a suspension foot-bridge over the Irvon, the gift of
Joseph Bailey, Esq., M.P. The carriage road is half a mile
further, but carriages cannot be driven all the way to the Wells.
After walking several hundred yards through cool woods you
reach the "pump-room," and a house. There are three very
efficacious springs, which combine the medicinal properties of
those at Llandrindod and Llanwrtyd, and although perfectly distinct—saline, chalybeate, and sulphureous—apparently originate
within a few feet of each other. The following is the description
given on the spot of the *Saline Spring*, which is of peculiar

character.   "An imperial pint contains 136 gr. of saline matter, consisting of muriates of soda, magnesia, and lime, with no sulphates, and a trace of iron, but not sufficient to designate it a chalybeate.   It is more like the Harrogate than other English water, but differs in not containing carbonic acid.   The sulphur exists only as sulphurated hydrogen, which entirely escapes when the water is freely agitated, or exposed to the air."   There are two other strong springs—*i. e.*, five in all—outside the building.

Builth is an admirable fishing station, both for trout and salmon; the sportsman has the rivers Irvon and Ithon within reach, as well as the Wye.   INN—The Lion.   A coach runs in the summer months from Brecon; and for some seasons a coach, called the Lily of the Valley, has run between Gloucester and Builth, also in the summer.   Market, Monday.   The Builth Poor Law Union includes 31 large parishes and townships!

LLANWRTYD.

Distant from	Miles.	Distant from	Miles.
Builth	14	Llanvihangel Abergwessin	5
Llandovery	12	Trecastle (over Epynt Hills)	13
Llangammarch	5½	Tregaron	18

A long valley, or undulating district, stretches between Builth and Llandovery in a direction west by south, bounded on one side by the Epynt Hills, and on the other by the vast group we have already sketched (*ante* p. 330).   The Irvon, one of the best but least known rivers in Wales, pursues a "devious" course along this comparatively low country, not far from the road, for more than half its length.   After leaving *Bedd Llewellyn*, there is nothing worth mentioning until you arrive at a comfortable roadside fisherman's Inn, at *Maes Cefyn-y-fford*.   At the village of *Llangammarch*, two or three miles further on, is a bridge across the Irvon, and a tolerable Inn.   Mr. Theophilus Jones, the learned historian of Brecknockshire, was a native of this parish, of which his father was vicar, and was buried here.   A large circular mound, supposed to be a *Roman camp*, may be traced near the old mansion of *Caerau*.   There is much open water and excellent fishing in the Irvon (which has throughout its course many tributaries, the chief of which are the Dylas and the Chwernwy), from hence to Llanwrtyd.

No one passing through these wide and tame lowlands would suspect the existence of the deep *Vale of Llanwrtyd*, running into the heart of the mountains, unless he were previously told of it. —The village strikes us as more thoroughly *Welsh* than anything we have seen. A primitive bridge, and "runs" of water—a nest of rude thatched cottages on a rocky strand, with thin peat smoke curling upward—a receding Vale, "bowered" with untouched tree and river scenery — wild round brown hills, with bluffs that *suggest* much—an air of profound repose—are the concomitants of this charming picture. There is a little Inn, called the Belle Vue, at the village, where some who "rough it" board and lodge; but about half a mile up the vale, on a terrace at the very edge of the Irvon, is *the* "Boarding House," *Dol-y-Coed*, formerly a seat of the family of Jones, at which most comfortable accommodations may be obtained. The general arrangements resemble those at Llandrindod : terms for board and lodging per week, at the first table, including the use of the waters, £1 15s. ; ditto at the second table, £1 3s. Persons desirous of furnishing their own provisions can have lodgings at *Dol-y-Coed*. The season begins in May. The mineral spring is not far off, amidst prettily-laid out grounds, and was discovered in 1732, near the Irvon, by the Rev. Theophilus Jones, vicar of Llangammarch. It is called in Welsh " Fynnon Ddrewllydd," owing to the fetid odour of its waters, which " are strongly impregnated with hepatic gas, a small portion of sulphate of iron, and a still smaller quantity of sulphate of soda. The water is a specific remedy in scorbutic and cutaneous diseases, relaxation of the fibres of the stomach, and in chronic disorders, and is considered by many skilful chemists who have analyzed it to be equal to that of Harrogate." —Sir R. Murchison states that the mineral springs here and at Builth " rise in the silicified and hardened schists at points where they are penetrated by trap rocks. Their origin is considered to be due to the decomposition of the vast quantities of sulphuret of iron which are collected at such points."

The church is exquisitely situated a mile up the glen, at the foot of a lofty wooded hill, called *Pen-y-Dinas ;* the house near *Dinas*, now occupied by a farmer, is a lately deserted seat of the Lloyd family.   There are walks up this hill, which commands a mountain prospect, and view up the vale, of very great beauty. The author of the " Mountain Decameron " compares the scenery here to that of Matlock.   A road along which a carriage may be driven (keep to the right of *Pen-y-Dinas)* runs to the twin churches of *Llanddewi Abergwessin*, and *Llanvihangel Abergwessin*, which stand on opposite knolls, on either side of the Irvon, at its confluence with the little river Gwessin.   The scenery from *Pen-y-Dinas* to this spot is truly beautiful; in some parts the river dashes over huge rocks ; and the ruddy colours of the hills, even in winter, would charm an artist.   The glen contains a solitary mansion, *Llwyndderw*, the seat of Captain Roberts. *Llanddewi* is the very rudest church we have seen in Wales ; no better than a cottage, 30 feet by 15, with three small common shutter windows, and without a belfry.   There are only 143 souls in this immense mountain parish.   Its opposite neighbour is almost equally primitive, but graced by a little grove of aged yews.   There is a public-house near, without a sign.   Drygarn mountain rises in the background.   The Irvon runs for ten miles into the hills. The following distances by the hill roads were given to us on the spot, and we suppose they are near the mark :—From Abergwessin to Tregaron, 13 ; to Builth, 13 ; to Rhayader, 13.

Llyn Carw.   This small lake is six or seven miles off in the mountains, almost due north, beyond *Drygarn*.   An Ordnance map or guide is essential.   It contains very large *red* trout; some of which weigh 3 or 4lbs. ; but although difficult of access, it is usually preserved.   The pool is nine miles from Rhayader, and 13 from Pontrhydvendigaid.

Perhaps the easiest mode of getting to Llanwrtyd is to proceed by mail to Llandovery, from whence the road ascends the pass of the Bran river.   *Glan Bran*, the seat and large estate of the ancient family of the Gwynnes', has lately been purchased by Mr. Crawshay Bailey, one of the " iron kings.' '

We shall retrace our steps to Builth, and leaving the Wye for
the present, cross the county to Brecon by one of its least interesting and least frequented roads.   Yet the Vale of the Honddû, and
Castle Madoc, with its glossy woods, contain some charming
scenery, often disfigured, however, by cultivation.

BRECON.

Distant from				*Miles.*	*Distant from*				*Miles.*
Abergavenny ..	..	..	..	20	Llandovery ..	..	..	..	21
Builth ..	..	..	..	16½	Llandilo Vawr, by Llandovery		..	33
Crickhowel ..	..	..	14	London, by Monmouth		..	..	177
Glyn Neath (Lamb and Flag)		..	23	Merthyr Tydvil	..	..	..	18½
Glasbury	..	..	..	11	Neath, by Pont Neath Vaughan		..	34
Hay ..	..	..	..	15½	Pont Neath Vaughan		..	..	20½
Hereford	..	..	..	35½	Trecastle	..	..	..	12

There are few towns more happily situated than Brecknock
(modernised to Brecon).   It stands in a fine valley at the confluence of the rivers Usk, Honddû, and Tarell (" Aber-Honddû"),
nearly in the centre of the county of which it is the capital, and
commands mountain scenery of the highest grandeur.   " I have
seen few places," observes Gilpin, " where a landscape painter
might get a collection of better ideas. "

This was an ancient British post or " city."   The Romans
formed one of their most important stations near, and the Normans soon perceived its natural advantages.   Bernard Newmarch
founded the present castle, A. D. 1094, in order to maintain the
ground that he had won [*ante* p. 351], and it was long one of the
chief seats of the Lords-marchers.   Very strong fortifications were
also constructed to defend the town, which remained entire until
the civil war of the seventeenth century, when with the castle they
were dismantled by the inhabitants, to avoid the horrors of a siege.

Churches.   There were two religious houses in Brecon before
the Reformation ; a Priory for six Benedictine monks, founded
by Bernard de Newmarch, and subordinate to Battle Abbey,
Sussex ; a House of Black Friars near the West Gate.   The
present "Priory" church was, according to Leland, built " afore
the priory was made ; " that is, built in part.   Newmarch no

doubt found an old church here. The revenues were £112 14s. 2d.
at the Reformation, and there are hardly any remains left of the
Priory. The Church, which stands in the midst of venerable
yews, is a large and interesting edifice, of irregular cruciform
design, with a massive square embattled tower, erected A. D. 1515,
containing eight bells. It has undergone injurious alterations at

various periods. The Chancel is of great
beauty, with a lofty five-light deeply-recessed
Early Pointed east window. The Marquis of
Camden, the holder of the rectorial tithes,
is bound to repair it, but it is in a dilapidated
condition. Within the altar rails is a remarkable grave-stone, which contains " a representation of the Crucifixion (the cross being
omitted) with two angels at the upper angles
of the stone censing the head of the Saviour ;
at his sides are the figures of the Virgin and
St. John ; and beneath them are four figures
kneeling, being the persons to whose memory
the stone was inscribed." This sort of sculp-
ture on grave-stones is exceedingly rare. The
following monumental inscription to the memory of a true patriot will be read with interest :

" Sacred to the memory of the right hon. John Jeffreys Pratt, Marquess
Camden, K.G., who died Oct. 8th, 1840, aged 81 years. During a long
life passed in the service of the public, and in the highest offices of the
state, he contributed by voluntary donations towards the service of his
country, £366,116 14s. 3d. This tablet to record his patriotism and virtues is erected by his affectionate niece, Lady Caroline Wood. ' A good
name is rather to be chosen than great riches.' "

A wooden screen divides the chancel from the transepts ; that
on the south side is called *Capel Cochiaid* or " Red-haired [*i. e.*,
Norman] Men's Chapel ; " the northern transept is styled " The
Chapel of the Men of Battle," and was once appropriated to the
inhabitants of the neighbouring village of that name. A Chapel,
called the " Vicar's Chapel," adjoins this transept, and is one of

the gems of the church. The nave, which has a clerestory, is
plain, and one of the oldest parts of the church ; it has a window
of the style of the fifteenth century.   There is a fine circular Norman font, with intersecting arches.   Most of the monuments,
although numerous, are not remarkable.   Length of the nave, 137
feet ; of the chancel, 62 feet.

St. Mary's Church, in the centre of the town, is a large struc-
ture, which was partly rebuilt temp. Henry VIII.   St. David's
Church stands in the suburb of *Llanvaes*, in which (next to the
Priory) is also the most interesting building in Brecon,

The COLLEGE OF CHRISTCHURCH.   A Dominican priory, which
existed here at the time of the Reformation, was converted by
Henry VIII. into a collegiate establishment, which he transferred
from Abergwilly, and on which he conferred a charter.   The
Bishop of St. David's is *ex-officio* dean, and there are a precentor,
treasurer, chancellor, and nineteen prebendaries.   Some eminent
persons, including Mr. Theophilus Jones, the historian of the
county, have been educated at this grammar school, from which
divinity students were admitted to holy orders without graduating
at Oxford or Cambridge, until Lampeter College was founded.
Brecon College is now a disgrace to the Principality.   The school
long existed only in name ; but eighteen boys were being educated
there when we visited it in 1848 ; the buildings are in a state
bordering on ruin.   The court on entering from the street was
formerly the nave of the church (of which a Norman doorway
remains), and was pulled down in Cromwell's day.   The present
church, which is in the Early Pointed style, with a very large
five-light east window, eleven windows on the north, and four
on the southern side, formed the choir, 60 feet long by 25 wide, and
was altered and restored by Bishop Lucy after the Reformation.
It is an interesting structure, but in wretched condition.   Divine
service was discontinued in the year 1838, after which the work
of decay and destruction went rapidly on ; at last the roof was
repaired at the end of 1847, and greased calico put into the eyeless
windows, but the weather still often occasions havoc.   There are
many mutilated monuments, including tombs of Bishops Bull,

Lucy, and Mannering ; and a splendid altar tomb, on which are effigies in the style of James the Second's time, of Richard Lucy, chancellor of the church (the bishop's son), and of his wife and child. Over the threshold of the door is an inscribed stone, now illegible, to the memory of the father of the celebrated *Sir David Gam*. There are twenty-three rude stalls, with grotesque misereries, in a state of decay, the incomes annexed to which vary from £60 down to £1 6s. 8d. ; but many fines are received on the renewal of leases ; nominal total, £387 2s. Several stalls are now vacant, and in the hands of the ecclesiastical commissioners. The Bishop's house or palace, now leased, is curious in an architectural point of view. The cloisters of the priory were in existence half a century ago ; and part of a Chapel (the " Aubrey Chapel ") attached to the church of St. Nicholas—which stood close at hand—is left, together with the chapter-room and vestiges of the refectory, and other parts of the old establishment.

The remains of the *Castle* in the beautiful grounds of the Castle Hotel are unimportant. The original design inclosed an oblong square, about 300 feet by 240 feet, and the keep—which is now the chief remain—is called Ely tower, " from having been the prison of Morton, bishop of Ely, and the scene of his conference with the crafty Duke of Buckingham respecting the houses of York and Lancaster," which led to the downfall of Richard III., who had imprisoned the bishop here.

Brecon looks picturesque at almost all points, and mainly consists of three long streets, which, with the suburb of Llanvaes, across the bridge over the Usk, stretch from point to point for about a mile. . Amongst the public buildings are the *County and Borough Halls ; Assize Courts*, which cost £12,000, and were opened in 1843 ; and extensive *Barracks*, that impart a lively character to the place, and which contain an armoury. There is always a considerable force in this central situation. A County Agricultural Society was established at Brecon as far back as 1755, and still flourishes. Races are held in the autumn.

Very few towns possess such fine *public walks* as Brecon. The Priory walks, which are connected with a house—on the site of the old Priory, of which there are some relics, including the gateway and outbuildings—belonging to the Marquis of Camden, are very extensive and picturesque, being carried through high woods along the banks of the Honddû.   They are open to the public; and there is another fine walk along the shore of the Usk.

The famous Sir David Gam, who is said to have saved the life of Henry V. at Agincourt, was born and lived at Newton, in the adjoining parish of St. David.—Mrs. Siddons was born at Brecon in 1755, at a public-house called the Shoulder of Mutton, whilst her parents were on a professional tour.

The view from Brecon bridge is beautiful.   The town and castle are seen to the greatest advantage from this side, and the majestic " Beacons" look near at hand to the southward.

HOTELS—The Castle, the Swan.   There are other comfortable Inns.   Chief Market, Saturday.   Population in 1841, 5,354.

Fishing near Brecon.   Mrs. Gwynne Holford has let the fishing on the Usk, for about four miles on the Buckland estate, to an individual who grants tickets at 5s. per day.   The Usk above Brecon, to the junction of the Yskir, belongs to Mr. Lloyd Vaughan Watkins, M.P., but visitors at the Castle Hotel have the use of a ticket, subject to regulations, from the 1st of February to the 1st July; the fishing is excellent.   The Yskir is slightly preserved ; we have heard that the Honddû often affords good sport.

Excursions.   To the summit of Brecknock Beacons ; to the Gaer ; to Llynsavaddon.

BRECKNOCK BEACONS.   Nearly six hours are required for an excursion to the summit of this hill king, once called Mount Denny.   If proper directions be obtained a guide is not requisite, although it is difficult to thread the irregular country at the foot, which is near the *Merthyr road.*   The structure of the mountain is so truly Alpine that it alone repays the fatigue of the ascent, independently of the view from the summit, which, although very impressive, perhaps hardly equalled our · expectations.   On the west is the Carmarthenshire or rather Brecknockshire Van ; nearer at hand, Mount Capellante ; on the south, Merthyr ; on the south-east, the Vale of Crickhowel, terminated by the " Sugar-Loaf," which looks a pigmy hill here ; on the north-east, the Hatterel hills and Cradle mountain ; on the north, the " low country" of Brecknockshire, backed by the Epynt and Radnor mountains. Leland states that " in a veri cleere day a manne may see a part of Devenshire and Cornwale"—we much doubt the latter. He speaks of the "faire well-spring on the veri toppe," and calls this and the group of hills around "Banne Brekenianc." A little below the summit, on the west, is a small lake called the *Llyn cwm Llwch*. The Taff takes its rise near. According to Bardic traditions the institutes of the order of the Knights of the Round Table were framed at a gathering here— hence the name of the highest peaks, *Cader Arthur*. A pic-nic party of fifty once dined on this summit. Fatal accidents have occurred amongst these wild steeps.

The Gaer. At the confluence of the river Yskir with the Usk, about three miles to the west of Brecon, are the remains of one of the earliest stations of the Romans in Britannia Secunda—and the parent of Brecon—now called the Gaer, or *Caer-Bannau*. It is seen from the Trecastle road, but the route to it is by a country track direct from Brecon on the north side of the Usk. This post was on the *Via Julia Montana*, now called Sarn Helen. You strike into the Roman causeway after walking for about a mile and a half, on the side of which, about half a mile from the *Gaer*, is a carved monumental headstone, about six feet high, to the memory of a Roman Soldier or Citizen and his wife, erroneously called by Camden and some other topographers " the Maiden-stone." Some time before reaching this stone, however, the lover of antiquities ought to explore some extensive *British Camps* of great interest. That on the top of *Venny Wood* is supposed to have been the site of a British city, and to have been occupied by the Romans. *Pen-y-Crûg*, a round hill opposite, is crowned by an oval military work, encircled by triple ramparts about 18 feet high ; its diameter varies from 600 feet to 430 feet. There is a third camp of smaller size in the vicinity, and ves-tiges of entrenchments, which show that this must have been one of the most important stations in the Principality. A

Maen Hîr, or pillar of great size, stands in a field on Battle farm, on rising ground, about a mile to the north of the " Maiden Stone." *Pennoyre*, a fine modern seat belonging to Mr. Lloyd Watkins, M. P., who has a very large estate in this district, is in the parish of Battle.—We leave the Roman Stone and walk down to the Yskir, wading the river to the church of Aberyskir—jumping ancient stepping stones where practicable— close to which is the *Gaer*, admirably situated in a military point of view.   It forms a " parallelogram of 624 feet by 456 ; the foundations of the wall which bounded this area are yet perfect, and its ruins in some places are from three to six feet high above the level of the ground, though much overgrown and concealed by underwood ; the north-western angle of the camp is now occupied by a farm-house and offices built chiefly from the ruins of the ancient wall." The pretorium is distinct, and marked at a distance by a modern tower, meant to look old.   Several gold and silver coins of Nero, Trajan, and other emperors, and many Roman bricks, marked LEG. II. AUG., have been found.   This legion acted under Julius Frontinus in the reduction of the warlike nation of the Silures, A. D. 76.—Pedestrians can follow a path by the Usk from hence, through the meadows, until they reach a bridge which leads to the Trecastle road.

The road from Builth to Merthyr Tydvil which intersects the county from north to south, and which we have already indicated as far as Brecon, embraces some sublime scenery in the latter part of its course.   The route from BRECON to MERTHYR, on which a slow omnibus plies, is one of the wildest in Wales : it first follows the course of the Tarell up *Glyn Tarell*, below the western steeps of the " Beacons ; " about eight miles from Brecon, at *Pont ar Taff*, the infant Taff vawr river is crossed, and its course followed all the way to Merthyr.   *Capel Nant Dû* (expressive name !), a humble edifice near the road, is a chapel of ease to Cantref, its mother church, situated ten miles off.   The road on the *right*, beyond Pont ar Taff, goes to Hirwain.   '

There are three "coach" roads out of Brecon; 1. to Trecastle and Carmarthen; 2. to Hay and Hereford [*see* WYE]; 3. to Crickhowel, Abergavenny, and Monmouth.

The TRECASTLE ROAD runs along the upper Vale of the Usk, through a fine country, with the stupendous mountain scenery of the "Beacon" group on the south. There are two branches from it through this mountain district: 1. the road to *Merthyr Tydvil*, already described; 2. the road *to the Vale of Neath*, on the left, several miles from Brecon, which must not be confounded with one to Devynock. We have already referred [p. 170] to the *Glen of Llià*. The stone *Maen Llià* is visible for five miles *on ascending* this pass; it is 12 feet high and 9 broad, and Mr. Theophilus Jones does not consider it Druidical. Cwm Dû turnpike, nine miles from Brecon, is almost the only house seen throughout a distance of ten miles. The descent into the Vale of Neath is described at p. 169.

We regain the Trecastle road. *Capel Bettws* is surrounded by a *grove* of yews. At the hamlet of *Pont Senni* (8½ miles from Brecon) which has risen since this mail-coach road was formed in 1819, the Senni, an excellent trout stream, joins the Usk. Fragments of *Castell Dû*, once the stronghold of the Constables of the vast *Forest of Devynock*, may be seen close to the road. *Devynock* Church and village are less than a mile off in the Vale of Senni. The parish is of great extent. A Druidical circle, called *Cerrig duon* or the "Black Stones," stands near the Ystradgunlais road, not far off the village.

The Usk affords charming pictures in proceeding to Trecastle, especially *Pont Pwl Gwyn*, near which the Cray joins its impetuous neighbour.

TRECASTLE. A large village in the parish of Llywel, at which there is an excellent Hotel, the Camden Arms. A Castle stood opposite the inn, but nothing is left except large earthworks. The Marquis of Camden has large estates in this district, and leave to fish in the Usk can be obtained by all who visit the hotel.

THE CARMARTHENSHIRE VAN. We add here additional particulars [*ante* p. 250] relative to this noble mountain, Trecastle being by far the best point both to make the ascent and to fish *Llyn Van Vach*. The Ystradgunlais road (to the Swansea Valley) is followed for two miles ; then proceed to the right until you enter the open at a gate, and leaving the road (the old road to Llangadock or Llandilo Vawr) keep up gradually, making for the projecting mountain head seen in the background, which is the north-west end of the true Carmarthenshire Van. *Llyn Vach* sleeps under this scarped steep, and is about seven miles in a straight line from Trecastle. The journey can be performed, with some deviations, on a pony. The Usk rises below *Llyn Vach* ; and the *Hutfar*, a trout stream crossed on the route, springs not far from *Llyn Vawr*.

We ascend the mountain at Llyn Vach, making a circuit of the "Carmarthenshire" Van, and proceeding to the "Brecknockshire Van" (the boundary line of the counties runs through the depression between), from whence there is on a very clear day *the finest view in Wales except that from Snowdon*, and, perhaps, Cader Idris —a fact which no one seems to be aware of. The position of the mountain enables it to command a large portion of Wales and the Bristol Channel. It would take some pages to adequately describe this entrancing prospect; we can but indicate a few objects in a circuit of fourten or fifteen counties. On the north : the Ellennith "sea" of hill tops, Plinlimmon, Cader Idris, and other Merionethshire giants; a glimpse of Carnarvonshire. Then, Radnor Forest ; Clee Hills, in Salop ; Black Mountains to Hay end—Pen Cader. Brecknock Beacon; Mount Capellante ; Mynydd Maen, in Monmouthshire. Coasts of Somerset and North Devon, from Exmoor to Hartland Point. Lundy Island. Nearer at hand : Vale of Neath and Glamorgan Mountains ; Swansea Valley and Bay; all Gower ; Burry River; Llanelly. Vale of Towy. Carreg Cennin Castle. Sweeping westward—Carmarthen Bay ; Tenby ; Caldy and St. Margaret's Islands ; Giltar Point ; St. Gowan's Head. Percelly Mountains. St. George's Channel on the far west.—We descend the Brecknockshire Van to *Llyn Van Vawr*, a superb lake, but, alas ! without fish.

Trecastle is 12 miles from Brecon, and 9 from Llandovery. We have crossed the Epynt Hills, *with a guide*, from hence to *Llan-urtyd* (13 miles), an exceedingly wild walk.

The VALE OF CRICKHOWEL. As the majority of tourists *ascend* this vale, we shall complete our itinerary of Brecknockshire, by indicating the prominent features of the road *to* Brecon, and its tributaries. The boundary of Monmouthshire is passed about three miles from Abergavenny, from which town the mountain scenery on either side is rather romantic.

CRICKHOWEL.

Distant from	Miles.	Distant from	Miles.
Abergavenny	6	Llanthony Abbey (through moun-	
Brecon	14	tains)	14
Llanvihangel Cwm Dû	4	Monmouth	22

Crickhowel is a very agreeably-situated and thriving little place. The views from the bridge of fourteen arches over the Usk afford a good idea of this delightful district. The church, which was founded in the thirteenth century, and dedicated to St. Edmund the King and Martyr, is of cruciform design, and distinguished by a tower, over which a spire — the only one in the county— forms a beautiful symbol. The transepts—Rumsey and Gwernvale Chapels—were once chantries belonging to proprietors of estates in the neighbourhood. The ancient family of Rumsey has, how-ever, ceased to exist here, but the Gwernvale Chapel is still kept up. Judicious restorations have lately been effected, including the removal of a low ceiling—a work of the last century—which disfigured the nave. It is stated that "the old custom of singing carols in the church at cock-crowing, on the earliest dawn of morning," has been continued at Crickhowel. The Castle once covered a space of more than two acres, but has been almost wholly destroyed ; some remains of the keep are to be seen on a mound. Population, 1,257. INNS—The Bear, the Beaufort Arms.

On the Breannog Mountain, nearly two miles to the north of the town, is a very interesting *British Camp*, called *Crûg Hywel* or "Howel's Rock," an irregular triangle, nearly 1,200 feet in circumference.

B B

The mineral basin of South Wales commences in the mountain region to the west of Crickhowel.

Amongst the antiquities in this neighbourhood is the *Turpillian Stone.* We have already [*ante* p. 157] drawn attention to Welsh Ogham characters, some of which are, in the opinion of Mr. J. O. Westwood (*see Archæologia Cambrensis,* No. 5), to be seen on this stone. It lies prostrate in a field about three-quarters of a mile from Crickhowel, near the farm of *Ty yn y wlad,* on the north side of the northern road from Crickhowel to Llanbedr. The inscription, which is nearly all in Roman capitals, runs thus: TVRPILLI IC IACIT PVVERI TRILVN DVINOCATI.

This is an admirable district for sporting ; and the valley contains many gentlemen's houses, including *Llangattock Park,* a hunting seat belonging to the Duke of Beaufort, and abodes of cottage comfort. At Llangattock are curious caverns. Some interesting antiquarian discoveries have been made in the grounds of Llangattock Park. In the summer of 1847 a Cairn was found, evidently the burying place of a warrior. A few months later several Roman coins were discovered, some of the Emperor Constantine ; and a smaller one, with a representation of the wolf sucking Romulus and Remus.

Fishing. The Usk is preserved throughout the greater part of the Vale of Crickhowel. The Duke of Beaufort possesses the largest portion ; but that below Crickhowel Bridge is reserved by his Grace, on an understanding with Major Stretton and Mr. Davies, of Court-y-gollen. His Grace, however, liberally grants tickets of leave to fish in his water above the bridge. The *Glanusk* water intervenes, for which application must be made to Mr. Bailey. This extends to a point where a large brook joins the Usk on the left side of the river, and a notice-post marks the re-commencement of the Duke's fishing, which extends for some distance beyond *Llangunider Bridge*, to which place we recommend anglers to proceed first. Much the best time for trout fishing in this river is the latter part of March and the beginning of April. We have obtained good flies from Mr. H. Williams, opposite the Angel Inn, Abergavenny.

BLACK MOUNTAINS. The range to the north-east of the Vale of Crickhowel, leading to Talgarth, are called the Black Mountains. This lofty group forms, in combination with the *Hatterel Hills* overlooking the Golden Valley in Herefordshire, a parallelogram, enclosing two long deep valleys. The nearest, through which the *Gruny Vawr* runs, is partly comprehended in a detached (the "Feudog") portion of Herefordshire, partly in Brecknockshire. It is exceedingly wild and secluded. The Vale of Ewias, which belongs to the Hatterel range, runs parallel to the Gruny Valley, from which it is separated by a dark and lofty ridge ; the vallies are expressively called by an ancient writer the " *two sleeves* of Gwent Uwchcold." *Pen Cader* can be easily distinguished by its peculiar head ; the river Gruny rises near its roots. Giraldus, and his translator and annotator, Sir R. C. Hoare, give an interesting account of these grand mountains, which Archbishop Baldwin and Giraldus penetrated when preaching the crusades ; a bridge which they passed on the Gruny is still called "*Pont Escob*," or "the Bishop's Bridge."

There is a horse road from Crickhowel (not passable for carriages) through mountain vallies, skirting the *Sugarloaf* to *Llanthony Abbey*.

We return to Crickhowel, and continue our ascent of its vale. After passing *Tretower* and *Glanusk*, the splendid seat and park of Joseph Bailey, Esq., M.P., we soon begin to ascend a long hill which leads to the *Bwlch* (pass), leaving the beautiful *Vale of St. Michael Cwm Dû* on the right, and overlooking the course of the Usk, *Llangunider*, and its bridge. There is a roadside Inn at the hamlet of *Bulch*, eight miles from Brecon. The scenery from hence to Brecon is truly exquisite, combining an air of rural comfort with that of mountain freedom to a degree which may be pronounced perfection. *Buckland Park*, a fine mansion under a very romantic hill on the left, a little below the *Bulch*, is the seat of Mrs. Gwynne Holford. The steeps of the Brecknock Beacons form a magnificent back-ground, and there are few scenes in North Wales which surpass this, when the lights are favourable.

Instead, however, of proceeding to Brecon, we shall return to the *Bulch* Inn, and follow the road which leads to Llyn Savaddon (Savathan), Llangorse, Talgarth, and Hay. If you want to proceed to Brecon, turn down a lane to the left, *near* Bwlch, which passes *Blaenllynvi Castle*. Low and broken walls, and a deep fosse, are all that are left to tell of this once important stronghold, which is supposed to have been the residence of Hwgan, Prince of Brycheiniog, early in the tenth century, and was afterwards the head of the Norman lordship of Welsh Talgarth. Leland speaks of it as "a veri fair Castel now dekeiying," and adds that "by it was a Borow Town now also in decay. Both longgid to the Earl of March."—The road from hence passes near the lake, and falls into the mail road to Brecon.

LLYN SAVADDON or Llangorse Pool, the *Clamosum* of Giraldus, is three miles long, and in some places more than a mile broad. The country people erroneously affirm that the river Llynvi runs through without mingling its waters with those of the lake. There are curious legends connected with Savaddon; amongst them, a story about a buried city. This pool was frequented by the Monks of Llanthony, and abounds with perch, trout, eels, and pike, some of the latter of which grow to the size of 50lbs. The bold hill of Talgarth forms a fine background to the scenery of the lake, which is, however, rather of a melancholy character.

————

Two miles above Crickhowel a road diverges on the right to Talgarth. TRETOWER, "the town of the tower," with its picturesque Castle, invites attention a mile onwards. It is believed that a Norman fortress replaced one of greater antiquity here. Owen

Glendower attacked and much injured it in 1403; marks of hasty repairs which followed—carved work built up—can be traced. The shell of a massive keep on a mound, part of two bastions and curtain walls, are left. Tretower was the property of the gallant Sir Roger Vaughan, who with Sir David Gam and others saved the life of Henry V. at Agincourt; Sir Roger was knighted on the field when in the agonies of death. The castle now belongs to the Duke of Beaufort.—There are, we are told, antiquities in *Tretower Court*, once the mansion of the Vaughans.

St. Michael Cwm Dû, which stands at the entrance of a beautiful valley, along the bowered brook Rhiangoll, is a mile further on. The body of the Church was rebuilt in 1830; the old tower was left. We give an engraving of a carved stone which is built into the south wall of the chancel, on account of the beauty of the cruci form pattern, and because many stones of this character seem to have been fashioned in Brecknockshire about three centuries ago, particularly in Brecon.

The bearings on the shields are English; the dexter arms are supposed to have belonged to a descendant of Reginald de Sully, one of Fitzhamon's twelve knights.—The Rev. T. Price, an eminent antiquary, is vicar of this parish.

Cwm Dû was a Roman station on the *Via Montana*. Jones's History of Brecknockshire contains a ground plan of various works which have been discovered at an oblong square *Camp*, built of hewn stone, called *Gaer;* coins of the lower empire have also been found, and many discoveries were made by the late Archdeacon Payne about half a century since. On Pentir Hill, opposite the church above Mr. Gwillim's farm-house, through a plantation, is a camp called *Coed-y-Gaer*, consisting of a quadrilateral area 140 yards long by 105 in breadth, very perfect on the north side, and supposed to be British, but occupied by the Romans. There are three farm-houses in the parish called *Gaer*. — Those tourists who have diverged to Llanvihangel Cwm Dû on their way to Brecon, may save a mile by enquiring for the field paths to *Bwlch*.

We follow the road to Talgarth from Cwm Dû, a *Pass*, under the shadowy bluffs of the Black Mountains.   TALGARTH is a populous village—once a good market town—in a very interesting neighbourhood.   There is an inn.   Its church has a square embattled tower, and is a structure of some consequence.   The parish contains 90,154 acres !   The little river Ennig joins the Llynvi, an excellent trout stream, near the village.   There are some slight *Druidical remains* and *British earthworks* in the neighbourhood on the hills.   Half a mile from Talgarth, on *Pendre* farm, is a fine earthwork, forming a segment of a circle—a place of refuge in sudden emergencies ; two miles to the rear of which, on a conical hill, commanding the pass to Crickhowel, is a very strong fortified post called *Dinas*, "which was attacked by Ethelfleda, daughter of Alfred the Great, and Countess of Mercia, who, after defeating Hwgan Prince of Brecknock, here took his wife with thirty of her attendants prisoners, and sent them into England. "   Leland states that Dinas was dismantled to prevent Owen Glendower from occupying it.   Dinas may be explored in proceeding from Crickhowel.—In the hamlet of Trevecca is *Trevecca House*, built by Howel Harris, a disciple of Whitfield's, for a community of persons, once 150 in number, besides children, which is now nearly deserted.—From Talgarth it is an easy walk to the Three Cocks Tavern, Glasbury, described in our Wye Tour — an excellent halting place.

THE WYE,

Like its sister the Severn, is of Highland birth, nurtured in a hollow, high up Plinlimmon, from whence it pursues a course— celebrated by pen and pencil—through the counties of Cardigan, Radnor, Hereford, and Monmouth, ultimately mingling its waters, as we have already seen, with the SEVERN SEA.

There are two distinct Wye Tours.   The first, from Steddfa Gerrig to the borders of Herefordshire ; the second, from Ross to Chepstow.   The former has not yet been estimated as it deserves, because it is off the beaten track—not so readily accessible as the other; but when railroads are extended to Hereford, the charming scenery of the Upper Wye will be within easy reach.

THE UPPER WYE TOUR.

Steddfa Gerrig, or the "Rest on the Stones," is a small hamlet on the Aberystwith road, from whence the infant Wye (in Welsh, *Gwy* or river) pursues its sportive course down a valley, encompassed by lofty and rather common-place green mountains, with interminable sweeping outlines. This portion of the river is in North Wales (Montgomeryshire), and we do not re-enter Southern Cambria until nearly half way between Llangurig and Rhayader. *Llangurig,* [see p. 339] is ten miles from the source of our heroine. The Inn is somewhat better than it used to be. The nature of the mail road, which is cut out of the hill-sides along the exact line that Nature has indicated, always excites interest—occasionally awe. The scenery from hence to Rhayader, with some tame exceptions, is full of the poetry of nature, and chiefly winds through romantic passes, with folding lines. There are frequent glimpses of the rapid Wye, now swollen by the Dernol—sweeet reaches with banks sometimes feathered by delicate copse. On the north bank, the Nanerth rocks, which consist of the craggy steeps of a hill three miles long, form the first "grand scene."

RHAYADER and its neighbourhood are described at page 340. The road from hence to Builth (14 miles) runs for more than half the distance close to the river, which has worn a deep bed through rocks, and forms many eddying pools and "runs" that excite the ardour of the angler. About two miles below Rhayader the gentle and romantic, but ofttimes passionate, Elan enters into a joyous alliance with our river, which now assumes an air of greater dignity. Four miles from Builth, near a pretty scene at *Pont ar Ithon,* the Ithon—another important stream—falls into the Wye, and just above Builth the Irvon adds to the consequence of our heroine, so that at Builth Bridge the stream is wide, but not stately; it has not yet been corrupted by association with the broad red plains of old England, but preserves, untouched, the freshness of youth—of the mountains from whence it springs.

There is no public conveyance between Rhayader and Builth; the road is secluded, full of the poetry of the pastoral life, with solitary homes on the hills. BUILTH and its associations have already claimed our best attention.   There is a road on either side of the river from Builth to Glasbury, and we advise persons of taste, who do not mind traversing rough lanes, nor going a few miles out of their way to explore fine scenery, to take the old road on the *northern side*.   Gilpin, the historian of the Wye, thinks that the prospect on approaching Aberedw is possibly "more beautiful than in any part of its course," and contrasts the character of the river here with that of the "solemn parading stream" which it ultimately becomes.

We shall first follow the north bank.   About four miles and a half below Builth is one of nature's gems—ABEREDW (Aberedow), where the interest excited by highly picturesque scenery is heightened by touching historical recollections.   Imagine a Highland glen of much beauty — through which a pure mountain stream awakens the echoes of the hills with its music—receding from the Wye, here characterised by grand rock scenery and graceful woods.   At the entrance of the dingle is a mound partly natural, partly artificial, the summit of which is surrounded with the mouldering walls of a *Castle*, much hidden by foliage.   This was LLEWELLYN's favourite hunting seat [*see* page 355].   *Aberedw Church* stands on an eminence a short way above the castle, opposite a lofty range of rocks, partly concealed by foliage, which forms a fine contrast to the delicate green of far-off hills.   The playful Edw winds round the steep bank of the churchyard.   It is a place to linger at.   An excavation in the rock, about six feet square, is called "Llewellyn's Cave;" and the rock scenery, which extends along the banks of the Wye, is highly romantic and curious.   We proceed along the road or lane—a route worth taking if it be only to visit *Pwll Du* (the Black Pit), which has been almost overlooked by tourists.   The best way is to ascend the heights to the "Great House" (Mr. Powell's), in the parish of Llanstephan.   We met with much civility there, and were guided to the river scene, which is not very easily found.   The little river *Machwy* has worn for itself a deep channel in its descent from the

mountains—very steep, narrow, and gloomy.   The earth assumes
a dark colour, and the descent down the slippery sides of the
dingle is one of the most fatiguing we ever encountered.
" Savage " rocks, slightly fringed with brushwood, impend over
the river, and one of vast size projects so abruptly across the
glen at right angles as to apparently close it.   Here stood a
fortification called the Castle of the Black Rock, of which little
else than the name remains ; but the surrounding peasantry
devoutly believe that it is the abode or favourite resort of fairies.
Some curious legends are to be picked up in this rude and
secluded neighbourhood.   According to tradition, one of the
ancient Welsh princes kept prisoners in a castle on the summit
of the rock, from whence they were not unfrequently hurled into
the tremendous pool below.   There is a difficult passage round
the foot of the black rock to a singular *Waterfall*, about forty
feet high, surrounded by accessories which very greatly heighten
its grandeur.   You feel astonished but hardly pleased in this wild
and gloomy hollow, and value sunshine when you leave its agitated caldron far below.—There is a smaller waterfall lower down.

The distant prospects, on returning to the Wye side, become
magnificent.   The steep and lofty *Black Mountains*, which blend
their summits with the *Hatterel* as they stretch eastward, sweep
for many miles gracefully, at a height of 2,000 feet, above a
broken wooded foreground, masses of foliage varied by tufted
ravines and nests of heather.   *Garth Hill*, an inconsiderable elevation—opposite to Erwood—on which there are traces of a British
camp, is passed on the journey onwards : then *Boughrood Castle*,
a square house near the site of an old fortress.   The river makes
a great horse-shoe bend, the largest throughout its course, just
below this place, and we enter the English looking village of
Glasbury, where there is a comfortable Inn, and skirt the park of
Maeslough Castle, the imposing seat of the De Winton's, as we
proceed to cross the river at Glasbury Bridge, where the romping
Wye has become a staid and almost glassy stream.   Gilpin describes the view from Maeslough as " wonderfully amusing,'' and
thinks that the situation of the house is, of its kind, the finest in
Wales.—The distance from Builth to the Three Cocks Tavern,

above Glasbury—which parish is situated partly in Radnorshire,
partly in Brecon—by the route we have been pursuing, is 21 miles.

We must now retrace our steps to Builth, and follow the high
road downwards, which commands many beautiful scenic effects,
but is a good deal hidden with foliage. At the ancient Ferry,
called *Cefyn Twm Bach* [*see* p. 355] is a little thatched hostelrie,
from whence a fisherman might cross to see Pwll Dû. This place
is called *Erwood*, and pedestrian tourists, who *can* rough it,
sometimes sleep here. Three miles onward is a modern house,
amidst fine woods, named *Llangoed Castle ;* then the miserable
village of *Llyswen*, where there is a tolerable Inn ; and a little
before reaching Glasbury, the road falls into that which runs
between Brecon and Hereford. The Three Cocks Tavern, by the
road side, 15 miles from Builth, is one of the most comfortable
fisherman's houses throughout Wales. There is a seat of Lord
Hereford's on the slope of the lofty hills above, which seen over
knolls covered with trembling foliage, or from the deep channels
of rivulets, form a dark solemn background to the whole. Those
who are in quest of fine scenery and antiquities should ascend the
mountain here, (obtaining, whenever they can, minute directions),
and proceed to *Llanthony Abbey*, distant 13 miles, down the *Vale
of the Honddû*, passing near *Capel y Fin*, ''the chapel on the
boundary '' [of three counties], at the foot of a lofty mountain, on
the left. The river Llynvi affords excellent fishing ; there is the
Wye close at hand, and *Llyn Savaddon* within easy reach.

There are no objects to detain us in the comparatively tame
country which stretches for four miles between Glasbury and HAY,
(''said to derive its name from the Norman French *Haier*, to
enclose, and *celli*, a grove of saplings,'') a market town just
within the borders of Brecknockshire, rather picturesquely situated on ground sloping to the Wye, which is crossed by a bridge.
À large stone bridge was swept away here by a flood, which
suddenly rose 15 feet, in 1794. A gothic gateway forms almost
the only relic of the ancient castle of Hay. There is a striking
view from the churchyard.

Two miles and a half below Hay, at a short distance on the
left of the road, are the graceful ruins of CLIFFORD CASTLE, the

birth-place of "fair Rosamond"—'cleped (says Holinshead) the "rose of the world" by Henry II.—whose "love-lorn tale" invests the spot with historic interest. It is, however, as picturesque in reality as it is in association. The fortress, which stands on a knoll near the Wye, was founded by Fitzosborne, first Earl of Huntingdon. The Clifford family—one of whom, Walter, was the father of Rosamond — afterwards became its possessors. Anne, Countess of Dorset, Pembroke, and Montgomery — whose masculine spirit is matter of history — was a celebrated member of the De Clifford family.

About a mile farther on the Wye enters the fertile plains of merry England, near Rhydspence. At *Bradwardine* there is a very beautiful river scene. The "*Golden Valley*" of Herefordshire—a district of rare beauty—stretches along the base of the Hatterel Hills on the right. The road from Hay to Hereford (20 miles) runs through a flat country, which offers little, except the fine seat and park of the Cotterell family, to interest the tourist.

KENCHESTER, said to be the *Ariconium* of the Romans, which is four or five miles distant from Hereford, will, however, detain the antiquarian. It is a vast station—well termed *Magna Castra*—covering upwards of fifty acres, with two openings to the west and two to the north. A few traces of the walls, which appear to have surrounded an irregular hexagonal area—of a temple at the east—of a niche of Roman brick and mortar called "the chair," are visible. Vaults, tesselated pavements, stone altars, coins, &c., have been discovered at various periods.

HEREFORD (*Here-ford*, pure Saxon for a "military ford") is a good old-fashioned English city, with a massive and venerable cathedral, churches, and a gem of a market-house. Nearly all the principal streets command some object of interest in each vista. The Cathedral, which contains much Saxon work, is now undergoing a complete restoration under the judicious superintendence of Mr. Cottingham. In 1847, the sum of £14,356 had been subscribed for the accomplishment of the undertaking ; the Bishop and Dean and Chapter then gave £3,500 in addition to a large amount which they had previously subscribed ; an outlay of £25,000 will effect *all* that can be wished. No less that 47,000 strangers had inspected the progress of the restoration up to the spring of 1847.—There is a delightful walk at Hereford adjoining the Wye, called the Castle Green—the Castle no longer exists—in the midst of which is a column designed to commemorate Nelson's victories. About a mile on the Hay road is the hexagonal shaft of a fine stone Cross, called the White Cross, erected in 1345 by Dr. Lewis Charlton, afterwards Bishop of Hereford, "as a market-place for the country people during the ravages of an infectious disorder with which the city was at that time visited." Its height including the base is 15 feet. Nell Gwyn, one of the favourites of Charles II., was born at Hereford, and the house, which stood in Pipe Lane, existed within the last twenty years ; Garrick also first drew breath here.

The hills near the city, named *Dinedor* and *Aconbury*, are within a pleasant walk, and often visited. The best course is to ascend Aconbury only, for it possesses a large Roman camp on its summit, and commands the finest prospect.

The Wye runs through a pastoral country—full of true English scenery—between Hereford and Ross, distant 14 miles.

THE LOWER WYE TOUR.

Oh, sylvan Wye! thou wanderer through the woods,
How often has my spirit turned to thee !
Once again I see these hedge-rows, hardly hedge-rows,
Little lines of sportive wood run wild ; these pastoral forms
Green to the very door ; and wreaths of smoke
Sent up in silence from among the trees !
With some uncertain notice as might seem,
Of vagrant dwellers in the houseless woods,
Or of some hermit's cave, where by his fire
The hermit sits alone.   WORDSWORTH.

So many persons make *Gloucester*—the ancient "key" to South Wales, and which will soon be a focus of Railways—the starting point for a Wye Tour, that we shall follow the example. The great object of interest at this "fair city" is its magnificent Cathedral. The tower and choir are almost unrivalled examples of the late Pointed or Perpendicular style. The great East window is the largest in the kingdom, and the crypt is Saxon, slightly altered by Norman architects.   The recently-restored church of St. Mary de Crypt—the ruins of Llanthony Priory, a little below the Docks—the New Inn, a vast " pilgrims' " house of the fifteenth century—the remains` of St. Catherine's or St. Oswald's Priory church—are also objects worth a stranger's notice.

The road to Ross—about to be superseded by a railway—runs through sixteen miles of as pleasant a country as a tourist need wish to begin with.   The great round hill crowned with firs is called "May Hill," and is a conspicuous object in several counties.

At last the "heaven-directed spire" of Ross rises in the distance, and we soon enter this comfortable-looking little town—a combination of the old-fashioned and the modern.   The history of John Kyrle has been celebrated ever since Pope wrote his famous poem.   The " Man of Ross " resided in a house opposite the market, distinguished by. an inscription in the wall ; he was born in 1637, and lived to the good old age of eighty-seven.

The church contains a monument to his memory—a bequest of Lady Kinnoul—erected in 1776, just above his burial place ; and monuments of the old family of Rudhale, one of whom defended Hereford against Cromwell.   There is an air of repose about the churchyard, although it belongs to a town.   The trees, as well as those in the adjoining " Prospect Walk;," were planted by good John Kyrle ; and a legend—which is all events pleasing—exists about these elms.   Two trees in the churchyard, near the wall which joined his pew, were wantonly cut down in the last century, but the roots forced their way through the pew, and now the foliage of elm branches which commence in the interior of the church may be seen through one of the windows.   "The Prospect" was laid out by Kyrle A. D. 1700.   It is an evening scene—a circumstance which critics seem to have overlooked ; the picture then gains breadth, and the mountain horizon over the deep shadowy river foreground acquires its true effect.

An old house in Church Lane, called " Gabriel Hill's Great Inn, " contains a chamber — now divided into two — in which Charles I. slept on his way to Raglan.

INNS—Barrett's Royal Hotel—a superb house, and the King's Head.   [See MONMOUTH AND HEREFORD RAILWAY.]

Before we proceed we must give a hint to pedestrian tourists. Walk to the entrance of Goodrich Court, on the Monmouth road ; afterwards cross from the Court to the ancient Castle, from which there is a path to the village of Goodrich, distinguished by the spire of its church.   Then enquire the way to *Huntsham Ferry*, a short distance below, beyond which a lane runs through the centre of the long narrow peninsula formed here by the Wye, to *Cymon's Yat,* which ascend.   From hence there is a truly refreshing walk of about five miles and a half, near the banks of the river, to Monmouth—soon to be defaced by a railway.   In 1387, Henry IV. was hastening across *Huntsham Ferry* on his way to Monmouth, in deep anxiety about his royal consort, whose confinement was near at hand, when he was met by a messenger who announced the birth of a prince—Harry the Fifth—and the safety of the Queen.   The King bestowed the ferry on the man as a guerdon.   The grant still exists.

GOODRICH COURT and CASTLE may be visited here by land or water.   The distance by the Monmouth road to the " Court " Gate-house from Ross is four miles.   The situation of this " romance in stone and lime,'' on an eminence near one of the sweetest reaches of the Wye, is truly graceful.   The elevation, designed by Mr. Blore in 1828, partly embraces specimens of the styles used during the period between the reigns of Edward I. and Edward III.   Sir S. Meyrick, whose sudden death in the spring of 1848 will be felt by the antiquarian world, placed his magnificent collection of armour and antiquities in a series of galleries, and adopted an excellent arrangement for the admission of the public.   Visitors each pay one shilling to the housekeeper, and write their names in a book on entering.

A description of the curiosities cannot be comprised within moderate limits, but details will be found in an excellent local guide to the building.   The collection of armour is the finest belonging to any individual.   The suit in Henry the Sixth's Gallery, which belonged to the Duke of Ferrara, celebrated from his association with Tasso, will perhaps strike visitors the most.   There are interesting relics of the civil war.   The plan adopted by Sir Samuel Meyrick in arranging this valuable collection has been severely

criticised. The "doll's faces" which are introduced have been
strongly objected to, and not without good reason; a complete
suit of *empty armour* is always impressive. This is not a place
for Madame Tussaud, although we believe that wood, not wax,
is the material chiefly used. The collection embraces many
specimens of weapons from the South Seas, and many Indian
equipments. One of the chambers is so arranged as to represent
a joust between Knights. The private apartments are not shown
to strangers; but they contain objects worth seeing, especially
pictures. The library, which is enriched with beautiful oak
carving, contains two miniatures by Holbein, viz., portraits of
Anne of Cleves and of Henry VIII., both painted for the fair
lady; also a portrait of Nell Gwyn, by Sir Peter Lely. The
furniture of each room is that of the style of a particular reign;
in the drawing room the characteristics of the period of Edward
II. are admirably preserved.—The Goodrich Court estate is now
the property of Colonel Meyrick, a nephew of the late possessor.

A sweet dingle intervenes between Goodrich Court and the
CASTLE, which stands on the brow of the opposite eminence. An
eminent antiquary well observes that "this fortification, although
not of large dimensions, contains all the different works which
constitute a complete ancient baronial castle." The general design
forms a parallelogram, defended by a round tower at each of the
angles, with an Anglo-Saxon keep. The entrance to the ruin
through a dark vaulted passage is its most striking feature: the
gloom sobers the mind—gives it the right tone for viewing a place
of desolation. The graceful chapel and stately hall then divide
attention with the keep, the walls of which are of great thickness. The hall is 65 feet long and 28 broad, and the windows
show that it was erected in the reign of Edward I. Another room
of almost equal size leads to the ladies' tower. It is worth while
descending to the fosse to see fine architectural effects. Ivy,
the "adorner"—sometimes the disfigurer—of a ruin, is at Goodrich aided by the clematis. A castle, which belonged to one
Godric, stood here before the Conquest; and the structure underwent alterations down to the reign of Henry VI. The most
memorable event in its history is the siege during the Civil War,

when it was obstinately defended for the King with great gallantry by Sir Richard Lingen. Colonel Birch invested it at the head of a strong Parliamentary force on the 10th of March, 1646, and the garrison defied him until the beginning of August, when famine subdued them. The Parliament then ordered the castle to be " slighted," and it has ever since been "silently decaying."

> " The echoes of its vaults are eloquent. The stones have voices,
> And the walls do live,—it is the house of Memory!"

The devoted loyalty and terrible persecutions endured by Thomas Swift, the parson of Goodrich, during the troubles of the seventeenth century, invest GOODRICH CHURCH with more than common interest. Dean Swift was a grandson of this admirable man—who was the head of an ancient family in the parish — and presented a chalice which had belonged to his ancestor to the church in 1726, which is still used in the administration of the Holy Communion there.

We return to Ross, where boats—the gondolas of the Wye—can be hired for the voyage to Monmouth, distant by water nearly 21 miles, by land 11 miles. The boat hire varies according to the size of the craft ; and the time occupied, *without stoppages*, is usually about five hours. An attempt was made in 1837 to introduce a small steamer on the river between Chepstow and Ross, but there is not always sufficient water in the summer. The river is navigable for barges up to Hereford—sometimes higher. The first object that excites attention after fairly embarking on " pleased Vaga," as the Wye is poetically called by Pope, is WILTON CASTLE, a stronghold of the Greys of the south, destroyed by the Royalists in King Charles' time, and afterwards the property of Thomas Guy, who left it to the trustees of his Hospital, to whom it now belongs. Wilton Bridge was built near the end of Elizabeth's reign. Before we proceed to indicate the objects of interest on our voyage, we shall copy the best general description of the Wye scenery that has ever been written (Mr. Coxe's), which will save much repetition :—" The effects of these numerous windings are various and striking ; the same objects present themselves, are lost and recovered with different accom-

paniments, and in different points of view...........:...The banks for
the most part rise abruptly from the edge of the water, and are
clothed with forests or are broken into cliffs. In some places they
approach so near that the river occupies the whole intermediate
space, and nothing is seen but woods, rocks, and water; in others,
they alternately recede, and the eye catches an occasional glimpse
of hamlets, ruins, and detached buildings, partly seated on the
margin of the stream and partly scattered on the rising grounds.
The general character of the scenery, however, is wildness and
solitude; and if we except the populous district of Monmouth,
no river perhaps flows for so long a course in a well cultivated
country, the banks of which exhibit so few habitations.''

The river bends suddenly under the wooded. steep of *Pencraig
Court*, and an exceedingly beautiful reach is opened, crowned by
the towers of *Goodrich*, one of the softest and most perfect scenes
of its kind. The tourist who has not previously visited the Court
and Castle should disembark here. The course of the stream
now becomes extremely sinuous for nine or ten miles. Near
Kerne Bridge, on the right amidst fair meads, are the fragments
of Goodrich or *Flanesford Priory*, worked up into farm buildings.
Bold hills — sometimes bare, sometimes wooded — succeed. At
Bishopswood on the left bank (behind which is *Ruardean)* a
rivulet divides the counties of Hereford and Gloucester, and from
this point downwards, until within a short distance of Monmouth,
the Wye forms a boundary line between those two counties.
Courtfield, the mansion of Mr. Vaughan—built on the site of a
house belonging to the Countess of Salisbury, at which, according
to tradition, Henry V. was nursed by her ladyship—rises on the
right bank. Many persons land a little below to inspect a monumental effigy in the primitive church called *Welsh Bicknor*, which
has until recently been supposed to represent the royal nurse, who
died in 1395, but Sir S. Meyrick and other modern antiquaries
doubt the fact. At *Lydbrook*—an outlet of Dean Forest—there
is a tramway for the conveyance of minerals, which runs up a
very steep narrow valley.

Two or three miles onward is one of the most singular and
enchanting scenes on the river. A mellow hill, called *Rosemary*

Topping, first appears on the left bank, but as you glide on, rapidly changes its position and becomes a wooded side screen on the right (the effect has been likened to the shifting of a scene in a theatre), opposite the majestic COLDWELL ROCKS — one of nature's most exquisite compositions. A walk by moonlight along the foot of this "fantastic" range affords very exquisite scenic effects. The river now makes a remarkable oval bend, sweeping for four miles and two furlongs round a peninsula, the neck of which is only six hundred yards broad. Many persons land at this neck, and send the boat on whilst they ascend *Cymon's* or *Symmond's Yat* (Gate), which impends from the hill side above; but some fine scenery is lost in consequence. At *Whitchurch* there is a nice little Inn and fishing stream.

We ascend the YAT. The view from the lofty summit of this singularly-shaped promontory is justly considered one of the "grand scenes" on the Wye. The mind is at first almost bewildered—if the day be clear—by the variety of objects which are suddenly seen. On either side are two river scenes of extraordinary beauty: to the right are the Coldwell Rocks, with the distant spire of English Bicknor Church amidst the heights of Dean Forest; on the left, a long placid reach of the Wye—full of dreamy repose—which commences at New Weir, just below. The eye then ranges over the spires of Goodrich and other village fanes — the ancient Castle and its ambitious neighbour — the "devious" windings of the Wye,—and the horizon is bounded on the north-east by the wavy line of the Malvern Hills, and on the north-west by the dark mountains of Wales. Morris Dancers usually celebrate their "revels" on Cymon's Yat at Whitsuntide. Traces of *Offa's Dyke* may be found in the Forest, near at hand, within the enclosure on the right of the lane. The rocky pillars on the left below *New Weir* (the salmon weir has been long removed) are strikingly beautiful. The large hill tattoed by stone quarries on the other side is called the *Great Doward*. We glide onwards amidst solemn woods, until a turn in the river brings the very romantic hill called the *Little Doward*—on the summit of which are traces of a British camp—into sight. Warmth of colour now distinguishes the scenery. The elegant "airy" open-work tower on the summit of the Doward was erected a few years ago by R. Blakemore, Esq., M.P., who resides at *The Leys*, near the river bank. A little Welsh church at Dixton, in Monmouthshire, seen on the right of the reach that leads to " delightsome MONMOUTH," always excites admiration. Many *coracles* [*see* p. 305] may be seen skimming about the river—which is famed for its salmon—here.

We have lingered at Monmouth early in our tour [*ante* p. 67]; but before we glide on, we must· say a few words about DEAN FOREST, a district which has been strangely overlooked by writers on the Wye. Those who visit the *Buckstone*, and possess curiosity or leisure, must feel moved by an impulse to penetrate the vast region of solemn woods which stretches before them. A large Forest is always invested with an air of mystery — sublimity. You may lose yourself in it. You may meet with some adventure. Wild animals 'or birds that shun the haunts of man are sure to cross your path. How fresh and soothing are the cool green woods ! How deep the solitude !—We recommend tourists to proceed through the town of Coleford to the *Speech House*,* distant about 8½ miles from Monmouth ; and to walk from thence —the path is often wet and miry — to the " White Oak," a monarch towering over subject woods. The scenery about *Parkend*, and along the road through Lydney by *Bream*, is also ex-

* This has always been a famous forest. In the middle ages it afforded a safe refuge to robbers, who used often to go afloat and plunder vessels on the Severn. The commanders of the Spanish Armada had orders "not to leave a tree standing in it" if, says Evelyn, "they should not be able to subdue our nation." Early in the reign of Charles I. the forest contained 43,000 acres. 14,000 of which were woodland ; but the devastations committed were so great, that in 1667 only 200 large oak and beech trees were standing. "To repair these mischiefs 11,000 acres were immediately enclosed, planted, and carefully guarded," and large additions have since been made. The plantations during the last twenty years in this magnificent nursery of navy timber (the quality of the oaks is the finest in England) have made very great progress. The Forest is divided into " walks," and placed under the care of officers and keepers. Iron mines were opened here by the Romans; and there are extensive and remarkable workings partly attributed to that people, near Coleford, Bream, and Littledean. These wild deserted *scowles* (that is their local name) can be penetrated for considerable distances. The mineral treasures of the Forest—coal and iron—are great ; and Foresters retain peculiar rights.

ceedingly beautiful ; besides the sylvan attractions, superb views
are sometimes obtained of the *Vale of the Severn.*   The largest
oak in the Forest (41 feet in girth) is at *Newland,* by which
village—there is a fine old church—strangers might return to
Monmouth.—There is a road, chiefly along high ground, near the
western edge of the Forest from Monmouth to Chepstow through
Clearwell, St. Briavel's, and *Tidenham Chase.   St. Briavel's
Castle*—an interesting ruin—was built by Milo Fitzwalter [temp.
Henry I.] to curb the incursions of the Welsh.   About a century
afterwards it reverted to the Crown by forfeiture.—*Offa's Dyke*
terminates at Beachley, and may be traced at a point where
it crosses the road at Buttington Tump.   We return from our
digression.

At Monmouth a fresh boat may be procured for Chepstow,
distant by water about 17 miles, by land 16.

Troy House, one of the seats of the Duke of Beaufort, is seen
on the right soon after leaving Monmouth, a little beyond the
spot where the Monnow joins the Wye.   A small river called the
Trothy, which runs through the grounds, also here falls into our
queenly stream.   Troy contains a carved chimney-piece, and other
antiquities from Raglan Castle, and relics or supposed relics of
Harry the Fifth—a cradle, a bed, and a suit of armour.   *Penalt*
Church, almost hidden by aged yews, nestles high up the right
bank ; the busy hamlet of Redbrook—at which there are works—
succeeds ; you pass Whitebrook, and then *Pen y Van* Hill and
Pilstone House on the right ; and *St. Briavel's Castle* is seen over
the distant heights, called the *Hudknolls,* under which is Bigsweir
House.   Soon after " shooting " the Suspension Bridge, of 160
feet span, a beautiful reach leads you to *Llandogo,* a picturesque
group of wild homes nestling under a vast hill, down the sides of
which there is in winter a waterfall called the *Cleddon Shoots.*
The banks of the sylvan river now become tidal,—mountain associations are lost, but the increasing beauty of the scenery makes
amends.   *Brockweir*—a little port where large trows from Bristol
transfer their cargoes of goods to the Wye barges—with its bustle,
its timber-yards and ships on the stocks (vessels of 500 or 600
tons are sometimes built here) seems out of place; but fortunately

the Wye makes another of its great horse-shoe bends just below, laving the feet of the hamlet of *Tintern Parva*, and then expectation is gratified, — HOLY TINTERN rises gracefully amidst a foreground of foliage. "As the Abbey of Tintern is the most beautiful and picturesque of all our Gothic monuments, so is the situation one of the most sequestered and delightful. One more abounding in that peculiar kind of scenery which excites the mingled sensations of content, religion, and enthusiasm, it is impossible to behold. There every arch infuses a solemn energy, as it were, into inanimate nature, and a sublime antiquity breathes mildly into the heart" (Bucke's Harmonies). [*See* p. 64.]

The scenery of the Wye from Tintern to Chepstow is full of pictures. The river meanders through steep wooded banks of great altitude, and on approaching the Wyndcliff sweeps boldly below the finest range of rocks throughout its course, the *Bannagor Crags*, round a pretty rural peninsula called Lancaut, which slopes from Tidenham Chase on the heights to the left. The little church of Lancaut (the parish only contains sixteen inhabitants) is a pleasing object. This great enclosed scene is the finest part of the Wye. The Wyndcliff lifts its head with dignity in the background ; the stupendous Bannagor Crags stand out of the woods with magical effect as the eye ranges round the landscape—"scathed, verdureless and shivered"—and "Nature has flung her leafage" over the solemn rock scenery of Piercefield, which closes the prospect. The series of rocks which give so much character to the Piercefield range are called the *Twelve Apostles* and *St. Peter's Thumb*, and one place is called the *Lover's Leap*.

The Tidenham Rocks at the edge of the road from Chepstow to Coleford were the scene of a marvellous exploit during the Civil War. Sir John Wyntour, an eminent royalist officer, was pursued from Lydney by a body of Parliamentarians, and galloped in desperation over this shelving precipice. His pursuers stood aghast, but Sir John is said to have escaped unhurt, and to have got clear off by swimming the river. The place is still called "*Wyntour's Leap*."

Piercefield Bay now opens its arms, and *Chepstow Castle*, crowning a rocky steep, completes a river excursion of thirty-eight miles, which when once seen can never be forgotten.

The length of the Wye from its source to Hay is forty-nine miles and a quarter ; from Hay to Ross, thirty-three miles and a quarter ; and from Ross to Chepstow, thirty-seven miles, seven furlongs, and sixty yards. The total length of the river is about one hundred and twenty-three miles.

We have already described Chepstow and its ruins, and we shall conclude our excursion with a visit to Piercefield (*see* p. 64).

PIERCEFIELD is one of the regions of romance of the last century—the " fairy-land " of the auctioneer. It is interesting as an example of the landscape-gardening of an age of false taste —of a time when man thought he could "improve" nature by "grottos" placed in absurd positions, by the introduction of gigantic figures, and by indifferent inscriptions. Still, it would be strange if the walk of three miles which winds along this fine park—placed in front of the most exquisite river scenery conceivable, and containing within its own limits several gems—should not contain a good deal to interest. Piercefield originally belonged to a family named Walters, who disposed of it in 1736 to Colonel Morris, father of Valentine Morris, a man of great benevolence of character, who was the chief " embellisher " of these rocks and woods. The history of poor Morris is full of melancholy vicissitudes. He was compelled to part with his "earthly paradise" on the Wye, to retire to the West Indies, where he acquired a fresh fortune, which he lost when governor of St. Vincent's owing to his generosity to *the nation*. He returned to England, languished several years in prison for debt, his wife lost her reason under the pressure, and he recovered his liberty too late to profit by an act of justice that had been shamefully delayed by the minister of the day. The old guide-books set forth with great preciseness a list of the principal views at Piercefield :—1. The Lover's Leap. 2. A seat near two beech trees on the edge of the precipice. 3. The Giant's Cave. 4. The Half-way Seat. 5. The Double View. · 6. The view above Pierce Wood. 7. The Grotto. 8. The Platform. 9. The Alcove.

We must hasten onward from Piercefield — which now belongs

to Nathaniel Wells, Esq., who has let the property to Mr. Wintle
—and ascend the WYNDCLIFF by the road that we have previously
described.

Cowper might have written, "God made the country, man
the town," from the top of this crag.   The eye ranges over
portions of nine counties, yet there seems to be no confusion in
the prospect ; the proportions of the landscape, which unfolds
itself in regular yet not in monotonous succession, are perfect ;
there is nothing to offend the most exact critic in "picturesque"
scenery.   The "German Prince" who published a tour in England
in 1826, and who has written the best description of the extraordinary view which the Wyndcliff commands—a view superior to
that from Ehrenbreitstein on the Rhine—well remarks that " a
vast group of views of distinct and opposite character here seem
to blend and unite in one. "   "As I stood on the brow of this precipice," observes an elegant writer (Archdeacon Coxe), " I looked
down on the fertile peninsula of Lancaut, surrounded with rocks
and forests, contemplated the hanging woods, rich lawns, and romantic cliffs of Piercefield, the castle and town of Chepstow, and
traced the Wye, sweeping in the true outline of beauty, from the
Bannagor Crags to its junction with the Severn, which spreads
into an estuary, and is lost in the distant ocean....I traced with
pleasing satisfaction the luxuriant vallies and romantic hills of the
interesting county (Monmouthshire) in which I stood, but I dwelt
with peculiar admiration on the majestic rampart which forms
its boundary to the west, and extends in one grand and unbroken
outline, from the banks of the Severn to the Black Mountains,

' Where the broken landscape, by degrees
Ascending, roughens into rigid hills,
O'er which the Cambrian mountains like far clouds
That skirt the blue horizon, dusky rise.' "

Let us attempt to fill up some of the *gaps* in this eloquent
outline.   On the south of the channel, beyond the Holmes, which
seem to float gracefully on the deep, Devonshire looms in the far
west, faced by the stern coast of Glamorgan which apparently
commences at Penarth Point near Cardiff.   Nearer at hand, on
the south side, is the vast upland region of Exmoor.   The Quan-

tock Hills—the Mendips—Dundry Tower—the country about Bath — the Wiltshire Downs — are seen in succession. The wooded promontory of Portishead keeps watch and ward at the portal of the channel right before you. Bluff Aust Hill rises doggedly on the eastern bank of the Severn. Thornbury Church Tower—Berkeley Castle, shaded by Stinchcombe Hill—stand in the midst of a region of oaks and elms, and green pastures. The smiling Vales of Gloucester and Evesham follow in succession,—bounded by the Cotswolds, which melt in the distance as the eye wanders to the pale north. We descend in a mood to read " sermons in stones, and good in everything."

ISLANDS OF THE BRISTOL CHANNEL.

FLAT HOLM. This island lies nearly in the centre of the Channel, a few miles below Cardiff. It is three miles and a half in circumference. There is a good farm-house and inn, and a Lighthouse, which bears a bright fixed light. Many persons visit the island, and in summer steamers from Bristol frequently make trips to it. Two miles to the S.S.E. is the

STEEP HOLM, a stern rock about 400 feet high, about a mile and a half in circumference. On the N.E. and S.W. sides are two narrow passages from pebbly beaches, difficult of access. There are several small tenements on the summit. Many persons, including Githa, the mother of King Harold, have sought an asylum here in past days ; and *Gildas,* the earliest British Historian, wrote his treatise " *De Excidio Britanniæ*" in this wild retreat. Rabbits and sea-birds abound.

BARRY ISLAND, on the coast below Cardiff, closely adjoins the mainland, from which it is separated by a narrow isthmus, dry at low water. It is a mile and a half in circumference, and contains a large and ancient farm-house. The name is derived from the de Barri's of Manorbeer, who were its possessors. [*See* p. 208.]—Steam Excursions are sometimes made to this island from Gloucester, Bristol, and other places.

CALDY ISLAND, two miles and a half from Tenby, is frequently visited from that place, and contains 650 acres of land, about 450 acres of which are included in a well-cultivated farm. It is a mile and a quarter long and about half a mile broad. In the reign of Henry I. Robert de Tours founded a *Priory* here, which was made a cell to St. Dogmael's. The remains, which are attached to offices at the back of a modern mansion, include the rude stone spire of the church, the refectory, and other apartments which are vaulted. The hospitable lord of the island, Cabot Kynaston, Esq., lives at Caldy in great comfort, and farms his own land. An ancient chapel about a quarter of a mile from the Priory was repaired a few years ago, and service is occasionally performed by a clergyman who crosses for the purpose. The island is nominally in the parish of Penally, but there are no rates. Many workmen, whose dwellings stand near the beach, find employment in the limestone quarries, which yield a handsome revenue to Mr. Kynaston. The Lighthouse was first lighted on the 26th of January, 1829, and is well worth visiting. It bears a stationary light from two tiers of reflectors (which are of copper, plated in the inside thickly with silver, and lighted with the common argand burner). There are two keepers, who watch all night by turns; the wicks require trimming every three hours.

Oysters, crabs, and lobsters are plentiful around the shores.

The outer road for shipping lies off the N.E. point, where vessels may anchor in 6 or 7 fathoms; a ledge of rocks runs from this point with 1½ and 2 fathoms over it, to the westward of which is the *Inner Road*, where vessels may ride sheltered from all but easterly winds.

ST. MARGARET'S ISLAND has been dissevered from Caldy by the force of the sea; and can be approached at low water of high spring tides, over a rough ledge of rocks. It is perforated by vast caverns; and there are the ruins of an ancient chapel, and some quarrymen's cottages on the summit.

SKOKAM ISLE is situated three miles from the mainland to the N.W. of St. Anne's Head, Milford Haven. It contains two hundred acres, and its shores are very bold, but access can generally be obtained at two small landing-places, called the North and South Haven. Many sheep are pastured here, and rabbits abound.—About six miles W.N.W. from Skokam, there is a lofty round rocky islet called *Grassholm*.

SKOMAR ISLAND rises about a mile and a half to the north of Skokam, from which it is separated by a strait, termed Broad Sound. It contains seven hundred acres, and a farm-house. There are multitudes of rabbits.

RAMSEY ISLAND is very lofty, and terminated at each end by a precipitous hill, which give it a majestic appearance. The mountain at the S.E. end is the loftiest, and commands a view of vast extent. Falcons, and immense numbers of sea-birds, including the puffin and the razor bill, breed here; and rabbits are plentiful. "The Choir," an amphitheatre of rocks, and a place called "the Organ," both derive their names from the noise made by the sea-fowl. Ramsey is three miles long, and in one part a mile broad, and contains much good land, and plenty of water. There is a farm-house. It is the property of the Bishop of St. David's. There were two chapels on the island, which in early times was a great resort of devotees. Several large cairns may be traced. About a league to the westward lie a group of seven insulated rocks, called " *The Bishop and his Clerks*"—the terror of mariners ; and two small islands closely adjoin Ramsey.

LUNDY ISLAND is much the most important of the channel group. It possesses a history marked by curious incidents ; it was once inhabited by a considerable community; and it is capable of affording valuable shelter to shipping. The length of the island exceeds three miles, but it is hardly a mile broad at any point. Captain Denham, who surveyed the Bristol Channel minutely a few years ago, thus indicates the nautical value of Lundy :—" This island is not only of service in stormy weather, but enables the mariner to dodge the ebb or flood stream, *under weigh,* according as the wind may be east or west, he having a three-mile board to fore-reach upon, to and fro on either side of the island, screened from the tide." On the eastern side there is, according to Captain Denham, a roadstead, with shelter for vessels of any size from the prevailing winds ; and the aid of pilot skiffs may almost always be obtained.

Lundy, which contains 2,000 acres, was purchased in 1842 by Mr. Heaven, late of Bristol, for £9,000. That gentleman has erected a good dwelling-house on the island, and resides there with his family. He has materially improved the only means of access—a pass to a small beach near the south-east point. A small vessel regularly plies to and from Clovelly, the distance from which is about 16 miles. The remains of some fortifications and of a chapel are to be traced here. The *Lighthouse,* erected in 1819, near the S.W. side, is a conspicuous object. The upper lamps are elevated 567 feet above low water level, and produce " an *intermittent light,* appearing bright for 10 seconds, at intervals of 22 seconds obscuration, visible in clear weather to an eye 10 feet above the water, 31 miles off. The *lower light* is steady, and may be seen 29 miles off," but only on the N.N.W. and W.S.W. sides.

LIGHTHOUSES. The Smalls Lighthouse, 70 feet high, which is elevated on pillars on a rock that is seen in fine weather about 5 feet above high water—the centre of a group of sunken rocks—is an extraordinary structure, distant about seven leagues from the south-western coast of Pembrokeshire : the sea sometimes runs between the pillars to the height of at least 20 feet.—The following is a list of the Lights in the Bristol Channel :—1. South Bishop ; 2. St. Anne's (Milford Haven) ; 3. Lundy ; 4. Caldy ; 5. Light-ship off Worm's Head ; 6. Light-ship near entrance of Burry River ; 7. Mumbles ; 8. Swansea Harbour ; 9 and 10. Nass Point ; 11. Flatholm ; 12. Usk ; 13. Lightship on English and Welsh Grounds (revolving) ; 14. Kingroad ; 15 and 16. Burnham ; 17. Ilfracombe ; 18 and 19. Appledore (Bideford Bay).

BRISTOL CHANNEL STEAM PACKET TABLE.

We have in most instances indicated the days of departure of the steamers from Bristol on the various Channel stations ; but as changes sometimes take place in the summer, it is advisable to refer to *Bradshaw's Railway Guide,* which is not, however, always to be literally depended on, as to steam-packet departures. Annexed is a list of departures at either end. None of the steamers, with one exception, run on Sundays.

Bristol to Portishead. To and fro daily (in summer).

Bristol to Chepstow. To and fro daily.

Bristol to Newport. Daily, (sometimes to and fro).

Bristol and Cardiff. Daily, (sometimes to and fro).

Bristol, Mumbles, and Port Talbot. Monday and Thursday ; *return,* Tuesday and Friday.

Bristol, Mumbles, and Neath. Twice a week each way.

Bristol, Mumbles, and Swansea. Tuesday, Thursday, Friday, and Saturday ; *return,* same days.

Bristol to Carmarthen by Tenby. Friday ; *return,* Tuesday.

Bristol to Tenby. Tuesday and Friday ; *return,* Tuesday and Saturday.

Bristol to Tenby, Milford, Pater, and Haverfordwest. Tuesday ; *return* from Haverfordwest, Friday. Also *from* Milford, "*Troubadour*" on Sunday.

Bristol to Ilfracombe (in summer) Tuesday and Friday ; *return,* Monday and Wednesday.

Swansea to Ilfracombe (in spring and summer) Monday, Wednesday, and Saturday ; *return,* same days.

Swansea to Milford and Liverpool. Wednesdays.

Swansea to Tenby, Thursday ; *return,* the same day.

Bristol to St. Ives (Cornwall), Monday, Tuesday, and Friday.

GLOUCESTER.—To *Swansea,* Tuesday and Thursday ; to *Cardiff,* Wednesday ; to *Newport,* Wednesday and Saturday.

NOTE ON FISHING.—Since the notice which appears (*ante* p. 153), relative to the Ogmore was printed, we have heard that the fishing in that river has greatly deteriorated. The *Ddaw* (Thaw), in the neighbourhood of Cowbridge, is much the best river in Glamorganshire ; it is preserved, but we believe that not much difficulty exists in obtaining leave to fish with the fly.—*Rhayader* : Fishermen who visit this place will find Edward Jones a most useful and intelligent guide.

INDEX TO PLACES AND PRINCIPAL SUBJECTS.

PRINTED BY F. G. CARRINGTON, GREY FRIARS, GLOUCESTER.

Lightning Source UK Ltd.
Milton Keynes UK
UKHW022314060223
416579UK00001B/471